The Greek Revolution in the Age of Revolutions (1776–1848)

The Greek Revolution in the Age of Revolutions (1776–1848) brings together twenty-one scholars and a host of original ideas, revisionist arguments, and new information to mark the bicentennial of the Greek Revolution of 1821.

The purpose of this volume is to demonstrate the significance of the Greek liberation struggle to international history, and to highlight how it was a turning point that signalled the revival of revolution in Europe after the defeat of the French Revolution in 1815. It argues that the sacrifices of rebellious Greeks paved the way for other resistance movements in European politics, culminating in the 'spring of European peoples' in 1848. Richly researched and innovative in approach, this volume also considers the diplomatic and transnational aspects of the insurrection, and examines hitherto unexplored dimensions of revolutionary change in the Greek world.

This book will appeal to scholars and students of the Age of Revolution, as well as those interested in comparative and transnational history, political theory and constitutional law.

Paschalis M. Kitromilides is Professor Emeritus of Political Science at the University of Athens and a member of the Academy of Athens, where he holds the chair of the History of Political Thought.

Routledge Studies in Modern European History

Emotions and Everyday Nationalism in Modern European History
Edited by Andreas Stynen, Maarten Van Ginderachter and Xosé M. Núñez Seixas

Black Abolitionists in Ireland
Christine Kinealy

Sinti and Roma in Germany (1871-1933)
Gypsy Policy in the Second Empire and Weimar Republic
Simon Constantine

German Neo-Pietism, the Nation and the Jews
Religious Awakening and National Identities Formation, 1815–1861
Doron Avraham

Child Migration and Biopolitics
Old and New Experiences in Europe
Edited by Beatrice Scutaru and Simone Paoli

The Rhine and European Security in the Long Nineteenth Century
Making Lifelines from Frontlines
Joep Schenk

Garibaldi's Radical Legacy
Traditions of War Volunteering in Southern Europe (1861–1945)
Enrico Acciai

The Creation of the Austro-Hungarian Monarchy
A Hungarian Perspective
Edited by Gábor Gyáni

Postwar Continuity and New Challenges in Central Europe, 1918–1923
The War That Never Ended
Edited by Tomasz Pudłocki and Kamil Ruszała

For more information about this series, please visit: https://www.routledge.com/history/series/SE0246

The Greek Revolution in the Age of Revolutions (1776–1848)

Reappraisals and Comparisons

**Edited by
Paschalis M. Kitromilides**

LONDON AND NEW YORK

First published 2022
by Routledge
2 Park Square, Milton Park, Abingdon, Oxon OX14 4RN

and by Routledge
605 Third Avenue, New York, NY 10158

Routledge is an imprint of the Taylor & Francis Group, an informa business

© 2022 selection and editorial matter, Paschalis M. Kitromilides; individual chapters, the contributors

The right of Paschalis M. Kitromilides to be identified as the author of the editorial material, and of the authors for their individual chapters, has been asserted in accordance with sections 77 and 78 of the Copyright, Designs and Patents Act 1988.

All rights reserved. No part of this book may be reprinted or reproduced or utilised in any form or by any electronic, mechanical, or other means, now known or hereafter invented, including photocopying and recording, or in any information storage or retrieval system, without permission in writing from the publishers.

Trademark notice: Product or corporate names may be trademarks or registered trademarks, and are used only for identification and explanation without intent to infringe.

British Library Cataloguing-in-Publication Data
A catalogue record for this book is available from the British Library

Library of Congress Cataloging-in-Publication Data
Names: Kitromilides, Paschalis, editor.
Title: The Greek Revolution in the age of revolutions (1776-1848) : reappraisals and comparisons / edited by Paschalis M Kitromilides.
Description: Abingdon, Oxon ; New York : Routledge, 2022. | Series: Routledge studies in modern history | Includes bibliographical references and index.
Identifiers: LCCN 2021007156 | ISBN 9780367471835 (hardback) | ISBN 9781032053660 (paperback) | ISBN 9781003033981 (ebook)
Subjects: LCSH: Greece--History--War of Independence, 1821-1829. | Revolutions--Europe--History--19th century. | Europe--History--1789-1815 | Europe--History--1815-1848.
Classification: LCC DF804.7 G74 2022 | DDC 949.5/06--dc23
LC record available at https://lccn.loc.gov/2021007156

ISBN: 978-0-367-47183-5 (hbk)
ISBN: 978-1-032-05366-0 (pbk)
ISBN: 978-1-003-03398-1 (ebk)

Typeset in Times New Roman
by MPS Limited, Dehradun

Contents

List of figures	viii
List of tables	ix
Rector's foreword	x
List of Contributors	xiii

The Greek World in the Age of Revolution	1
PASCHALIS M. KITROMILIDES	

PART I
Resonances of the Age of Revolution I   17

1	Revolutions in Europe (1776–1848)	19
	ANNIE JOURDAN	
2	The Greek Revolution and the Age of Revolution	32
	DAVID A. BELL	
3	Greece, Spain, and the theory of emancipation in early European liberalism	43
	JOSÉ MARIA PORTILLO VALDÉS	
4	Austria and the 1820s revolutions: Between the heritage of the Congress of Vienna and political change	53
	MIROSLAV ŠEDIVÝ	

vi *Contents*

PART II
Resonances of the Age of Revolution II 65

5 Transnationalism and cosmopolitanism in the 1820s:
Philhellenism(s) in the public sphere 67
ANNA KARAKATSOULI

6 Greece and the liberal revolutions of 1820–1823 in
southern Europe 82
JOHN DAVIS

7 Greece and 1848: Direct responses and underlying
connectivities 95
CHRISTOPHER CLARK AND CHRISTOS ALIPRANTIS

8 "Che dura prova è tentar di greca aquila il dorso".
The Greek War of Independence and its resonance in
Sicilian culture of the 19th century 109
FRANCESCO SCALORA

PART III
**Reverberations of Revolution in Eastern and Southern
Europe** 123

9 Russia and Greece in the Age of Revolution 125
SIMON DIXON

10 The decade prior to the Greek Revolution: A black
hole in Ottoman history 139
H. ŞÜKRÜ ILICAK

11 The Serbian, Greek, and Romanian Revolutions in
comparison 150
HARALD HEPPNER

PART IV
Revolutionary Waves in the Greek World I 157

12 From the revolts to the Greek Revolution: Economic–
political realities and ideological visions among the
Greeks (end of the 18th C.–1821) 159
OLGA KATSIARDI-HERING

Contents vii

13 The vigilant eye of the Revolution: Public security and
police in revolutionary Greece 173
VASO SEIRINIDOU

PART V
Revolutionary Waves in the Greek World II 189

14 Internal conflicts and civil strife in the Serbian and the
Greek Revolutions: A comparison 191
MARIA EFTHYMIOU

15 The sea and nation-building: Between a privately-
owned merchant fleet and a revolutionary National
Navy, 1821-1827 203
GELINA HARLAFTIS AND KATERINA GALANI

16 Economy and politics in the correspondence of the
Neapolitan consuls in Greece 216
ANNA MARIA RAO

PART VI
Aspirations of Freedom in the Greek World 233

17 The vision of the rebellious Greeks for a democratic
and liberal state: the constitutions of the Greek
Revolution 235
SPYROS VLACHOPOULOS

18 Ideals of freedom in the Greek Revolution and the
political discourse of modernity 245
KONSTANTINOS A. PAPAGEORGIOU

Index 262

Figures

5.1 Articles mentioning Greece/Greeks/Turkey/Turks in French
    newspapers in 1821–1830   74
5.2 Digitized books and pamphlets of Greek interest, 1821–1830   75

Tables

5.1	Articles mentioning Greece/Greeks/Turkey/Turks in French newspapers in 1821–1830	73
15.1	Main naval expeditions, 1821–1827	206

Rector's foreword

As rector of the National and Kapodistrian University of Athens (NKUA), the oldest higher education institution in Greece (1837), it is with great pleasure and genuine emotion that I salute the publication of this volume. Adapted from the proceedings of the conference, The Greek Revolution in the Age of Revolutions (1776–1848): Reappraisals and Comparisons, which was organized by our university and held in a virtual-only format on 11–12 of March 2021, this volume represents a unique contribution to the study of the Greek Revolution as a national and international event.

As is customary with such important commemorations, the bicentennial of the Greek Revolution (1821–2021) provides an exceptional occasion for new research approaches, which broaden knowledge and understanding of this major event. By transcending national borders, this commemoration enables us to consider this particular national experience in the context of the critical period of political and social upheaval and ideological change that has been canonized in international historiography as the "Age of Revolution", extending from 1776 to 1848. The Greek Revolution was a pivotal event in the period of repression following the defeat of the French Revolution in 1815. Its outbreak in the period of international repression of the liberal movements acted as a singular reminder of the value of the struggle for freedom and contributed significantly to the revival and the dissemination of democratic ideals throughout the world.

Greece emerged as the first modern sovereign nation-state in southeastern Europe and the eastern Mediterranean. This achievement influenced the revolutionary and ideological movements that were manifested among neighbouring peoples and provided a model for all other national communities in the region to envision their own future.

The central issues discussed in the pages of this volume include the Revolution of 1821 as a diplomatic event, its kinship with other revolutions of the same period, and its legacies and their reverberations; the rise of nationalism in combination with the liberal movements of that period and the heritage of Enlightenment ideas; the international Philhellenic movement; and the Revolution in the framework of Ottoman history and its juxtaposition with the history of the rest of the Balkan Peninsula and the anterior uprisings in the region.

The reappraisal of the Greek revolutionary experience and its comparison with other revolutionary movements across Europe at that the time, as it unfolds in this volume, illustrates various facets of the Age of Revolution to advance the understanding of the revolutionary phenomenon on a global scale. This is largely due to the novel contributions made by the volume's several authors, all of whom are prominent scholars and specialists with great expertise in their respective subjects. Their contributions shed light on the various aspects of a complex and multilateral issue.

Both the conference and this volume are part of the initiatives undertaken by the NKUA to commemorate the bicentennial. The works presented, including conferences, lectures, publications, research programmes, exhibitions, and artistic events, contribute concurrently to dialogue on the trajectory of the Greek nation-state from the early nineteenth century to the dawn of the twenty-first century.

As Greece's first university, the NKUA has a predominant position within the country's intellectual and cultural landscape; thus, its role in commemorating the bicentennial is important to the university's overall history and academic contribution. The establishment of a higher education institution constituted one of the revolutionaries's visions, which was fulfilled in 1837 with the creation of the NKUA. Since that time, our university has functioned as a guardian of the legacy of the 1821 Revolution.

As rector of the NKUA, I wish to thank particularly the Greek and foreign colleagues who have participated in the publication of this volume. These scholars have contributed greatly to the thoroughness and originality of this volume by lending their authority and profound scholarly expertise. In addition, the contribution of the members of the conference's academic committee is deeply appreciated. Constituting the cornerstone of this publication, these colleagues worked with zeal and scholarly dedication under my chairmanship to successfully organize and conclude the conference under the distressing conditions of the COVID-19 pandemic. They include Nikos C. Alivizatos, Maria Efthymiou, Evanthis Hatzivassiliou, Anna Karakatsouli, Vangelis Karamanolakis, Olga Katsiardi-Hering, Paschalis Kitromilides, Paraskevas Konortas, Anastasia Papadia-Lala, and Nassia Yakovaki.

Particular mention and thanks are extended to Olga Katsiardi-Hering, a Professor Emerita of our university, who sparked the initial idea for this conference and strove tirelessly for its realization while contributing to the organization of this volume during its early stages. Finally, I would like to express my warmest thanks to Paschalis M. Kitromilides, a professor emeritus of the NKUA, who shouldered the burden of editorial work on this volume and contributed immensely to the success of the entire endeavour by providing his internationally acknowledged scholarly authority and extensive knowledge of the subject. The conference was made possible thanks to the kind sponsorship of Piraeus Bank, with which we have had a harmonious and fruitful collaboration during the organization of a series of events for the commemoration of the bicentennial.

xii *Rector's foreword*

The pages that follow are dedicated to the comparative study of this unparalleled event of modern Greek history and its international contextualization. We believe that initiatives such as this contribute to further development of scientific knowledge and mark a decisive step forward for the expansion of reflection and communication among various academic environments at this critical time for humanity as a whole.

Meletios-Athanasios Dimopoulos
Professor of Medicine

Contributors

Christos Aliprantis, European University Institute and Ludwig Maximilian University, Munich

David A. Bell, Sidney and Ruth Lapidus Professor of History, Princeton University

Christopher Clark, Regius Professor of Modern History, University of Cambridge

John Davis, Professor of History Emeritus, University of Connecticut (USA), and Senior Research Associate, Department of History, University of Warwick (UK)

Simon Dixon, Sir Bernard Pares Professor of Russian History, University College London

Maria Efthymiou, Professor of Modern Greek History, National and Kapodistrian University of Athens

Katerina Galani, Institute for Mediterranean Studies/Foundation for Research and Technology-Hellas (FORTH) and Hellenic Open University

Gelina Harlaftis, Director, Institute for Mediterranean Studies, University of Crete

Harald Heppner, Professor Emeritus, Society for Eighteenth Century Studies on South Eastern Europe, University of Graz

H. Şükrü Ilıcak, Institute for Mediterranean Studies, University of Crete

Annie Jourdan, Associate Professor of European Studies, University of Amsterdam

Anna Karakatsouli, Associate Professor of European History and Civilization, National and Kapodistrian University of Athens

Olga Katsiardi-Hering, Professor Emerita of Modern Greek History, National and Kapodistrian University of Athens xiv *Contributors*

Paschalis M. Kitromilides, Professor Emeritus of Political Science, National and Kapodistrian University of Athens and Academy of Athens

Konstantinos A. Papageorgiou, Professor of the Philosophy of Law, National and Kapodistrian University of Athens

Anna Maria Rao, Professor Emerita of Modern History, Università degli Studi di Napoli Federico II

Francesco Scalora, Research Fellow, University of Padova and Harvard Center for Hellenic Studies in Greece

Miroslav Šedivý, Institute of Historical Sciences, Faculty of Arts and Philosophy of the University of Pardubice, Czech Republic

Vaso Seirinidou, Assistant Professor of Modern Greek History, National and Kapodistrian University of Athens

José Maria Portillo Valdés, Professor of Contemporry History, University of the Basque Country, Spain

Spyros Vlachopoulos, Professor of Constitutional Law, National and Kapodistrian University of Athens

The Greek world in the Age of Revolution

Paschalis M. Kitromilides

The conceptual and substantive historical problems inherent in the two historiographical categories making up the title of this chapter force me to begin with some disclaimers. I cannot hope in this introductory survey to accomplish much more than an approximate clarification of the two historiographical categories in question; indeed, to remember John Locke, to attempt to "clear ground a little" and "remove some of the rubbish that lies in the way to knowledge".[1] I wish to recall in this connection the urge of the foremost representative of the Greek Enlightenment, Adamantios Korais, who liked to remind his reader of the advice of the ancient Athenian philosopher, Antisthenis, as recorded by Epictetus, who pointed out that the beginning of wisdom amounted to the clarification of names. This offers Korais the occasion for the following comment:[2]

> Those wise men had understood that the vagueness of words generates disorder in ideas and this in turn disorder in actions

A bit of good advice to all of us, including historians, who give in easily to the temptations of theorizing and to all the confusion this tends to breed. With this in mind, let us turn to some reflections concerning the meaning of the two terms "Greek world" and "Age of Revolution".

I should like to point out that I am not using the term Greece or Greek nation to describe the subject I propose to examine. Greece in the period of the late 18th and the early 19th century up to 1821, was a term of historical geography or, to borrow Metternich's characterization of Italy, merely a "geographical expression",[3] unconnected with a political entity. It did not feature on the political map of Europe as a recognizable unit.

The Greek nation on the other hand, in the absence of a state, was still an incipient historical and political idea, with many uncertainties as to the precise historical agent that might be recognized as the embodiment of the idea. Yet, during the long centuries that had followed the fall of Constantinople and the disappearance of the Eastern Roman Empire, there had been a Greek-speaking population dispersed over a huge territorial space in Southeastern Europe, Asia Minor, and the islands of the

2 Paschalis M. Kitromilides

Eastern Mediterranean, which formed a community, with fluid human and linguistic boundaries to be sure; it was a community which, nevertheless, cohered to a remarkable degree around the ecclesiastical institutions ministering to its religious faith. This cultural community was described by Iosipos Moisiodax, an eighteenth-century thinker endowed by remarkable perspicacity, as the "diasporas of the Greeks".[4]

It is worth dwelling on this term as a lens into the self-understanding of Greek culture on the eve of the "age of revolution". Iosipos Moisiodax himself, as his name makes abundantly clear, was a "convert" to Greek culture through education and ordination in the ranks of celibate clergy, having been born in a Vlach (Aromunian)-speaking village on the south bank of the Danube delta. As one from a non-Greek ethnic background who had become Greek by choice on his way to educational and social mobility, Moisiodax developed into an acute commentator on Greek culture, its problems and its prospects. Writing in 1761 about the condition of "Greece" following the fall of Constantinople, he stresses the evils besieging the captive society, first and foremost among them "the most pernicious dissension". In the same breath, he hastens to clarify what he means by Hellas/Greece: "when I say Greece, I mean all the diasporas of the Greeks".

This is how he thinks the community of Greek speakers extending within but also beyond the frontiers of the Ottoman Empire in Europe and Asia could be most precisely described: diasporas of the Greeks, a population recognizable by its cultural characteristics, primarily its language, dispersed in space. Moisiodax had traveled widely in the historical space of the diasporas of the Greeks and he had a clear perception of that to which he was referring: "I have lived in many parts of Greece and I know what I am talking about", he asserts at another locus in the same pioneering text of social and cultural criticism.[5]

At the time Moisiodax was writing, the Greeks as a community, or in their own language a γένος, were dispersed in the mountains and plains of the Greek peninsula, in the great urban centres around the Eastern Mediterranean, in the islands of the Aegean and Ionian seas and the great islands of Crete and Cyprus, along the Western and Northwestern coast but especially in the Pontic coastal and highland regions of Northeastern Asia Minor. Politically, the great majority of all these communities, which understood themselves primarily in terms of their religious identity as Orthodox Christians, were subject to the Ottoman Empire. In addition to the Ottoman-ruled mass of the γένος, there was a pocket of Greek-speaking Orthodox Greeks who lived in a leftover of Western rule in the Venetian-held seven Ionian islands, from Kythira in the south to Corfu and its offshore islets in the north. Beyond these continental and insular territories there was a wide network of Orthodox communities, whose members spoke Greek or Vlach (usually both), extending deep along the great Macedonian rivers into Southeastern Europe in the South Slavic lands and in the Romanian principalities north of the Danube and into the Habsburg

The Greek world in the Age of Revolution 3

domains in Central Europe, forming a tight network of emigrant Orthodox communities in Northern Italy, especially Venice, Trieste, and Livorno, and in the new Russian territories north of the Black Sea from Bessarabia to the shores of the Caspian Sea. In the Levant, there were Greeks in all the great port cities and in the great seats of ecclesiastical organization in the Fertile Crescent and in Egypt, primarily in Alexandria, Cairo, Jerusalem, and Damascus.

These were the "diasporas of the Greeks" to which Iosipos Moisiodax refers as a specification of what Greece meant to him. This was the Greek world on the threshold of the period of change and upheaval that later on was going to be described as the age of revolution. A community widely dispersed in space, which meant openness to the world around it into which it penetrated and to which it was exposed. This broad exposure opened so many windows to the culture of the time, the secular ideas and values of the Enlightenment.

Yet, this widely based and dispersed population remained a community, in fact, a "polity" whose main body in its original heartlands remained in captivity, but possessed, nevertheless, the marks of cohesion and distinctiveness that set it apart as a nation. This early understanding of the captive Orthodox community as a distinct nation was articulated shortly after Moisiodax's diaspora definition, by Dimitrios Katartzis, an articulate Encyclopedist scholar and high official at the court of the semiautonomous principality of Wallachia. Writing in the 1780s, Katartzis puts forward for the self-understanding of the Greeks an extremely revealing definition of what it means to form a political community, for which he uses the term nation, *ἔθνος*.[6] He begins with Aristotle's definition of citizenship as participation in decision-making and exercise of public office in an organized community (*Politics* 1275a 20–25) and points out that although subject to another alien nation, the Greeks were not in a condition similar to that of the Helots of ancient Sparta.[7]

> We are not like them thanks be to God and yes maybe we do not partake in the administration of the state of our rulers in everything, but nevertheless we are not totally excluded from it either. Therefore we constitute a nation and we are bound together by our ecclesiastical leaders who also connect us with the highest authorities; in many things they are also our political leaders; many of our civil laws, which are called habits, and all of our ecclesiastical laws which are subsumed under religion enjoy the recognition of the imperial authority ... Many from our community carry top dignities and offices ... All these participate in the government and they are covered by Aristotle's definition and with them necessarily all those under them, ... that is all Orthodox Greeks.

This is the community of the Greeks, still called *Romioi* by Katartzis, who uses a traditional denomination based on religious premises: they are the

4 Paschalis M. Kitromilides

community of Orthodox Christians descending from the subjects of the Eastern Roman Empire. What is important in this account is the assertion that this religious community could be recognized as a nation aspiring to its own state. Thus, an explosively modern concept is introduced in the description of the captive polity of the Orthodox community. Katartzis insists on the understanding of the community as a captive polity. To make his point completely clear he offers some important clarifications:[8]

> our polity, because it cannot show to the same extent, like those sovereign ones, its love and care for its citizens, doesn't it nevertheless show it to the extent it can? Then if our polity cannot do all that it owes to us, is this a reason for us to think that we do not have duties toward it? On the contrary we ought to love our defective and weak polity more than independent nations love their own polities which flourish under the rule of law.

What emerges from Katartzis's account is the image of a community with its distinctive social and political structure, marked by its lay and ecclesiastical dignities and striving to bring itself into the modern age by redefining its culture and intellectual life. The attempt at cultural redefinitions included a drastic turn to the vernacular as the language of culture, learning, and education. This was Katartzis's top priority on his agenda of cultural change. A parallel major concern was the incorporation of modern Enlightenment culture, especially encyclopedism, into Greek learning. His aspiration was to move the nation forward by means of a creative fusion of the two. Katartzis was arguing for cultural change through reform and opening up of the collective mind, but he remained skeptical and shied away from the prospects of a drastic break with the past and from overturning the present of Greek society in ways that might prove self-defeating.[9]

It was precisely such attitudes, which were attaining remarkable maturity on the eve of 1789, that were overtaken by the coming of the Age of Revolution. The tremours of the new age were brought into Greek political thought and into the perception of the Greek world by a younger associate and disciple of Moisiodax and Katartzis, Rhigas Velestinlis. Rhigas represents the paradigmatic Greek and Southeast European exemplar of the Age of Revolution. A Jacobin and follower of the radical democratic Enlightenment in his published works and revolutionary plans for the overthrow of Ottoman despotism, Rhigas added a broader and more inclusive perspective to the perception and understanding of the Greek world voiced by his forerunners. Moisiodax's diasporic vision was certainly an integral component of Rhigas's own understanding, which he recorded on his great map of Hellas. However, next to the diasporas of the Greeks, he could perceive and record in his revolutionary appeal other communities defined primarily by their languages, nations in-the-making that were invited to join the Greeks in the revolution and in the new

The Greek world in the Age of Revolution   5

democratic republic that would unite them on the basis of free and equal citizenship.[10]

To Katartzis' s perception of the Greek world as a nation in captivity defined by both language and religion and by its political structure, Rhigas added an expanded sociological make-up. To the urban and cultured environments and to the hierarchy of social dignities, he added a recognition of the massive peasant component, which formed the nation's basis and its inexhaustible human resource. The peasantry, illiterate and uncouth, was subjected to multiple forms of social injustice and exploitation by Ottoman masters and fellow Christian primates. From its bosom sprang the various forms of primitive social protest, which inscribed a revolutionary dynamic into Greek and, more broadly, Balkan society under alien rule.

The radical Enlightenment and the Age of Revolution added new meanings to varieties of primitive social protest represented by the *klephts* in the Greek-speaking regions of the Balkans and by the *haiduks* further north. Their oral poetry and songs registered the sense of injustice and the aspiration of redemption in a long tradition lost in pre-modern times.[11] The coming of the Age of Revolution recast in modern ways what has been described as the "Balkan revolutionary tradition", which went back to the late 15th and the 16th century, and which included in its dynamics the primitive social claims of the mountain rebels.[12] Now, in the Age of Revolution, these claims and aspirations, which voiced the moral outrage of the subjugated society, were finally articulated in national terms; and this turned out to be a powerful, indeed irresistible force, that could move societies to revolution and, indeed, brought the Greek world and its Southeast European hinterland into the revolutionary age.

In his revolutionary pamphlet, Rhigas did not fail to appeal to the formations of resistance that were shaping up in the mountains of Greece, enlisting the sons of peasant society. He urged them to close ranks under the banner of the revolutionary movement and to fight for the liberation of their compatriots and the defense of the sacred inalienable rights of all.[13]

The survey of the condition of the Greek world through the prism of Greek political thought in the age of revolutions cannot be complete without a serious look at the pertinent ideas of Adamantios Korais. A classical scholar and political thinker, who belongs to the broader world of the European Enlightenment, besides being a "Greek radical enlightener", in Jonathan Israel's characterization,[14] Korais guided political reflection in the Greek Enlightenment tradition to its maturity.[15] Nothing expressed better the achievement of maturity than Korais' s understanding of the community of Greeks as a modern nation, defined generically by its language and culture but articulated politically by the aspiration of freedom and independence. Korais had been primarily interested in and deeply preoccupied with questions of language and educational reform and by the broad issue of Greek παιδεία, which he saw as an invaluable heritage but at the same time in urgent need of extensive restructuring and reform on the models of

6 *Paschalis M. Kitromilides*

Enlightenment philosophy. All this, however, he considered as the necessary preparation of the most serious and important prospect before the Greek nation, its liberation and accession to sovereign statehood. Korais visualized this on the model of the "first new nation", as it was to be described by a leading twentieth-century political scientist,[16] the United States of America, or the "republic of the Anglo-Americans", as Korais himself called it.

In the most important statement of his political thought, his 1823 commentary on the *Provisional Constitution of Greece*, Korais repeatedly invoked the model of the Anglo-American polity, especially the constitutional protection of individual rights and civil liberties as the best guide in the construction of a free republic in liberated Greece.[17]

Korais's political thought and his conception of the Greek nation could be seen to represent a point of confluence of the ideological traditions of the age of revolutions; it registered the strong impact of American liberalism, what has been called the "expanding blaze" of American revolutionary ideas on European thought,[18] and the debate on the French Revolution as the framework for the redefinition of European politics as the politics of modernity. The impact of the American blaze of freedom on Korais's political thought is recorded epigrammatically in his assertion that the Greeks, in drafting their future constitution, "should follow in everything the political system of the Anglo-Americans, a system attested by the judgment of all political philosophers and by the strongest of all proofs, experience, as the most perfect among contemporary polities governed under the rule of law".[19] Korais's idea of the Greek nation amounted to the model of the modern nation-state, and his hope for his contemporary Greeks was to achieve their establishment and international recognition as a nation-state in the "century of the liberation of peoples".[20]

Korais's concept of the nation-state is a distinctly modern notion, primarily on account of the centrality of the American constitutional model in its definition, which determines the liberal-democratic character of state organization expected to guide it in practice. One particularly instructive testimony of Korais's liberal democratic expectations of the new nation-state concerns the treatment of ethnic and religious minorities in the new state, Muslims and Jews. They must be treated with humanity and kindness and be prepared through civic education to be accorded fully equal citizenship and, of course, full freedom in the exercise of their religious faith.[21] Such was the Greek nation-state visualized by Korais as the fitting future for the Greek world. It is obvious that this vision and the conceptualizations on which it was based would not have been imaginable outside the climate of expectations and the prospects opened for the Greeks by their revolution.

By recovering the reflection of the Greek world in the mirror of Greek political thought, we can follow the evolution of the conceptual self-understanding of the Greeks in the age of revolutions. From Moisiodax's diasporic perception through Katartzis' s conditional recognition of a nation-in-captivity defined by its civil and ecclesiastical dignities to Rhigas's vision of a radical multicultural republic and to Korais's concept of a modern liberal democracy, we can discern the Greek world on a trajectory of social transformation and consciousness-raising that, amidst the convulsions of the age of revolution, was leading it from a protracted "Medieval" slumber into the world of modernity, with all its passions, contradictions, and expectations, first and foremost of which was the hope of freedom.

I should now turn to the second historiographical category in my title, the Age of Revolution. The idea denotes an age dominated by violent upheaval and overthrow of the established order in many parts of the Western, or Atlantic world, as one of the originators of the idea preferred to call it. All these violent risings against established authority were seen to follow a shared logic and to be inspired by the same ideals, making it conceptually reasonable and historically tenable to integrate them into a unitary pattern of political change transforming the Western world. The chronological range is broadly now understood to extend from the American Revolution of 1776 to the European revolutions of 1848, with its pivotal climax in the revolutionary decade 1789–1799 in France. This had been an extremely influential historical conceptualization, already in the making in the 1950s under the shadow of the Cold War. It owed its genesis and elaboration to two truly great historians, one continental European and one American, Jacques Godechot and R. R. Palmer.

Godechot, originally a distinguished historian of the institutions of re-volutionary France, introduced the concept of "la Grande Nation", whereby he referred to the expansion and radiation of the ideas and practices of the French Revolution in Central, Eastern, and Southern Europe and overseas, in territories of the French empire, such as the future Haiti, but also more broadly in the Americas. It was this expansion of French revolutionary ideas and the influence of revolutionary and Napoleonic France that shaped the Age of Revolution.[22] To this understanding, Princeton historian, R. R. Palmer, whose broader interest lay in world history, added a pronounced American dimension. Palmer pointed out that the events in France and their widely felt impact in the rest of Europe formed part of an even broader phenomenon of revolutionary change and political transformation, which extended over the entire Atlantic world and whose earliest articulate ex-pression was the American Revolution. This is how what Palmer called "the democratic revolution" was set in motion in the West and, through the convulsions of several decades, produced the contemporary world.[23]

For R. R. Palmer, the age of the "democratic revolution" extended roughly from 1760–1800, while Godechot more or less saw "la Grande Nation" reaching its limits and coming to an end with the defeat of the French Revolution and Napoleon in 1814–1815. Both of them, in trying to develop an inclusive and comprehensive perspective on the revolutionary age, did not fail to mention the Greek experience represented by Rhigas Velestinlis as a witness of the revolutionary spirit in the distant Southeastern periphery of Europe.[24]

8   *Paschalis M. Kitromilides*

The term "Age of Revolution" itself, with an expanded chronological horizon up to 1848, is due to a British historian with a remarkable cosmopolitan background, Eric Hobsbawm. He coined the term in the title of his most important work, in my judgment, published in 1962. Hobsbawm added as a primary component of his narrative an important social dimension, which, he considered, the earlier political histories of the age had downgraded. For him, the "age of revolution" was shaped by the twin explosions of two volcanos, the Revolution in France and the Industrial Revolution in Britain. Their combined effects reshaped European history and society and, by extension, through the channels provided by the worldwide European empires, the rest of the world. To R. R. Palmer's mostly political approach that focused on the revolt against aristocracy across the Atlantic world, Hobsbawm projected a history of class struggle, with the "conquering bourgeoisie" as its protagonist but also marked by the increasingly asserted presence of the working class.[25]

This was established as a dominant historiographical "paradigm", in Thomas Kuhn's sense of the term. The original conceptualization of the age of revolution has been variously criticized over the years, especially since the 1990s. One line of criticism has pointed to the "Eurocentric" logic of the overall approach and its affinity with Cold War ideological attitudes. A further criticism has pointed to the broader world beyond its North Atlantic core, upon which the age of revolution approach had originally concentrated its attention.[26] These have been valid criticisms, which proved remarkably fertile for historical research. They generated an expansion of focus and reflection, which placed first Latin America and the Caribbean on the agenda of the historiography of the age of revolution, with the Haitian revolution of 1804 recovered as an emblematic expression of a whole historical age. The reappraisal of the original set of ideas and of the historiographical practice they had informed, led eventually to a literally "global" expansion of reflection on the age of revolution, premised on the logic of the interconnectedness of revolutionary movements, especially across the Eurasian continent and the Americas.[27] Criticism and rethinking have greatly enriched and refined the historiographical paradigm of the age of revolution, as suggested by important recent contributions by David Armitage, David Bell, Jonathan Israel, and many others.[28] The paradigm, nevertheless, still holds ground and through its repeated renewals shows that it can inform, in productive ways, historical research.[29]

The adoption of the globalized perspective on the age of revolution in recent scholarship should not obscure some comparatively older but pioneering pointers in earlier scholarship. One such suggestion came half a century ago from Elie Kedourie, a truly insightful historian of political ideas and an ingenious thinker on nationalism. By expanding in a global direction, by looking at Asia and Africa, his own original interpretation of nationalism in the European world, Kedourie recognized the significance of the Greek experience, which he characterized as the first instance, more precisely, the

The Greek world in the Age of Revolution   9

beginning, of the radiation of Western secular and liberal ideas on a global scale. Kedourie pointed out that the seminal lecture by Adamantios Korais, "Memoir on the present state of civilization in Greece", delivered to the Société des Observateurs de l'Homme in Paris on 6 January 1803 was, in fact, an eloquent witness to the origins of the process of globalization of Western ideas.[30]

The central component of the secular and liberal ideas, the origin of whose globalization according to Kedourie can be traced back to the thought of scholars like Korais, was the modern idea of the nation. Thus, nationalism, the aspiration of self-determination of national communities defined primarily by their language, can be seen to form a critical factor shaping in decisive ways the age of revolution. More precisely, it might be said that the various processes of intellectual change, marking the transition from pre-modern and pre-national forms of collective consciousness and identity to the lively awareness of belonging to national communities and the concomitant claims of collective and individual liberty, constituted integral constituents of the dynamics of the age of revolution. The rise of the "cult of the nation" was, in fact, the hallmark of the age. This has long been recognized.[31] In view of the evidence of the Greek Revolution as a nation-building project, it could be added that new directions of research on the Age of Revolution should not disregard the critical significance of nationalism and the articulation of national sentiments and identities as a fundamental aspect of the rise of modernity and a factor of great dynamism in cultural and political change.

The process whereby these ideological changes were witnessed in Greek historical experience and articulated in the crucible of the Greek revolution provides a paradigmatic example of the globalization of the Western model of nation-building and can provide both insights and corrections to pertinent mainstream historical reflection. The conceptual value and historiographical significance of the evidence of the Greek Revolution consist in the specificity it provides to the more general trends of the age and the lively evidence of the transformation through revolutionary action of a people sociologically marked by diversity and disunity into a modern nation.

The global geographical focus could, thus, be combined and indeed deepened by reconsidering manifestations of the age of revolution, which had surfaced off the main stages of revolutionary action while the high drama was unfolding. In areas on the European periphery, movements of cultural, social, and eventually political change produced results that represented revolutionary breaks with the past of the regions in question and were inscribed integrally in the logic of the age of revolution. The manifestations of revolutionary change on the European periphery have been noted and briefly recorded in the classic accounts of the age of revolution by Godechot, R. R. Palmer, and Hobsbawm. The challenge that arises for us today in light of the critical reappraisals of the age of revolutions that have so productively probed anew many of the original questions, premises, and

10   *Paschalis M. Kitromilides*

conceptualizations, involves an invitation to rethink conventional understandings and expand and deepen scholarly treatments of the subject. Connecting such rereadings with the globalized perspective on revolution can offer new interpretations of the age but also adjustments, corrections, and a more realistic appraisal of evidence.

The aspiration of the present volume has been to attempt such reappraisals of the Age of Revolution by focusing on the Greek Revolution of 1821 as an integral expression of that age of upheaval, conflict, and change. The contributors approach the Greek Revolution in the age of revolution on three levels of analysis: comparative history; regional history of revolution in Eastern, South, and Southeastern Europe as the immediate context of revolutionary impulses among the Greeks; and in-depth examination of neglected aspects of revolutionary experience and politics in the Greek case.

The broader comparative perspective on the Greek Revolution is set by Annie Jourdan's study of the fate of revolution in France and elsewhere in Europe and the fluctuations of revolutionary waves, which even after the defeat of the revolution in France and elsewhere in Western Europe managed to rekindle the revolutionary age on the European periphery through the action of veterans and other disgruntled radicals in search of other revolutionary causes. David Bell contributes an analytical model for the comparative study of revolution through the logic of the three concepts of structural homologies, contagion and disruption, thus placing the Greek revolution in a long-term historical perspective. The affinity of the revolution in Greece with its contemporaneous revolutions in Spanish America is revealed by Jose Maria Portillo Valdés by means of a consideration of the liberal theory of emancipation, as elaborated by Dominique Dufour du Pradt. The Age of Revolution was shaped by an often explosive combination of domestic pressures, claims, and movements of political change with international antagonisms and diplomatic complications derived from power politics. Miroslav Šedivý illustrates all this by proposing a reevaluation of Austrian policies and diplomacy focusing specifically on the Greek Question, as personified by Chancellor Prince von Metternich, one of the emblematic figures of the age.

The transnational aspects of the age, as represented primarily by Philhellenism, are discussed by Anna Karakatsouli. The paper reminds us that the concept of transnationalism, which was introduced in international relations theory in the 1970s as a pioneering idea, can have broader applications, which can prove quite fertile in historical analysis. Another characteristic phenomenon of transnational action, specifically in the years preceding 1821, is represented by the phenomenon of secret societies, which span underground politics in Europe after the defeat of the French Revolution. One of the most successful among them, the Philiki Etaireia, which, between 1814 and 1821, was actively engaged in the final stages of the

The Greek world in the Age of Revolution   11

preparation of the revolution for the liberation of Greece, is frequently referred to in the pages of this collection.

The cataclysmic events of 1848–1849, which came as a climax and at the same time as the closing curtain of the drama of the age of revolution, are drawn into the purview of our collection by Chris Clark and Chris Aliprantis. No matter how many times that dramatic story has been told, it cannot be exhausted and the narrative in this collection makes that clear by pointing to the transnational networks through which revolutionaries operated in that biennial drama. Their comparative perspective allows the authors to bring forward the convergences in state-building between Greece and other European states, especially those in German-speaking Central Europe, in the period leading up to the revolutionary outbreak in 1848. As a footnote to the chapter, it might be added that there was a Balkan dimension to the drama of 1848 with the revolution in Bucharest, brought about by the radicals of the "generation of 1848", who were genuine heirs of the ideals of the age of revolution.[32]

The regional history of the age of revolution in Eastern, South, and Southeastern Europe is surveyed in our collection by authoritative studies, which invariably bring out the transnational dimension of revolutionary movements in those regions. Perceptions and responses to the Greek revolution emerged as a constant recurrence in that transnational dynamic. John Davis illustrates this nexus by looking at the intriguing question of how the liberation movements in Southern Europe reshaped British identities, thus pointing to a British component of age. A very important, if often forgotten, witness of the revolutionary age was Russia, drawn into our collection by Simon Dixon. Russia's presence is conventionally brought forward in the diplomacy of the Age of Revolution, but, as Simon Dixon reminds us, there was a lot more beyond diplomacy as the two Orthodox societies, Russia and Greece, converged in multiple and interlocking ways. The Greek Revolution inspired hopes and invited active support by Russian Philhellenes, including the leading poet of the age, Alexander Pushkin. The Russian equivalent to the Greek secret society, Philiki Etaireia, the Decembrist movement, however, with its tragic failure, showed that the odds against liberal change in autocratic Russia were much greater than in rebellious Greece.

The Ottoman context of the Greek Revolution is laid out by Sükrü Ilıcak in his survey of a chain of uprisings and centrifugal movements in the Ottoman Empire, which proved significant in diverting the Ottoman Sublime Porte's attention and thus allowing the revolutionary movement among the Greeks to develop and survive. The Greek Revolution and the loss of Greece turned out to be an important challenge that eventually set the Empire on the road of reform later in the nineteenth century.

Anna Maria Rao and Francesco Scalora open up the Italian world for us and its responses to the Greek Revolution, thus documenting still another transnational ideological network of the period in South Europe. Both authors

12 *Paschalis M. Kitromilides*

discuss new and hitherto unexplored primary sources, thus adding considerable originality to our collection. We hear about the reports of the consul of the Kingdom of Two Sicilies in the Kingdom of Greece in the 1830s, an important testimony on the fate of liberty in the new state, and of the multiple responses to the Greek liberation movement in Sicilian culture throughout the nineteenth century.

The Greek Revolution had its neighbours and parallels in Southeastern Europe. Harald Heppner and Maria Efthymiou draw two other Balkan revolutions into the picture by attempting well informed and penetrating comparisons of the revolutionary phenomenon in Serbian, Romanian, and Greek societies, pointing out the shared characteristics but also the specificities that can explain the divergences between them, including the different outcomes in each of the three cases. Maria Efthymiou, in particular, in her comparison of the Serbian and Greek Revolutions directs attention to the dynamics of civil conflicts, which invariably characterize large-scale revolutionary upheavals, thus illustrating a well-established feature of theories of revolution, going back to the pioneering work of Crane Brinton.

A group of distinguished Greek historians enriches the collection with their studies of important, if neglected in some instances, aspects of the revolutionary experience of the Greeks. The studies, which represent a good sample of the quality of historical scholarship in contemporary Greece, add depth to the overall consideration of the Age of Revolution attempted by the collection as a whole and constitute in themselves an argument why the Greek Revolution deserves to be canonized and integrated more systematically into pertinent scholarship. Olga Katsiardi-Hering provides a complete survey of the emergence and growth to maturity of the liberation movement in the Greek world from the 1770s to 1821 and the gradual articulation over this period of a clear vision of a new Greece as a free nation.

A unique feature of the Greek revolution was the importance of the sea in the liberation struggle and the decisive contribution of the significant insular part of the Greek world to nation-building. Gelina Harlaftis and Katerina Galani discuss the evidence of recently completed research in Greek and European archives on the construction of a Greek navy as part of the nation-building project in the revolutionary period. The paper brings out one important specificity of the Greek Revolution among all other revolutions of the age, which is the critical role of the maritime factor, which made it a revolution acted out and eventually won on both land and sea.

The largely forgotten social history of the Greek Revolution transpires in the chapter by Vaso Seirinidou on crime and police formation in revolutionary Greece. The subject has never been treated before and the evidence discussed adds a fascinating perspective of history from below on the high drama of the Revolution. This particular contribution can be read as an opening of our project to theories of political change focusing on the role of police in state-building and nation-building in European history.[33]

The Greek world in the Age of Revolution 13

A significant part of statecraft in the Greek Revolution was transacted by the national assemblies, primarily those of 1821–1822, 1823, and 1827, which, by means of the constitutions they drafted, attempted to give form to the dynamics of revolutionary action through the introduction of the structures and institutions of a modern state. What was decisive in this task was the normative political culture it introduced in the society in revolt by projecting the principles and values of democratic liberalism, the rule of law and respect for civil liberties and human rights, as the desirable political model that would guarantee the fighting nation's freedom. This important dimension of the Greek Revolution is introduced in our collection by Spyros Vlachopoulos. Konstantinos Papagergiou closes the collection with a subtle analysis of ideas of freedom as elaborated by the three foremost political theorists of the Neohellenic Enlightenment. Writing from the perspective of normative political theory, he reminds readers of this collection that over an extended period of gestation and on the battlefield of revolutionary action, the Greek struggle for liberation, with its enormous costs and sacrifices, was inspired and guided by the indomitable ideals of freedom, human rights, and self-determination of individuals and communities, which had guided European modernity.

What emerges from the specialized studies in the collection is first the significance of the Greek Revolution as an international event. David Bell very perceptively remarks in his own chapter that the Greek Revolution could be seen in a long-term perspective as the most international of all revolutions in the age because it was the one revolutionary outbreak in which so many other powers and movements internationally were entangled.

What could be seen as a distinctive feature of the Greek Revolution in the broader context of European history in the first half of the nineteenth century, in "Metternich's Europe" as it has been aptly described,[34] involved the revival of revolution in Europe after the defeat of the French Revolution and the Restoration following the Congress of Vienna. The entire phenomenon of historical action represented by the Greek Revolution – its planning at the heyday of reaction and repression, its outbreak and persistence over a ten-year period amidst incredible odds and setbacks, and its internationalization through the Philhellenic movements around the Western world and through Great Power diplomacy – revived the Age of Revolution by heartening liberal hopes and national claims everywhere and thus prolonging the age to 1848. The several papers in this collection illustrate in concrete and authoritative ways the flow of events, which marked the revival of revolution in Europe through the drama of revolutionary action in the cause of the liberation of Greece.

Notes

1 John Locke, *An Essay concerning Human Understanding*, ed. P. H. Nidditch (Oxford, 1975), 10.

14 *Paschalis M. Kitromilides*

2 Adamantios Korais, *Προλεγόμενα στους αρχαίους Έλληνες συγγραφείς* [Prolegomena to ancient Greek authors], vol. I (Athens, 1984), 495.

3 See Miroslav Šedivý, *The Decline of the Congress System. Metternich, Italy and European Diplomacy* (London, 2018), 32.

4 Paschalis M. Kitromilides, *The Enlightenment as Social Criticism. Iosipos Moisiodax and Greek Culture in the Eighteenth Century* (Princeton, 1992), 49. See further idem, "Diaspora, Identity, and Nation-Building", in *Homelands and Diasporas. Greeks, Jews and their Migrations*, ed. Mina Rozen (London and New York, 2008), 322–331.

5 Kitromilides, *The Enlightenment as Social Criticism*, 21. On the important subject of Greek diaspora at the time Moisiodax was writing see Mathieu Grenet, *La fabrique communitaire. Les Grecs à Venise, Livourne et Marseille 1770–1840* (Athens and Rome, 2016) and Olga Katsiardi-Hering and Maria A. Stassinopoulou, eds., *Across the Danube. Southeastern Europeans and their Travelling Identities (17th–19th C.)* (Leiden and Boston, 2017).

6 Dimitrios Katartzis, *Τα ευρισκόμενα* [The surviving works], ed. C. Th. Dimaras (Athens, 1960), 44.

7 *Ibid.*

8 *Ibid.*, 45.

9 See C. Th. Dimaras, "D. Catargi, 'philosophe' grec", *La Grèce au temps des Lumières* (Geneva: Droz, 1969), 26–36.

10 P. M. Kitromilides, "An Enlightenment Perspective on Balkan Cultural Pluralism: The Republican Vision of Rhigas Velestinlis", *History of Political Thought* 24 (2003): 465–479.

11 See Albert B. Lord, "The Heroic Tradition of Greek Epic and Ballad: Continuity and Change", in *Hellenism and the First Greek War of Liberation (1821–1830): Continuity and Change*, eds. N. P. Diamandouros et al. (Thessaloniki, 1976), 79–94. See further, Roderick Beaton, *Folk poetry of modern Greece* (Cambridge, 1980), 102–111, 168–171.

12 D. Djordjevic and Stephen Fischer-Galati, *The Balkan Revolutionary Tradition* (New York, 1981), 14–15, 31–32, 41–42, 54–55, 69–71, 74–76. On the agents of primitive social protest see the perceptive remarks by Traian Stoianovich, *Balkan Worlds. The First and Last Europe* (New York, 1994), 165–168.

13 Rhigas Velestinlis, *Απαντα τα σωζόμενα*, vol. V, ed. P. M. Kitromilides (Athens, 2000), 33–35.

14 Jonathan Israel, *The Enlightenment That Failed* (Oxford, 2019), 1051.

15 For a survey of Korais's political thought see Paschalis M. Kitromilides, *Enlightenment and Revolution. The Making of Modern Greece* (Cambridge, MA and London, 2013), pp. 175–199.

16 Seymour Martin Lipset, *The First New Nation. The United States in Historical and Comparative Perspective* (Garden City, New York, 1967). Lipset was responding to the wave of academic interest in the emergence of "new nations" out of the dissolution of colonial empires in Asia and Africa and reminded writers on "political development" in the 1960s and the 1970s that there had been a serious precedent to all that in the case of American independence. On the rise of "new nations" see Rupert Emerson, *From Empire to Nation* (Cambridge, MA., 1960).

17 See Adamantios Korais, *Σημειώσεις εις το Προσωρινόν Πολίτευμα της Ελλάδος* [Notes on the Provisional Constitution of Greece], 2nd edition, ed. Paschalis M. Kitromilides (Athens, 2018), 85–89, 100–102, 106–107, 109–115, 188–195, 203–204.

18 In the terms of Jonathan Israel, *The Expanding Blaze: How the American Revolution Ignited the World, 1775–1848* (Princeton, 2017).

The Greek world in the Age of Revolution   15

19 Korais, Σημειώσεις, 117. Another characteristic testimony of the impact of the "American blaze" on Greek political thought at the time of the Greek Revolution was the translation of the Declaration of Independence and the US constitution by Anastasios Polyzoidis in 1824. See A. Polyzoidis, Κείμενα για τη δημοκρατία 1824-1825 [Texts on democracy 1824-1825], ed. Ph. Peonidis and Elpida Vogli (Athens, 2011), 99–106.
20 Korais, Σημειώσεις, 196.
21 Ibid., 95.
22 Jacques Godechot, "La Grande Nation". L'expansion de la France révolutionnaire dans le monde, 1789–1799, 2nd edition (Paris, 1956, 1979).
23 R. R. Palmer, The Age of the Democratic Revolution, vol. I: The Challenge (Princeton, 1959); vol. II: The Struggle (Princeton, 1964). On the significance of the historiographical contributions of J. Godechot and R. R. Palmer cf. the critical appraisals by Wolfgang Schmale, "Révolution française, révolution occidentale" and Annie Jourdan, "Les révolutions républicaines d'occident (1770–1779/1800). Propositions d'analyse en termes de configuration", La Révolution française. Idéaux, singularités, influences, ed. R. Chagny (Grenoble, 2002), 3-10 and 219–235, respectively. Marc Belissa, "De l' ordre d' Ancien Régime à l'ordre international: approches de l' histoire des relations internationales", in La Révolution à l'œuvre: perspectives actuelles dans l' histoire de la Révolution française, ed. Jean-Clement Martin (Rennes, 2005), 217–227, esp. 221–222 connects the works of Palmer and Godechot with the emergence of a new from of 'international history' in the post World War II period, signaled especially by the imposing eight-volume Histoire des relations internationales, ed. Pierre Renouvin (Paris, 1953-1958).
24 Godechot, op. cit., vol. I, 197–200; Palmer, op. cit., vol. II, 334–335.
25 Eric Hobsbawm, The Age of Revolution 1789–1848 (London, 1962). See esp. pp. 44–73, 202–217, 238–257.
26 See especially David Armitage, "Foreword", in R. R. Palmer, The Age of the Democratic Revolution, Princeton Legacy Library reprint (Princeton, 2014), xv–xxiv.
27 For relevant examples see David Armitage and S. Subrahmanyam, eds., The Age of Revolutions in Global Context c. 1760–1840 (Houndmills and New York, 2010). See additionally, Peter Hill, "How global was the age of revolutions? The case of Mount Lebanon, 1821", Journal of Global History (2020): 1–20, which argues that political economy rather than the impact of French revolutionary ideas should be seen as the causal factor shaping the age of revolution on a global scale. The impact of political economy as a causal factor in social and political change, however, needs to be mediated in conceptual and ideological terms, which at the time could only emanate from sources such as the ideas of the "Age of Revolution".
28 The debates generated by Jonathan Isreal's imposing tetralogy on the Enlightenment bear directly on the conceptualization of the Age of Revolution. The critical review by David A. Bell, "Where do we come from", The New Republic, March 1, 2012, is quite suggestive in this regard. Israel himself has devoted two further volumes to the subject of the Age of Revolution. See Revolutionary Ideas. An Intellectual History of the French Revolution from the Rights of Man to Robespierre (Princeton, 2014) and The Expanding Blaze.
29 See, for example, David Bell and Yair Mintzker, eds., Rethinking the Age of Revolutions. France and the Birth of the Modern World (Oxford, 2018).
30 See Elie Kedourie, ed., Nationalism in Asia and Africa (New York: Meridian, 1970), 37–48. Korais's text on 153–188.
31 See, for example, David A. Bell, The Cult of the Nation in France. Inventing Nationalism 1680–1800 (Cambridge, Mass., 2001), 167–197, on the significance of

16 *Paschalis M. Kitromilides*

producing a common national language as the unifier of the nation. Hobsbawm, *The Age of Revolution*, 163–177 provides an important appraisal of nationalism as a fundamental factor in revolutionary change.

32 See John C. Campbell, "The Influence of Western Political Thought in the Romanian Principalities, 1821–1848. The Generation of 1848", *Journal of Central European Affairs* IV (1944): 262–273 and Dan Berindei, "L'idéologie politique des revolutionnaires roumains de 1848", *Nouvelles études d'histoire* IV (1970): 207–221. On the flow of revolutionary events see Keith Hitchins, *The Romanians 1774–1866* (Oxford, 1996), 230–272.

33 Cf. the pioneering study by David H. Bayley, "The Police and Political Development in Europe", in *The Formation of National States in Western Europe*, ed. Charles Tilly (Princeton, 1975), 328–379.

34 As coined by Mack Walker, ed., *Metternich's Europe 1813–1848* (New York, 1968).

Part I

Resonances of the Age of Revolution I

1 Revolutions in Europe (1776–1848)

Annie Jourdan

Despite the numerous publications discussing European revolutions, little has been presented on those of the seventeenth century, and much remains to be said on those of the eighteenth and nineteenth centuries[1]. One may wonder why some countries remained immune to the five revolutionary waves that followed each other. For example, the first wave occurred in the 1780s, which includes the American Revolution as an extension of the European revolution given the intensity of transatlantic communications at that time. The second wave, which hit in the 1790s, affected much of Europe on the heels of the French Revolution and culminated in the uprisings of the 1820s. Thereafter came the 1830s wave and, finally, the 'People's Spring' of 1848. Surprisingly enough, some important countries such as Prussia, and Austria, did not participate in the waves of the 1820s and the 1830s, nor did Great Britain – or, more accurately, England, given that Ireland tried time and again to liberate itself from British rule.[2] I am not going to provide a definitive answer to this important question, although it needs to be asked.[3] Obviously, Great Britain is an exception in the European constellation because the country experienced two seventeenth-century revolutions that produced a number of liberal institutions such as bills of rights, writs of *habeas corpus*, and other private and public liberties. Britain was and has remained a model for Europe during the following centuries, as we will see later in this chapter. Conversely, countries governed by enlightened despots had more difficulty enforcing liberal laws in their government. The only reforms approved by these despots tended to strengthen their power and rationalize their states in the hope of increasing their resources. Such was the case of the Austrian Emperor Joseph II and the Prussian King Frederic the Great. In the Holy Roman Empire, Belgium was the only province to enter into a revolution; the others failed to resist official repression. Such was the case for Hungary.

One can also ask why recent historians are so fond of the term 'Atlantic Revolution', given that non-Atlantic countries were the first to be affected by the revolutionary phenomenon. Those that come to mind are Corsica in the 1750s, Poland in the 1790s, and then Italy, the Rhineland, the Republic of Geneva, and Switzerland which are Mediterranean or continental

20 *Annie Jourdan*

countries. In the 1820s, indeed, more Mediterranean nations were touched by revolution, notably Spain, Naples, Piedmont, and Greece. Although it is not strictly a Mediterranean country, Portugal was also affected.[4] The popularity of the term 'Atlantic Revolution' suggests that an Americo-centrism may be replacing the old-fashioned Eurocentrism by focusing on the South American and Caribbean revolutions at the expense of the European uprisings. Additionally, with the rise of global history, thanks to Bayly's works and successes, the Atlantic Revolution is considered to be a global revolution despite the fact that it is difficult or almost impossible to discover any Asian, African, or Russian echoes. Following the work of Eric Hobsbawm, Michael Lang has proven this point successfully.[5] Since 2004, I have chosen to call them Western revolutions using the plural form because each was unique. However, this appellation is also open to criticism and dismissal as yet another centrism. To conclude on this point, since 1776, revolutions occurred in both the Atlantic and the Mediterranean but also on the continent.[6] Regardless of the name, however, the relevance was more Western and transnational than global.

Analysis of revolutionary waves has the undeniable advantage not only of discovering connections, which seem to function as ricochets, but also of making a distinction among them. Yet even if it produced the same effects in different countries, revolutionary contamination did not necessarily stem from the same causes of discontent and did not necessarily have the same consequences. This is true even though the expectations of the patriots were identical, at least between 1789 and 1799 and probably until 1848 with some qualifications. In fact, except for those in the United States between 1776–1786, which were separate cases,[7] the first revolutions of the 1780s were mostly conservative. They strove to restore ancient liberties and customs, especially in Belgium, the Netherlands, Geneva, and Switzerland, that seemed to be threatened by the reforms of enlightened despots in Belgium/France, or by the autocratic laws enforced by magistrates in Holland/Geneva/Switzerland. Other causes of discontent could have included the loss of independence, or at least the fear of losing it. This could have driven states to strengthen national unity, as in the cases of Corsica in the 1750s and Poland in the 1790s and during the 1820s wave in Italy against Austria and in Greece against the Ottoman Empire. In contrast, revolutionaries in both North America and South America sought emancipation from their colonial masters.

These revolutionary waves can be studied from several perspectives.[8] In a recent book review, David A. Bell reminds us that to understand global connections, historians have to consider several factors on different levels including direct or indirect influences, the different time scales, and the different reasonings behind public and individual decisions. In short, history is not just 'a matter of the ripples on the surface of events, but of the current beneath them, and the slow, steady tides'.[9] All these dimensions must be taken into account by historians.

Revolutions in Europe (1776–1848) 21

In this essay, I try to understand what was really going on in Europe by studying the different constitutional plans and texts implemented or devised by European revolutionaries and then comparing them with those of the first revolutions. This can offer us far more information than any political discourse and gives an overview of the claims of the dominant coalitions. In addition, by comparing these claims with those of 1776 or 1789/1793, as well as with one another, we can reveal how the connections have functioned and have led to rejection, misunderstanding, acceptance, and inspiration or correction and adaptation.

The first wave

In the 1780s, despite the precedent of the American Revolution, which had recently proclaimed and enforced the rights of men,[10] most European countries were asking only for e-establishment of their original rights – rights that were seen as having been violated by their respective governments. Even in France, where the American constitution was translated in 1783 with the approval of the French king, thinkers such as Condorcet were not venturing as far as the Americans in their request.[11] Rather than asking for absolute revolutionary Liberty with capital L, they requested only a few particular liberties. Everything changed between 1788 and 1789, when France itself, the most densely populated and powerful country on the continent, underwent a revolution. Consequently, discussions of bills of rights and constitutions proliferated, and the new American Republic was updated to alternately become a positive or negative reference. This suggests that until that time, Europe had not fully understood the degree of radical innovation born from the American War of Independence (1776–1783). Thanks to French events and to the debates of the National Assembly, these revolutionary creations came to be better understood, and they inspired the Europeans. Among these creations, the need for a bill of rights and a written constitution – both bastions against arbitrary power – prevailed. The 1780s had been an incubation period more than a radical impulse. One can detect this in the limited constitutional plans made in the 1780s by Dutch patriots or in the comments made by patriots such as Mandrillon, a French merchant living in Holland.[12] The same was true for Belgian patriots, who asked for radical reforms only after 1789. From that point onwards, everything changed. Patriots followed the trend and asked for more natural rights and popular participation. French and foreign patriots also became aware of at least two models: a federal republic attractive to European federalists, such as the idea of creating the Belgian United States, and a centralized republic appealing to all who dreamed of union and unity. In contrast, only a few patriots at that time considered the British monarchy to be an appropriate solution. Louis XVI's minister Necker was among these patriots, as were the so-called monarchiens. In all concerned countries, the federal and central options were both debated and adapted to local contexts. For instance, the

22 *Annie Jourdan*

Dutch political debate rejected French 'centralized unity' in favour of de-centralized unity, which went against the American absolute federalism.[13] Meanwhile, European patriots had realized the importance of creating a written constitution and a universal bill of rights by this time, and they understood that they had to involve the people to win the battle.[14]

The French Revolution and Europe

We now turn to the relationships between France and her European neighbours, since the French Revolution had a great impact on the continent both during and after this major event. During the first years after the fall of the Bastille, as is well known, successive French governments oscillated between the desire to emancipate oppressed peoples and the need to favour national interest. At that time, Geneva was the only European country to revolutionize itself, taking advantage of the French annexation of Savoy in November 1792. The following February, its bill of rights was ready, and in 1793, a democratic constitution was implemented. At the end of 1792, the Rhineland was invaded by French troops and was occupied until July 1793, whereas Belgium was 'liberated' from the Austrians by the army of Dumouriez and was occupied until his defeat in April 1793. Meanwhile, France had annexed several enclaves including Corsica, Avignon, Savoy, and Nice on the pretence that their people wanted to become French. But the French government hesitated on the fate of the Belgians and Germans,[15] questioning whether these territories should be annexed or remain independent.[16] France's military defeats in 1793 put an end to these questions. It was not until French military resurgence in 1795 that the problem of 'liberated territories' arose again.

At the end of the Thermidorian Convention in September 1795, following two French victories, only two countries had achieved their own revolutions: the United Provinces of the Netherlands and the Republic of Geneva; Belgium was eventually annexed to France. It is important to note that these three countries had already experienced moderate revolutions in the 1780s. Their patriots sought revenge and closely followed what was going on in Paris in the hope that France would help them to return home and seize power. Moreover, two of them were already republics, albeit oligarchies, with a great republican tradition. This could explain why they were so quick to achieve their own revolutions. When the French Revolution broke out and the Dutch, Belgian, and Genevan refugees were able to return to their countries, they did so with dreams of revenge against their former oppressors. In addition, they had formulated and continually focused on numerous plans during their exile based on declaratory and constitutional concepts as well as ideas about legal codification. However, none of their visions were similar to the French ones. Each was adapted to a specific national character, as they themselves asserted.[17] This point was not always as obvious at it appears to be today. Historians in the 1960s–1980s have largely neglected this aspect and have emphasized the unilateral influence of France far too much.

In Italy, the situation was quite different. Some states such as Tuscany and Lombardy had already been reformed and modernized by their Austrian rulers. Conversely, Rome and the Papal States, Piedmont–Sardinia and Naples–Sicily still repressed everyone who strove for changes, whereas the republics of Venice and Genoa had become more oligarchic.[18] The situation was revolutionary only among some intellectuals just after the French Revolution began; the same was true in Germany and to a larger degree in the Rhineland. In Switzerland, the French and Genevan revolutions had stirred up democratic aspirations, or at least libertarian ones among inhabitants who suffered from a lack of liberty and Bern's imperialism. Although authorities forbade the tricolor cockade and refused to recognize the French Republic, extensive changes were sought by patriots, including members of the Helvetic Club in Paris, where Swiss refugees met regularly. Until 1796, when the refugee Frederic César de la Harpe arrived in the French capital and Bonaparte was creating new republics in Italy, France refused to intervene because a neutral Switzerland had many advantages.[19] Among other benefits, it protected France's eastern frontiers from Austria. But Bonaparte's victories and his so-called sister republics put an end to this policy. Once Bonaparte had created the Cisalpine Republic in Lombardy, he needed to protect his creation, and he realized that he had to obtain the Swiss canton of Valais. Some time later, he sought to reunite the Italian Swiss territories to 'his' republic. Meanwhile, La Harpe and his colleague Peter Ochs tried to convince the French Directory to help them overthrow the Swiss governments. At the end of 1797, they had written a draft constitution with the involvement of Bonaparte.

The key point is that until Bonaparte's victories, there were only two free (sister) republics: the Genevan and the Batavian republics. Although the Batavian Republic had to accept French troops on its territory, these forces did not intervene until asked to do so by the Dutch authorities. Until January 1798, France allowed the Batavian Republic to adopt its own constitution and form of government as long as it remained a republic. Yet, two years had passed, and the Dutch had rejected the first 1797 constitutional plan. Everything was provisional in the entire country, which was rather negative for the Franco–Dutch alliance. Meanwhile, Bonaparte had changed the face of Italy without the permission of his government, which wanted to exchange Italian territories for Belgium and the left bank of the Rhine. Bonaparte had created the Cisalpine Republic and stimulated the modernization of the Genoese Republic while conspiring against the aristocratic Venetian Republic. The Campo Formio treaty recognized the new order and provided that the French would also occupy Venice's Ionian Islands Corfou, Cephalonia, Zante, Santa Maura (Lefkada), and Cerigo (Kythira). Geopolitics resulted in other changes because the new territories needed to be protected, which meant that the French army was responsible

24 Annie Jourdan

for looking after far more spaces. By the late 1790s, France was engaged in a complex and risky challenge that was aided by foreign patriots such as Giuseppe Ceracchi, a Roman sculptor, and Buonarotti, a Tuscan Jacobin. At the beginning of 1798, the French Directory went one step further by accepting the Egyptian expedition of Bonaparte. This proved to be a huge mistake because it alienated both Russia and Turkey and provoked a far stronger anti-French coalition than the first one. Meanwhile, other generals were imitating the young hero and seeking to establish their own republic. General Hoche, for instance, hoped to establish a Cisrhenan Republic in the Rhineland but died just before the plan was finalized. Rome was occupied and transformed into a republic in the French mold, whereas the Helvetic Republic was proclaimed, and Geneva was annexed to France. Chaos was increasing on the continent and even in Ireland, where a violent uprising took place in 1798 in conjunction with an attempted French invasion. Both failed lamentably. Moreover, turned upside down by Bonaparte, Italy became a scene of ambitions and disturbances as well as despoliation and plundering. In short, the entire peninsula was in a state of chaos that was exacerbated by the predatory behaviour of the new Italian republics toward their neighbours (e.g. the Cisalpine dreamed of conquering Genoa).

Finally, in 1798–1799, some French generals transformed or tried to transform the last traditional Italian states into democratic republics. Although Championnet was successful in Naples, Joubert's attempt in Piedmont and Sérurier's plan in Lucca were both in vain. Aware of the dangers of further Italian democratization, the Directory forbade the creation of new republics in November 1798. By then, however, it was too late.[20]

Furthermore, what had been desired by the majority of Dutch and Genevan people was rejected in other contexts, especially when imposed by foreign occupation and accompanied by violence, looting, and depredation. In Italy and Switzerland, the new order divided the inhabitants against each another. Civil war loomed. The same thing almost happened in the Ionian Islands, where the citizens did not really understand what the French wanted from them.[21] Worst of all, the aggressive policy of the French Directory in 1798 spooked the great powers, including Turkey and Russia. What England had failed to accomplish several years earlier – a strong coalition of European powers against France – the Directory's aggressive policy brought to fruition! This policy had disastrous consequences for France and its allies. Italy was lost; Switzerland split into two hostile factions of pro-French and pro-Austrian; and the Helvetic Republic almost died. During this tragic crisis, the Batavian Republic alone resisted and survived. This dramatic situation helps to explain why some French politicians wanted to change the regime and strengthen the executive power, but they made a new mistake when they asked Bonaparte to help them. The Coup of 18 Brumaire sounded the knell of the republic in France even though it remained nominal until 1806. Thereafter, another history began with Bonaparte at the helm, a history for which he is responsible and whose preface was written from 1797

The 1820s in Europe

When the "Corsican ogre" died in 1815, the expectations aroused by the French Revolution were still alive. Under the Restoration (1815–1830), the so-called liberals wanted to complete what remained to be done. As the journalist of the liberal *Mercure Surveillant*, Charles de Ceulleneer contended, "the Revolution is not finished and threatens all of Europe with a universal fire" if the governments refused to grant national representation and constitutional liberties to the people.[23] A new generation was taking over these aspirations and

asked for a liberal government and the rule of law. Among the members of this international movement were Italian, Spanish, Portuguese, and Greek patriots. The third wave was on its way. These patriots met all over the continent, including London, Paris, and Brussels. A Greek committee was everywhere present, and in Brussels it was supported by the Belgian banker François Rittweger.[24] They recruited volunteers to send to respective countries to fight the people's oppressors. Among them was the famous Spanish general Francisco Mina, who in 1820 implemented the 1812 Cadix constitution in Spain. The same constitution was also adopted in Portugal, Naples, and Piedmont during the revolutions of 1820–1821.[25] The 'volcano is still active', as another witness wrote. In France, royalists observed these signs of spreading revolution with alarm. They concluded that every idea of reform that hinted at a return to 1789–1799 had to be resisted at all cost. Therefore, the legacy of the revolution was Janus-faced, especially in France. For liberals and radicals, it was an example to be repeated, a promise to be fulfilled. For conservatives and royalists, it was the hydra's seed that needed to be crushed before it could germinate and develop into an invincible monster.

What did revolutionaries strive for in the 1820s? The promises of the French Revolution! That is, fundamental liberties guaranteed by a written constitution, genuine national representation, separation of powers, and the pre-eminence of law over all other authorities. But they also strove for national independence. The Republican Revolution of the 1790s, which was supported by the people, was followed by a period of liberation of the colonized peoples from the colonizers, which Jeremy Adelman referd to as an 'imperial revolution'.[26] But instead of being directed by lawyers and intellectuals, as it had been during the American and French revolutions, this new style of revolution was far more often led by generals and their armies in Latin America and in Europe, where Napoleon's former officers fought against the 'oppressors'. Good examples of this type of adventurer are General Fabvier, who fought in Spain against conservatives in 1823 and in Greece for independence in the following years, and General Lallemand,

26 *Annie Jourdan*

who invaded Spanish Mexico in 1818 and served in Spain and in Greece. This 1820s wave appeared to combine revolutionary legacy *and* Bonapartist legacy! In fact, all of the losers of 1789–1815 banded together against the victorious Restoration, so these two legacies actually did fuse after 1815. Greece is a good example of this situation, as are the South American revolutions. Is it so surprising when one knows that a great number of French generals and officers joined their European or American counterparts in the hope of finding action and because they felt nostalgic for the Great Adventure of the Revolution and Empire? With this conclusion, I do not mean to imply that the French generals actually did this; rather, they inspired a new type of revolution that would have severe consequences in the future. Known as the 'pronunciamiento', this form of revolution represented a new type of political upheaval that was led by the army.[27]

A new model

By this time, a new model was spreading across revolutionary Europe: the Spanish Constitution of 1812. With this constitutional monarchy based on national sovereignty and religion, bills of rights disappeared and with them, the natural rights of man.[28] Liberty and equality remained but only as civil rights and as constitutional freedoms; there was one legislative body and a separation of powers between it and the monarch. This Spanish model, which combined local traditions and history with positive laws, was rejected by the Spanish king as a 'copy of the revolutionary and democratic principles of the French Constitution of 1791'; nonetheless, he was forced to accept it during the three-year reign of liberalism in Spain (1820–1823). In Spain, Portugal, Naples, and Piedmont, this model dominated.[29] In Restoration France (1814–1830), something quite different happened – something Pierre Rosenvallon referred to as the 'English moment'.[30] This featured a mixed regime founded on national sovereignty and hereditary monarchy but with two legislative bodies: a House of Lords and a House of Commons. The constitution was called a Charter, given by the king to his subjects just as that in England. Although ministers became responsible, the king was not, and he was afforded the right of dissolution. In our context, this means that a model that seemed to have become obsolete since 1789 could resurface and become relevant again. Metternich certainly thought it was, and he described it as inspired by Great Britain, but 'adapted to suit the new needs'. In contrast, he disapproved of the Spanish liberal constitution as dangerous for thrones and social peace. For Metternich, indeed, the Spanish model was too close to the French one.[31]

In Greece, the first revolutionary constitutions (1822, 1823, and 1827) were also different. As in Spain, there was a single legislative body and a reference to national religion. Here, too, no natural rights were evoked. Only the 'public right of the Greeks' was accepted: equality before the law, meritocracy, and civil rights. The Greek constitutions also enshrined the

Revolutions in Europe (1776–1848) 27

right to be heard by the court and to be judged publicly, and they abolished torture. A great difference between the French Constitution of 1791 and the Spanish one of 1812 was that the executive power would not be exercised by a king but by a collegial body of five men, such as that in France in 1793 and 1795. The Greek constitutional text of 1827 introduced a president to be chosen by the legislative body,[32] which marked the first time this institution became a reality in Europe.[33] It might have been inspired by the American example, just as the Greek Act of Independence (January 1822) echoed the American Declaration of 1776.[34] The first president was Ioannis Capodistrias, who had already played a leading role in the Septinsular Republic between 1803 and 1807. Interesting, too, are several articles that seem to have been inspired by French codification such as civil code, military code, and commercial code as well as articles on the national guard, public justice, and justices of the peace. More allusions to the French revolutionary texts can be found, such as the proclamations that the Greek state would be 'one and indivisible' and that 'the sovereignty lies in the nation and that power issues from and exists only for it'. Article 99 of the 1827 Constitution is explicit because it mentions that codification would be founded on French legislation. However, the Greek constitutions, like those of France (1814) and Spain (1812), omit any mention of natural rights. The only rights the Greeks were to enjoy were limited to life, honour, property, and personal liberty under the law (1827). They were also granted the right to express themselves and to publish, while nobility would be suppressed. This French-style constitution did not please the Holy Alliance or England, and in 1830, during the fourth revolutionary wave, the Greek Republic had to become a hereditary monarchy.[35] The same thing happened in Belgium, which was forced to accept a king, and in Spain, where French bayonets ended the constitutional experiment and restored the unreconstructed Ferdinand VII to the throne in 1823. The revolutions of the 1830s had initial revolutionary aspirations but produced regressive results. Europe was becoming monarchist again.[36] The only progress was that all of these monarchies were constitutional except for that in Greece, whose king first refused to grant his people a founding text. Only Republican Switzerland escaped this fate. Republicanism had fallen into disgrace and was dismissed as a synonym of democracy.[37]

Several important changes were finally enacted during the fifth wave (1848). This transnational revolution affected the European continent, including Germany, Italy, Poland, Hungary, Austria, Switzerland, and France. Spain and Portugal were spared, whereas Great Britain, Belgium, and Greece remained quite peaceful. The November 1848 French Constitution speaks volumes about contemporary expectations. Natural rights were invoked anew; fraternity had priority over liberty and property and for the first time became part of the French national motto of 'Liberty, Equality, Fraternity'. Under this motto of fraternity, the rights to work, education, and protection were proclaimed, and the French Republic was revived. For the first time since 1793,

28 Annie Jourdan

France acknowledged its revolutionary inheritance, but only for a short time because Napoleon's nephew soon followed his uncle's example and in 1852 assassinated the Second French Republic. In other countries, such as Italy and Germany, a first step was made in the realization of national unity against foreign 'oppressors'. Indeed, in most European countries including Hungary, Romania, and Poland, this revolution was more of an independence war against imperial powers than it ever was in France. But for these nations, too, the 1848 revolutions failed, and no new republic was created except in France.[38]

Conclusion

These revolutionary waves reveal that there was no single model and that each wave had its own characteristics. Among the models, one can distinguish the English, American, French, and the Spanish ones, with each learning from the mistakes of those that came before. As Mazzini contended, for instance, it was time to renew French tradition and 'Italianize' the movement. Germans rejected this same French tradition and aspired to a 'legal revolution' – whatever that may have been. Because the French Revolutionary model had been disqualified by France's tragedies and Napoleon's imperialism, Restoration Europeans preferred not to be associated with something French. Indeed, when some French institutions were borrowed, they were never touted as such. Even though the Spanish constitution appeared to be similar to the first French one, its legislators tried to avoid acknowledging this, preferring instead to mention British inspiration and Spanish tradition. French terminology was modified and Hispanicized. This, while each move in Paris had an electrifying effect beyond France, Gallican influence had to be concealed.[39]

Other interesting conclusions can be drawn. The first is that borrowing could concern different texts and sources. For example, while the Greek Act of Independence remained original, it had many things in common with the American Declaration of 1776, and its constitutional texts showed some similarity to the French and the Spanish ones. This is understandable since each country had its own priorities according to its contingencies and culture. One thing is sure, however: the revolutions of the 1820s and 1830s were not as generous as those of the 1790s. Gone were the social rights and political liberties, the social guaranty and the right to work, and the right to financial support and protection. Universal suffrage became taboo. What remained were the right to be educated and the freedom to express oneself. The very fact that natural rights were no longer mentioned also means that the people no longer had the right to rise up against its government – even though the new regimes themselves had arisen from revolution!

The composition of revolutionary coalitions was also changing. In 1776 or 1789, almost every citizen was involved. During the Restoration era, a shift occurred that pushed forward officers and soldiers as well as and secret societies. Inspired by freemasonry and counter-revolutionary associations, these secret societies tried to win civil society over to their cause and overthrow the governments by relying on an international network of revolutionaries. This was quite evident during the Greek Revolution, in which volunteers from Europe fought for Greek independence. At that time, there was no question of nationalism; the revolutionary cause was universal. This was true even in Russia, where officers who were in Spain in 1823 took the Greek side before trying to revolutionize their own country in December 1825.[40] But this was not enough to defeat the conservative coalition of royalist Europe. In the 1820s, the Holly Alliance proved strong enough to stop these uprisings. France stopped it in Spain; Austria stopped it in Italy, and Prussia stopped it in Germany. By the end of the decade, however, something had changed. The French king sent 14,000 soldiers to Greece to help fight against the country's oppressors with the agreement of Russia and England. This dealt an unexpected blow to the Holly Alliance.

The 1830s wave was quite similar, although it was more a conclusion of the 1820s uprisings than an actual turning point. Greece and Belgium were proclaimed independent but had to accept hereditary monarchy. For the latter, it was successful, and constitutional Belgium remained peaceful during the following years. But the new Greek King Otto, in contrast to Leopold of Belgium, refused to enforce a constitution and governed as an absolute ruler. The consequences were general discontent followed by a military coup in September 1843. This finally persuaded Otto to grant a constitution to his people. In France, the political situation was quite different. The great revolution was revived in 1830 and divided the French once again. Some wished to return to 1789; others wanted 1793. Some wanted a republic; others wanted a constitutional monarchy. The monarchists won. Consequently, instability persisted throughout the period of 1830–1848.

In actuality, the greatest shift happened in 1848, when the revolutions brought together a massive coalition of liberals and radicals. For some months, European patriots believed that their expectations would be realized. In France, a generous republican constitution was implemented that promised political and social rights reminiscent of those in 1793. But four years later, the Second French Republic was again overthrown by a new Bonaparte, and these rights abolished. In Europe, all revolutions were reduced to nothing, making it difficult to maintain liberty, equality, and fraternity.[41] However, all three of these French motto ideals would remain popular expectations across the Western world. For want of these 'godly' principles, oppressed peoples would turn to nationalism. It was another way of obtaining independence and entering another stage. In addition, it had become clear that global connections do not necessarily provoke revolutions across the world even though they may inspire political, social, technical, legal, or cultural changes.

30 *Annie Jourdan*

Notes

1 On the seventeenth century revolutions, see the recent book by Edmond Dziembowski, *Le Siècle des revolutions, 1660–1789* (Paris, 2019), which, however focuses on the 1688–1689 revolution and does not tackle the Cromwell period.
2 Thanks to the Great Reform Act of 1832, perhaps.
3 See for instance Eric J. Hobsbawm, *The Age of Revolutions* (London, 1962).
4 Certainly, I have not forgotten about Haiti or South America and its successive revolutions between 1810 and 1825. However, they are not the focus here. Further information is given by Rafe Blaufarb in *The Revolutionary Atlantic: Republican Visions 1760–1830. A Documentary History* (Oxford, 2017). For information on the Mediterranean, see M. Phlip & J. Innes, eds, *Re-imagining Democracy in the Mediterranean (1780–1860)* (Oxford, 2018).
5 Michael Lang, 'Globalization and its History', *Journal of Modern History*, 78 (2006): 899–931.
6 If Corsica is included, this wave can be considered to have started in the 1750s.
7 One could say that although the results of the American Revolution went far past its initial intentions, 1787–1789 rectified some of the 'excesses' of the previous revolutionary decade.
8 See the chapter by David A. Bell in this volume.
9 David A. Bell, 'Did Britain win the American Revolution?', *New York Review of Books*, issue 23, April 2020.
10 Great Britain had implemented a bill of rights in 1688, but they addressed only British subjects.
11 Compare Condorcet's *De l'Influence de la Révolution américaine* (Paris, 1786) with his *Lettre d'un citoyen des Etats-Unis* from 1788 to see the evolution of his views.
12 See A. Jourdan, *La Révolution batave entre la France et l'Amérique* (Paris, 2008), 53–58.
13 Jourdan, *La Révolution batave*, 161.
14 Genevan patriot and best friend of Brissot, Etienne Clavière thought that the Dutch patriot revolution was doomed to failure because the people were not involved.
15 Edward J. Kolla, *Sovereignty, International Law, and the French Revolution* (Cambridge, 2017). Marc Belissa, *Repenser l'ordre européen. De la société des rois aux droits des nations* (Paris, 2006).
16 A vote in Belgium seemed to indicate that the inhabitants wanted to be part of France. A first step was made in this direction before Dumouriez was beaten.
17 For more qualification and references, see my *La Révolution batave*.
18 Stuart Woolf, *A History of Italy (1700–1860). The Social Construction of Political Change* (London, 1979).
19 On Switzerland, see my *Nouvelle histoire de la Révolution* (Paris, 2018), 428–463.
20 Antonino de Francesco, *L'Italia di Bonaparte, Politica, statualità e nazione nella penisola tra due revoluzioni, 1796–1821* (Turin, 2011).
21 See the *Correspondence* of Ioannis Capodistrias for a qualified overview. In the 1820s, the Greeks had a better understanding of French reforms. Meanwhile, Greek brokers had popularized the revolutionary ideas and reforms. The most important was Rhigas Velestinlis (Pheraios), who was executed with his seven companions in an Ottoman jail in Belgrade in 1798.
22 Among these creations, one can quote a public justice, justice of the peace and jury, law codification, written constitution and fundamental rights including civil and no longer civic or political.
23 Charles de Ceulleneer, *Défense du Mercure surveillant* (Brussels, 1816).
24 There were many more Greek committees on the continent, in London and in Paris. I mention the Brussels committee because it is less known. Thanks to the

Revolutions in Europe (1776–1848) 31

Dutch king and his son, Brussels indeed became a revolutionary centre. See Archives nationales de France, F7–6651 (Lettres de Bruxelles).

25 See Matthew Brown & Gabriel Paquette, eds, *Connections after Colonialism. Europe and Latin America in the 1820s,* Tuscaloosa (Alabama), 2013.

26 Jeremy Adelman, 'An Age of Imperial Revolution', *The American Historical Review* 113 (2008): 319–340.

27 Rafe Blaufarb, 'The French Revolutionary Wars and the Making of American Empire', in *The French Revolution in Global Perspective*, ed. by Suzanne Desan, Lynn Hunt & W. M. Nelson, Ithaca & London, 2013, pp. 148–162, and Irene Castells, 'Le libéralisme insurrectionnel espagnol (1814–1830)', *Annales historiques de la Révolution française*, no. 336 (2004): 221–233. For other influences and adventurers, see Matthew Brown, *Adventuring through Spanish Colonies. Simon Bolivar, Foreign Mercenaries and the Birth of new Nations* (Chicago, 2012).

28 This was already the case in the first Bonapartist Constitution of 1799.

29 Jean-Baptiste Busaall, *Le spectre du jacobinisme. L'expérience constitionnelle française et le libéralisme espagnol (1808–1814)* (Madrid, 2012), and Joaquim Varela Suanzes-Carpegna, 'La Constitution de Cadix dans son contexte espagnol et européen (1808–1823)', *Jus Politicum*, no. 9 (2013): 1–25.

30 Pierre Rosanvallon, *La Monarchie impossible. Les Chartes de 1814 et de 1830* (Paris, 1994), 57–64.

31 Stéphane Pierré-Caps, 'La Constitution de Cadix et le droit constitutionnel européen', *Revue Civitas Europa*, no. 29 (2012): 5–21.

32 These texts in French and the Act of Independence can be found online at Digithèque MJP: https://mjp.univ-perp.fr/constit/gr.htm

33 South-America had followed the United States on this point and took over republicanism as well as federalism.

34 The Constitution of 1827 mentions a single elected executive for seven years. The legislative power is now sitting four to five months and is no longer permanent. I would suggest that this new text with its references to codification and a strong executive was inspired more by the Napoleonic regime than the first Greek constitutions with their collegial executive. Here, we can distinguish French and American inspirations. See also David Armitage, *The Declaration of Independence. A Global History* (Cambridge, MA, 2008), 108, 148.

35 Anne Couderc, 'L' Europe et la Grèce, 1821–1830. Le concert européen face à l'émergence d'un État-nation', *Bulletin de l'Institut Pierre Renouvin*, no. 42 (2015): 47–74.

36 The antique Dutch Republic had become a monarchy in 1806 when Napoleon created a Dutch throne for his younger brother Louis. In 1814, with English support, the son of the last stadholder, William I replaced Louis. This was the first step in the monarchization of Europe. This process ended with the creation of monarchies in Belgium and Greece, whereas Italy returned into autocratic royal or princely hands.

37 As suggested above, republics are not always democratic, but the restoration powers did not make this distinction.

38 John Breuilly, 'The revolutions of 1848', in *Revolutions and Revolutionary Tradition in the West, 1560–1991*, ed. David Parker (London & New York, 2000), 109–131.

39 Breuilly, 'The revolutions of 1848', 125–128.

40 Julia Grandhaye, 'La république des décembristes. Pour une histoire de la modernité politique en Russie (1760–1870)' (Ph.D. thesis, University of Panthéon-Sorbonne, Paris I, 2008).

41 Breuilly, 118–120.

2 The Greek Revolution and the Age of Revolution

David A. Bell

The Greek Revolution took place in the midst of an extraordinary wave of revolutions that swept across the Western world. As the great Italian historian Franco Venturi asserted many years ago, even before Massachusetts Minutemen and British redcoats began shooting at each other on the Lexington Green in April 1775, revolutionary upheavals had already taken place in Corsica, Geneva, and other European locales.[1] Americans and Britons were still at war in the early 1780s when revolutionary activity began in the Netherlands, and scarcely six years after the achievement of American independence, the convocation of the Estates General at Versailles in 1789 set off the immense explosion of the French Revolution. And long before the debris from that explosion had fallen back to earth, further European upheavals took place in Liège, the Austrian Netherlands, the Dutch Republic, Poland, Ireland, and the parts of Germany and Italy occupied by French revolutionary forces. Across the Atlantic, revolutionary turmoil shook France's slave colonies in the Caribbean and in the largest of these, Saint-Domingue, the greatest and most successful slave revolt in history eventually led to the formation of the independent state of Haiti. Revolutionary conspiracies formed in various parts of Spain's vast American empire and, following Napoleon Bonaparte's occupation of the Spanish metropole in 1808, revolutionary independence movements arose throughout this empire as well. The Greek Revolution took place nearly simultaneously with upheavals in Portugal, Italy, (again) Spain, and, after the achievement of Greek independence the wave continued to roll through the 1830s, notably in France, Belgium, and Poland. If we continue the story to 1848, we have to add further revolutions in several Italian states, France, the German confederation, Prussia, Austria, Hungary, Denmark, Poland, and the Romanian principalities.[2]

Each of these revolutions had features that were *sui generis*. Local traditions, practices, and conditions triggered and shaped each of them. At the same time, however, the international revolutionary context mattered immensely, as well. Revolutionaries everywhere made reference to events in other countries. They copied each other's language, symbols, and practices. Think only of the Greek flag of 1833, with its obvious echo of the flag

The Greek Revolution and the Age of Revolution 33

adopted by the American revolutionaries, or the numerous tricolor flags of the period that echoed the revolutionary tricolor of France. Charismatic revolutionary leaders in one part of the world became models for leaders elsewhere. None of these revolutions, the Greek Revolution very much included, can be understood without a grasp of this larger context and of the various factors that connected the different revolutions of this revolutionary age to each other.

In a recent work, I have suggested that there exist three distinct modes of analysis for understanding this context and for connecting different revolutions to each other.[3] First, there is the study of *structural homologies*. If similar structural conditions exist in different places, they can generate similar tensions, which can provide the basis for similar revolutionary upheavals. Second, there is the study of what might be termed *contagion*: the way the movement of news, concepts, practices, and often people, transmit revolution from one locale to another. Finally, there is the study of *disruption*. A revolution in one place causes such severe disturbances in the politics, economics, and/or social structure of another that it triggers revolutionary activity there, even when shared structural conditions or direct contagion are not present.

These three categories of historical analysis are in no way exclusive of each other. To understand fully the connections between different revolutions, and the larger revolutionary context, we need to employ all three. However, they also require quite distinct approaches. The study of structural homologies is an exercise in comparative history. Depending on the structures in question, it generally involves the analysis of economics, social structure, or political institutions. The most famous student of structural homologies was of course Karl Marx, who claimed that revolutions result when changes in the mode of production generate tensions between social classes that, in turn, provoke revolutionary actions. If revolutions took place at roughly the same time in different places, it was because these places had reached roughly similar stages of economic and social development, resulting in roughly similar class conflicts.[4] In the twentieth century, distinguished scholars, such as Barrington Moore and Theda Skocpol, pursued broadly similar lines of inquiry inspired by Marx.[5] R.R. Palmer, the author of the most important study to date of the "age of revolution," also had a heavily structural approach. His work, which limited itself to the United States and Europe between 1760 and 1800, argued that rising new social formations across the Atlantic world attacked the power of aristocratic elites, in the context of political struggles between monarchies and older "constituted bodies," such as estates and *parlements*.[6]

The study of revolutionary contagion above all involves intellectual and cultural history – and also, in the case of revolutionary actors, biography. This approach was already highly developed more than a century ago when Georg Jellinek and Émile Boutmy debated the intellectual origins of France's Declaration of the Rights of Man and Citizen.[7] David Armitage has carefully

34   David A. Bell

traced the global influence of a single document, the American Declaration of Independence, while Boris Kolonitskii has paid close attention to the use of French Revolutionary symbols in the Russian Revolution.[8] In a massive, enormously erudite, highly ambitious and also highly problematic study of the "age of revolution," Jonathan Israel has argued that a single current of ideas – what he calls "radical Enlightenment" – represented the most important connection between the period's different revolutionary episodes.[9] Janet Polasky, meanwhile, has illuminated the role of "itinerant revolutionaries" who helped to transmit ideas and practices from one country to another.[10]

The study of revolutionary disruption is, by its nature, more varied, and more focused on contingent events. It has proven particularly attractive to recent practitioners of global history, who often seek to trace global patterns of change while eschewing "grand narratives" of the Marxist variety. Christopher Bayly's sweeping history of the modern world, for instance, emphasizes such factors as the way that the debt incurred by the French monarchy while helping the United States achieve independence unintentionally helped to provoke a French national bankruptcy, which in turn helped to trigger the French Revolution.[11] A recent study of the worldwide impact of the American Revolution (which the author claims "devastated the globe"), credits this event with disruptions so massive that they eventually caused everything from the independence of the Spanish American mainland states to the rise of Russia to great power status, and China's decline.[12]

I am in no sense an expert in the history of the Greek Revolution. In what follows, I rely wholly on the expertise of others, and would in no sense claim to be making new revelations about the dramatic and complex events that resulted in the creation of an independent Greek state. My far more modest aim is simply to suggest how the categories of analysis described above could be applied to the Greek case, largely by pointing to similarities between the Greek case and that of the revolutions of the period that I know better – the North American, South American, Haitian, and above all the French.[13]

Structural homologies

Karl Marx, and the long historiographical tradition he inspired, saw changes in the economic mode of production as the key shared structural change behind the revolutions of the late eighteenth and early nineteenth centuries – and especially the French Revolution of 1789. Subsequent historical work has long since brought this conclusion into question, although a current of neo-Marxist analysis has revivified debates by foregrounding the rise of a capitalist consumer economy in the period.[14] Regardless, this particular sort of structural change is not one that current historical work sees as central to understanding the origins of the Greek Revolution. Although Greek commerce and commercial networks flourished in the late eighteenth and early nineteenth centuries, and Greek-speaking merchants in the Ottoman Empire grew in wealth and influence, it is hard to argue that these merchants constituted the nucleus of an incipient capitalist bourgeoisie, still less a revolutionary one. Nor did Greece experience a widespread consumer revolution, comparable to that of Western Europe, in this period.[15] Recently, some historians of the revolutionary Atlantic have drawn attention to shared changing cultural practices in the period, centered on institutions such as literary salons, lending libraries, and learned academies.[16] Here again, it is hard to make a case that such developments occurred to a sufficient extent in Greece. Orthodox Christian academies played an important part in the diffusion of Enlightenment thought in the Greek-speaking world and in the Balkans more generally, but these were traditional institutions of long standing.[17]

There is, however, a different sort of structural issue that historians have recently come to see as crucial for the "Atlantic Revolutions" of the period, and that has considerable relevance to the Greek case. This structural issue, political rather than economic or cultural at heart, was the almost unbearable strain placed upon the great multi-national empires of the period by intensified imperial competition for territory, glory, and control of the burgeoning wealth generated by global commerce.[18] The most important competition of the period in the Atlantic world took place between Britain and France, as they fought a series of wars throughout the eighteenth century. Britain, thanks to its superior naval abilities and its stronger, more supple fiscal-military state, largely emerged the victor by 1763, forcing France to relinquish the vast territories it had claimed in mainland North America, largely driving it from India, and leaving it with few overseas possessions beyond its prosperous island slave colonies in the Caribbean.[19] This victory, however, placed an enormous strain on British finances, and on its over-extended military: between 1757 and 1763 alone, the British public debt rose 70%.[20] As a result, in the years after 1763 the British government imposed punishing new taxes on its North American colonies while placing strict new limits on those colonies' westward expansion into indigenous territory. Colonial opposition to these measures led directly to the American Revolution. France took advantage of this turmoil within its rival's empire to renew hostilities. However, the cost of sending an expeditionary force across the ocean, as already noted, greatly increased an already crushing French national debt, which France's creaky and outmoded fiscal institutions proved incapable of managing. The resulting national bankruptcy led directly to the outbreak of the French Revolution in 1789. During the same period, the strains of imperial competition forced Spain as well to impose higher taxes on its American possessions and to increase the power and influence of Spanish-born officials at the expense of American-born white (Creole) elites. In Madrid, policymakers increasingly came to see the monarchy's far-flung possessions as a cohesive and taxable "commercial machine." These moves contributed to scores of fiscal revolts, and to the major

36 David A. Bell

Túpac Amaru rebellion of 1780-82 in Peru, although not in the short run to sustained independence movements.[21]

In southeastern Europe and the Middle East, a strikingly similar set of pressures, born out of imperial competition, put the Ottoman Empire under increasing strain in the late eighteenth and early nineteenth centuries. The most important competition was with Russia, whose long series of aggressive wars against the Ottomans (1768-74, 1787-92, 1806-12) resulted in large-scale territorial losses (notably of Crimea) and a corresponding loss of influence and prestige. In 1770, Russia directly sponsored a failed Greek revolt. The strain was further exacerbated in 1798 when France invaded and quickly conquered Egypt (then under indirect Ottoman rule), while also giving Greeks in the Ionian Islands a limited degree of self-rule. While both these changes were soon reversed, the moment marked the arrival of a much stronger Western European presence in the Eastern Mediterranean, and a further challenge to Ottoman imperial structures.[22]

Historians agree that the efforts of the attempts by successive Ottoman rulers to address these strains formed an important part of the background to the Greek Revolution. Already in 1789, upon coming to the throne, Sultan Selim III introduced controversial reforms such as the creation of the new, western-style volunteer military force called the *nizam-I cedid* (the "New Order"). Its creation spurred hostility in the Janissary Order, forcing Selim to cultivate the support of Christians in the empire, including granting them the right to bear arms and form militias. When the Janissaries tried bloodily to re-establish their authority in Serbia in 1804, they provoked the first great Balkan revolt of the period and the formation of Karadjordje's 30,000-strong partisan army – an event recognized as a precursor to and inspiration for subsequent Greek uprisings.[23] Between this period and the 1820s, the Ottoman authorities sometimes tried to strengthen local grandees in the empire in order to obtain funds and support for imperial competition, but also struck back against grandees they perceived as a threat, as exemplified in the move against Tepedenenli Ali, Pasha of Yannina, in 1820.

The intensified imperial competition also created opportunities for revolutionary states to enlist powerful allies for their independence struggles, playing empires off each other. The United States depended on French support during its revolutionary war, while the future state of Haiti, under Toussaint Louverture, cultivated relations with Britain and the United States in order to take its distance from its French colonial masters. Britain unofficially provided aid to several of the South American states struggling for independence against Spain. In a similar vein, although Alexander I of Russia initially denounced Greek rebellions, Russia nonetheless served as an important base for the insurgents; ultimately British, French, and Russian intervention, of course, proved decisive for the actual achievement of Greek independence. With Russian Black Sea trade (especially grain exports) growing massively in the first decades of the 1820s, Russia took an ever-closer interest in Ottoman affairs.[24]

Contagion

As already noted, the movement of ideas, documents, practices, and political actors played an absolutely crucial role in connecting the Atlantic revolutions of the period. The many different branches of intellectual and cultural history, from the "Cambridge School" to *Begriffsgeschichte* to anthropological approaches have all contributed to our understanding of the process.[25] In some cases, while the ideas, documents, practices, and actors in question could have a deeply radical, subversive effect in the places where they arrived, they had not themselves arisen in explicitly revolutionary situations. This was the case, for instance, with many works of the Enlightenment that circulated widely in Europe and the Americas. In other cases, however, these things bore the mark of revolutionary origins, and could hardly fail to be seen as calling for the spread of revolution to new parts of the globe. When Manuel Gual and José Maria España distributed a clandestine translation of the French *Declaration of the Rights of Man and Citizen* in Venezuela in 1797, they did so with the clear intent, understood by all, of starting a revolution akin to the French one in South America.[26] Similarly, when Thomas Paine, author of the great American revolutionary pamphlet *Common Sense*, arrived in Paris in 1792 and stood for election to the revolutionary French National Convention, he did so in the explicit hope of joining the greatest of the Atlantic revolutions together into a single movement.

Already in the mid-eighteenth century, Greek intellectuals such as Evgenios Voulgaris and Iossipos Moisiodax had introduced key ideas and texts of the Western European Enlightenment to Greek-speaking elites, including texts that justified rebellion against unjust authority – in large part through the medium of the Orthodox academies.[27] In the 1790s, Rhigas Velestinlis, while also influenced by local political tradition, explicitly called for a French-style revolution in Greece, and the foundation of a Hellenic republic. His *Rights of Man* took inspiration from the French *Declaration of the Rights of Man and Citizen*, and he modeled his planned republic in part on the never-implemented radical French constitution of 1793. Like revolutionaries across Europe, Rhigas proposed a tricolor flag for his new state, and a national anthem akin to the Marseillaise.[28]

Just as important as foreign revolutionary texts and symbols were revolutionary concepts of rights, citizenship, and the nation. While the Greek concept of *patris* long pre-dated the age of revolution, during the 1820s, as it has been recently argued, a revivified concept of *ethnos* came to stand not just for an ethnic group, but to represent this collectivity as the ultimate source of political sovereignty, in the manner powerfully expressed by the French revolutionary Emmanuel Sieyès in his great 1789 pamphlet *What is the Third Estate?*. By the 1820s, this language of national sovereignty had also been powerfully echoed and amplified by the national revolts against Bonaparte in Portugal, Spain, and Germany. In addition,

38   *David A. Bell*

the Greek revolutionaries of this decade invoked a language of natural rights that closely echoed texts of the French Revolution. For instance, the French of the 1790s frequently spoke of "reconquering" natural rights and "regenerating" their nation. In 1821, the Messenian Senate declared: "We now celebrate a deliverance which we have sworn to accomplish, or else to perish... that we may... reconquer our rights and regenerate our unfortunate people."[29] Like the French revolutionaries, the Greeks adopted a model of citizenship based on active participation in the revolution.

From the point of view of revolutionary "contagion," the most remarkable aspect of the Greek events was the unusually large role played by "itinerant revolutionaries." In the eighteenth century Atlantic world, a few figures of this sort had certainly achieved great prominence – Thomas Paine most of all; also Francisco Miranda, the Venezuelan revolutionary who served for a time as a general in the French revolutionary armies, and the German noble Anacharsis Cloots, whose participation in the French Revolution was cut short by the guillotine in March, 1794.[30] But these men had relatively few emulators. In the 1820s, by contrast, hundreds – if not thousands – of foreign volunteers, of whom Lord Byron was the most famous, traveled to Greece to participate in its Revolution, while organizations such as the London Philhellenic Committee contributed funds and supplies to the revolutionaries. The reasons for foreign enthusiasm were over-determined. The eclipse of revolutionary movements elsewhere in Europe – and in particular the defeat of revolutionaries in Spain and Italy in the early 1820s – left liberals with few other movements in which to place their hopes. At the same time, exiles from Spain, Italy, and other locales that had fallen under the grip of political reaction traveled to Greece, as did unemployed military veterans of the Napoleonic Wars from both sides. Christian Orthodox rebels against Ottoman rule from elsewhere in southeastern Europe naturally found common cause with the Greeks. Also, the spread of the Romantic movement in art and literature generated massive sympathy for the rebels, as seen both in the poetry of figures like Shelley and Byron, as well as in the tableaux of Delacroix. The Greek Revolution, in fact, has a plausible claim to being the most genuinely international of all the revolutions of the "age of revolution."[31]

Disruption

The intensity and geographic extent of turmoil in the Atlantic world between the 1770s and 1820s dwarfed anything seen since the early sixteenth century (when the start of the European Reformation coincided with the conquest of the Aztec and Inca empires by the Spanish). In Europe, nearly every state experienced major changes to its regime, its borders, or both. An Atlantic space dominated by four European empires (Britain, France, Spain, and Portugal) was transformed into a space where a bevy of independent states contended for influence, along with the British empire. Under these conditions, events in one part of the globe could very easily set off powerful ripple effects in another.

The French Revolution, in addition to spreading its ideas and texts widely and starting a new series of imperial wars, had vast disruptive effects throughout the Atlantic world. Most immediately, the revolution in the metropole disrupted the fragile order of France's Caribbean colonies, in which a small minority of white settlers tyrannized over a vast population of enslaved people and smaller numbers of free people of color. By giving the colonies elected assemblies, the revolution provoked violent conflict for control of these bodies, including a rebellion by free people of color claiming the full citizenship seemingly promised by the *Declaration of the Rights of Man and Citizen*. Within two years of 1789 in the colony of Saint-Domingue, the resulting chaos made possible the largest slave rebellion in history. The resulting series of wars eventually led, 13 years later, to the transformation of this colony into the free, independent, Black state of Haiti.

The single most spectacular set of disruptive effects occurred when Napoleon Bonaparte invaded Portugal in 1807, and then Spain a year later. Spain's colonies in the Americas refused to acknowledge the sovereignty of Napoleon's nominee for the Spanish throne – his brother Joseph Bonaparte – and proclaimed their loyalty to the Bourbon king Ferdinand, now a prisoner in France. They refused, however, to give obedience to the institutions in Spain resisting Napoleon, and within a few years these tensions with the metropole provoked full-scale wars for independence.[32]

Beyond increasing the strain of imperial competition on the Ottoman Empire, the Napoleonic Wars had multiple disruptive effects that contributed to the outbreak of the Greek Revolution, as well. The most important of these was the achievement of autonomous rule by the Ionian Islands, first under Russo-Turkish protection as the Septinsular Republic between 1798 and 1807, and then as the United States of the Ionian Islands under British protection after 1815. These unexpected developments provided an example of Greek self-rule for the first time since 1453 and fostered the emergence of a cadre of figures – most importantly Ioannis Capodistrias, who would prove crucial to the establishment of the new Greek state.[33]

Events elsewhere in the Mediterranean in the early 1820s also had important ripple effects that contributed to the Greek Revolution. At the Congress of Vienna that followed Napoleon's defeat, the great powers designed the "Concert of Europe," by which they would coordinate their policies so as to preserve peace and stability and to prevent revolutionary upheavals. It was this arrangement that initially led France, Britain, and Russia to oppose the Greek independence struggle.[34] Yet at the start of the 1820s, liberal forces tried to take power in Portugal and Spain, while a revolution broke out in the Kingdom of the Two Sicilies in southern Italy. The great powers, acting through the Concert of Europe, tried to suppress this activity. In Spain, they sponsored military action by the conservative

40 *David A. Bell*

Restoration government of France to aid King Ferdinand in putting down the Spanish liberals, but the combination of events forced the powers to recognize that they could not tamp down revolutionary change everywhere at once and this realization led them to take a more measured approach as the Greek Revolution continued.[35] Ultimately, when combined with the strongly philhellenic sentiments of British and French public opinion, and the Russian volte-face on Greek affairs, this pressure led to the great power intervention in favour of the Greeks, culminating in the naval Battle of Navarino. At the same time, of course, the powers did everything possible to ensure that the Greek Revolution took a conservative turn, culminating in the nomination of Otto of Bavaria as King.

Consequences

Just as the outbreak and course of the Greek Revolution cannot be understood without placing it in the larger context of the "age of revolution," so the events in Greece influenced later revolutions in their turn, in each of the three ways discussed above.

To begin with, the Greek Revolution helped further heighten the sort of imperial competition that put all the rival empires under strain. Most immediately, it represented a massive blow to the Ottoman Empire, which increasingly came to deserve the sobriquet of the "sick man of Europe," and found itself losing territories formerly under its control to Egypt, to Russia, and, in North Africa, to France. Russian designs on Ottoman territory eventually helped lead to the Crimean War of 1853–56, a conflict that exposed many of the Russian empire's weaknesses and ended in a debilitating draw. As a result, the Greek Revolution not only encouraged independence struggles elsewhere in the Ottoman Balkans, but also less directly contributed to the conditions under which independence movements could grow in Russia as well.

At the same time, the example of the Greek people achieving national independence provided direct inspiration to nationalist movements throughout Europe and beyond. Not only was Greece the first new European state of the period to win full independence (although Serbia became effectively independent in 1817, it remained in theory subject to Ottoman suzerainty), the enthusiasm of the Philhellenes for the cause attracted enormous additional attention. The movements for unification in Italy and Germany, and the movements for independence in the Ottoman, Russian, and Austrian Empires all paid homage to the Greek example.[36]

Finally, the Greek Revolution contributed to later revolutionary events through its disruptive effect on the post-Napoleonic European order. By leading the great powers (Britain, France, Russia, Prussia, and Austria) to shift their policies from blocking the emergence of new national states to helping these new states to emerge in an orderly way, other national movements were encouraged to seek great power support. Indeed, many of

The Greek Revolution and the Age of Revolution 41

these movements (notably in Italy) managed to play the great powers off each other very successfully. In this way as well, the Greek Revolution acted as a catalyst for other revolutionary national movements across the continent.

Notes

1 F. Venturi, *The End of the Old Regime in Europe, 1768–1776: The First Crisis*, trans. R. Burr Litchfield (Princeton, 1979).
2 On this larger revolutionary context, see D.A. Bell, "The Atlantic Revolutions", in *Revolutionary World: Waves of Upheaval in the Global Age*, ed. D. Motadel (Cambridge, 2020); W. Klooster, *Revolutions in the Atlantic World: A Comparative History* (New York, 2009); J. Israel, *The Expanding Blaze: How the American Revolution Ignited the World, 1775–1848* (Princeton, 2017).
3 Bell, 'The Atlantic Revolutions'.
4 See G. A. Cohen, *Karl Marx's Theory of History: A Defence* (Princeton, 1978).
5 B. Moore, *Social Origins of Dictatorship and Democracy: Lord and Peasant in the Making of the Modern World* (Boston, 1966); T. Skocpol, *States and Social Revolutions: A Comparative Analysis of France, Russia and China* (Cambridge, 1979).
6 R. R. Palmer, *The Age of the Democratic Revolution: A Political History of Europe and America, 1760–1800* (Princeton [1959–1964], 2014).
7 See discussion in K. M. Baker, "The Idea of a Declaration of Rights", in *The French Idea of Freedom: The Old Regime and the Declaration of Rights of 1789*, ed. D. Van Kley (Stanford, 1994), 154–196.
8 D. Armitage, *The Declaration of Independence: A Global History* (Cambridge, MA 2007); B. I. Kolonitskii, *Simvoly vlasti i bor' ba za vlast': K izucheniu politicheskoĭ kul'tury rossiĭskoĭ revoliutsii 1917 goda* (Saint Petersburg, 2001).
9 Israel, *The Expanding Blaze*. See also the series by Israel beginning with *Radical Enlightenment: Philosophy and the Making of Modernity, 1650–1750* (Oxford, 2002).
10 J. Polasky, *Revolutions without Borders: The Call to Liberty in the Atlantic World* (New Haven, 2016).
11 C. A. Bayly, *The Birth of the Modern World, 1780–1914* (Oxford, 2004).
12 M. Lockwood, *To Begin the World Over Again: How the American Revolution Devastated the Globe* (New Haven, 2019).
13 See D. A. Bell, *Men on Horseback: The Power of Charisma in the Age of Revolution* (New York, 2020).
14 See notably W. Sewell, Jr., "The Rise of Capitalism and the Empire of Fashion in Eighteenth-Century France", *Past and Present* 206/1 (2010): 81–120; Id. "Connecting Capitalism to the French Revolution: The Parisian Promenade and the Origins of Civic Equality in Eighteenth Century France", *Critical Historical Studies* 1/1 (2014): 5–46.
15 See T. W. Gallant, *The Edinburgh History of the Greeks, 1768 to 1913: The Long Nineteenth Century* (Edinburgh, 2015).
16 See N. Perl-Rosenthal, "Atlantic Cultures and the Age of Revolution", *William and Mary Quarterly* 74/5 (2017): 667–696.
17 See P. M. Kitromilides, "Orthodox Culture and Collective Identity in the Ottoman Balkans during the Eighteenth Century", *Oriente Moderno* (new series) 18/1 (1999): 131–145; Id., *Enlightenment and Revolution: The Making of Modern Greece* (Cambridge, MA, 2013).
18 See notably J. Adelman, *Sovereignty and Revolution in the Iberian Atlantic* (Princeton, 2006).

42   *David A. Bell*

19 See J. Brewer, *The Sinews of Power: War, Money and the English State, 1688–1788* (London, 1989).
20 W. S. Dunn, Jr., *The New Imperial Economy: The British Army and the American Frontier, 1764–1768* (Westport, CT 2001), 15. For a comparative account, see D. Stasavage, *Public Debt and the Birth of the Democratic State: France and Great Britain, 1688–1789* (Cambridge, 2003).
21 Klooster, *Revolutions in the Atlantic World*, 122–127; G. Paquette, *Enlightenment, Governance and Reform in Spain and its Empire, 1759–1808* (New York, 2008); and Fidel José Tavárez, "The Commercial Machine: Reforming Imperial Commerce in the Spanish Atlantic, c. 1740–1808" (Ph.D. dissertation, Princeton University, 2016).
22 See Gallant, *The Edinburgh History of the Greeks, 1768 to 1913*; M. Sotiropoulos and Antonis Hadjikyriacou, "Patria, Ethnos and Demos: Representation and Political Participation in the Greek World", in *Re-Imagining Democracy in the Mediterranean, 1780–1870*, eds. J. Innes and M. Philp (Oxford, 2018), 99–126.
23 D. A. Bell, 'Armed Forces', in ibid., 253–270.
24 Gallant *The Edinburgh History of the Greeks, 1768 to 1913*, chapter 3.
25 See discussion in K. M. Baker and D. Edelstein, eds., *Scripting Revolution: A Historical Approach to the Comparative Study of Revolutions* (Stanford, 2015).
26 See C. Michelena, *Luces revolucionarias: de la rebelión de Madrid (1795) a la rebelión de La Guaira (1797)* (Caracas, 2010).
27 See P. M. Kitromilides, *The Enlightenment as Social Criticism. Iosipos Moisiodax and Greek Culture in the Eighteenth Century* (Princeton, 1992).
28 P. M. Kitromilides, "An Enlightenment Perspective on Balkan Cultural Pluralism. The Republican Vision of Rhigas Velestinlis", *History of Political Thought* 24 (2003): 465–479; Israel, *The Expanding Blaze*, 495–500.
29 Quoted in Sotiropoulos and Hadjikyriacou, 111.
30 See Polasky, *Revolutions without Borders*.
31 See W. St Clair, *That Greece might still be free: The Philhellenes in the War of Independence* (Oxford, 1972).
32 See on this subject especially Adelman, *Sovereignty and Revolution in the Iberian Atlantic*.
33 See Gallant, ch. 3.
34 See B. Vick, *The Congress of Vienna. Power and Politics after Napoleon* (Cambridge, MA, 2014).
35 M.S. Miller, "'Liberal International'? Perspectives on Comparative Approaches to the Revolutions in Spain, Italy, and Greece in the 1820s", *Mediterranean Studies* 2 (1990): 61–67.
36 See D. Hastings, *Nationalism in Modern Europe: Politics, Identity and Belonging since the French Revolution* (London, 2008), 51–88.

3 Greece, Spain, and the theory of emancipation in early European liberalism

José Maria Portillo Valdés

Ten years ago Paschalis Kitromilides complained – justly, I must say – about the role assigned by western academic powers to the studies on Modern Greece as an "ethnic" appendix of the historical mainstream dominated by the canonic idea of modernity that never crossed east of Austria or south to the Balkans. I know it is not at all a relief, but this canonic conception of modernity does not usually cross the Pyrenees either. As it happened to Modern Greece, Modern Spain always had a troublesome relationship with the standardized interpretation of Modernity. If, as Kitromilides argued, the "ethnification" of Modern Greece is better perceived confronting it to the academic canonization of Ancient Greek, something similar can be observed in the case of Spain confronting the canonization of early modern Spain (from the late fifteenth to the beginning of the eighteenth centuries) with the "peculiarization" of Modern Spain, a space traditionally considered beyond the limits of the experience of modernity.[1]

The consequence of this, as has been noted, is that Spain (and the Spanish World) and Greece (and South-Eastern Europe) very rarely count when it comes to describing the main historical processes of European and Western History. This was more commonly the case until the last decades of the twentieth century; open any of the main histories of modern political thought and you will see that references to these "extremes" of Europe fade as you approach modernity[2]. It must be said that some progress in the inclusion of the "extremes" in a European historical account has been made in the last two decades. It is due, first, to the improvement of scholarship in Latin American, Spanish, or Greek academies, and also to the social and political need for a better and more complex understanding of Europe.

The fact is that the more we know from these European extremes, the better we understand the intricate paths to modernity in Europe. To say this in Kitromilides's own words, we are now on our way to construct a new European historiographical canon that definitively cannot be based on the idea of Northwestern modernity. Important as it is, I would say that – historiographically speaking – the future points to an integration of a variety of paths and experiences of modernity into a single European narration of it.

44 *José María Portillo Valdés*

Europe is federal, its history is federal too and its historiography should accommodate for a federal narration.

Guided by this aim, I would like to raise three main points in my contribution to this book. First, I will reflect on the relevance of both "imperial knots" of Spain and Greece for the historical interpretation of the crisis of early modern empires and the birth of modern nations and states. My second point has to do with the necessity of a theory of emancipation as a complement for the historical understanding of early liberalism in the context of imperial and monarchical crisis. Finally, I would like to point to some possible points of confrontation between these two European experiences of modernity on both sides of the Mediterranean.

Greece and Spain as imperial knots

One of the reasons for the marginalization of the Spanish and Greek modernities has to be found in their respective situation in the imperial organization of modern Europe. The Spanish Catholic monarchy as the most extended Atlantic empire and Greece as the evidence of the European extension of a non-Christian empire certainly caused a problem of interpretation to the theorists of empires in the eighteenth century.

Generally speaking the European Republique des Lettres saw in the Spanish monarchical empire the counter-example of the civilized idea of empire. If we go to the reading of the most popular book as a way of getting introduced to the knowledge of political systems in Europe, *The Spirit of the Laws*, the picture is quite eloquent. For the French influential author, two main aspects characterized the Spanish monarchy. On the one hand its enormity and on the other its religious constitution.

The first condition problematized the interpretation of the Spanish monarchy, and Montesquieu considered it from a double point of view. Like any other extended empire, it tended to despotism, but it was still a monarchy. Treating the properties of monarchy,[3] Montesquieu added a brief specific chapter on the "particular" character of the Spanish monarchy to state that it could not be enlisted under the despotic regimes but that it certainly tended to, precisely due to the imperial involvement of the Castilian monarchy since the sixteenth century (Book I, chapter 18).

The other condition, the religious constitution of the Spanish monarchy, referred to its nature as a Catholic monarchy in which the Church and the clergy had a notable ascendancy and influence. On this point, Montesquieu had ambivalent sentiments: on the one hand what he labeled as "clericracy" reinforced the anti-libertarian nature of the Spanish monarchy and, on the other hand, the clergy constituted the only remaining "intermediate body" able to face monarchical despotism.

This double condition configured Montesquieu's Spain as a strange body in the midst of European civilization. As a European monarchy, it was in some respects similar to the monarchy of France and, as the French

The theory of emancipation 45

monarchy did, it tended to dangerously dissolve the "intermediate bodies" that traditionally existed and tempered the monarchical power. As a huge transcontinental empire, based on the ruins and devastation of the conquered lands, however, it looked more like the stereotype of the evil empire, the Turkish. Definitely for Montesquieu Spain was, not only geographically but above all constitutionally, in between England and Turkey.

As historiography has shown, Montesquieu was not specifically interested in Spain or in England. Both monarchies served rather as exempla with which the French monarchy (the real concern of Montesquieu) should learn what to do (England) and what to avoid (Spain). In the latter case, the acquisition of a large empire was decisive. The French intellectual drew a couple of interesting consequences from this analysis. The first was that the Spanish monarchy presented a completely strange situation regarding the regular relationship between the metropolis and the dominated lands. Contrary to modern empires, Montesquieu argued, Spain conceived her empire as an ecumenical project and as a source of gold and silver. The main leitmotif of the "Catholic Monarchy" (as it was usually referred to) was spreading the Catholic faith, as many theoreticians of the Spanish empire asserted before Montesquieu. Montesquieu would mock this characteristic of the Spanish kings: "The King of Spain was Catholic in good faith, that is, with a religiosity that well accommodated his ambition".[4] It was also a very common idea that the Spanish exhausted the American mines, not to the benefit of Spain but to the disgrace of it due to the circulation of metals coming from America and passing through into the hands of other European bankers, moneylenders, and merchants.

That is the reason why Montesquieu asserted that "The Indies and Spain are two powers under the same master, but the Indies are the principal, while Spain is only an accessory".[5] This was a situation that made Spain a controversial European kingdom up to the point that some political thinkers, among them Montesquieu himself, considered that "The Spanish and the Portuguese are still in tutelage in Europe".[6] In 1769, analyzing the general situation of Europe, Edmund Burke, took for granted that something of the like already happened as the "Spanish minister received his instructions not from Madrid, but from Versailles".[7] The effectiveness of this consideration about the Spanish monarchy would be visible in 1808 when Napoleon put it under the tutelage of the French empire.

It must be said that among European intellectuals there were other approaches to the situation of the Spanish monarchy in the context of European civilization. William Robertson, the Scottish historian, for example, reproduced in his *History of America* much of the common ideas about the relationship between the extraordinary imperial expansion of Spain, its decline, and the despotic character of its government. Robertson added a particularly interesting point of view to the usual analysis about the Spanish American dominions insisting on the fact that the Spanish faced an extraordinary situation unknown to European powers of the sixteenth century when Castile bumped into a new world. The constitutional solution to this situation consisted precisely in considering America out of the reach of any constitutional limitation: "The fundamental maxim of Spanish jurisprudence with respect to America is to consider what has been acquired there as vested in the crown, rather than in the state". As a consequence, it allowed an "interposition of the crown" in the regulation of commerce and the internal government of America. There were certainly cities, Indian towns, and many other corporations but only for their interior regulation and without any public political relevance. "In whatever relates to the public and general interest the will of the sovereign is law. No political power originates from the people".[8]

Robertson however, did not hesitate to end his analysis with a sort of present-day history. Published in 1777, he could consider the evolution of the reforms introduced in the government of the empire by the Bourbon dynasty, especially those implemented by the minister José de Galvez for Charles III, after the experience of the consequences of the Seven Years war. His conclusion was more optimistic than Burke's since he relied on the capacity of the Spanish people to adapt themselves to the principles of commercial society: "The sentiments and spirit of the people seem to second the provident care of their monarchs, and to give it greater effect. They have adopted more liberal ideas, not only with respect to commerce but domestic policy". Liberal at this moment meant not a political attitude but a trend towards modern sociability.

This opinion was commonly shared by other European intellectuals by the end of the eighteenth century. A characteristic, well-known topos is the ruthless judgement on Spain made by Nicolas Masson de Morviliers for Panckoucke's *Encyclopédie méthodique* (1782) questioning any significant progress in Spain since the time of El Quijote. At the end of his article, however, he also detected some possibilities due to the reformist policy of Charles III. Masson was one of the sources of Greek geographers Daniel Philipidis and Gregorios Constantas, who also insisted on the possibility of a social and cultural renaissance of Spain.[9]

Whatever the possibilities of a Spanish renaissance could be, European thinkers of the late Enlightenment coincided in questioning the adaptation of Spain and the Spanish monarchy to the standards of European civilization. As though they were giving ammunition to the argument made by Theodor Adorno and Max Horkheimer in 1944, European thinkers of the Enlightenment universalized a concept of modernity as the unique possible modern civilization in which Spain could hardly fit. It was not at all impossible that she could finally accommodate the requirements of the theory, but the general impression that permeated European historiographical, philosophical, and political discourses was more related to the ideas of backwardness, despotism, and obscurantism. Just as it was the case in other European territories (Greece, for example, or south Italy). Dislocation from modern civilization was the first step in a process of orientalization

The theory of emancipation   47

performed by romanticism and in many cases assumed by the orientalized themselves. The first European tourists went to Spain in the nineteenth century attracted by an exotic country made out of Arab remains, Gypsies, and bandits. Any Spanish "Europeanness" absolutely lacked of interest.

Revolution as emancipation

Like other Atlantic empires, the Spanish monarchy experienced a crisis, which, during the first three decades of the nineteenth century, drastically transformed it. By 1830, the Spanish monarchy saw her territory reduced seventeen times; all colonial possessions (except the Iberian territories), the Canary Islands, Cuba, Puerto Rico, and the Philippines, went independent from the Spanish monarchy.

Different from other Atlantic imperial crises, the Spanish one began with the coincidence of a dynastic and an imperial crisis that brought about a constitutional crisis. As in the United States or France, early constitutionalism was a result of the imperial crisis, but in the case of the Spanish monarchy, the merging of a dynastic and a constitutional crisis made early liberalism a versatile experience. The majority of the Spanish American territories searched for different forms of autonomy and home rule before going through independence; although some, like Venezuela, opted for independence since 1811.[10] There were monarchical constitutions, above all during the early period of the crisis, and also openly republican projects. There were, however, two common elements to all those constitutions and constitutional projects in the Spanish Atlantic: all of them integrated the idea of a national Catholic religion and all of them used, in one sense or the other, a language of emancipation.

Let us first focus on the language of emancipation. The word *emancipación* was widely used by the ideologues of early constitutionalism all along the Spanish Atlantic not only to denote separation or independence from the monarchy. Above all, the concept of emancipation allowed them to explain why and how it was possible to introduce a radical transformation in the relationship between the king and the varied collection of *pueblos* of the monarchy.

Most of the leaders of the Spanish American territories, and the European Spaniards as well, acquired a notion of the meaning of emancipation by studying civil law at the Spanish universities in America and Europe. Some of the books regularly used on both sides of the monarchy can give us a clear notion of it while explaining differences between *personas*. Among them, a basic distinction was made between emancipated and dependent persons. There were two conditions, necessarily concurrent, to be considered emancipated: "those persons who in addition to be free are also independent", as it was put by Ramón Lázaro Dou, a Catalan professor of law in 1800. Both conditions, asserted some years later by José María Álvarez from the University of Guatemala, made a person *sui juris*, in contraposition to those

48   *José María Portillo Valdés*

who lacked one of the mentioned conditions (to be free and independent at the same time) who were to be considered *alieni juris*.

The difference between emancipated and dependents was operative above all inside the *oikos*. The first kind of persons, who could only be free males since women could be free but never independent, depended on their own law for the government of the household. José María Álvarez equated them to "absolute sovereigns" in their small family-kingdoms. However, since society was conceived as a collection of *oikoi*, the condition of being emancipated could eventually become relevant in public terms. By the end of the eighteenth century, most of the reformist thinkers on both sides of the monarchy proposed to give some public relevance to this *repúblicos*.

It is worth paying some attention to the transfer of this idea from civil to constitutional law. The key text here is, of course, Emmerich de Vattel's *Droit de gens* where we can find the first necessary step. De Vattel conferred the concept of emancipation to the collectivity of the emancipated individuals stating that since society was formed by free and independent persons, nations as well had to be considered free and independent from each other. This comparison between individuals and community proved to be crucial in North America when, for the first time, the idea of emancipation was used with an evident constitutional purpose: "That these United Colonies are, and of right ought to be, free and independent States" as following the Virginia Convention Richard Lee proposed and Congress approved in 1776.

Thus, a traditional civil law wording – emancipated as free and independent person – went from *ius civile* to *ius gentium* and finally, by the end of the eighteenth century, to the new constitutional law. In a context like that of the Spanish monarchy, this transition is datable to the moment in which a monarchical and dynastic crisis coincided with an imperial crisis. The absence of the king and the cession of the sovereignty to a foreign dynasty (to Napoleon) brought about a situation never before experienced. The need to figure out solutions gave some reformists the opportunity to interpret the crisis actually as a constitutional crisis of the monarchy and, consequently, to propose a radical reform of it. The emancipation of the nation was a precondition for any constitutional reform based on the idea of national sovereignty.

As I said before, the variety of constitutional responses in the Spanish Atlantic was outstanding.[11] All of them, however, coincided in including in the very first articles the same wording we have seen transiting from civil to constitutional law: "The Spanish nation is free and independent, and neither is nor can be the property of any family or person" or "The Peruvian Nation is forever free and independent from any foreign power". *Libre e independiente*, free and independent, was for early Hispanic liberals the key concept that allowed nations to act as sovereigns.

This idea constituted an axis around which evolved much of the political debate during the crisis of the Spanish Atlantic. Theorists of the Spanish

The theory of emancipation 49

monarchy usually represented it as a union between the king and each of the *pueblos* (kingdoms, provinces, lordships, cities) with nothing constitutionally relevant in between.[12] It is crucial that traditional Spanish doctrine considered that there was nothing similar to a "kingdom of Spain" that could be represented in a single institution (like the parliament of England, later Britain, or the General Estates of France). There had been some representative assemblies – the Cortes – for each of the original kingdoms of the monarchy – Castile, Aragon, and Navarre – but not a Cortes of Spain.

As the dean of the church of Córdoba in Rio de la Plata, Gregorio Funes, observed, the renunciation of the sovereignty by Charles IV and Ferdinand VII in favour of Napoleon broke the chain that had kept together the head of the monarchy and the *pueblos*. From that moment on there were basically two possibilities: some institution (the Council of Castile, a Regency or a General Junta) could take the place of the king, or a constitutional change should be implemented. The first option proved to be unfeasible since none of the possible institutions to replace the king had the legitimacy to do that. The second option required a previous process of emancipation to create the nation and relocate the sovereignty on it.

Revolutionary and conservative emancipation and why Greece was significant for Spain

Excepting those who defended a return to the traditional monarchical system, there was an extended consensus on the need for emancipation. However, there were different interpretations about the extent and consequences of it contributing to shaping different liberal ideologies. The more progressive interpreted emancipation as a complex process that involved both the nation and the society. They thought, on the one hand, that emancipation was not only a contestation of the paternal superiority of the monarch, but also that it was a recovery of the sovereignty and the legislative power by the nation. For them, emancipation was not, as classical civil law envisaged it, a concession made by the king as the father of their pueblos, but an act of the nation itself. Even for those who still recognized Ferdinand VII as their legitimate king, the monarchy should be considered as reinstituted by the nation and the king as the leader of a constitutional government.

Critics of the first Hispanic constitutions highlighted negatively the republican character of them, including the Cádiz constitution, which, in fact, was monarchical. They were right because it was one of the main characteristics of the radical emancipation thought. On the other hand, and coherently with this republican substratum, it also extended the need for emancipation to society, defending the need for replacing the complexity of a universe of different corporations with their own rights and statutes with a society of heads of households – *pater familiae* – organized in towns, provinces, and nation. They specifically advocated the suppression of the *fueros* (particular rights) of the clergy and the military.

50 *José María Portillo Valdés*

Early liberals who championed this perspective on emancipation – as the Venezuelan leader Juan Germán Roscio or the Spanish influential theorist Francisco Martínez Marina – also supported the idea of a national Catholic religion. This was the clearest limit to the idea of emancipation accepted by early Hispanic liberals in practically all the constitutional projects produced in the Spanish Atlantic during the first decades of the nineteenth century. In 1825, commenting on the recent Chilean constitution of 1823, the ex-Catholic now-Anglican priest José María Blanco-White, criticized the article replicated all over the Hispanic world, stating the exclusivity of Catholicism as the "unique and true religion of the nation".

From a liberal perspective, Blanco maintained that the Hispanic societies could not be considered truly emancipated until they accepted the principle of toleration. The article published by Blanco brought about a notable debate extending from Chile to Colombia, Venezuela, and Spain. Juan Egaña, who had been influential in the drafting of the Chilean constitution of 1823, responded to Blanco's argument using an argument that was very common among early Catholic liberals: the Hispanic societies actually did not need toleration because they were societies "with a national God".

In the majority of the Hispanic societies, the debate about the convenience of an opening to religious toleration date from the thirties of the nineteenth century and was promoted by the second liberal generation who had decided to extend the concept of emancipation beyond the limits of religion. Depending on the particular country, it took some decades or even a century to separate religion and politics, and, which was even more complicated, to establish the ideal type of an individual considered independently of their religious beliefs.

Emancipation was also a concept accepted by moderate reformers in the context of the imperial crisis of the Spanish monarchy. The moderate theory of emancipation assumed that the Hispanic societies that formed the huge Spanish monarchy had already arrived at a state of maturity, which made it impossible to preserve the monarchy, united as it had been for the previous three hundred years. Their interpretation of the situation generated by the merging of a dynastic and an imperial crisis differed from the liberal perspective in the sense that moderates used a theory of emancipation more strictly attached to the principles of civil law. For them, emancipation was a process that ideally should have been initiated by the king himself. Following the "natural" process of the emancipation of a son, the king should detect when his *pueblos* were in a position to create their own "household" or state.

Manuel de la Bárcena, a moderate Criollo priest, gained a seat in the Spanish parliament in 1820 representing the kingdom of New Spain. When the Mexican deputies were about to leave the Spanish Cortes for Mexico, he addressed the king, Ferdinand VII, pleading: "Be the last act of your paternal government the emancipation of New Spain".[13] The moderate idea of emancipation consisted essentially in a transference of paternal authority from the king to the newly created state and its leading elite. Moderates tended to adopt the interpretation that local elites could simply be subrogated in the role of the king so that they could programme and control any associated process of social change.

European moderate political thought found in this theory solid support for a general interpretation of the Spanish crisis. The most accurate narration of the independence of Greece published in Spanish, due to the journalist Marcos Manuel Río y Coronel, adopted the point of view of a moderate interpretation of emancipation. Published under the second absolute government of Ferdinand VII in 1828, Río y Coronel took for granted, as was usual in Europe, that by the beginning of the nineteenth century the Greeks were awakening to a new era of civilization while the Turkish empire remained in its "state of ignorance".[14]

Some years before Río y Coronel wrote his history of the Greek revolution, Dominique Georges Dufour du Pradt published a treatise, immediately translated into Spanish, that linked the Greek and the Spanish American rebellions.[15] De Pradt had previously written extensively on Spanish America, advocating a moderate interpretation of emancipation. His argument was especially attached to the principles of traditional civil law, arguing that Spanish América, as now Greece, evidenced their maturity through the means of civilization while Spain, like the Turkish empire, showed the opposite. "Spain is the Christian Turkey", concluded de Pradt.[16]

De Pradt's use of a moderate theory of emancipation, however, did not necessarily lead to the acceptance of radical independence. On the contrary, de Pradt accepted the possibility of a mediated emancipation of both spaces, Spanish America and Greece, depending on the interest of Europe. In fact, his main concern was not the independence of Mexico, Chile, or Greece but how it affected the *Ius Pubblicum Europaeum*.

Since the British crisis of 1776, plate tectonics of the European imperial system started to move in different directions: the Portuguese monarchy reinvented it as a tropical empire, Napoleon attempted a republican empire, and the British looked for a reconstruction of their empire as a maritime power. For its dimensions, but above all for its conceptual situation right at the borders of the European civilization, the crisis of the Spanish empire posed a problem for European intellectuals and political thinkers about how to interpret the consequences of emancipation. As in the case of Greece, however, the main concern for moderate theorists was how to make a transition from a *Ius Pubblicum Europaum* based on the Atlantic empires to a new system of States (and, eventually, new empires) without affecting the balance of power.

Notes

1 Paschalis M. Kitromilides, "Paradigm Nation: The Study of Nationalism and the "Canonization" of Greece", in *The making of Modern Greece: nationalism*

52 *José María Portillo Valdés*

romanticism and the uses of the past (1797–1896), Roderick Beaton and David Ricks eds. (London, 2009), 21–31.

2 For a sample check Mark Goldie and Robert Wolker, eds., *The Cambridge History of Eighteenth-Century Political Thought* (Cambridge, 2008).

3 Montesquieu, *The Spirit of the Laws* (cited from *The Complete Works of M. De Montesquieu* vol. I [London, Evans and Davis, 1777]) Book VIII.

4 Montesquieu, *My Thoughts*, ed. Henry C. Clark (Indianapolis, 2012), n. 620.

5 Montesquieu, *Spirit of the Laws*, cit. 21, XXII.

6 Montesquieu, *My Thoughts*, n. 2020.

7 Edmund Burke, *Observation on a Late State of the Nation* (London, 1769) in Edmund Burke, *The Works of the Right Honorable Edmund Burke* (London, 1834), 85.

8 William Robertson, *History of América* (Dublin, 1777), vol. 2, book VIII.

9 Paschalis Kitromilides *Enlightenment and Revolution. The Making of Modern Greece* (Cambridge, MA, 2009), 103.

10 Jaime E. Rodríguez, *The Independence of Spanish América* (New York, 1998); Hilda Sabato, *Republics of the New World: The Revolutionary Political Experiment in Nineteenth-Century Latin America* (New Haven, 2018).

11 Javier Fernández Sebsatián, "Friends of Freedom: First Liberalism in Spain and Beyond", in *In Search of European Liberalisms. Concepts, Language, Ideologies*, eds Michael Freeden, Javier Fernández Sebastián and Jörn Leonhard (New York, 2019).

12 Pablo Fernández Albaladejo, *La crisis de la monarquía* (Madrid: Marcial Pons-Crítica, 2010); Annick Lempèriére, *Entre Dios y el rey, la república. La ciudad de México de los siglos XVI al XIX* (México DF, 2013).

13 Manuel de la Bárcena, *Manifiesto al mundo. La justicia y la necesidad de la independencia de la Nueva España* (México, 1821).

14 Marcos Manuel Río y Coronel, *Compendio histórico del orige y progresos de la insurrección de los griegos contra los turcos* (Madrid, 1828), I, 79.

15 M. De Pradt, *Vrai système de l'Europe relativement à l'Amérique et à la Grèce* (Paris, 1825).

16 M. De Pradt, *Verdadero sistema de la Europa con respecto a la América y la Grecia* (Paris, 1825), 103.

4 Austria and the 1820s Revolutions: Between the heritage of the Congress of Vienna and political change

Miroslav Šedivý

The Greek Revolution was unquestionably one of the most important affairs between the Napoleonic Wars and the revolutionary year of 1848. Contemporaries as well as historians have often agreed that it represented an important violation of the post-war order established at the Congress of Vienna in 1815, notwithstanding that the Ottoman Empire did not formally belong to it due to its omission in the Final Acts of the Congress. Less certain, however, is the agreement on the definition of this violation: it usually depends on the perspective used for the evaluation of the immediate as well as the long-term impact of the revolution. European liberals and democrats saw in it an open revolt against absolutist despotism, the same endeavour that was defeated in Spain and Italy at the beginning of the 1820s and frustrated at the same time in the German Confederation; the fact that the Greeks were finally successful when they overthrew the sultan's supremacy served as encouragement among those Europeans longing for political modernization. Another kind of violation was connected with the deterioration in the relations among the five dominant European powers which split into two contradictory camps in the late 1820s, pro-Greek and anti-Greek, with the armed intervention of the former – Great Britain, Russia, and France – being assessed as the first modern humanitarian intervention.

The exceptional historical importance of the Greeks' struggle for independence was also acknowledged by Austrian Chancellor Klemens Wenzel Nepomuk Lothar, Prince of Metternich-Winneburg, who, after his political downfall in March 1848, wrote a short account of the uprising in the form of a memoir; he regarded it as one of the most important international events during his long political career, referring to its significant impact on the political situation not only in the Ottoman Empire but also generally in Europe.[1] The existence of this memoir clearly shows that he regarded this affair as so important that he felt it necessary to reflect on it, which gives rise to the crucial question: Why did he consider the revolution to be so significant not only for the Greeks and Turks but also for the people living in the signatory countries of the Final Acts of the Congress of Vienna? Providing an answer is all the more important because it helps to explain the motives of his active involvement in the Greek Question during the 1820s and his support of the sultan against the Greek insurgents, as well as against the three great powers intervening on their behalf. Resolving these issues is the principal aim of this text, which simultaneously reveals another violation of the heritage of the Congress of Vienna made by the Greek Revolution, namely of the legal framework of the post-Napoleonic international order guiding the relations among European countries. In accomplishing this task, the European contextualization will be useful, and particularly the Italian context used for better clarification of the so to speak legal thesis introduced above.

In historical works, Metternich and 'his' Austria have often been depicted almost as villains opposing humanity, freedom, and progress with their support of the sultan against the Greeks. Metternich's Near Eastern policy in the 1820s was therefore usually viewed as a black and white story in which scholars tended to extremes, usually with the denigration of Metternich, but it is also possible to find him depicted as a man with hidden pro-Greek sentiment.[2] Actually, all these one-sided evaluations must be questioned and replaced by an attempt to offer a more balanced view, for which extensive knowledge of primary, often archival, sources, is always essential – as has already been proved in the great scholarly works about Metternich written by Robert D. Billinger, Enno Kraehe, Alan J. Reinerman, and last but not least Wolfram Siemann.[3]

It is above all necessary to emphasize the fact that Metternich was personally neither a friend nor foe of the Greeks. As a rationally thinking man formed by the period of Enlightenment, his personal reaction was motivated by a realist evaluation of the situation in the Ottoman Empire, and he made a distinction between the Greeks as human beings and their political aspirations. He was not personally hostile towards them, in much the same way that he was not against Muslims or Jews. To prove the contrary, historians have often quoted his statement from 6 May 1821 that in the Ottoman Empire "three or four hundred thousand are hanged, slaughtered or impaled... it scarcely matters' as evidence of his 'callousness' or 'incomprehension'".[4] The problem is that these words have been taken out of context; what Metternich actually did was describe the sorrowful situation in the Ottoman Empire seized by the massacres committed by both Christians and Muslims, saying precisely: "Beyond our eastern border three to four hundred thousand hanged, garrotted, beheaded do not count for much".[5] This opinion on the value of life in regions of the Ottoman Empire resulted from his extensive knowledge of the history of the Greek Revolution since its very beginning, but his reaction in no way meant that he condoned the bloody scenes; on the contrary, he disapproved of all of them not only in the first year of the uprising but also later.[6] On 9 May 1821, he added to his statement of three days before: "The Greek affair will cost rivers of blood. God himself only knows how it will end. Constantinople is exposed to the excesses of Mussulman anarchy

Austria and the 1820s Revolutions 55

... The whole population has taken up arms; they massacre and insult the Christians indiscriminately".[7] With his great analytical skills, Metternich was able to foresee the well-known massacres of the Muslims in Tripoli, as well as of the Greeks in Chios, and he wrote prophetically before these two principal disasters took place:

> You see that the war in these countries [Morea and Epirus] is pulsating with the opportunities that revolutionary movements normally present, but these will not fail to take on the most barbaric character when they are associated with people such as the Turks and the Greeks in the nineteenth century. You have seen a deplorable event in Navarino. The massacre of the Turkish prisoners-of-war will influence the Turks in the same way as the Greeks will be influenced by the excesses which the Janissaries seem to have perpetrated on the religious in the convent that served as an asylum and defence for the Arnauts after the defeat of Iordaky's forces.[8]

The claim that Metternich's anti-Greek policy was not motivated by any personal prejudice can be easily supported by his appeals to the Ottoman sultan. He hastened to warn Mahmud II against the unjust and excessive brutality, fanaticism, and eventual extermination of the Greeks, in his opinion a proceeding not only against humanity but also against the precepts of Islam. He also condemned the execution of the Greek patriarch and advised humane conduct, amnesty for the insurgents, and administrative improvements. There is no reason to regard these warnings and counsel as insincere, although they were naturally in part motivated with consideration of Russia, as well as public opinion in Europe, and proof can be found in his practical – one can say humanitarian – deeds. Metternich not only tolerated but also explicitly agreed with the activities of the Austrian agents with the aim of helping the suffering Greeks, as well as, in other cases, the Muslims. Although the Austrian merchant navigation in the Mediterranean Sea suffered greatly from the activities of the Greek pirates, the Austrian Levant squadron behaved according to its principles when the captured Greek pirates were not handed over to the Turks, which would have equalled handing them over to their certain execution, but were instead taken for trial in Trieste. The Austrian Empire served as a safe haven for the Greeks who had not participated in the insurrection but were forced to leave their homes due to the war and flee to the Austrian territories. The instigator of the Revolution, Alexander Ypsilanti, after his flight to the Austrian Empire and imprisonment there, was treated much better than ordinary prisoners; it was Metternich who long desired his release following his pledge to emigrate to the United States, which did not happen because both Alexander I and Nicholas I rejected the idea. Metternich also readily agreed with the collection of money in the Austrian Empire for the suffering Greeks on condition that the money would be given not to the fighters but to destitute people.[9]

56   *Miroslav Šedivý*

Due to his realism and knowledge of the facts, Metternich did not share the one-sided pro-Greek sympathies of the Philhellenes, and he would also have hardly agreed that the decision of Britain, Russia, and France to intervene in Greece could be called a humanitarian intervention, which it surely was not because it was primarily their mutual mistrust and jealously that led them to become active in the Greek cause; any humanitarian regard was extremely limited in the decision-making of the cabinets in London, St Petersburg, and Paris. Generally, historians working with primary sources and familiar with the decisions made by these governments like Davide Rodogno, Oliver Schulz, and John Bew[10] refuse to see their interference as humanitarian while other scholars like Gary J. Bass, Reinhard Heydenreuter, and Matthias Schulz are the promoters of this idea.[11]

Metternich's policy in the Greek Revolution was a simple outcome of his conservative worldview and Austria's geopolitical needs; he sided with the sultan because he wished to preserve the Ottoman Empire intact. In other words, he was a political but not personal opponent of the Greek insurgents. In this case, however, one must clarify that the issue of internal politics – the conflict of absolutism and constitutionalism – was not the most important factor in his attitude. Although he disliked what he considered the disloyalty of proponents of change towards their legitimate monarchs and the example they were giving to European revolutionaries, he acknowledged the need for reforms to improve life. That his concern for their plight was genuine is obvious from his correspondence and has generally been proved by later scholarly works about his reformatory policies in Austria, Italy, and the Ottoman Empire.[12] Less definite is his support of a kind of Greek home rule (*Selbstverwaltung*) as he claimed later in his memoir,[13] something he also suggested at the end of the Napoleonic Wars for the Austrian Lombard-Venetian Kingdom; in his own writing from the 1820s, he did not entirely exclude autonomy for Greece, but this topic is still awaiting impartial research. Nevertheless, it is certain that at the end of the decade he – and not the three pro-Greek powers – preferred the full independence of Greece because, first, he did not want to see Greek autonomy becoming a wooden horse for foreign interference in Ottoman internal affairs, especially on the part of Russia, and, second, he knew perfectly well that autonomy was unacceptable for the Greeks and would therefore be merely a temporary solution causing future trouble to the sultan. He even considered a federation according to the pattern of the United States of America with a president at its head to be the most suitable political system for Greece to overcome the regional loyalties and animosities of its inhabitants, and he saw his former political foe, Ioannis Capodistrias, as the best candidate for presidency.[14]

The final victory of the Greeks became a symbol of change for contemporaries, but for Metternich hardly one of political modernization. For him, the whole question was primarily about the general peace that he had helped to restore with great effort in 1814–1815. According to him, the

Greek Revolution represented a serious threat to it, and not solely from just the geopolitical point of view with the inherent concern that Russia would exploit the uprising to gain greater influence or even territories in the Balkans when the tsar decided to become involved in the Greek Question (which finally happened later in the 1820s). There was a second, and no less important, perspective through which Metternich observed the affair: the legal one. He feared that the support and victory of the revolution would undermine the legal principles which had been adopted by European governments at the end of the Napoleonic Wars for peace and crisis management, representing thus a legal basis for the organization of interstate relations within the post-Napoleonic international order. That this aspect of the Greek Revolution, if not crucial, was at least extremely important for him is clear from his emphasis in his later memoir that his promotion of legal principles was connected with the defence of the law,[15] and it is fully proved in his correspondence from the 1820s.[16]

The fact mentioned at the beginning of this text that the Ottoman Empire was not legally a member of the post-Napoleonic order was unimportant for the Austrian chancellor. For the sake of pan-European peace and according to his deep-rooted conviction that the law served everyone regardless of power or religion, he claimed that the same principles observed in the relations among Christian countries were also to be respected in their relations with the Ottoman Empire or, more specifically, its legal authority represented by the sultan. This standpoint corresponded again not only with Austrian needs but also to Metternich's worldview that had manifested itself during the Congress of Vienna wherein he wished to achieve a stable and lasting peace, not only by restoring the eighteenth-century balance of power but also by laying the foundations of legal principles ensuring justice in international affairs. These principles were to be identical for large as well as small countries not only among the predominantly Christian states but also the Ottoman Empire, as was shown by his attempt to bring it to the round table and ensure the sultan's signature under the Final Acts of the Congress.[17]

Although the sultan refused to join the negotiators in the Austrian capital and remained outside the Congress order, Metternich saw no reason why the European countries could not apply the same legal rules towards the Ottoman Empire as generally accepted among themselves, if they wanted to maintain the very stability of the European states system and if they expected the Ottoman Empire to act according to the same law in return, as a Prussian envoy in Vienna reported in connection with the Greek Revolution in June 1827:

> Metternich strongly opposes the principle introduced by the French government that, in the matter of the distinction between suzerainty and sovereignty, it is not necessary to define them so precisely with the Turks who do not understand the difference themselves; he thinks that if one

58   *Miroslav Šedivý*

> believes one can deviate from the treaties and from the principles of law
> with regard to the Turks, one no longer has the right to demand of the
> Porte [the Ottoman government] that it observes them on its part.[18]

That this opinion was meant seriously is confirmed by other statements by
Metternich criticizing the arrogance of Europe towards overseas nations;
for example, when French journalist and politician Prosper Duvergier
de Hauranne wrote in 1840 about France's relations with the "half-savage
governments ... *for whom the law of nations is still an empty word*",
Metternich underlined the part on the law and wrote in the margin: "M. D.
de H. should tell us what value *the law of nations* has in his eyes!" [the
emphasis of Metternich's own words in original].[19]

With his defence of the sultan's sovereign rights, Metternich was trying to
preclude foreign interference in Ottoman internal affairs, but at the same
time he was protecting the whole legal heritage of the Congress of Vienna,
and he did so in the same way as in other affairs, including those of Italy.
According to him, if the principles of public law were not universally
obeyed, the result would be the destabilization or even collapse of the whole
structure of European politics. The principle that was to be respected above
all was that of state sovereignty, which made him believe that the independence of states was inviolable. The only exception was the situation
when a country was threatened with revolution, and, in such a case, other
countries could intervene solely on behalf of the legitimate government and
not the insurgents. The government was represented by a ruling authority,
usually the monarch; as long as this ruler was regarded as legitimate, in
other words, acknowledged as the subject of international law, it was
deemed necessary not to violate his rights, including the inviolability of his
territory and his full powers in domestic affairs. Although Metternich
agreed with the 1820 Troppau Protocol enabling foreign intervention to
suppress a revolution in another country even without the formal invitation
of the legitimate government, he always preferred to act only after such an
invitation to legalize foreign interference. Exactly for this reason, he demanded and obtained the invitation appeals for the Austrian interventions
in the Kingdom of the Two Sicilies and Piedmont in 1821 and others in
Modena, Parma, and the Papal States ten years later. It was in this way that
he contributed to the modification of the intervention principle in the Treaty
of Berlin of October 1833 when Austria, Prussia, and Russia agreed that
military support of foreign governments was conditional upon the formal
request of the latter.[20]

The Greek Revolution represented just one of several chapters in this legal
dispute, but it was undeniably a crucial one for both its extent and outcome.
The question of international law together with the issue of sovereignty had
featured continually in the debate among European powers on their coexistence with the Ottoman Empire since 1821. It became particularly important in 1826 and 1827 when Great Britain, Russia, and France began to

Austria and the 1820s Revolutions 59

meddle in Greek affairs, which finally led to their military intervention against the sultan. According to Metternich what they did from a legal point of view was take advantage of the exclusion of the Ottoman Empire from the so-called family of European nations and use legal double standards in their relationships with it and other – more 'civilized' – European countries, which enabled them to disregard the Ottoman Empire's sovereignty and conduct themselves towards it from a position of power. This conduct represented a kind of about-turn since, in the case of the Greek Uprising, the three great powers were ready to violate the rights of a legitimate authority, while during the early 1820s revolutions in Italy and Spain they had agreed that the legitimate governments were represented by the monarchs and, therefore, a general consent existed between them on the validity of the Austrian interventions in the Kingdom of the Two Sicilies and Piedmont and France's in Spain, which they opposed.[21] The difference in the attitudes assumed by Great Britain, Russia, and France toward the Greek uprising during 1826–1827 led Metternich to sharp criticism of the duplicity of their conduct when they infringed upon the sovereignty of another country in a manner "scarcely justifiable according to the simplest principles of the respect to the independence of countries"[22] and in a manner that, moreover, they would never have allowed to be used against themselves in a similar case: "What would England or Russia say to an agreement ... which would take place between France and Austria and which would basically establish that His British Majesty or the Russian emperor would be deprived of an insurgent Ireland or Finland?"[23]

Metternich was often scorned for his insistence on his conservative principles and his allegedly anachronistic approach to international relations and the problems of the period. However, with regard to the Greek Revolution, his Austria basically did not differ from the other great powers – which actually did not pursue any modern pro-nationalist policies in the Near East or anywhere else, but simply used double standards. The near future proved this, at least in the case of Russia, when Nicholas I refused with indignation the British and French offer of mediation in the Polish November uprising in 1830–1831, something which he had pressed for in the Greek case. A British reaction in the event of any eventual foreign interference in its own Irish affairs could hardly be different and, furthermore, the British government agreed with Metternich's notion of the need to respect Ottoman sovereignty when France attacked Ottoman Algeria in the spring of 1830, which was seen in Britain as a threat to its own interests in the Mediterranean Sea.[24]

The role of the Greek Revolution in the political-legal heritage of the Congress of Vienna was not forgotten with the establishment of the Greek Kingdom in 1832 and was actually remembered in European society in two different ways. The first was a negative one as the violation of monarchical sovereignty; this opinion became more widespread when the French troops occupied Ancona in February 1832. The French presence in this papal town,

60   *Miroslav Šedivý*

without the consent of the 'Holy Father', represented an obvious violation of the public law of Europe and was denounced across Europe and certainly not only by conservative elites. The Europeans experienced for themselves what they had merely heard about in previous years in connection with the conduct of some great powers in areas unprotected by the legal precepts of the European states system. Unsurprisingly, the occupation of Ancona brought to mind the intervention of Great Britain, Russia, and France in the Ottoman Empire on behalf of the insurgent Greeks in 1827 leading to the destruction of the sultan's fleet at the Navarino Bay since this 'incident' had also occurred at a time of peace between the allied powers and the sultan.

The French invasion of Algeria in 1830 was also recalled two years later for the same reason; Charles X seized this North African Ottoman province without a declaration of war. Since the Ottoman Empire was not included in the family of European nations and was also regarded in the West as an alien and inferior civilization, the Europeans could easily cope with the great powers' actions in Greece and Algeria. In the case of the leader of the Catholic world, however, the situation was completely different; the French invasion was regarded not only as barely credible but also unacceptable. The occupation of Ancona showed the Europeans that the way the great powers proceeded in areas located outside the European states system could also be applied towards the states formally under its protection. It was thus no coincidence that the criticism of the French incursion into the Papal States often contained references to the Battle of Navarino and the occupation of Algeria, in particular when France was directly involved in both of them.[25] For Metternich, the French occupation of Ancona represented an obvious transfer of 'illegal' conduct from Greece and Algeria to Italy, and he recalled the Greek Revolution in the same respect in the spring of 1840 when Britain illegally seized Neapolitan commercial vessels in the so-called Sulphur-War against the Kingdom of the Two Sicilies; he strongly disapproved of the British proceeding that was not authorized by the law of nations and he linked it to parallels in the past: "This is Copenhagen, Navarino and Ancona, and therefore, something we will never understand!"[26]

While some people, like Metternich, remembered the Greek Revolution in a negative way because it contributed to the erosion of the legal structure established in 1815, there was a second group that regarded it in a positive way exactly for the same reason. This view was connected with the popular debate about the improvement of the existing international order, a discussion provoked in the 1820s by the Greek Revolution and distinctive among Italian political emigrants who criticized the same order. They promoted the idea of 'national sovereignty' and used legal argumentation in their attacks against what they saw as the great powers' oligarchy imposed on the smaller countries at the Congress of Vienna without the latter's consent and to their detriment. Under the premise that all countries regardless of their material strength enjoyed the same sovereign rights, they demanded the reform of the post-Napoleonic order. New international law was to be introduced to ensure this equality and more justice and peace in relations among all states. The example of the Greek Revolution served for them as a pattern worthy of following, especially when it became successful and showed that change in the international order was possible. It was an obvious transfer of a positive geopolitical experience from Greece to an Italian-speaking milieu, and this transfer became all the more important when the unsuccessful Italian revolutions of the early 1820s could not offer such an experience.[27]

All this made the Italians even more aware of the significance of the Eastern Question for the future of not only the Ottoman Empire but also of Europe, of which the most immediate evidence was the wave of various visions of the reorganization of Ottoman territory and its impact on territorial changes in the Apennines. The recognition of the significance of Near Eastern affairs for the Italian cause continued to be present in Italian society and was exploited in the 1840s by the moderate patriots in their programme of national unity.[28] Unsurprisingly, it was also the time when the memory of Greek Revolution was revived in Italian society, at least among the liberals and democrats who saw the nation as the main entity of the public law of Europe. They remembered the success of the Greeks primarily not as the victory of political modernization or a humanitarian intervention, but as a successful breach into the political-legal heritage of the Congress of Vienna. The Greek victory was to be imitated by Italians and other Europeans in their effort to replace the old international order with a new and better one, namely a Europe of free nations ensuring greater fairness and a more stable peace within the whole European family. To quote just one example for all, the Florentine newspaper *Alba* wrote on 23 January 1848 that Europe was accustomed to acknowledging the 'right' of *fait accompli* and that

> ... the public law of Europe is a fiction, a lie: we are under the empire of force; the reason is at the tip of the sword, justice is in victory. There, where the insurrection was victorious, as in Greece, France, Belgium, Spain and Portugal, Europe bowed before the right of the strongest; there where it was defeated, as in Poland, Europe glorified the victorious powers and made a God of the cannon. The treaties of 1815 will be the iron yoke of Italy until Italy has the strength to break them: once they are broken, Europe will accept the fait accompli and recognise right in the triumph.[29]

This argument helped the Italians to vindicate their revolutionary and bellicose actions in 1848.

The Greek Revolution represented a revolt not only against the Ottoman supremacy but also against the political-legal roots laid at the Congress of Vienna, although it must be repeated here that neither the Ottoman Empire nor Greece formally belonged to the post-Napoleonic order. The fact that the Greeks were successful and even supported by some European powers

62 Miroslav Šedivý

made them pioneers of change, and European revolutionaries used their successful uprising as a weapon against the congress heritage. It became all the more important in 1848 when the demand for change was connected not only with social, economic, and constitutional issues but also with the desire to reform the whole international order, an ambition particularly expressed in Italy where the war declared by Piedmont on Austria in March (and supported by a considerable number of Italians) represented a serious violation of that order. It was symbolic that in the same month Metternich fell from power and Austria became a victim of this first open war in Europe since 1815 (not counting the Ottoman Empire). From his own perspective of an architect and guardian of this order, he lost his first battle in Greece and went on to lose the whole war later in Italy. This obvious political-legal link between the 1820s and 1848 also makes it clear why, in retrospect, he obviously evaluated the Greek Uprising as having been more serious than the Italian revolutions of the 1820s and why he decided to turn his attention back in time and write his brief memoir on the former when he was no longer an active player in European politics.

Notes

1 Metternich, *Die Geschichte des Aufstandes der Griechen*, 1848 [or afterwards], Národní archiv, Prague [henceforth: NA], Rodinný archiv Metternichů, Acta Clementina [henceforth: RAM-AC] 8, 2/12.

2 For Metternich's alleged sympathies with the Greeks see K. Nikolaides, 'Die Politik des Fürsten Metternich gegenüber der großen Revolution von 1821', *Oesterreichische Rundschau* 18 (1922): 778–789.

3 R. B. Billinger, *Metternich and the German Question. State's Rights and Federal Duties, 1820–1834* (Newark, 1991); E. E. Kraehe, *Metternich's German Policy*, vols. 1 and 2 (Princeton, 1963, 1983); A. J. Reinerman, *Austria and the Papacy in the Age of Metternich*, vols. 1 and 2 (Washington, 1979, 1989); W. Siemann, *Metternich. Stratege und Visionär. Eine Biographie* (Munich, 2016).

4 Most recently M. Jarrett, "No Sleepwalkers. The Men of 1814/15", *Journal of Modern European History* 13/4 (2015): 437.

5 R. von Metternich-Winneburg, ed., *Aus Metternich's nachgelassenen Papieren*, Band 3 (Vienna, 1882), 438.

6 Metternich to Lebzeltern, Vienna, 3 December 1821, Haus-, Hof- und Staatsarchiv, Vienna [henceforth: HHStA], Staatenabteilungen [henceforth: StA], Russland III, 45; Metternich to Lebzeltern, Vienna, 6 October 1825, HHStA, StA, Russland III, 71.

7 Metternich to Esterházy, Ljubljana, 9 May 1821, HHStA, StA, England 166.

8 Metternich to Lebzeltern, Vienna, 8 October 1821, HHStA, StA, Russland III, 45. See also Metternich to Esterházy, Vienna, 18 and 20 July 1821, HHStA, StA, England 166; Metternich to Vincent, Vienna, 5 August 1821, HHStA, StA, Frankreich 244; Krusemark to Frederick William III, Vienna, 28 July 1821, Geheimes Staatsarchiv Preussischer Kulturbesitz, Berlin [henceforth: GStA PK], Hauptabteilung III [henceforth: HA III], Ministerium des Auswärtigen I [henceforth: MdA I], 5995; Caraman to Pasquier, Vienna, 16 December 1821, Archives du Ministère des affaires étrangères, Paris [henceforth: AMAE], Correspondance politique [henceforth: CP], Autriche 402.

Austria and the 1820s Revolutions 63

9 M. Šedivý, *Metternich, the Great Powers and the Eastern Question* (Pilsen, 2013), 402–407. For the Greek emigrants in Trieste see also the recent and excellent analysis by O. Katsiardi-Hering, *La presenza dei Greci a Trieste. La comunità e l'attività economica (1751–1830)*, volume 1 (Trieste, 2018), 343–368.

10 J. Bew, "From an umpire to a competitor. Castlereagh, Canning and the issue of international intervention in the wake of the Napoleonic Wars", in *Humanitarian Intervention. A History*, eds. B. Simms and D. J. B. Trim (Cambridge, 2011), 117–138; D. Rodogno, *Against Massacre. Humanitarian Interventions in the Ottoman Empire, 1815–1914: The Emergence of a European Concept and International Practice* (Princeton and Oxford, 2012), 79–89; O. Schulz, *Ein Sieg der zivilisierten Welt? Die Intervention der europäischen Großmächte im griechischen Unabhängigkeitskrieg (1826–1832)* (Berlin, 2011), and "This Clumsy Fabric of Barbarous Power. Die europäische Außenpolitik und der außereuropäische Raum am Beispiel des Osmanischen Reiches", in *Das europäische Mächtekonzert. Friedens- und Sicherheitspolitik vom Wiener Kongreß 1815 bis zum Krimkrieg 1853*, eds. W. Pyta (Cologne, Weimar, and Vienna, 2009), 273–298; Šedivý, *Metternich, the Great Powers and the Eastern Question*, 395.

11 G. J. Bass, *Freedom's Battle. The Origins of Humanitarian Intervention* (New York, 2008), 48–49; Reinhard Heydenreuter, "Die erträumte Nation. Griechenlands Staatswerdung zwischen Philhellenismus und Militärintervention", in *Die erträumte Nation*, eds. R. Heydenreuter, J. Murken, and R. Wünsche (Munich, 1995), 60; M. Schulz, *Das 19. Jahrhundert (1789–1914)* (Stuttgart, 2011), 92.

12 For relevant scholarly texts see endnote 3 in this chapter.

13 Metternich, *Die Geschichte des Aufstandes der Griechen*, 1848 [or afterwards], NA, RAM-AC 8, 2/12.

14 A. von Prokesch-Osten, ed., *Geschichte des Abfalls der Griechen vom türkischen Reiche im Jahre 1821 und der Gründung des hellenischen Königreiches. Aus diplomatischem Standpuncte*, vol. 2 (Vienna, 1867), 391, 445.

15 Metternich, *Die Geschichte des Aufstandes der Griechen*, 1848 [or afterwards], NA, RAM-AC 8, 2/12.

16 For more on Metternich's interpretation of the public law and the intervention into the war between the Turks and the Greeks see for example Metternich to Bombelles, Vienna, 13 November 1826, HHStA, StA, Russland III, 75; Metternich to Apponyi, Vienna, 25 September, 17 and 30 October 1826, HHStA, StA, Frankreich 261; Metternich to Apponyi, Vienna, 31 March and 11 June 1827, HHStA, StA, Frankreich 264; Metternich to Zichy, Vienna, 14 June 1827, HHStA, Staatskanzlei, Preußen 125; Caraman to Damas, Vienna, 1 April 1827, AMAE, CP, Autriche 408; Wellesley to Canning, Vienna, 1 November 1826, The National Archives of the United Kingdom, London [henceforth: TNA], Foreign Office [henceforth: FO] 120/82; Wellesley to Canning, Vienna, 30 April 1827, TNA, FO 120/85; Wellesley to Dudley, Vienna, 14 June 1827, TNA, FO 120/86; Tatishchev to Nesselrode, Vienna, 11 June 1827, Arkhiv vneshnei politiki Rossiiskoi Imperii, Moscow, fond 133, Kantseliariia, opis 468, 11873; G. de B. de Sauvigny, *Metternich et la France après le congrès de Vienne*, vol. 3 (Paris, 1970), 1097–1098.

17 M. Šedivý, "An Insupportable Burden. The Eastern Question and the Failure of the 1815 Order", in *Der Wiener Kongress 1815/15. Band I: Internationale Politik*, eds T. Olechowski, B. Mazohl, K. Schneider, and R. Stauber (Vienna, 2019), 135.

18 Maltzan to Frederick William III, Vienna, 10 June 1827, GStA PK, HA III, MdA I, 6008.

19 P. Duvergier de Hauranne, "De la Convention du 13 Juillet et de la Situation actuelle de la Franc", *Revue des Deux Mondes* 27 (1840): 711, Chancellor Metternich's Library, Chateau Königswart, book number 15-C-21.

64 *Miroslav Šedivý*

20 M. Šedivý, "The Principle of Non-Intervention Reconsidered. The French July Monarchy, the Public Law of Europe and the Limited Sovereignty of Secondary Countries", *Nuova Rivista Storica* 103/1 (2019): 75–108.

21 M. Šedivý, *The Decline of the Congress System. Metternich, Italy and European Diplomacy* (London and New York, 2018), 84–85.

22 Metternich's remarks to the Protocol of 4 April 1826, attached to Metternich to Esterházy, Vienna, 4 June 1826, HHStA, StA, England 175.

23 Ibid.

24 M. Šedivý, "Metternich and the French Expedition to Algeria (1830)", *Archiv orientální. Quarterly Journal of African and Asian Studies* 76/1 (2008): 15–37.

25 Foster to Palmerston, Turin, 20 February 1832, TNA, FO 67/86; Talleyrand to Sébastiani, London, 9 March 1832, AMAE, CP, Angleterre 636; Apponyi to Metternich, Paris, 13 March 1832, HHStA, StA, Frankreich 281; Garibaldi to Bernetti, Paris, 2 March 1832, G. Procacci, ed., *Le relazioni diplomatiche fra lo Stato pontifico e la Francia, II serie: 1830–1848*, vol 2 (Rome, 1963), 141; N. Jolicoeur, *La politique française envers les états pontificaux sous la monarchie de juillet et la seconde république (1830–1851)* (Brussels, 2008), 263; P. Silva, *La Monarchia di Luglio e l'Italia: Studio di storia diplomatica* (Torino, 1917), 207; H. von Srbik, *Metternich. Der Staatsmann und der Mensch*, vol. 1 (Munich, 1925), 676; F. Wolfram, "Besetzung und Räumung Ankonas durch Frankreich 1832–1838 (unpublished dissertation, Universität Wien, 1930), 79–80.

26 Metternich to Neumann, Vienna, 25 April 1840, HHStA, StA, England 230. See also Lerchenfeld to Ludwig I of Bavaria, Vienna, 11 May 1840, Bayerisches Hauptstaatsarchiv, Munich, Ministerium des Äußern, Österreich 2409.

27 M. Isabella, *Risorgimento in Exile. Italian Émigrés and the Liberal International in the Post-Napoleonic Era* (Oxford, 2009), 99–106.

28 G. Galasso, *Il Regno di Napoli. Il Mezzogiorno borbonico e risorgimentale (1815–1860)* (Torino, 2007), 590; Isabella, *Risorgimento in Exile*, 18 and 31.

29 *L'Alba*, no. 128, 23 January 1848, 509.

Part II
Resonances of the Age of Revolution II

5 Transnationalism and cosmopolitanism in the 1820s: Philhellenism(s) in the public sphere[*]

Anna Karakatsouli

The Philhellenic movement is undoubtedly the most studied feature of the Greek Revolution in international bibliography. The men who, in Europe as well as in the United States, raised public awareness about the Greek struggle for independence and contributed with money, pamphlets, artistic works, and – in many instances – their lives, too, offer a wide field for historical research. Their contribution is recorded in books and memoirs, newspaper articles, private and State documents, all primary sources in languages other than Greek readily accessible to the international scholarly community. As a result, the production focusing on the Philhellenes has grown disproportionally to all other aspects of the Greek struggle for independence. Despite this impressive scholarly work, the Greek War of Independence remains excluded from the Age of Revolutions. The area traditionally covered by relevant studies extends to both shores of the Atlantic but stops firmly at the border of the Ottoman world.[1]

Moreover, British, French, German, or American volunteers to the Greek cause have been examined thus far largely as if they were independent actors operating along mutually exclusive national boundaries and cultures. This approach, however, cannot do justice to the rich human connections and exchanges of ideas, inspiration, information, and resources that abound during this formative postwar period of "flux and hiatus", according to C.A. Bayly.[2] Most importantly, it does not consider the fact that the transition to a nation-state world at the beginning of the nineteenth century was only a distant glimmer. We are still well into the age of empires and it would better fit the reality of the times if we placed 1821 Greece at an "imperial crossroad",[3] juggling between Ottoman, Tsarist, Habsburg, British, and French imperial plans and possibilities, ambitions, and constraints.

Typology

We commonly distinguish between four types of foreign interest in the Greek struggle for independence: a. Military engagement of the liberal army and naval officers who came to fight in Greece, b. Humanitarian action by European and American philanthropy committees gathering

68 *Anna Karakatsouli*

funds and provisions to assist the Greek population, c. Financial activity of bankers, investors, and speculators who hastened to set up high risk but also extremely profitable loans, and d. State intervention by the Great Powers, openly from the Battle of Navarino in 1827 onwards but acting undercover much earlier. To avoid traditional national classifications, we propose here two alternative analytical categories, one geographical, and another political and social. We should first distinguish Philhellenes acting inside and outside of Greece. In the first category, we place the ones who came to Greece as fighters, conspirators, or humanitarian agents and had first-hand experience with the land and its people. They share significant common features; they are for their greatest part ex-army officers on half-pay, often in disgrace for their political beliefs in their country of origin. They defend the superiority of tactical warfare over the guerilla tactics of the Greeks, they pursue their own agenda, and in most cases, they look upon the locals with disdain. In the second category belong all those who supported the Greek struggle from afar by writing books and dramas; painting pictures and composing music; or through newspaper articles, pamphlets, parliamentary debates, and public meetings, but who may have had a bigger impact on the final outcome. This is more than a spatial division. Personal contact with local warlords and war tactics in Greece critically affected attitudes towards the fighting Greeks and the Greek cause. Additionally, we see Philhellenism operating at two political and social levels: as a radical movement of suppressed liberalism 'from below' close to revolutionary romanticism that rallied transnational cosmopolitan mobilization, and at the same time as a tool 'from above' serving State policies.

Chronology

Switzerland (Bern) and Germany (Stuttgart) were the first countries in which philhellenic committees were formed before the end of summer 1821. The movement expanded rapidly and appeals began to appear in the press, at first cautiously putting forward religion and European kinship with Greece and carefully suppressing political motives. The first volunteers left for Greece with enthusiasm as soon as news of the revolt reached Western Europe in spring 1821. Ships were called at Marseilles, Trieste, and Ancona to buy arms and ammunition and to board individuals, as well as organized groups. It was a motley crowd that rushed to the Morea: unemployed army officers and ex-soldiers of the vast conscript armies that had been fighting against each other between 1792 and 1815, political exiles, romantic artists, runaway students, fortune seekers, and adventurers. These unexpected volunteers were met with surprise and bewilderment by the locals.[4] Greek warlords were not prepared to incorporate men from abroad into their armed groups nor were any barracks, uniforms, or weapons available to

Philhellenism(s) in the public sphere 69

offer them. The volunteers had to find out that even the widespread rumor that Greeks had adopted the Marseillaise as their national anthem was 'fake news'.[5] After wandering aimlessly in the Peloponnesian countryside, usually left to themselves to find food and shelter, a special battalion had finally been created, the Battalion of the Philhellenes. It would soon be decimated at the Battle of Peta in July 1822. Bitterly disappointed, horrified by the wild plundering and murder scenes they had witnessed at Tripolitsa and elsewhere, survivors returned as best they could to their home countries. They made it their duty to prevent others, credulous as they themselves had been, from making the same journey to Greece. They wrote articles and books and seriously affected the philhellenic flux of volunteers until 1824–1825.

An unexpected event, the death of Lord Byron in Missolonghi in April 1824, marked a major turning point for the philhellenic movement. Byron was a cult figure for romantic souls all over Europe. His death was seen as the end of the golden age of poetry, the last act in "the astonishing creativity of the Romantic age" and it was generally believed thereafter that "there was no market for poetry".[6] His body was brought back from Greece in July for two weeks of public funeral rites and burial in Nottinghamshire.[7] A flood of biographies began to appear – although his own *Memoranda* of 1819–1824 (the basis of a biography) perished in the flames of Murray's fireplace with the consent of Byron's close friends John Cam Hobhouse and Thomas Moore to whom the poet had entrusted his manuscript[8] – and public opinion interest in the Greek cause was re-vivified. Moreover, after the French invasion of Spain in 1823 and the restoration of the absolutist monarchy in Portugal, the Greek War of Independence was the last refuge in Europe for scattered revolutionaries. Almost every volunteer in the second wave of Philhellenes of 1824 and 1825 was a professional soldier in search of employment with long years of active experience behind him on the battlefields of Europe. They enrolled at a critical moment for the Greek insurgents, when the Egyptian army of Ibrahim Pasha was in control of much of the Peloponnese while the Greeks themselves were in the grip of the civil war. Distinguished officers, such as Sir Richard Church and Charles Fabvier, devoted their efforts to the formation of a regular Greek army. During 1824 and 1825, a succession of prominent Italian exiled revolutionaries also made their way from England to Greece, partly hoping to use a portion of the proceeds of the two Greek loans to keep the cause of Italian liberalism afloat. The third and last massive foreign intervention to assist the Greeks no longer concerns military action but humanitarian aid, and this was the first international operation of that kind. The American relief expeditions of 1827 and 1828 distributed loads of food and clothing to non-combatants and, thus, ensured the survival of the starving population exhausted by years of fighting and devastation.

70   *Anna Karakatsouli*

"The printing press as an agent of change"[9]

In this paper, we focus on the presence of Philhellenism in the public sphere and more specifically, in the realm of publishing activity. Books, pamphlets, and newspaper articles about the events in Greece did not aim at some 'niche' philhellenic or Christian-faith market, but they were channeled via existing radical networks. It has already been asserted that, during the 1820s, liberal Philhellenism approached issues like the political and moral status of modern Greek nationhood "exclusively on the basis of modern political considerations".[10] As such, turning to print culture in the age of global communication may shed new light on the close entanglement of philhellenic activism with home politics in the countries concerned. The philhellenic movement profited greatly from innovations in printing and publishing entering then into the industrial era. Steam-powered iron presses, stereotype printing, and mechanized paper manufacturing processes sped up production and increased the amount of printed matter in circulation from 1820 onwards. Production growth and the spread of readership made the press appear "most influential and potentially threatening", especially at times of political unrest.[11] We consider these changes in the print industry one of the "circumstances peculiar to the times that made Europeans acutely sensitive to revolution and many of them more sympathetic to the Greek than to that of other nations", as formulated by Virginia Penn.[12]

Georgian Britain

The reign of the Hanoverian kings (1714–1830) was broadly an era of great change in Britain as cities grew, as trade expanded, and as consumerism and popular culture blossomed.[13] With the Napoleonic and post-Napoleonic period, however, the British Isles witnessed radicalism, popular agitation, and repression, including trials for seditious and blasphemous libel. The Six Acts of 1819 passed by the Parliament after the Peterloo massacre to counter "the treasonable, blasphemous, and seditious branch of the press" imposed high taxes and harsh punishments on news and opinion articles alike.[14] Stamp, paper, and other duties were introduced to prevent the wide circulation of 'dangerous' ideas and information among the 'lower classes' curtailing the flowering of cheap radical print.[15] Nevertheless, there were still 52 London papers and over 100 other titles in the early nineteenth century.[16] State repression remained mostly ineffective and did not prevent an active philhellenic press from developing. The new domain of public opinion was kept informed about the struggle in Greece through the columns of *The New Monthly Magazine* established in 1814 by Henry Colburn as a "virulently Tory publication"[17]; the long-popular *The London Magazine*, an old monthly magazine of news, commentary, and satire published since 1732 – but that had been revived by a new editor, John Scott, in 1820 and reached the height of its literary prosperity publishing poetic luminaries such as William Wordsworth, Percy Bysshe Shelley, John Clare, and John Keats[18]; and, the *Westminster Review* founded by Jeremy Bentham in 1823, the official organ of the political group of Philosophical Radicals. Access to the radical press offered a wide and supportive audience to the Greek struggle for independence beyond private discussions and sensibilities, however seminal these may have been (the Byron-Shelley circle perhaps being the most famous one).[19] Articles from this period could be categorized as 'conflict reportage'; they concern chiefly travel accounts and first-hand experiences in belligerent Greece, such as the "Adventures of a foreigner in Greece", "The Siege of the Acropolis of Athens in the years 1821-22 By an Eye-Witness", "Adventures of an English Officer in Greece", or "Greece in the Spring 1825".[20] Lengthy political analyses were usually reproduced in book form through the usual channels of radical thought.

Radical printers continued, despite a sustained campaign of intimidation and prosecution, to produce cheap papers defying the four-penny stamp tax. In 1821, the printing press was "the best weapon a man can yield against tyrants", as proclaimed by Richard Carlile, radical agitator and a printer himself.[21] A number of book publishers specialized in works about the ongoing struggle in Greece, producing both memoirs and pamphlets. Among the most prolific ones we may include, Henry Colburn, who used to print in book format the long articles previously published in his monthly magazine; George B. Whittaker, the publisher of John Bowring, Edward Blaquiere, and Giuseppe Pecchio[22]; Hunt and Clarke,[23] the last two reaching the peak of their production in the years of the Greek Revolution; James Ridgway, the radical London pamphlet publisher and bookseller who published *The Cause of Greece, the Cause of Europe* as early as 1821, a translation from the German original by Heinrich Gottlieb Tzschirner (a Protestant theologian from Saxony)[24]; and, last but not least, John Murray, one of the most important and influential publishing houses in Britain, founded in 1768, which published Byron, Jane Austen, and Sir Walter Scott.[25] Titles of Greek interest were made a common part of their catalogues. The Greek cause was promoted and integrated into the radical culture of the 1820s, debated among other fiery current issues such as suffrage, parliamentary reform, or Corn Laws. The collusion extended to the spaces of the radical movement. It is no accident that the London Greek Committee set its headquarters at the old Crown and Anchor Tavern in the Strand, "an established space on London's cultural landscape, ... appropriated by successive generations of radicals".[26] Greece meant much more than a local insurgency; it became a tool for expressing "radical political ideas for Europe's future".[27] Since Ancient Greece offered the model for republican political institutions, Modern Greece might serve as the perfect forum for new republican ideas.

Restoration France

The restored Bourbon monarchy placed book and press publishing under close surveillance and censorship with the rationale that "the press had to be protected from its own potential abuses".[28] After the revolutionary period, free communication of ideas and opinions and the power of the press was now to be restrained. The caution-money system remained valid to prevent the press from "becoming at first seditious, and later tyrannical", according to Guizot. This meant that newspaper publishers were required to deposit a significant sum of money to secure permission for publication. Although discussion of freedom of the press "figured highly in the political and constitutional debates that followed the restoration of the monarchy in 1814",[29] the laws of March 1822 established prior authorization for political press articles and introduced the infamous 'délit de tendance', making an illegal offence not only of the opinions explicitly expressed but also of the general spirit the court might deduce from a selection of articles spanning over an indefinite period of time.[30] The reactionary policy of the Richelieu government led to polarization into liberal and royalist groups. Moreover, changes in the electoral law left no chance for the liberals to legally access power. Secret societies flourished while genuine conspiracy plots (but also intense conspiracy anxiety) dominated the French political arena. Everything, the liberal polemicist Abbé de Pradt affirmed in 1825, "was now reducible to a single question: 'for or against the Revolution, before or after the Revolution'".[31]

In this atmosphere of mutual fear and mistrust, Philhellenism became a rallying symbol for the opposition, both liberal and royalist, criticizing the government for its indifference and inaction towards the suffering Greeks.[32] Several factors may explain the momentum of the Greek cause. After 1823 and its successful intervention in Spain, France had gradually regained a position of power and turned its focus to the Levant, seeking to restore equilibrium in European politics.[33] Initially, Philhellenism in France organized on a philanthropic basis through the action of the *Société de la Morale Chrétienne* founded in Paris in 1821 to promote noble causes such as the abolition of slavery and of the death penalty, assisting widows and orphans, suppressing gambling and drinking, etc. At the beginning of 1823, the Society created a relief committee (*Comité en faveur des Grecs réfugiés en France*) to raise money for Greek refugees in France, and, in February 1825, a new committee, (*Société philanthropique en faveur des Grecs*), usually known as the Paris Greek Committee, entitled this time to collect funds that could be used to buy guns and ammunition. The prestige of the Committee was greatly enhanced by the adherence of Chateaubriand, the romantic writer who "dominated the literary scene in France in the first half of the nineteenth century"[34] and had served as Foreign Minister to the restored Bourbons.[35] In contrast with the London Greek Committee, which always rested on a narrow political base, the Paris Committee gradually extended its membership and influence to an ever wider spectrum of opinion. Originally, the Committee

Philhellenism(s) in the public sphere   73

seems to have been largely composed of Liberals and Orleanists, but with the accession of Chateaubriand, it became a truly national movement.

News arriving in September 1825 of the Greek Act of Submission to Great Britain seriously alarmed political circles in France who tried to minimize its scope, even to deny the accuracy of the reports.[36] The creation of a British protectorate in Greece was considered a direct threat to French commercial activities in the Levant; suspicions were even raised that it masked other "secret and dreadful" plans of British expansion as far as Latin America, and the whole affair was linked to Cochrane's recruitment as Admiral of the Greek Fleet.[37] Fears raised by British intervention in Greek affairs provoked a major shift in government policy and public opinion. As it has been argued, growing French support for the Greek cause should be attributed to the pressure in international politics.[38] The French philhellenic movement grew to become "the largest demonstration of militant philhellenism" and reached its greatest strength in 1826 at the very time when the English Philhellenes – following the loan bubble of 1822–1825 and the stock market crash of 1825 – were at their lowest point.[39]

Philhellenic articles appeared mainly in opposition newspapers, such as the anticlerical *Constitutionnel* ("the largest newspaper on the continent of Europe"[40]), which offered its premises for the collection of funds deposited "en faveur des Grecs"; *Le Globe,* established in 1824 by Pierre Leroux and the printer Alexandre Lachevardière as a Romantic literary journal and which became political and liberal in tone after 1828 as well as the official paper of Saint-Simonianism in 1830; or the royalist *La Gazette de France* and *Le Drapeau blanc,* the latter displaying on the first page the dubious slogan: "Vive le Roi! Quand même...".[41] References to Greece rose sharply during the revolutionary decade and peaked in 1826 with nearly 2,900 articles mentioning Greece or Greeks (Table 5.1, Figure 5.1).

Table 5.1 Articles mentioning Greece/Greeks/Turkey/Turks in French newspapers in 1821–1830

	GREEKS	GREECE	TURKS	TURKEY
1821	2179	969	1773	1142
1822	1973	934	1551	914
1823	1268	641	814	495
1824	1525	861	849	496
1825	1988	1618	889	435
1826	2876	2021	1214	754
1827	2253	1667	989	815
1828	1891	1979	2016	1475
1829	1628	1890	1919	1377
1830	1497	1963	1010	737

(Source: Retronews, BNF)

74 *Anna Karakatsouli*

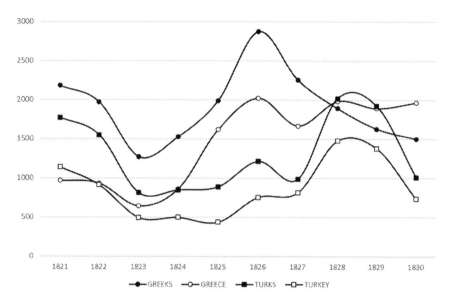

Figure 5.1 Articles mentioning Greece/Greeks/Turkey/Turks in French newspapers in 1821–1830.
(Source: Retronews, BNF)[42]

The sharp peak in 1825 and 1826 is also confirmed when we consider global book and pamphlet production of philhellenic content. Our research indicates a clear increase in titles of Greek interest during that time span, as shown in the sample count in Figure 5.2:

This is only a fraction of information about philhellenic book production worldwide. This climax, however, is confirmed on a variety of occasions. The Paris season 1825–1826, for instance, was astonishingly rich in artistic creations of Greek inspiration covering all fields of cultural production. Philhellenic press and art had become fashionable again in the conjuncture of Lord Byron's death.[43] Even Lamartine, who rejected vividly what he saw as Byron's religious negation, published in 1825 *Le Dernier Chant du pèlerinage d'Harold*, a fictional version of Byron's last months.[44] Byron's death rekindled the dwindling public fervor for the Greek cause; romantic ascendancy addressed an active and politically committed public.

That year, presented to the public were the famous ode by Victor Hugo, "The Heads of the Seraglio"; the five-act tragedy, *Leonidas,* by Michel Pichat at the Théâtre Français, which made a huge success with the famous Talma at the leading role; and, a philhellenic dithyramb signed by the 23-year-old Alexandre Dumas on the occasion of his theatre review for this specific performance. In April 1826, the "flamboyant and controversial performer", Tommaso Sgricci[45], an Italian poet and widely acclaimed stage improviser who was touring Paris, had been asked by the public to

Figure 5.2 Digitized books and pamphlets of Greek interest, 1821–1830.
(Source: 1821 Digital Archive, RCH)

improvise a tragedy on *The Fall of Missolonghi*, the breaking news from Greece. Sgricci tried to avoid such a political topic, protesting that the information had not been confirmed yet. Upon the insistence of the audience, he complied in the end and improvised a poetic drama that "brought down thunders of applause".[46] Sgricci was aware of what was happening in Greece. Close to the Pisa circle of Byron and the Shelley's a few years earlier, in the winter of 1820–1821, he had met with Alexander Mavrokordatos and even helped Shelley become familiar with the themes and style of Ancient Greek tragedy while he composed *Hellas*.[47] At the beginning of May 1826, Sgricci presented *The Fall of Missolonghi* in London, but this time he refused to improvise. Instead, he gave a dramatic reading from the printed version of his drama in verse that had been published in book form soon after its first presentation in Paris, much to the disappointment of his English public.[48]

Music was also appropriately represented. Rossini gave his first French opera at the Salle Le Peletier of the Paris Opéra, *Le Siège de Corinthe*, on 9 October 1826. The opera was based on the reworking of some of the music from *Maometto II*, the composer's rather unfortunate opera commissioned in 1820 by the Teatro di San Carlo in Naples. Enhanced with two ballets to better seduce the French public and transplanted to the Peloponnese with a new title, the opera finally succeeded and was performed in several countries during the next decades. That same year, a young composer, Héctor Berlioz, then 23 years old, set to music the poem, "La révolution grecque: scène héroïque", written by his close friend, the lawyer Humbert Ferrand. Last but

76   *Anna Karakatsouli*

not least, Parisian art lovers enjoyed that year three fresh paintings by Eugène Delacroix, "The Combat of the Giaour and the Pasha", "A Turkish officer killed in the mountains", and the magnificent allegory "Greece on the Ruins of Missolonghi"; as well as the "Taking of Missolonghi" by Ary Scheffer, drawing teacher to the children of the Duke of Orléans and a keen observer of politics in Europe, also known as a prominent Philhellene; and Alexandre Colin's "Massacre of the Greeks".[49] They were all exhibited at the Galerie Lebrun's *Exposition en faveur des Grecs.*[50]

In contrast to the close policing of the daily and periodical press, book censorship abolished in 1815 had not been reintroduced.[51] The Restoration kept tight control over the printers' operation through weekly reports of their activity and the obligation of a prior declaration of all printed matter before legally putting it to sale. From 1815 to 1826 book production in France was on a continuous and steady rise. The need to reconstruct libraries destroyed during the revolutionary years, the import from Britain of the first completely iron hand presses that increased output to 250 sheets per hour, and the strong attachment of the French public to reading for leisure led to a remarkable expansion of the book trades – printing, bookselling, and the activities related to them.[52]

Ambroise Firmin-Didot (1790–1876), official printer of the French Academy and the King's Printer ("Imprimeur du Roi") in 1829–1830, was a key figure for the promotion of the Greek cause. A printer-publisher with an illustrious family tradition in book trade behind him and an editor and a Greek scholar taught by Koraes, Didot was also a committed Philhellene and the secretary of the Paris Greek Committee. In his early years, he had spent some time at the school of Kydonies in Asia Minor and then had been attached, in 1816, to the French Embassy in Istanbul.[53] Before returning home, he made an extensive tour through Greece, Asia Minor, Syria, Palestine, and Egypt, of which he published an account in 1821. Didot donated an iron printing press to the fighting Greeks and published several titles on the subject. In a catalogue packed with official legal texts and the proceedings of the Chamber of Peers, Didot displays a systematic interest in Greece and his editorial choices cover a wide spectrum of Greek subjects comprising political works, as well scholarly and literary ones. We identified fifty such titles for the period 1821 to 1830. His yearly output doubles for the years 1826–1827, translations of Ancient Greek texts not included. Didot published, among others, the *History of Greece* by Pouqueville (*Histoire de la Grèce*, 1824); studies of the Venus of Milo, only recently discovered and transferred to Paris; Claude Fauriel's collection and translation of Greek folk songs (1824); Allan Cunningham's translation of Byron's *Don Juan* third Canto (*La Grèce*, 1821), as well as an anonymous *Irregular Ode on the death of Lord Byron* (1825); the translation of the letter of Lord Erskine to Lord Liverpool on behalf of the cause of Greek independence in 1822, the year of its first publication in England by Murray; and Constantinos Polychroniadis' pamphlet

Considérations sur la guerre actuelle entre les Grecs et les Turcs, par un Grec (1821), and the *Dithyrambe sur la Liberté* by Dionysios Solomos, which was to become the Greek national anthem after 1865, in a bilingual edition of 1825. From June 1826 onward, Firmin Didot launched a special journal for the documents released by the Paris Greek Committee, the *Documents relatifs à l'état présent de la Grèce publiés d' après les communications du comité philhellénique de Paris*. It lasted until February 1829, having printed ten issues. When, in 1827, the Académie Française bestowed its annual poetry award to the *Liberation of the Greeks* (*L'Affranchissement des Grecs*) by Pierre-Auguste Lemaire, a Latinist and Dean of the Faculty of Letters at the University of Paris, it was Didot who published the poem situated in Epidaurus on the opening day of the Greek National Assembly, 6 April 1826. Furthermore, as a corollary to the 1828 French Expedition to the Morea, a new category of books emerged in Didot's publishing activity. In response to the rising demand for textbooks of the Modern Greek language in 1829, Didot frères put into circulation two new titles, a method of teaching Greek for French speakers and a short guide of the Greek pronunciation and orthograph, plus a grammar book in 1830.[54]

Numerous French printers and booksellers were also active in the trade of books about current affairs in Greece. Le Normant, the printer of the *Journal des Débats* –an influential newspaper of great authority "read by the royalist bourgeoisie open to modern ideas",[55] – published *The Remarques politiques sur la cause des Grecs* by Panayotis Kodricas in 1822 and Chateaubriand's *Note sur la Grèce* in 1825. In 1824, Tournachon-Mollin published Maxime Raybaud's two-volume *Mémoires sur la Grèce pour servir à l'histoire de la Guerre de l'Indépendance*. Victor Tournachon (1771–1837) had joined the Revolution on the first day. Because of his liberal views, his press was closely watched by government censors.[56] Béchet Aîné put into print the best-selling analyst Dominique de Pradt, an eccentric member of the high clergy with an acute sense of political affairs who dedicated no fewer than eight books to the war in Greece.[57] Lastly, we should mention the two Parisian publishers and booksellers specializing in international book trade, Galigniani and Bossange Frères[58], who published English authors writing about the Greek struggle, such as William Parry and Edward Blaquiere.[59]

Conclusion

The extensive network between book trade establishments originally set up during the Revolutionary era served communication needs and transfer of ideas also under the Restoration. It has been argued that after 1815 the liberal press created a vivid common space of shared sensibilities and collective perceptions about politics and society.[60] We have seen how the rapidly growing publishing industry of the beginning of the nineteenth century allowed for the wide dissemination of the Greek cause through both liberal

78 Anna Karakatsouli

and royalist opposition channels. Moreover, the artists' and poets' ardour for the Greek Revolution suitably served "the tendency of the post-1815 Radical Enlightenment to evolve, in the face of general opposition,...in a veiled fashion."[61] In this transitional period, the inclusion of articles, books, and pamphlets about the struggle for Greek independence in the columns of opposition newspapers, as well as in the catalogues of printers and booksellers of this affiliation, turned the Greek Revolution into a regular issue of the current political agenda. As an efficient tool for expressing underground dissidence, it was at the same time confirmed as an indisputable part of the global connections that formed the modern world.

Notes

* I wish to thank the Research Centre for the Humanities (RCH) and the 1821 Digital Archive project (https://www.rchumanities.gr/en/1821-about-the-project/#) on which the collection of data for this paper is partly based.

1 Bryan Banks, Cindy Ermus, "About *Age of Revolutions*, or The Allure of Revolution", *Age of Revolutions*. Accessed 15 June 2020, https://ageofrevolutions.com/about-or-the-allure-of-revolution/.

2 C.A. Bayly, *The Birth of the Modern World, 1780–1914* (Oxford, 2004), 125.

3 Credits to Yanni Kotsonis, 'Greece as an Imperial Crossroad, 1797–1830', Seeger Centre for Hellenic Studies, Princeton University, Feb 11, 2020, https://hellenic.princeton.edu/events/lecture-yanni-kotsonis-greece-imperial-crossroad-1797–1830

4 Anna Karakatsouli, *Μαχητές της ελευθερίας και 1821: Η Ελληνική Επανάσταση στη διεθνική της διάσταση* [Freedom fighters and 1821: The Greek Revolution in its transnational dimension] (Athens, 2016), 193–209.

5 Claude Denis Raffenel, *Histoire des événements de la Grèce depuis les premiers troubles jusqu'à ce jour; Avec de notes critiques et topographiques sur le Péloponnèse et la Turquie, et suivie d'une notice sur Constantinople; une carte du Théâtre de la Guerre est jointe à l'ouvrage*, Paris, 1822, 10.

6 David Stewart, *The Form of Poetry in the 1820s and 1830s: A Period of Doubt* (Cham, Switzerland, 2018), 2–3.

7 Angela Esterhammer *Print and Performance in the 1820s: Improvisation, Speculation, Identity* (Cambridge, 2020), 2–4.

8 Murray found the text "abominable", "horrid and disgusting" and despite the prospect of huge profits he decided to sacrifice it to safeguard Byron's honour and fame. See Susan J. Wolfson, *Romantic Interactions: Social Being and the Turns of Literary Action* (Baltimore, 2010), 246–247. Later Moore wrote his own *Life of Byron* published by Murray in 1835.

9 We borrow here the title of Elizabeth Eisenstein's groundbreaking work *The Printing Press as an Agent of Change: Communications and Cultural Transformations in Early-modern Europe*, 2 vols. (Cambridge, 1980).

10 Margarita Milliori, "Europe, the classical *polis*, and the Greek nation: Philhellenism and Hellenism in Nineteenth-Century Britain", in *The Making of Modern Greece: Nationalism, Romanticism, and the Uses of the Past (1797–1896)*, eds by Roderick Beaton and David Ricks (London and New York, 2013), 66.

11 Hannah Barker, *Newspapers and English Society, 1695–1855* (London and New York, 2000), 10.

12 Virginia Penn, "Philhellenism in Europe, 1821–1828", *The Slavonic and East European Review* 16 no. 48 (1938): 638.

Philhellenism(s) in the public sphere 79

13 "Georgian Britain", *The British Library*. Accessed 15 June 2020, https://www.bl.uk/georgian-britain

14 Katie Carpenter, 'The Six Acts and Censorship of the Press', *The History of Parliament: British Political, Social, and Local History*. Accessed 15 June 2020, https://thehistoryofparliament.wordpress.com/2019/08/20/the-six-acts-and-censorship-of-the-press/.

15 Daniel Allington, David A. Brewer, Stephen Colclough, Sian Echard, eds, *The Book in Britain: A Historical Introduction* (Hoboken, New Jersey, 2019), 262.

16 Barker, *Newspapers*, 1.

17 David Higgins, 'The New Monthly Magazine', *The Literary Encyclopedia*. First published 22 October 2006, accessed 29 February 2020, https://www.litencyc.com/php/stopics.php?rec=true&UID=1682.

18 'History', *The London Magazine*. Accessed 15 June 2020, https://www.thelondonmagazine.org/about-us/.

19 Paul Stock, *The Shelley-Byron Circle and the Idea of Europe* (New York, 2010).

20 *The London magazine*. n.s. v. 5 1826 May–Aug., https://babel.hathitrust.org/cgi/pt?id=mdp.39015033845572&view=1up&seq=482; *The London Literary Gazette and Journal of Belles Lettres, Arts, Sciences, Etc.*, February 1826, https://play.google.com/books/reader?id=gQEFAAAAQAAJ&hl=el&pg=GBS.PA144-IA1; William Henry Humphreys, *The New Monthly Magazine and Literary Journal*, 7 (1826). https://play.google.com/store/books/details?id=RzcaAQAAIAAJ&rdid=book-RzcaAQAAIAAJ&rdot=1 Giuseppe Pecchio, *The New Monthly Magazine and Literary Journal*, vol. 14 (London, 1825). https://play.google.com/books/reader?id=CYJHAAAAYAAJ&hl=el&pg=GBS.PR1.

21 Christina Parolin, *Radical Spaces: Venues of popular politics in London, 1790–c. 1845* (Canberra, 2010), 208.

22 "G. and W. B. Whittaker, Publisher", Open Library, *Internet Archive*, accessed 15 June 2020. https://openlibrary.org/publishers/G._and_W._B._Whittaker.

23 Laurel Brake, Marysa Demoor, *Dictionary of Nineteenth-century Journalism in Great Britain and Ireland* (London, 2009), 124; "Hunt and Clarke Publisher', Open Library, *Internet Archive*, accessed 15 June 2020, https://openlibrary.org/publishers/Hunt_and_Clarke;

24 Ralph A. Manogue, "The Plight of James Ridgway, London Bookseller and Publisher, and the Newgate Radicals 1792–1797", *The Wordsworth Circle* 27, no. 3 (Summer 1996): 158–166. https://doi.org/10.1086/TWC24042936. Title of the original, printed in Leipzig earlier that same year: *Die Sache der Griechen, die Sache Europa's*; 'James Ridgway, Publisher', Open Library, *Internet Archive*, accessed 15 June 2020, https://openlibrary.org/publishers/James_Ridgway.

25 'John Murray, Publisher', Open Library, *Internet Archive*, accessed 15 June 2020, https://openlibrary.org/publishers/John_Murray.

26 Parolin, *Radical Spaces*, 14.

27 Paul Stock, *The Shelley-Byron Circle and the Idea of Europe* (New York, 2010), 175–197.

28 Jeremy Jennings, "A note on freedom of the press in Restoration France", *Journal of Modern Italian Studies* 17:5 (2012): 571. DOI: 10.1080/1354571X.2012.718562.

29 Jennings, "A note": 570.

30 Ioannis Dimakis, *La Guerre de l'indépendance grecque vue par la presse française (période de 1821 à 1824)* (Thessaloniki, 1968), 27.

31 G. Cubitt, "Conspiracism, Secrecy and Security in Restoration France: Denouncing the Jesuit Menace", *Historical Social Research* 38 no. 1 (2013): 108, 113. https://doi.org/10.12759/hsr.38.2013.1.107-128

32 Dimakis, *La Guerre*, 22.

80   *Anna Karakatsouli*

33 Anna Karakatsouli, 'The French Involvement in the Greek War of Independence', *Historein*, Special issue "1821 - What made it Greek?What made it Revolutionary" 20 (2021), forthcoming.

34 Peter Gay, 'The Complete Romantic', *Horizon* 8/2 (1966): 12–19.

35 The famous pro-Greek pamphlet by François-Réné Chateaubriand *Note sur la Grèce, ou Appel en faveur de la cause sacrée des Grecs*, was put in print in 1825 only after its author had been suddenly dismissed of his ministerial post in June 1824.

36 *Journal des débats politiques et littéraires*, 17 September 1825, 2; *Le Drapeau blanc*, 17 September 1825, 1.

37 *La Quotidienne*, 11 September 1825, 3.

38 Albert Boime, *Art in an Age of Counterrevolution, 1815-1848*, Chicago, 2004, 209-210.

39 Larry Neal, "The Financial Crisis of 1825 and the Restructuring of the British Financial System", 22nd Annual Economic Policy Conference at the Federal Reserve Bank of St. Louis, October 16-17, 1997, *Lessons from Financial History*. Research Gate, accessed 6 June 2020. https://www.researchgate.net/publication/5 047144_The_Financial_Crisis_of_1825_and_the_Restructuring_of_the_British_ Financial_System.

40 D. L. Rader, *The Journalists and the July Revolution in France: The Role of the Political Press in the Overthrow of the Bourbon Restoration, 1827–1830* (Berlin, 2013), 19; Christian A. E. Jensen, *L'évolution du romantisme: L'année 1826* (Geneva, 1986), 18.

41 Dimakis, *La Guerre*, 31-32.

42 Data collected from *Retronews*, Le site de presse de la BNF, https:// www.retronews.fr/. The rising trend in the years 1828–1829 may reasonably be attributed to topical circumstances, namely the presence of the French expeditionary force in the Morea under the commands of General Maison.

43 Paul Joannides, "Colin, Delacroix, Byron and the Greek War of Independence", *The Burlington Magazine* 125, no. 965 (1983): 495–500. Accessed May 31, 2020. www.jstor.org/stable/881314.

44 Joanna Wilkes, "'Infernal Magnetism': Byron and Nineteenth-Century French Readers", in *The Reception of Byron in Europe*, ed. Richard A. Cardwell (London, 2004), 26; Peter Cochran, *Byron's European Impact* (London, 2015), 130.

45 Angela Esterhammer, "Improvisational Aesthetics: Byron, the Shelley Circle, and Tommaso Sgricci", *Romanticism on the Net* 43 (2006), accessed 15 June 2020. https://doi.org/10.7202/013592ar.

46 *The Literary Gazette*, 10 (1826): 249, accessed 15 June 2020, https://bit.ly/3eAdjly.

47 Jacqueline Mulhallen, *The Theatre of Shelley* (Cambridge, 2010), 178, 189–193.

48 Esterhammer, *Print and Performance*, 80–82. The Italian edition of 1827 is available at https://archive.org/details/lacadutadimissol00sgri/page/n9/mode/2up (accessed 15 June 2020).

49 Jonathan Israel, *The Expanding Blaze: How the American Revolution Ignited the World, 1775–1848* (Princeton, 2017), 508.

50 Antonio Baltassare, "The Politics of Images: Considerations of French Nineteenth-Century Orientalist Art (ca. 1800- ca.1880) as a Paradigm of Narration and Translation", *Narrated Communities – Narrated Realities: Narration as Cognitive Processing and Cultural Practice*, eds. Hermann Blume, Christoph Leitgeb, and Michael Rössner (Amsterdam, 2015), 223.

51 Isabelle de Conihout, "La Restauration: Contrôle et liberté", in *Histoire de l'édition française, Tome 2: Le livre triomphant, 1660–1830*, ed. Roger Chartier and Henri-Jean Martin (Paris, 1990), 709.

52 De Conihout, 'La Restauration': 732–733.
53 Gonda van Steen, *Liberating Hellenism from the Ottoman Empire: Comte de Marcellus and the Last of the Classics* (New York, 2010), 82–83.
54 *L'Interprète du Français en Grèce, ou Méthode pour parler la langue grecque moderne...* par D'Orient de Bellegarde et J.-B. Delgay, sous la direction de Mgr Joannikos (Paris, 1829); *Exposition abrégée de la prononciation grecque et de l'orthographe*, par Théocharopoulos Georges, Paris, 1829; *Grammaire grecque universelle, ou Méthode pour étudier la langue grecque ancienne et moderne*, par Georges Théocharopoulos, de Patras. Première partie. Lexicologie, Paris, 1830. Theocharopoulos was the pseudonym of two Hellenists: Wladimir Brunet de Presle (1809–1875) and Félix-Désiré Dehèque (1794–1870).
55 Dimakis, *La Guerre*, 31.
56 Victor Tournachon was also the father of the photographer Felix Nadar. See Maria Morris Hambourg, "A Portrait of Nadar", *Nadar*, Metropolitan Museum of Art 1995, 3.
57 Felkay Nicole, "VII. Madame veuve Béchet (1801–1880)", *Balzac et ses éditeurs, 1822–1837. Essai sur la librairie romantique* (Paris: Éditions du Cercle de la Librairie, 1987), 161–178.
58 Diana Cooper Richet, "L'imprimé en langues étrangères à Paris au XIXe siècle", *Au siècle de Victor Hugo: la librairie romantique et industrielle en France et en Europe*, Issues 116–117, *Revue française d'histoire du livre*, ed. by Frédéric Barbier (Geneva, 2003), 203–235.
59 Edward Blaquiere, *Histoire de la révolution actuelle de la Grèce: Son origine, ses progrès, et détails sur la religion* (Paris, 1825); William Parry, *The Last Days of Lord Byron* (Paris, 1826).
60 Jeremy D. Popkin, "The Book Trades in Western Europe during the Revolutionary Era", *The Papers of the Bibliographical Society of America* 78, no. 4 (1984): 403–445; Corinne Pelta, "La Presse libérale sous la Restauration: Emergence d'une écriture collective", in *Presse & plumes: Journalisme et littérature au XIXe siècle, sous la direction de Marie-Ève Therenty et Alain Vaillant*, ed. Michel Arrous (Paris, 2004), 32–35.
61 Israel, *The Expanding Blaze*, 508.

6 Greece and the Liberal Revolutions of 1820–1823 in Southern Europe

John A. Davis

Greece and the *trieno liberal* 1820–1823

The links between the liberal revolutions in Spain, Portugal, and Italy from 1820–1823 and the Greek revolution were close but complex. In March 1820, a mutiny by Spanish soldiers in Seville forced king Fernando VII reluctantly to restore the constitution that had been conceded to the Cortes of Cadiz in 1812 during the war again Napoleon but withdrawn in 1814 at the time of the Bourbon Restoration. Similar events followed in Portugal and then in Naples, where the Spanish king's cousin, Ferdinand I, also agreed to adopt the Spanish constitution. Shortly afterward, Sicily joined the revolution, and the seizure of the fortress of Alexandria by a group of liberal army officers, led by Santorre Santarosa in March 1821, marked the start of a short-lived attempt at revolution in Piedmont.

The Austrian Chancellor Prince Metternich was well aware that the revolutions in Spain, Naples, Piedmont, and Portugal were the consequences of the absolutist policies that had been adopted by restored rulers, but, in the aftermath of the repressive Carlsbad Decrees imposed on the German states in 1819, there could be no accommodation with even moderate political demands. In response to requests from France and Russia, Metternich convened an international congress, which met first at Troppau (November–December 1820) and then Laybach (January 1821), where the representatives of the Powers authorized Austrian military intervention in Italy to suppress the revolutions.[1]

The decision had been taken before there was news of the Greek uprisings of February and March in the Peloponnese and in the Danubian provinces, although these helped remove any lingering doubts on the part of the Russian Tsar about armed intervention in southern Europe. By the end of March, Austrian intervention brought the revolutions in Naples, Sicily, and Piedmont to end, while in Portugal and Spain the constitutional governments faced growing internal division and unrest. On the pretext of restoring order two years later, France dispatched an army described by the French foreign minister and poet Chateaubriand as "100,000 sons of St Louis" to restore the absolutist Spanish ruler.[2]

Revolutions of 1820–1823 in Southern Europe 83

The survivors of the failed southern European revolutions faced a future of extended exile. Many Italians headed for Spain and Portugal at first, but after 1823 moved on to Switzerland and Paris, and then to London. By then the hopes of European liberals had come to rest on the outcome of Greek revolts against Ottoman rule, as evidenced by the thousand and more who volunteered to join the Greek insurrections between 1821–1823. They came from all over Europe – especially from Germany, Switzerland, and Poland, with smaller numbers from Italy, France, and Britain – to assemble in Marseilles, the only Mediterranean port from which ships were still permitted to sail to the eastern Mediterranean. Most were students, but among them, there were many professional soldiers from the cohort left unemployed after the Napoleonic wars, some of whom had previously served in the armies of the constitutional governments in Italy, Spain, and Portugal.[3]

Whatever their backgrounds or motives, the volunteers believed that the Greeks were engaged in essentially the same struggles and shared the same values as the European liberals. No one expressed those hopes more passionately than Lord Byron, whose conversion to the Greek cause between 1821 and 1824 reflected a political itinerary followed by many others. Ever since, scholars have tried to explain the strength of literary and political philhellenism in western Europe, although many recent studies have underlined the often deeply contradictory values embedded in western philhellenism. For their part, to maximize foreign support, many of the leaders of the Greek Revolution consciously tailored their own political programmes to accommodate European liberal principles.[4] However, much less attention has been paid to the ways in which expectations of the Greek Revolution played a central part in contemporary reflections on the deep flaws in the 'liberal international', revealed by the failures of the earlier liberal revolutions.

A 'liberal international'?

Unlike the Greek revolution, the revolutions in Spain, Portugal, Naples, Sicily, and Piedmont failed, but unlike other failed revolutions they did not provide inspiration to resume the struggle. One reason was that many of the surviving protagonists were profoundly disillusioned by their experiences and in their often voluminous memoirs written in exile (in Paris and London, in particular) they harped on the weaknesses and flaws which, from the start, bedeviled the revolutions and pursued fierce personal vendettas against their fellow revolutionaries. Even more important were the reactions of the next generation of revolutionaries, who had nothing but contempt for the *trienio liberal*. In Italy, the republican Giuseppe Mazzini was the most scathing critic and his new revolutionary society, *Young Italy,* founded in 1832, was explicitly premised on a rejection of everything that the earlier liberal revolutions had embodied. Mazzini hailed the revolution in Greece as

84   *John A. Davis*

an inspiration for nationalists everywhere, but he rejected the narrow, elitist aims of the leaders, and the cloak and dagger tradition of the secret societies that had been key elements of the revolutionary movement in Naples, Sicily, Piedmont, and Spain in the *trienio liberal*. He decried both the folly of attempting to make absolutist rulers constitutional monarchs, as well as the federalist leaning of the liberal revolutions. In place of the liberal appeal to local and what he deemed to be merely municipal patriotism, Mazzini aspired to mobilize the masses and to create a revolutionary movement that was to be open, national, and popular. The antithesis, in fact, of the earlier liberal revolutions, which were led by soldiers, relied on support from armies commanded by the rulers and looked to achieve independence at a local level only within the structure of the existing states.[5]

If the liberal revolutions of 1820–1821 in Italy were discredited by failure, this was the case in Spain and Portugal, too, which had subsequently fallen victim to civil wars and where reactionary Carlism continued to undermine the constitutional government.[6] Nor have the liberal revolutions found greater sympathy amongst more modern historians. Paul Schroeder, for example, in his study of European geopolitics in this period made an exception for Greece but wrote off the revolutions in Spain and Italy, commenting that they "made some unsatisfactory situations in Europe marginally worse". Greece was different only because the threat of a renewed war between Russia and the Ottoman Empire posed a greater challenge to the post-Congress of Vienna European order than the liberal revolutions.[7]

Prince Metternich was equally dismissive, as revealed by his incautious reactions to the news of the revolution in Naples in June 1820: "A people that is still half barbarous, ignorant, superstitious without limit, ardent and passionate like Africans, that knows neither how to read or write and whose final word is the stiletto, offers a fine example of the application of constitutional principles!"[8]

The Austrian Chancellor's arbitrary division of Europe into a civilized north and a barbarous south was widely shared by contemporaries, however, which contributed to the marginal significance attributed by historians to the *trienio liberal*. It is only more recently that the remarkable transnational dimensions of the *trienio liberal* have attracted the attention they deserve, and Maurizio Isabella was among the first to underline the case for the 'liberal international' that set the southern European revolutions of 1820–1823 on a geographical canvas spanning from South America to the Balkans and Russia.[9]

The trans-Atlantic connections were inseparable in the cases of the revolutions in Spain and Portugal. The mutiny in Seville in March 1820 began when troops destined to suppress the revolts in the Spanish colonies refused to embark, while the subsequent course of the Spanish and the Portuguese revolutions was shaped by events in Spanish America and Brazil. However, even where the colonial connection was absent, the liberal revolutions shared common demands: constitutional monarchy, an end to absolutism,

Revolutions of 1820–1823 in Southern Europe 85

and independence from foreign subordination. Despite Metternich's disdain, the defenders of the post-Napoleonic international order were quick to identify the international dimensions of the challenge. When an elite cavalry regiment mutinied in St Petersburg in December 1820, it was immediately linked to the international liberal conspiracy, as were the more explicit aims of the Decembrist conspiracy after the death of Tsar Alexander I in 1825. The leaders of the Greek Revolution also consciously identified their cause with the wider liberal international.

One of the clearest demonstrations of the shared political aims of the liberal international was the adoption of the 1812 Spanish constitution in Portugal (briefly), in Naples, and in Piedmont. Originating as a declaration of Spanish resistance to Napoleon, outside of Spain the Constitution of Cadiz was widely seen as a statement of national independence and representative government; yet, it differed from earlier French constitutions in important ways, not least because it was untainted by any hint of Jacobin Republicanism and popular or direct democracy. The sovereign, not the people, was the representative of the nation, subject to constitutional constraint, though, and, hence, to representative government.[10]

An additional attraction was the Constitution's emphasis on local rights and autonomies, the *fueros* that had played a critical role in Spanish history and embodied the complex balance between central and local power. Indeed, the Spanish equivalents of the Italian Carbonari called themselves *Comuneros*, but local autonomies were no less important in southern Italy than in Spain. Defence of regional autonomy had become an integral element in resistance to the centralization and bureaucratization of power realized in the French reforms imposed during the period of Napoleonic rule in Italy. Hence, in Italy, the Spanish constitution embodied both defence of local autonomies and resistance to foreign occupation that had a long history. In the eighteenth century, for example, many Neapolitan writers traced the origins of southern Italy's loss of independence back to the Roman conquest of the indigenous southern peoples and their civilizations. It was no accident that, during the course of the brief constitutional experiment in the Italian South, the pre-Roman names for the provinces were revived as an explicit refutation of a centralizing logic that extended from the Romans down to the French, which, after the Restoration, the Bourbon rulers had chosen to perpetuate.[11]

The 1812 Constitution was neither a clear nor a concise document, but that in many ways facilitated its adoption and adaptation. Its appeal was also closely linked to what Italian historian, Giorgio Spini, called "the myth of Spain", which had grown up around popular support for armed resistance to the French. Four Horsemen. Riding to Liberty in association strengthened the autonomist interpretation of the Constitution, without aligning it in any way with democratic principles, and provided liberals in southern Europe and in South America with a platform designed to rally all ranks of society around a representative monarchy, the church, and established religion in the common pursuit of independence and national solidarity.[12]

86   *John A. Davis*

Understood as a declaration of opposition to French occupation and for national independence, the Spanish constitution articulated themes that resonated strongly in Italy, where opposition to Napoleonic autocracy and imperialism had spread in the closing years of the empire, especially in the south. When Joachim Murat replaced Joseph Bonaparte as king of Naples in 1808, a National Parliament was promised but never convened. Meanwhile, in 1812 in Sicily, where the Bourbon rulers spent the decade of French occupation of the mainland under the protection of the British navy, the British had forced the monarchy to concede a constitution. This only increased demands for constitutional government on the mainland, which, despite pressure from his most loyal generals, Joachim Murat repeatedly refused. This had occurred in Spain when, in 1815, the Bourbon monarchy was restored in Naples and the Sicilian constitution of 1812 was abolished, giving new impetus to the demands for representative government.

In contrast to the later revolutions of 1848–1849, the liberal revolutions of 1820 in southern Europe had been planned. In southern Italy, clandestine meetings between local and regional leaders of the Carbonarist lodges resulted in unanimous agreement to adopt the Spanish constitution of 1812, and it was through the same societies that the Neapolitan leaders maintained contact with sympathizers in Barcelona and Turin. In southern Italy, the *Carbonari* were especially well represented in the army, and one of the early leaders of the Neapolitan rebellion, General Guglielmo Pepe, had previously organized provincial militias with their help to maintain order once the revolution started.[13]

However, the Spanish Constitution also provided the southern liberal revolutions of 1820–1823 with a set of targets that went well beyond the Vienna settlement and the expansion of Austrian power in Italy. Opposition to British and French commercial and naval ambitions in the Mediterranean did not end with the defeat of Napoleon's imperial project. As the invasion of Spain in 1823 indicated, France remained a significant player in Mediterranean politics and trade even before the invasion of Algeria in 1830, while Britain had emerged from the Napoleonic wars as the leading Mediterranean naval and commercial power, thanks to the acquisition of Malta and the Ionian Islands.[14] This was at the root of north-south liberal antagonisms that were exposed by the revolutions in southern Europe and were brought into sharper focus by the new circumstances of the Greek Revolution.

The Greek Revolution and the liberal international

After 1823, many of the surviving protagonists were unsparing in highlighting the contradictions the southern revolutions had exposed.[15] The most glaring lay in the failure of Spanish and Portuguese liberals to recognize, never mind accommodate, the liberal demands of those resisting

Spanish and Portuguese colonial rule in Spanish America and Brazil. The same errors were repeated in southern Italy, where the Neapolitan liberals refused to negotiate with Sicilian demands for autonomy and the fraternal principles of the liberal international had not been effectively put into practice. In Italy, the Piedmontese rebels did not coordinate their actions with the Neapolitans, who were themselves on the point of armed conflict with the Sicilians as the Austrian army approached in March 1821. Portugal offered no support to the liberal government in Spain, while both the British and French governments adhered strictly, if hypocritically, to neutrality, and both tacitly condoned Austrian intervention in 1821. In 1823, it was France that brought the Spanish revolution to a close and ensured the failure of a Portuguese revolution.

The Spanish Constitution had not offered solutions to the tensions between international and local aims. In Portugal, it had quickly been replaced by a similar but more specifically Lusitanian constitution, while in Italy the Sicilians invoked the earlier British constitution of 1812. The Greek leaders also chose to underline the national origins of the provisional constitution adopted at Epidaurus and were wary of the interventions of Jeremy Bentham and his cohort.[16]

Nonetheless, many southern European liberals saw in the Greek struggles for independence ways to overcome the obstacles that had condemned the revolutions of the *trienio liberal* to failure. Public support for the Greek cause in Britain and France contrasted with the lack of foreign support for the earlier liberal revolutions, a point underlined by Edward Blaquiere in his introduction to the account of the revolutions in Spain and Portugal by the Piedmontese exile, Count Pecchio.

Blaquiere was the model of a liberal internationalist who, after service in the British Navy in the Mediterranean during the Napoleonic Wars, had become a close follower of Jeremy Bentham and, in 1823 with Bentham and John Bowring, founded the London Greek Committee. His high expectations of the Greek cause were set out in his introduction to the *Anecdotes of the Spanish and Portuguese Revolutions,* published in 1823 by the Piedmontese exile, Giuseppe Pecchio. Another model liberal internationalist, Pecchio's exile after the failure of the Piedmontese revolution had taken him first to Portugal and Spain where he attempted to organize an international liberal militia, although the "Cosmopolitan Corps" in Catalonia attracted fewer than two hundred exiles from Piedmont.

Count Pecchio's account of the revolutions in Spain and Portugal was published in 1823 before the Iberian revolutions had collapsed, and provided Blaquiere with an opportunity to promote the Greek Revolution as the way forward for European liberals.

'It is now clearer than ever that the preservation of European freedom and the stability of British power depends on the stand which the Peninsula and Greece shall make against the Holy Alliance'.[17]

88   *John A. Davis*

Like Pecchio, Blaquiere was fully aware of the fractures in the liberal international, and he criticized their failure to acknowledge the demands of the Spanish South American colonies and Brazil to acquire the independence "that they cannot possibly prevent". Calling on the Portuguese and the Spanish to unite, he urged them to give full support to the cause of the "independence of Greece, Classic Greece, that country which has shown itself worthy of its own renowned ancestry and whose sons continue to perform prodigies unexcelled even in the Peninsula".

While the Greek Revolution confirmed Blaquiere's conviction that the "constitutional system" was the essential "premise for political regeneration", but his fiercest criticism was directed at the British government and more specifically the "party in the cabinet that is guilty of slavish acquiescence to the liberticide views of the despots".[18] The critical task for supporters of the liberal international was, therefore, to find ways of persuading the British government to apply progressive liberal policies to foreign policy.

The idea that the success of the liberal international depended on winning over British public opinion was strongly promoted by another Italian political exile in London, Guglielmo Pepe. One of the leaders of the 1820 Naples revolution, General Pepe had a proud history of military service and political activism. Pepe came from a Calabrian military family and was the youngest of 23 brothers. A 16-year-old officer cadet in Naples when the Republic was proclaimed in 1799, he immediately declared his support and was imprisoned, but escaped to Marseilles and later returned to Naples, where he rose to high military rank under Joachim Murat, king of Naples 1808–1815. He served with Murat's forces against the anti-French insurrections in Spain, where he established contact with many leading Spanish liberals and, upon returning to Naples, was one of the senior generals who unsuccessfully tried to persuade Joachim Murat to concede a constitution in 1814 and again in 1815. At the Bourbon Restoration, Pepe was furloughed but reinstated in 1818 and given military command of the two provinces where the 1820 revolution would start. Pepe played a direct part in the outbreak of the revolution but once the constitution was granted he became embroiled in bitter quarrels with his fellow officers and the successive Ministers of War, Michele Carrascosa (with whom he would later fight a duel in London) and Pietro Colletta. In February 1821, he attempted to halt the Austrian advance at Rieti but was defeated. He, too, made his way to London via Madrid and Lisbon.[19]

In exile, Guglielmo Pepe became a leading voice of the liberal international. An account of the revolution in Naples was published in London in 1822 and was quickly translated into French, Spanish, and German, but a more detailed account appeared in the London *Pamphleteer* in 1824.[20] The issue explicitly linked the southern European revolutions of the previous years with the Greek Revolution, and, along with Pepe's article, contained two essays on Byron, one by Sir Walter Scott, and an anonymous essay on "Considérations sur la guerre actuelle entre les Grecs et les Turcs".[21]

Pepe's title was "The Non-Establishment of Liberty in Spain, Naples, Portugal and Piedmont to which is added a comparison between the successful revolution of North America, the partly successful one in France and that which is now the object of Greece..." In the first part of the essay, like Blaquiere and Pecchio, he underlined the failure of the liberal leaders to cooperate and coordinate their actions, but he staunchly defended the internationalist and liberal objectives of the revolutions, whose failure he attributed not to any defects in the liberal project but to international circumstances.

These, he believed, were best revealed by comparison with the French and North American revolutions. The French Revolution of 1789 was, Pepe claimed, the only revolution to date "that really deserves that name because it was perfect and lacked only in the people that fund of sound political knowledge possessed by the Anglo-Americans for its preservation". In France, the ruling dynasty had been completely overthrown, the legislative and the executive branches had been separated to guarantee political and civil liberties, and the clergy had been "entirely annihilated", while the French people "were all placed in a situation to feel interested in the revolution". Last, but not least, the French revolutionaries had inherited a powerful army and navy with which to defend their revolution.[22]

Pepe's treatment of the North American revolution was more sketchy and he claimed that the "real proceedings of the American Revolution are little known". Nonetheless, he underlined in particular that the American colonists had been able to count on significant support for their cause in England and above all from Britain's enemies, Spain and France. Pepe then turned to the Greek revolution, whose consequences he, in 1824, believed "may perhaps hereafter prove not inferior to those produced by the revolution of the United States and that of France". Among the circumstances that set the Greek revolution apart, he listed the "Provisional Constitution", which demonstrated that the Greeks already had what Pepe termed "political knowledge", meaning that their leaders had accepted the principles of the liberal international. Second, he claimed that "no nation, except the Jews, ever had such cause to detest the yoke of a foreign nation as the Greeks of or time". No other contemporary European country could claim to have experienced comparably "barbarous oppression". Then he turned to religion, contrasting southern Europe, where religion had been the enemy of the revolutions, with the Greek case where religion was an "inspirational force for resistance". Another advantage was that the Greeks had no "aristocracy or great Despots" to overcome and were "well prepared for military activity" whereas the Turks were "torpid and disinclined to gymnastic exercises". Finally, the areas where the Geek revolution had its strongest support, "the Islands of the Archipelago, the Peloponnese, now called the Morea, and the countries comprehended between the Isthmus of Corinth and the Straits of Thermopylae" meant that the insurgents possessed a large merchant fleet.[23]

90   *John A. Davis*

Pepe's assessment of what made the Greek case exceptional in the context of the southern European revolutions of 1820–1823 reflected many of the tropes of western philhellenism, although, like Byron, his admiration was not only for the Ancient Greeks but also for the Greeks of his own time. Like most contemporary commentators, however, Pepe's references indicated only too clearly his lack of first-hand knowledge of the circumstances of the Greek insurrections or the situation in the Balkans under Ottoman rule, while his comments on the "inspirational" and a unifying force of religion in the struggles against the Turks did little more than echo contemporary stereotypes. Yet, to dismiss Pepe's reflections as factually misinformed would be to miss the point of his memoir, in which the selection of circumstances likely to make the Greek Revolution succeed served primarily to explain why the revolutions of the *trieno liberal* had failed but could still be saved.

Pepe drew attention first to the changed international situation resulting from the anticipated collapse of the Ottoman empire that would cause Russian expansionist ambitions to directly threaten Britain's position in the Mediterranean. When faced by the earlier liberal revolutions in Madrid, Lisbon, Naples, and Turin in 1820, Britain, like France, had supported the *status quo* but now self-interest must lead Britain to support the Greek cause.[24] That underlined the need to work on shaping public opinion, but Pepe was an insecure political exile in London and his criticism of the British government was necessarily guarded; however, it had deep roots and, even before the revolution of 1789 in France, many southern Italian writers had been denouncing British colonial and commercial ambitions to establish a Mediterranean "Thessalocracy".[25] Britain's subsequent interventions had served only to accentuate those fears. In 1799, Nelson's fleet had crushed the Neapolitan Republic and left its leaders to the vengeance of the restored Bourbon monarchy, while during the Napoleonic occupation of the mainland, British control of Sicily from 1806–1815 had aroused suspicions of Britain's underlying colonial ambitions.[26]

As in Portugal, opposition to foreign occupation in southern Italy was directed against both the French and the British and increased when, in 1815, the Bourbon government accepted discriminatory commercial treaties imposed by Britain and France.[27] Indeed, Pepe was in no doubt that in 1820–1823 Britain had "turned the scale against Italy and Spain", but he now believed that the Greek cause showed how the freedom of the press could be used to mobilize public opinion against the government's anti-liberal policies. Since it was clear that "even Greek Christianity is to be preferred to Mahometanism", he believed that the Greek cause should be represented as a conflict of Christians against Muslims and he called on "the friends of freedom in England" to mobilize public support for the Greek cause to drive "the degenerate Turks out of Europe and check the expansion of the Russian Colossus".[28]

The idea that Britain and Greece were Christian nations engaged in a common struggle to liberate the Mediterranean from Islam was shared by other members of the London Greek Committee, although it was treated with great suspicion by many fellow liberal internationalists.[29] Both Byron and Ugo Foscolo, for example, were wary of the religious element in western philhellenism and considered religion to be little more than a pretext for foreign invention, to which they were strongly opposed. Foscolo, for example, fully supported the Greek cause and had discussed at length the constitutional projects for the Ionian Islands that, following the Napoleonic wars, had become British Crown territories, but he believed that a national revolution must be carried out by the people and that foreign assistance or invention was invariably compromising.[30] Byron was even more wary and mindful of the growing influence on public opinion in Britain of the evangelical Protestant Clapham Sect and its influential parliamentary spokesman, William Wilberforce. The public campaign organized by the evangelicals in 1813 led parliament to force the East India Company to abandon its non-interventionist religious policies and permit Anglican missionaries to proselytize in the Company's jurisdictions and establish an Anglican bishopric in India (the 1813 Charter Act). The same proselytizing principles were present in the revival of the theme of the anti-Muslim crusades in the works of Tory populist authors, amongst them Byron's great rival, Robert Southey.[31]

Pepe's emphasis on the need to mobilize public support in Britain for the Greek cause pointed to a critical contrast with the earlier southern European revolutions, however. In 1820, the Queen Caroline affair had distracted attention in Britain from foreign events, but Pepe recognized that while there was sympathy for Portugal because of ancient alliances and for Spain for its resistance to Napoleon, there was less sympathy when it came to the Spanish, the Portuguese, or the Italians. Even a cursory survey of the memoirs on the Iberian and Italian revolutions by British liberals reveals the deep antipathies toward the "backwardness" of Catholic Mediterranean cultures and especially to Roman Catholicism.[32] As Marilyn Butler pointed out, the popular uprisings against the French in Spain were admired more by the followers of Burke than by liberals like Byron and Francis Jeffrey, who viewed the Spanish insurgents as "rightist, Catholic and ideologically uncongenial to them". In the first two Cantos of Childe Harold (October 1809–March 1810), written after his visits to Spain and Greece, Byron was already portraying the Greek cause as the alternative and, despite the fact that he was in Italy during the 1820–1821 revolutions, Byron's support, in the words of his most recent biographer, did not go beyond the poetic.[33]

Conclusion

Pepe's remained an ardent supporter of the Greek cause, but his speculations about the possible outcome of the Greek Revolution in 1824 offered a

92   John A. Davis

detailed and often pragmatic analysis of the flaws in the liberal international that had caused the southern European revolutions of 1820–1823 to fail. He blamed internal divisions, but above all the lack of international solidarity. The Greek cause illustrated how the international situation had changed in ways that aligned support for it with Britain's self-interests as a Mediterranean power. Nevertheless, Pepe acknowledged that awareness of the fact that Britain's self-interest lay in supporting the Greek cause would only happen once public opinion was mobilized. His interest in the critical role that evangelical sentiment might play in shaping public opinion was, in many ways, prescient but only served to underline the obstacles posed by British anti-Catholicism to a closer north-south liberal dialogue.[34] Catholic Portugal, Spain, and Italy did not attract the sympathies that a still embryonic British public opinion might extend to Christian Greeks. As well, sympathy for the Greek cause could not overcome the tensions in the international liberal project posed by British and French ambitions in the Mediterranean. Over the following decades, successive British governments refused to countenance demands for representative government in Malta and the Ionian Islands,[35] while the coming of the July Monarchy in France in 1830 was accompanied by the occupation of Algeria. In that context, for many southern European liberals, the Greek bid for independence was above all evidence of new and dynamic processes of independent commercial and political development, which promised to realize an alternative liberal Mediterranean world.[36]

Notes

1 See Paul W. Schroeder, *The Transformation of European Politics 1763–1848* (Oxford, 1994); Richard Stites, *The Four Horsemen. Riding to Liberty in Post-Napoleonic Europe* (Oxford, 2014).

2 For recent surveys of the extensive new writings on the southern European revolutions of 1820–3 (the *trienio liberal)* see the essays in Maurizio Isabella and Konstanina Zanou, eds., *Mediterranean Diasporas: Politics and Ideas in the Long Nineteenth Century* (London, 2016); James Miller, "Modernizing the Mediterranean; The Liberal Thread", *Contemporanea* 23, no. 1 (January–May 2020): 133–158.

3 William St Clair, *That Greece Still Might be Free: The Philhellenes in the War of independence* (London, 1972), 65–73; W. Bruyère-Ostells, *La Grande Armée de la liberté* (Paris, 2009); G. Pécout, "The international armed volunteers; pilgrims of a Transnational Risorgimento", in *Journal of Modern Italian Studies* 14/4 (2009): 413–426 For the most recent biography see Roderick Beaton, *Byron's War. Romantic Rebellion, Greek Revolution* (Cambridge, 2013); and Idem, *Greece. Biography of a Modern Nation* (London, 2019). On the political exiles see Maurizio Isabella, *Risorgimento in Exile. Italian émigrés and the liberal international in post-Napoleonic Europe* (Oxford, 2009); Grégoire Bron, "Learning Lessons from the Iberian Peninsula; Italian Exiles and the Making of a Risorgimento without People", in Isabella and Zanou, *Mediterranean Diasporas*, 59–76.

4 Miller (2020); Beaton, *Byron's War*; K.E. Fleming, *The Muslim Bonaparte: Diplomacy and Orientalism in Ali Pascha's Greece* (Princeton, 2008); Isabella, *Risorgimento in Exile*; Maria Todorova, *Imagining the Balkans* (Oxford, 1997).

Revolutions of 1820–1823 in Southern Europe 93

5 Franco Della Peruta, *I Democratici e la Rivoluzione italiana. Dibattiti ideali e contrasti politici all'indomani dell'1848*, (Milan, 1958); Nadia Urbinati, "Mazzini and the making of republican ideology", *Journal of Modern Italian Studies* 17/2 (2012): 183–204; Gilles Pécout, 'Philhellenism as political friendship; Italian volunteers in the 19th century', *Mediterranean Journal of Modern Italian Studies* (2004): 405-427.

6 For Spain, see Jordi Canal, *El Carlismo. Dos siglos de contrarevolución en Espagna*, (Madrid, 2000); Cortezo Lopez-Gordon, Maria Victoria et Jean-Philippe Luis (dir.), *La naissance de la politique moderne en Espagne* (milieu du XVIIIe-milieu du XIXe) (Mélanges de la Casa de Velazquez, 2005), Nouvelle série, Tome 35-1; Javier Fernandez-Sebastian and Conzalo Capellan, "Democracy in Spain; An Ever Expanding Ideal", in *Re-imagining Democracy in the Mediterranean 1780–1860*, ed. J. Innes, and M. Philp (Oxford, 2018), 53–76; On Portugal see Ramos, Rui "Democracy without People; the Rise of Democratic Liberalism in Portugal", in *Religion, Revolution and Popular Mobilization*, ed. J. Innes and M. Philp (Oxford, 2018), 77–98; Gabriele Paquette, "An Itinerant Liberal: Almeida Garret's Exilic Itineraries and Political Ideas in the Age of the Southern European Revolutions (1820–34)", in Isabella and Zanou, *Mediterranean Diasporas*, 43–58.

7 Schroeder, *The Transformation of European Politics 1763–1848*, 606–628.

8 John A. Davis, *Naples and Napoleon. Southern Italy and the European Revolutions (1780–1860)* (Oxford, 2006), 296.

9 Isabella, *Risorgimento in Exile*; but see also Miller (1990); the term was first used half a century ago by the Spanish historian José Luis Comellas Garcia-Llera (1963). On Greece, Paschalis Kitromilides, *Enlightenment and Revolution* (Cambridge, MA, 2013).

10 Andrea Romano, "L'influenza della carta gaditana nel costituzionalismo italiano ed europeo", in *La Costitución de Cadiz de 1812. Hacia los origines del costitucionalismo iberoamericano y latino*, ed. A. Aguiar (Caracas, 2004), 351–373; on Naples, see Davis (2006) and Werner Daum, "Significato e eredità del decennio francese (e inglese) (1806–1815)", *Il Regno di Napoli e il Regno di Sicilia in una prospettiva di storia costituzionale comparata* (Momenti della storia di Napoli e del Mezzogiorno d'Italia, 5) (Napoli, 2007).

11 John A. Davis, "The Spanish Constitution of 1812 and the Mediterranean Revolutions (1820–25)", *Bulletin for the Association of Spanish and Portuguese Historical Studies* 37/2 (2012), article 7.

12 Giorgio Spini, *Mito e realtà della Spagna nelle rivoluzioni italiane del 1820–1* (Rome, 1950).

13 Davis (2006), G. Gabrieli, *Massoneria e carboneria nel Regno di Napoli* (Rome 1982); G. Leti, *Carboneria e massoneria nel Risorgimento italiano* (Genova, 1925).

14 Robert Holland, *Blue-Water Empire. The British and the Mediterranean since 1800* (London, 2012); Maurizio Isabella, "Liberalism and Empires in the Mediterranean: The View Point of the Risorgimento", in *The Risorgimento Revisited. Nationalism and Culture in Nineteenth Century Italy*, ed. Silvana Patriarca and Lucy Riall (London, 2012), 232–254; Maurizio Isabella, "Mediterranean Liberals? Italian Revolutionaries and the Making of a Colonial Sea ca 1800–30" in Isabella and Zanou, *Mediterranean Diasporas*, 70–96.

15 See, for example, Bron in Isabella and Zanou, *Mediterranean Diasporas*.

16 See Paquette in Isabella and Zanou, *Mediterranean Diasporas*. On Bentham see F. Rosen, *Bentham, Byron and Greece: Constitutionalism, Nationalism and Early Liberal Political Thought* (Oxford, 1992) and Idem, 'Edward Blaquiere 1779–1832' (DNB).

94 *John A. Davis*

17 Giuseppe Pecchio, *Anecdotes of the Spanish and Portuguese Revolutions*, with an Introduction by Edward Blaquiere Esq (London, 1823), v; on Pecchio see Isabella, *Risorgimento in Exile.*
18 Ibid., xiv.
19 See Silvio de Majo, "Guglielmo Pepe", in *Dizionario Biografico degli Italiani*; see also John A. Davis, Introduction to Pietro Colletta, *History of the Kingdom of Naples*, Edinburgh, 1859 (facsimile edition) (London, 2009).
20 See Isabella, *Risorgimento in Exile*; Bron (2016).
21 *The Pamphleteer,* Vol xxiv (London, 1824).
22 Ibid., 258, 260.
23 Ibid., 268–270.
24 Shroeder, 610–614.
25 The term was used by G. M. Galanti, but Vincenzo Cuoco reflected similar hostility: see Davis 2006, Antonio De Francesco, *Rivoluzioni e costituzioni. Saggi sul democratismo politico nell'Italia napoleonica 1796–1821* (Napoli, 1996).
26 See, for example, Michele Amari in Amelia Crisantino, ed., Introduzione agli "Studi su la storia di Sicilia della metà del XVIII secolo al 1820" di Michele Amari (Quaderni Mediterranea: Richerche storiche 14, Palermo, 2010).
27 On Portugal see Paquette in Isabella and Zanou, *Mediterranean Diasporas.*
28 Guglielmo Pepe, "The Non–Establishment of Liberty in Spain, Naples, Portugal and Piedmont, to which is added comparison between the successful revolution of North America, the partly successful one in France and that which is now the object of Greece ..." in *The Pamphleteer*, Vol. XLVI (London, 1821): 221–275.
29 Rosen, *Bentham, Byron and Greece*; Beaton, *Byron's War.*
30 On Foscolo see; E Biagini, "Liberty, Class and Nation-Building. Ugo Foscolo's 'English' Constitutional Thought 1816–1827", *European Journal of Political Theory* 5, no. 1 (2006): 34–49; Isabella, *Risorgimento in Exile.*
31 Marilyn Butler, "The Orientalism of Byron's Giaur", in *Beyond the Limits of Fiction*, ed. F. Beatty and V. Newey (Liverpool, 1988), 78–92; see also Boyd Hilton, *The Age of Atonement: The Influence of Evangelicalism on Social and Economic Thought 1795–1865* (Oxford, 1988) and Boyd Hilton, *A Mad, Bad & Dangerous People? England 1783–1846* (New Oxford History of England, Oxford, 2006/2013).
32 See Grégoire Bron, "Learning Lessons from the Iberian Peninsula: Italian Exiles and the Making of a Risorgimento Without People, 1820-48", in Maurizio Isabella and Konstantina Zanou, *Mediterannean diasporas*, 59-76.
33 Butler, "The Orientalism of Byron's Giaur"; Beaton, *Byron's War*, 64–6.
34 Spini, *Mito e realtà della Spagna nelle rivoluzioni italiane del 1820–1*; Maurizio Isabella, "Religion, Revolution and Popular Mobilization" in Innes and Philp *Re–imagining Democracy in the Mediterranean 1780–1860*, (Oxford, 2018), 231–252.
35 Miles Taylor, "The 1848 Revolutions and the British Empire", *Past & Present* 166 (2000): 146–180; see also John A. Davis, "Britain and the Two Sicilies in Il 'decennio inglese' 1806–1815", in *Sicilia. Bilancio storiografico e prospettive di ricerca,* Michela D'Angelo, Rosario Lentini, Marcello Saija, eds (Palermo, 2020), 79–92.
36 Isabella *Risorgimento in Exile*; Maurizio Isabella and Konstanina Zanou, eds., *Mediterranean Diasporas: Politics and Ideas in the Long nineteenth Century*, (London, 2016); Pécout (2004); Dominique Kirchner Reill, *Nationalists who Feared the Nation. Adriatic Multi-Nationalism in Habsburg Dalmatia, Trieste and Venice* (Stanford, 2012); Kostantina Zanou, *Transnational Patriotism in the Mediterranean* (Oxford, 2018).

7 Greece and 1848: Direct responses and underlying connectivities

Christopher Clark and Christos Aliprantis

Introduction

Among the most interesting themes of recent writing about the revolutions of 1848 are the forms of connectedness, impact, response, contagion, transfer, and emulation that made the near-simultaneity of so many geographically dispersed revolutions possible in 1848. Claus Møller Jørgensen has reflected on the "trans-urban interconnectivities" along which political models circulated in mid-nineteenth-century Europe.[1] Kurt Weyland has posited cognitive "causal mechanisms" that powered the proliferation of revolutionary unrest across diverse political settings.[2] Attention has focused on the agents who carried the tidings of revolution from one location to another both nationally and transnationally – François-Xavier Martischang has examined the *commissaires*, who acted as envoys for the new administration in the localities. Others have studied those 'passeurs de la frontière' who crossed national boundaries: Delphine Diaz has written on the foreign fighters who served on the Parisian barricades, Anne-Claire Ignace on the international volunteers who turn up in virtually every major armed struggle of the mid-century revolutions, and Ignácio García de Paso has illuminated the transnational affiliations of the Spanish revolutionaries of 1848.[3] A literature that was once focused overwhelmingly on specific urban and territorial theatres is now enthralled by the trans-national connections between them.

Seemingly Greece does not fit into this scenario because it experienced no revolution in 1848. The few local revolts in 1847–1848 do not seem to offer an equivalent of the generalized European revolutions.[4] The socio-economic setting was rather different in Greece. The probe was not that there was no industrialization, but rather that the transformation of manufacturing in western Europe, with the emergence of supra-regional market networks and a deepening division of labour, had not taken place. 1840s Greece lacked anything resembling a cohesive proletariat, skilled or unskilled. There were no cities over twenty thousand – Athens was just approaching this threshold. There were no latifundia and thus no landless rural class, but rather a world of often struggling smallholders. And this was a world deeply fragmented by

96 *Christopher Clark and Christos Aliprantis*

clientelist networks whose focus was emphatically local, and whose localism was accentuated by the exigencies of geography.[5]

Moreover, this rather archaic social structure was coupled with a strikingly advanced political and constitutional order. The Constitution of 1844 recognized the King, not the people or the nation, as the source of authority, but it also guaranteed universal suffrage, without an electoral college.[6] This meant a chamber full of local notables elected by peasants: a state of affairs that tended sporadically to empower precisely the archaic and localist structures and mentalities of the countryside.[7] Whether or not we regard the 1844 constitution as success in practical terms, it did create a parliament, with parties affiliated to the respective great powers (Anglophiles, Francophiles, Russophiles) and it did give the elites a means of articulating their diverse interests vis-à-vis the monarchy.[8]

All this suggests that the Greek mid-century experience may have been sui generis. And Greek historians have, by and large, shown a fondness for arguments that stress the uniqueness of the Greek narrative. It would be a mistake, though, to leave the matter there. After all, every European landscape was unique, or at least special. Additionally, the profound structural difference between Sicily and Belgium, or Cadiz and Turin did not mean that there was no traffic in ideas or political practices between them.

More importantly, if we look more closely at Greece in the spring and summer of 1848, we *do* find a rich vein of press commentary on European events.[9] So, we are going to reflect upon the contours of those Greek reflections in 1848. However, in addition to reflecting on Greek responses, we also want to ask whether there is any evidence to suggest an underlying connectivity between western and central Europeans in and after 1848, on the one hand, and the developments in Greece on the other. We say *underlying* connectivities because, as Anna Ross has pointed out, it is in the nature of transnational transfers that they are often not avowed or acknowledged – especially at the political apex; statesmen and their advisers borrow or emulate foreign practice without acknowledging that this is what they are doing.[10] Statisticians and urban hygienists may have been proud of being lodged within transnational networks. Statesmen and ministers, generally speaking, were not, which means we sometimes have to proceed inferentially. Thus, we want to think about two different kinds of responses. First, commentary that is self-consciously part of the process of transnational communication and reflection, and second, processes of emulation or convergence that may suggest that Greece followed a path common to the post-revolutionary states, even if it did not experience a revolution per se.

The 1848 revolutions and Greece: Direct responses

In considering the relation between Central Europe and Greece in the age of revolutions, most scholars have focused their attention on the Greek war of independence and the movement of Philhellenism in the 1820s.[11] This bond appeared to be particularly strong in Germany, where most philhellenic fighters came from.[12] Nevertheless, the impact of the later revolutions of 1830 and 1848 in Greece has apparently troubled historians little, while the potential and underlying connectivities between the German (and Italian) national movements and Greece have been likewise neglected. In a way, the relation between Germany and Greece appears reversed in 1848 in comparison to the 1820s; the earlier German liberals sought political inspiration in an (imaginary) Greece and in the daring constitutions of the Greek rebels.[13] On the other hand, public commentators in 1848–1849 Greece looked to the revolting German and Italian states with admiration because they saw in the plans of German and Italian national unification a potential guide for the territorial expansion of the Hellenic kingdom and the realization of Greek irredentism.[14] In both cases, the multinational Habsburg and Ottoman Empires were presented as the common foe; as autocratic and anachronistic entities, who were bound to withdraw under the pressure of the advancing national movements. As with the militant Philhellenes a few decades earlier (albeit on a much smaller scale), a few Greeks did travel to Italy to join forces with the Piedmontese troops in their fight against Austria in 1848, and also with Garibaldi's Expedition of the Thousand in 1860.[15] These movements constituted parts of a much wider trend of international revolutionary volunteers based on the principles of democratic liberalism and transnational solidarity in favour of national movements.[16]

When it comes to the Greek press, even a cursory glance reveals mixed reactions to the February revolution in Paris and the subsequent movements in Vienna and Berlin in March. The most important organs for the reading Greek public in Athens were the liberal and pro-western dailies, Αθηνά (Athena) and Ελπίς (Hope), as well as the conservative and pro-Russian Αιών (Century).[17] Liberal Athenian circles welcomed the regime change in France, without neglecting to congratulate themselves on the fact that, as they saw it, France had at last obtained in 1848 the constitutional liberties that Greece had already achieved through the constitution of 1844.[18] On the other hand, the Greek middle classes were appalled by the June days in Paris, condemned «το απαίσιον δόγμα του κομμουναλισμού και του κοοπερατιβισμού» – the awful doctrine of communism and cooperativism – and welcomed Louis Napoleon's later rise to power.[19] Greek observers were quick to ascribe the lack of a revolutionary upheaval to the different social and political conditions of the country. In France, the intellectual and educator, Scarlatos Vyzantios (Σκαρλάτος Βυζάντιος), noted: "the nation, the poor suffer, it is a misfortune, it is miserable" yet, he went on to argue, "there is no comparison between our Greeks and them: the Greek is free in every respect, and his happiness depends on it, while the French is a slave, the property of capital, he works for the landlord, for the rich".[20]

98   *Christopher Clark and Christos Aliprantis*

Administrative convergence between western Europe and Greece: Statistics

If we expand our field of vision and examine Greek developments in the post-revolutionary era, do we find any evidence of a convergence that might hint at transfers explicit or hidden? In order to clarify the kind of claim we want to make, we need to pause for a moment and consider the larger European scene after 1848. Whether or not we think of the revolutions as a failure, it is clear that they ushered in a period of intensified innovation.[21] Indeed, there are good reasons for thinking of this period as the second high-water mark of administrative renewal after the Napoleonic era. Can Greece be accommodated in this panorama?

The beginnings of Greek state formation have been intensively examined by Greek historians, and yet, the 1840s and 1850s are less well understood. Here, we are referring to government not in the sense of a monarchical regime with a specific sequence of cabinets and ministers, but about the administrative practices established and elaborated in Greece during the middle decades of the nineteenth century. If we look at this part of the Greek state machinery, we can indeed locate some traces of convergence with the wider European post-revolutionary model.

We could start with the early development of the Greek statistical service. Here we should point out that this era witnessed across Europe a wave of intense innovation in the field of official statistics and in the status of statistical knowledge as a way of conceptualizing the field of political action, of "seeing like a state", to borrow James Scott's epithet.[22] In Spain, the old conservative *moderado* statisticians merged with their radical *progresista* counterparts to form a new Junta Central de la Estadistica in Madrid under the auspice of the Unión Liberal. A similar merger took place in Paris. In the German states, too, we see statisticians who had been proscribed as political dissidents in the 1840s being drawn into government or asked to found new statistical central offices.

The Bureau of Public Finance (BPF), the main Greek central state service occupied – among others – with the conduct of statistical surveys and the collection of data, was founded in 1834 as part of the interior ministry by Ioannis Kolettis, who was keen in following international developments.[23] The linkage between the early statistical science in western Europe and Greece is also evidenced by the fact that a number of exiled French saint-simonians, and most notably François d'Eichtal, who had sought refuge in Greece, were offered employment there.[24] As with other parts of the Mediterranean, in Greece too, saint-simonians found the opportunity to test their novel ideas of economic reorganization and, more specifically, proto-type agricultural colonies.[25] Despite its initially ambitious agenda, the Bureau was handicapped by its limited resources. This meant practically that colonization plans were soon given up and its officials focused instead on the gathering of statistical data on the population, agriculture, and industry.

In the following years, Spyridon Spiliotakis (Σπυρίδων Σπηλιωτάκης) was appointed head of the BPF, who, in his long tenure (1837–59, 1861–64), embodies the evolution of early state statistics in the Greek kingdom. His repetitive complaints to his superior interior ministry reveal the lack of material resources and the reluctance of the higher authorities to respond to his calls for a more energetic statistical policy in spite of the admirable working ethos of the Bureau's officials.[26] Such complaints, though, should not be regarded as typical of ostensible Greek underdevelopment in public administration, especially given its very recent beginnings. Even polities with far superior resources and state apparatuses, such as Prussia, the Habsburg Empire, or the smaller German states, experienced too continuous problems of bureaucratic inertia and decision-making passivity not only before but also after 1848, as well.[27] Comparisons between Greece and the lesser German states are sound given the Bavarian origins of the Greek public administration as well as the similarities in territorial and population size, unlike the much bigger Great Powers. Although the BPF had in principle main functions (compilation of data related to commerce, agriculture, population mobility, etc.), its primary one was to observe the change in population size, which also brought its officials in touch with the vast majority of the population.[28]

Until 1850, the Greek Bureau of Public Finance used local policemen and priests to go door to door and compile data on each household. The local municipal police forces were thus mostly entrusted with the gathering of evidence related to the population, its size, and whereabouts.[29] The earlier statistics in the 1830s and 1840s were conducted in a rather simplistic manner; that is, by simply adding and deleting births and deaths to and from the existing population without taking into consideration other important factors, for example, migration. The process seems to have been fairly decentralized: local authorities gathered the data, while the central bureau merely incorporated them into a table. From around 1850, however, changes began to emerge. The statistical survey of March 1861 is considered a landmark in this case because Greek statistics acquired from then on a "scientific" character. This meant that the main aim was not a mere population count, but also to highlight the people's professions, gender, age, citizenship status, confession, ethnicity, and marital status.[30] Another major difference in comparison to earlier censuses was that its results were published in a special, detailed edition the following year and were thus rendered available to the public, instead of the previous concise notes published in the Government Gazette (Εφημερίδα της Κυβερνήσεως). Novelties were also noted as regards the census' methodology; instead of the past practice, which involved the local police and clergy, after 1861, a municipal committee was formed in each district to carry out this duty, while in Athens, the populace was given questionnaires about the aforementioned categories.

These new techniques constituted loans from equivalent French, British, and Belgian census practices. A similar process was repeated once again in the next census of 1870.

Not only the Bureau of Public Finance but also other state services began to publish statistical data towards the end of the 1850s, thus increasing the sense of a new era in Greek statistics. Tables on Greek commerce in 1851–53, a comprehensive report on secondary education in 1828–55, and a survey on political justice for 1857–58, all published by the respective ministries, indicate that the Bureau was not alone in a process of making the Greek public administration more open to the public.[31] To these state-sponsored publications, one should also add various private initiatives to gather and publish local statistical materials, which witnesses the gradual familiarization of the Greek public to the science of statistics.[32]

These novelties were not owed to an increase of the kingdom's broader administrative efficiency or resources, which remained largely unchanged in the period under consideration. What began to change instead was the wider international environment and scientific advances. Anxious about being left behind, Greek statisticians got keenly in touch with international developments wishing not only to improve their technical skills and methods but also to convincingly project Greece's material progress abroad. Since the early 1850s, two new international institutions influenced the development of Greek statistics: the international exhibitions and the international statistical congresses. Both became fora where countries came to compete against each other wishing to demonstrate greater material achievements.[33] Thus, they usually functioned as mechanisms of self-assurance for the largest industrial powers, such as Great Britain and France, since the first exhibitions took place in London in 1851 and in Paris in 1855. Smaller countries, though, found themselves bound to demonstrate their competence too amidst rising international antagonism and constant comparisons. Greece was of course not excluded, especially given that the young kingdom was expected to show certain achievements two decades after obtaining independence. The Greek government formed a special committee to oversee Greece's representation at the 1851 exhibition in London, where, quite expectedly, also Spiliotakis participated as its secretary.[34] Four years later, he was also dispatched in the international exhibition of Paris as Greece's special emissary, while he also carried out the duty of representing the country in the second world statistical congress, which was also taking place then.[35] En route to his mission, Spiliotakis carried along his survey containing the Greek statistical data he had gathered so far, "Renseignements Statistiques sur la Grece". This account aimed at strengthening Greece's position in the exhibition and also serving as the official contribution to the statistical congress.

Greece kept participating in the subsequent international exhibitions and congresses mainly through the personnel of the Bureau of Public Finance, which formed a bridge between the Greek public administration and scientific developments abroad. Spiliotakis represented Greece in the 1867 exhibition in Paris, while his successor as head of the Bureau, Alexandros Mansolas, acted likewise in the 1873 and 1878 exhibitions as well as in the 1869, 1872, and 1876 statistical congresses.[36] Spiliotakis presented the results of the 1861 and of the later censuses in the 1867 exhibition so that he could ensure the widest possible visibility of the Bureau's findings. It remains important to note that the official state statistical publications of the kingdom appeared often in a bilingual form (Greek and French) in order to be accessible to an international audience and encourage transnational comparisons. Greece took early steps toward an at least theoretical convergence with the new statistical normativity in western Europe, being the first among the Balkan states to do so.[37] This "dialogue" with international realities took other forms as well and was most notably reflected on the exchanges of official statistical bulletins between Greece and other countries such as France and Belgium.[38] Greece followed suit without too great a delay in the broader practice of formal exchanges in western Europe, which had evolved after the Napoleonic wars and was accelerated after the 1830s.[39]

Administrative convergence between western Europe and Greece: Human mobility and border controls

A pattern of perhaps slow and yet evident convergence of Greece with western and central European scientific and administrative practices can be traced in other fields, too. Administration of borders and human mobility, and control of migration is such a field of paramount significance given the importance of territoriality in modern state formation. During the revolutionary and Kapodistrian periods, the nascent Greek state had attempted to enforce mobility controls across the (fluctuating) borders and regulate arms usage.[40] Yet, these efforts were unsuccessful due to the extremely limited resources of the Greek authorities and the widespread lawlessness throughout the Greek territories. When the German archeologist, Ludwig Ross, arrived in Greece in 1832, he remarked with some surprise that nobody asked him for any identification. Ross compared negatively these circumstances of apparent disarray to the Bavarian and Austrian scrutinized passport and border controls that he went through when he was en route to Greece.[41] King Othon's government and new bureaucracy were aware of such unfavourable comparisons and put serious effort into controlling mobility across the borders and identifying the population at least in the major urban centers. The outcomes of this ambitious agenda could not be visible immediately and, as with statistics, it took until the late 1840s and the 1850s, when changes in the institutional framework and the language of the administration regarding mobility became evident.

In light of the increased rates of people's mobility across Europe, including Greece from the 1840s and 1850s onward, the Greek authorities sought to take appropriate measures. The interior ministry and the Athens police were reminded that all newcomers in the capital had to carry valid passports and report to the police headquarters following their arrival.[42] Given its nature as a maritime kingdom, the regulation was extended to the harbours as well, where the port police officials had to compile lists of the ship passengers arriving and departing from their vicinity and forward these materials to the interior ministry.[43] Ministerial degrees related to the mobility of vagabonds, paupers, and beggars were even more frequent and kept forbidding their settlement in Athens, regardless of them having passports.[44] The ministry had those considered dangerous for public order kept under police surveillance, although the effectiveness of this measure can be doubted.[45] In fact, the recurrent appearance of similar strict regulations only attests to the incapacity of the police to adequately deal with the problem of a growing destitute population immigrating to the capital city in search of better prospects. Likewise, the interior ministry and police authorities met with limited success when they tied to compile lists of the arriving and departing individuals in the kingdom's major cities in the late 1850s as these wandering masses hardly obeyed police and domestic passport regulations.[46]

Athens and – to a lesser degree – Patras began experiencing waves of domestic migration and problems of urban overcrowding after the 1840s, which triggered the aforementioned state responses.[47] Paupers (φαυλόβιοι) were portrayed in the interior ministry and police circulars as a "wound" to the social body, which had to be imminently isolated and put under control before "infecting" the rest of the population or causing upheavals.[48] The use of medical vocabulary to depict social problems was common in the bureaucratic jargon of many European states at that time. What remains important concerning state bureaucracies, both in Greece and elsewhere, is the usage of such symbolic language as an at-times substitute of physical force employed to legitimize policies of social exclusion and surveillance.[49]

Finally, while the formation of this state apparatus has been strongly associated with the Bavarian and more broadly western European expertise imported in Greece in the 1830s, the above evidence indicates that state-building followed an autonomous course even after foreign advisers left the country after 1843. Greek administrators manned these recently built institutions and developed in due course a respective professional ethos. Quite telling for the relative autonomy of this young bureaucracy is the fact that the interior ministry kept issuing such passport ordinances without an apparent break after Othon's dethronement and well into George I's reign.[50] After three decades of relatively uninterrupted function, the state apparatus had become self-reliant enough to resist the instability born out of regime change in 1862–63, which was not the case with the much weaker revolutionary and Kapodistrian administrations that had fainted easily.

None of these societal phenomena and respective state responses constituted a Greek exceptionalism. There was also a great deal of continuity in administration in western and central Europe, despite regime changes and revolutions during the same period.[51] The metropolitan police authorities of major European capitals such as London, Berlin, or Vienna were charged with compiling lists of people's arrivals and departures in order to oversee population changes at least since the Napoleonic years and with a growing intensity after the 1840s.[52] Surely, this expanded state vigilance is largely owed to domestic migration because these cities were becoming prominent centers of national industry and commerce, which applies to the overlapping categories of both working labour and vagabonds. These developments affected sea communications, too, and the port police authorities in coastal urban centres, such as Marseille, were similarly instructed to watch over sailors, craftsmen, tradesmen, and, in general, newcomers since the 1830s.[53] As the Social Question became more intense throughout Europe, these growing city populations fed fears of social unrest in either London, Paris, or Berlin, which became evident in 1848.[54]

Certain similarities and analogies between administrative practices in Greece and elsewhere in Europe can be noted in the ways borderlands were run vis-à-vis neighboring polities. In this case, despite nationalist narratives that have focused on supposed Greek-Ottoman tensions across the Thessalian frontier, it seems that between the 1840s and the 1860s a de facto stability had been achieved.[55] Local semi-state and state actors from both sides of the border had helped establish this fragile balance, seeking to prevent large-scale interruptions of their everyday realities with potentially unpredictable and devastating consequences. This regional stability had legal and police parameters and entailed regular and joint border policing by mixed Greek-Ottoman patrol units as well as extraditions of fugitive outlaws. Yet, these circumstances were not born out of an experience-driven local understanding, rather from an institutional framework agreed between the Greek and Ottoman central governments. Notwithstanding these ad hoc beginnings, a bilateral treaty on border security was signed in 1856 under British and French pressure, which formalized several among the aforementioned unofficial border police measures.[56] This development thus strengthened a tendency towards the bureaucratization of border security institutions and practices between Greece and the Ottoman Empire.

Elsewhere, for instance, in central Europe, similar measures were implemented at the same time. Again, regional circumstances could defy standard nationalist narratives. Between the 1830s and the 1870s, the Prussian and Austrian governments became engaged in information exchange regarding police and criminal affairs across their borders, exchanging bulletins of wanted fugitives and agreeing to their mutual extraditions.[57] Based on an 1864 bilateral border security convention, mixed police groups were appointed to patrol the borders, and gendarmerie units were allowed passage across alien territory to pursue fleeing criminals, a practice that continued after the 1866 war.[58] Even if local cooperation was, in this case, a product of central administrative decisions, both the Austro-Prussian and the Greek-Ottoman cases reveal that seemingly unlikely collaborations between otherwise sworn rivals could be possible when local circumstances dictated so and

104 *Christopher Clark and Christos Aliprantis*

with specific aims. It seems that all parties regarded perpetual instability and even conflict across their borders as highly detrimental, and they preferred ad hoc, discreet understandings of regional security and mobility controls, thus avoiding unforeseen difficulties and perhaps economizing their resources for more focused and decisive confrontations such as the Austro-Prussian (1866) and the Greek-Ottoman (1897) wars.

Conclusion

One might be thinking at this point: what does this have to do with the transnational impact of 1848? Our answer is that one of the consequences of the upheavals of 1848 across Europe was a technocratic turn in governance that affected many areas of administrative activity. This technocratic turn was post-revolutionary in two senses: first, it involved in many cases the integration into government of civil-society based forms of expertise that had previously occupied a politically marginal position. It was the revolution, for example, that opened the door into government for statisticians of radical or saint-simonian views.

In Greece, the mechanism was different. It was not the revolution as such that produced the turn to technocracy, but the state as the paternalistic carrier of processes of policy transfer; this was not a case of the direct 'impact' of a European revolution on Greece – in general, the metaphor of impact is problematic – but rather of parallel processes of state-to-state transfer that allowed Greece to experience a post-revolutionary administration without having experienced a revolution, or, at least, not a revolution of the European type.

Finally, two concluding remarks are in order. First, any conclusions we might want to draw from these observations are emphatically provisional, since the 1850s remain in Greece, to an even greater degree than across the rest of Europe, the least well researched decade of the 19th century – a great deal of further work is required before we can trace with any confidence the outlines of a history of Greek administration and state-building in this era. Second, it should be pointed out that reframing the 1850s in this way means pulling the focus away from diplomacy, geopolitics, and the dreamscape of the *Megali Idea*, narratives which have been crushingly dominant in historical awareness of this era in Greek history. It means thinking of Greece as a state among states, peculiar and unique in many respects, like all its European fellows, but also caught within patterns of emulation and convergence whose horizons were emphatically European.

Notes

1 C. Møller Jørgensen, "Transurban Interconnectivities: An Essay on the Interpretation of the Revolutions of 1848", *European Review of History* 19/2 (2012): 201–27.

Direct responses and underlying connectivities 105

2 K. Weyland, *Making Waves. Democratic Contention in Europe and Latin America since the Revolutions of 1848* (Cambridge, 2014), 99–123.

3 F.-X. Martischang, "Administrer autrement? Les commissaires du Gouvernement provisoire en 1848"; D. Diaz, "J'ai fait mon service comme un brave citoyen français. Parcours et récits de combattants étrangers sur les barricades parisiennes en février et juin 1848"; A.-C. Ignace, "Le volontaire international, acteur du printemps des peoples"; I. García de Paso, "Borderless Revolution: The Transnational Network of Spanish Revolutionaries in 1848", *Les acteurs européens du "printemps des peuples" 1848.* Colloque international du cent soixante-dixième anniversaire, Sorbonne Université, Paris, 31.05.2018–02.06.2018.

4 M. Sakellariou, "Hellenism and 1848", *The Opening of an Era, 1848: An Historical Symposium*, ed. F. Fejtö (London, 1948), 377–393.

5 K. Kostis, *History's Spoiled Children. The Formation of the Modern Greek State* (Athens, 2013); C. Chatziiosif, *Η γηραιά σελήνη. Η βιομηχανία στην ελληνική οικονομία, 1830–1940* [The old moon. Industry in Greek economy, 1830–1940] (Athens, 1993).

6 J. A. Petropulos, *Politics and Statecraft in the Kingdom of Greece, 1833–1843* (Princeton, 1968); N. Alivizatos, *Το σύνταγμα και οι εχθροί του στη νεοελληνική ιστορία, 1800–2010* [The constitution and its enemies in modern Greek history, 1800–2010] (Athens, 2011), 71–107.

7 C. Lyritzis, *Το τέλος των 'τζακιών'. Κοινωνία και πολιτική στην Αχαΐα του 19ου αιώνα* [The end of powerful families. Society and politics in nineteenth-century Achaia] (Athens, 1991).

8 Petropulos, *Politics*, 455–500; G. Hering, *Τα πολιτικά κόμματα στην Ελλάδα, 1821-1936* [Political parties in Greece, 1821–1936], 2 vols. (Athens, 2004), I, part iii.

9 L. Louvi, *Η Ευρώπη των Ελλήνων. Πρότυπο, απειλή, προστάτις, 1833–1857* [Europe of the Greeks. Model, threat, protector, 1833–1857] (Athens, 2020).

10 A. Ross, "Down with the Walls! The Politics of Place in Spanish and German Urban Extension Planning, 1848–1914", *Journal of Modern History* 90 (2018), 292–322.

11 There is a huge literature on Philhellenism. Suggestively: W. St Clair, *That Greece Might Still Be Free: The Philhellenes in the War of Independence* (Cambridge, 2008 [1972]); L. Droulia, *Philhellénisme: Ouvrages inspirés par la guerre de l' indépendance grecque 1821–1833. répertoire bibliographique* (Athens, 1974); N. Klein, *L' humanité, le christianisme, et la liberté: Die internationale philhellenische Vereinsbewegung der 1820er Jahre* (Mainz, 2000).

12 R. Quack-Eustathiades, *Der deutsche Philhellenismus während des griechischen Freiheitskampfes, 1821–1827* (Munich, 1984).

13 J. Irmscher, "Der Deutsche Philhellenismus als politisches Anliegen", *Byzantion* 36/1 (1966): 74–96; C. Hauser, *Anfänge bürgerlicher Organisation: Philhellenismus und Frühliberalismus in Südwestdeutschland* (Göttingen, 1990).

14 A. Noto, "Le 'nazioni sorelle': Affinità, dirersità e influenze reciproche nel Risorgimento di Italia e Grecia", *Il Risorgimento Italiano e i movimenti nazionali in Europa*, ed. G. Altarozzi and C. Sigmirean (Rome, 2013), 43–68.

15 A. Liakos, *L' unificazione italiana e la grande idea. Ideologia e azione dei movimenti nazionali in Italia e in Grecia, 1859–1871* (Florence, 1995), 87–129.

16 G. Pécout, "Une amitié politique méditerranéenne: le philhellénisme italien et français au XIXe siècle", *La democrazia radicale nell'Ottocento europeo*, ed. M. Ridolfi (Milan, 2005), 81–106.

17 D. Stamatopoulos, "War and Revolution: A Balkan Perspective. An Introduction", *European Revolutions and the Ottoman Balkans. Nationalism, Violence and Empire in the Long Nineteenth-Century*, idem (ed.) (London, 2020), 1–18.

18 *Εθνική*, 14 October 1848.

106 *Christopher Clark and Christos Aliprantis*

19 *Αιών*, 10 November 1848.
20 Quoted in: K. Lappas, *Πανεπιστήμιο και φοιτητές στην Ελλάδα κατά το 19°αιώνα* [University and students in Greece during the nineteenth century] (Athens, 2004), 494n113.
21 C. Clark, "After 1848: The European Revolution in Government", *Transactions of the Royal Historical Society* 22 (December 2012): 171–197.
22 J. Scott, *Seeing Like a State: How Certain Schemes to Improve the Human Condition Have Failed* (New Haven, 1998).
23 ΦΕΚ Α 18/1834: *Εφημερίς της Κυβερνήσεως*, 22 Μαΐου/3 Ιουνίου 1834: "Διάταγμα περί συστάσεως Γραφείου της Δημοσίας Οικονομίας παρά τη επί των Εσωτερικών Γραμματεία της Επικράτειας"; more broadly G. Bafounis, *Στατιστική και πλάνη είναι λέξεις συνώνυμοι... Η ελληνική στατιστική του 19ο αιώνα* [Statistics and error are synonyms ... Greek statisitcs in the nineteenth century] (Athens, 2006), 28–36.
24 D. Vikelas, "Ο Γουσταύος Έιχταλ εν Ελλάδι" [Gustave Eichtal in Greece], *Διαλέξεις και αναμνήσεις* (Athens, 1893), 257–331; C. Aliprantis, "Lives in exile: foreign political refugees in early independent Greece (1830–53)", *Byzantine and Modern Greek Studies* 43/2 (2019): 243–461, especially 248–249.
25 O. Abi-Mershed, *Apostles of Modernity. Saint-Simonians and the Civilizing Mission in Algeria* (Stanford 2010); P. Pilbeam, *Saint-Simonians in Nineteenth-Century France: From Free Love to Algeria* (London, 2014).
26 Bafounis, *Ελληνική στατιστική*, 119–130.
27 A. Green, *Fatherlands. State-Building and Nationhood in Nineteenth-Century Germany* (Cambridge, 2001); W. Heindl, *Josephinische Mandarine: Bürokratie und Beamte in Österreich, II: 1848–1914* (Vienna, 2013).
28 Bafounis, *Ελληνική στατιστική*, 77–83.
29 S. Spiliotakis, *Στατιστικαί πληροφορίαι περί Ελλάδος* [Statistical information about Greece] (Athens, 1859), 5.
30 All details about the 1861 census can be found at G. Bafounis, ed., *Στατιστική της Ελλάδος. Πληθυσμός του έτους* 1861 [Statistics of Greece. Population of the year 1861] (Athens, 1991).
31 Bafounis, *Ελληνική στατιστική*, 110; M. Chouliarakis, *Στατιστική βιβλιογραφία περί Ελλάδος, 1821–1971* [Statistical bibliography on Greece] (Athens, 1971).
32 For example, I. Dekigallas, *Γενική στατιστική της νήσου Θήρας* [General statistics of the island of Thera] (Hermoupolis, 1850); G. Angelopoulos, *Στατιστική Πειραιώς* (Athens, 1852). Furthermore, several occasionally published statistics on various topics.
33 P. Greenhalgh, *Ephemeral Vistas: The Expositions Universelles, Great Exhibitions and World's Fairs, 1851–1939* (Manchester, 1988); N. Randeraad, "The International Statistical Congress (1853–1876): Knowledge Transfers and their Limits", *European History Quarterly* 41/1 (2011): 50–65.
34 There are uncatalogued files referring to the Greek participation in the 1851 exhibition in the archive of the interior ministry: ΓΑΚ, Βιομηχανία, files: 1851/1, 1852/2, 1873/2, 1877/1.
35 Spiliotakis was also assisted in his mission by the Greek general consuls in London and in Marseille: Bafounis, *Ελληνική στατιστική*, 112–113.
36 A. Mansolas, *Δύο άρθρα δημοσιευθέντα εις την Εφημερίδα των Συζητήσεων και την Αλήθειαν καθ' όσων εγράφησαν εν τη Κλειοί κατά του εν τη Παγκοσμίω Εκθέσει της Βιέννης τμήματος της Ελλάδος* [Two articles published in *Ephimeris ton Sizitiseon* and *Alitheia* in response to what was written in *Cleio* about Greece's section in the Vienna World Exhibition] (Athens, 1873); Th. Retsinas, *Το ελληνικόν τμήμα εν τη εκθέσει των Παρισίων του* 1878 [The Greek section in the Paris exhibition of 1878] (Piraeus, 1879).

Direct responses and underlying connectivities 107

37 G. Lonergan, "Counting citizens: The transfer and translation of census categories from the international statistical congresses to the principality of Bulgaria (1872–1888)", *Nationalities Papers*, 46/4 (July 2018), 556–574.

38 ΓΑΚ, Υπουργείο Εσωτερικών, Στατιστικά, files: 1860/1 and Εφημερίδες-Περιοδικά, file: 1880/1.

39 Official exchanges entailed a variety of fields. The Prussian and Austrian states for instance were engaged in a process of exchanging documents related to police affairs with most other European states increasingly since the 1840s: for example, Geheimes Staatsarchiv Preußischer Kulturbesitz (GStA PK), I. HA Rep. 77, Tit. 609 Nr.1: Polizei-verwaltung in einzelnen fremden Staaten; Österreichisches Staatsarchiv, Haus, Hof- und Staatsarchiv (HHStA), Administrative Registratur, Fach (F) 51: Statistik, Krt.1, Fach 52: Sicherheitswesen, Polizei und Schub, Krt.4.

40 N. Diamandouros, *Οι απαρχές της συγκρότησης σύγχρονου κράτους στην Ελλάδα 1821–1828* [The origins of modern state-building in Greece 1821–1828], transl. K. Kouremenos (Athens, 2002), 210–220; B. Gounaris, "Blood Brothers in Despair: Greek Brigands, Albanian Rebels and the Greek-Ottoman Frontier, 1829-1831", *Cahiers balkaniques* 45 (2018), 1-20.

41 L. Ross, *Erinnerungen und Mittheilungen aus Griechenland*, Berlin, 1863, p. 13.

42 For example, Αρχείο της Ιστορικής και Εθνολογικής Εταιρείας της Ελλάδας (ΑΙΕΕ), Interior ministry to state prefects, No.147, 16 October 1854; Athens police to police authorities, 24 January 1857. The Interior ministry began issuing passports on March 1835 and thereafter issued repeatedly instructions asking authorities to conduct frequent passport controls, an indication that violations were common.

43 ΑΙΕΕ, Interior ministry to the police authorities, No. 20.160, 3 October 1849; No.3,278, 16 August 1852.

44 ΑΙΕΕ, Athens and Piraeus police to state prefects, No. 3,882, 20 December 1849; Athens and Piraeus police to police authorities, No. 2,919, 19 February 1852; Athens and Piraeus police to state prefects, No. 2, 866, 24 April 1855; Athens and Piraeus police to police authorities, No. 10,776, 9 December 1855.

45 ΑΙΕΕ, Interior ministry to state prefects, No. 143/21,837, 4 October 1854.

46 ΑΙΕΕ, Athens and Piraeus police to police authorities, No. 25, 6 January 1858.

47 On the demographics of both cities: G. Paraskevopoulos, *Οι Δήμαρχοι των Αθηνών*, 1835–1907 [Mayors of Athens, 1835–1907] (Athens, 1907), 173–189; N. Bakounakis, *Πάτρα. Μια ελληνική πρωτεύουσα στο 19°αιώνα, 1828–1860*, [Patras. A Greek capital city in the nineteenth century] (Athens, 1988), 47–59.

48 See, for instance, ΑΙΕΕ, Athens police to police authorities, No. 2,919, 19 February 1852.

49 See the Prussian example: A. Lüdtke, *'Gemeinwohl', Polizei und 'Festungspraxis'. Innere Verwaltung und staatliche Gewaltsamkeit in Preußen, 1815–1850* (Göttingen, 1982).

50 ΑΙΕΕ, Athens and Piraeus police to state prefects, No. 77, 22 October 1862; No. 4, 3 January 1864.

51 A. Fahrmeir, *Citizens and Aliens: Foreigners and the Law in Britain and the German States, 1789–1870* (New York and Oxford, 2000); Q. Deluermoz, *Policiers dans la ville: La construction d' un ordre public à Paris 1854–1914* (Paris, 2012).

52 See, for instance, the London and Berlin cases: S. Palmer, *Police and protest in England and Ireland, 1780–1850* (Cambridge, 1988), 450–500; A. Funk, *Polizei und Rechtsstaat: Entstehungsgeschichte der preußischen Polizei 1848–1914* (Frankfurt, 1986); GStA PK I HA Rep.89 Geh. Zivilkabinett jüngere Periode Nr.14947. Das Polizeipräsidium zu Berlin 1844–1854, Bd. 1, where date on migration to and from Berlin in the 1840s. The Düsseldorfcase is also indicative of

108 *Christopher Clark and Christos Aliprantis*

how the provincial city authorities dealt with these challenges: E. Spencer, *Police and the Social Order in German Cities. The Düsseldorf District 1848–1914* (DeKalb, IL, 1992).

53 É. Temime, "Immigration et police portuaire à la fin du XIXe siècle. Le cas de Marseille", *Police et migrants. France, 1667–1939*, ed. Blanc Chaléard (Rennes, 2001), 251–262.

54 W. Langer, "The Patterns of Urban Revolution in 1848", *French Society and Culture since the Old Regime*, eds E. Acomb and M. Brown (New York, 1966), 90–118.

55 The analysis on the Thessalian frontier is based on G. Gavrilis, *The Dynamics of Interstate Boundaries* (Cambridge, 2008), 37–65 and idem, "The Greek-Ottoman Boundary as Institution, Locality, and Process, 1832–1882", *American Behavioral Scientist*, 51/10 (June 2008), 1516–1537.

56 D. Özkan, "The Final Phase of the Greek Revolution: Delimitation, Determination and Demarcation of the First Greek Borders in Ottoman Sources", in *European Revolutions and the Ottoman Balkans*, ed. D. Stamatopoulos, 111–138, especially 126.

57 GStA PK, III. HA, MdA, III, Nr.9543. Übereinkommen mit Österreich über gegenseitige Mitteilung einer gerichtlichen Übersicht der schweren Polizeivergehen und Kriminaluntersuchungen. Gegenseitige Mitteilung der Gerichts- und Verwaltungs-Behörden.

58 ÖS, HHStA, Administrative Registratur, F52, Krt.3. The text of the Austro-Prussian convention can be found in *Reichs-Gesetz-Blatt für das Kaiserthum Oesterreich. Jahrgang 1864* (Vienna, 1864), 157–159 and in *Gesetz-Sammlung für die Königlichen Preußischen Staaten vom Jahre 1864* (Berlin, 1864), 107–110.

8 "Che dura prova è tentar di greca aquila il dorso". The Greek War of Independence and its resonance in Sicilian culture of the 19th century

Francesco Scalora

For a Palingenesis

"Che dura prova è tentar di greca aquila il dorso" (How difficult it is to try mounting the Greek eagle's back). With these words, the Sicilian poet, Mario Rapisardi (Catania 1844–1912), grasps the importance of the Greek Revolution, dedicating ample space to the memory of that historical event in the Canto VIII, entitled "Le Rivoluzioni", of his poem *La Palingenesi*. The work, published in 1868, on the eve of the First Vatican Council, was printed in Florence, at that time the capital of Italy.[1]

Ingenious, rather than brilliant, in concept, the poem was well-received due to the young poet's generous audacity, which, in times of religious, moral, and political stagnation, and in the fervour provoked by the Roman issue, contemplated a Christian *palingenesis*: a revival of the evangelical spirit, and a close harmony between science and faith, Church and State. Bringing to light the merits and defects of a Risorgimento narrated in a free and easy manner, of an external rather than inner harmony, Rapisardi singles out from the bas-reliefs of history those moments that, in his opinion, strongly contributed to the renewal of humanity.[2] From the biblical tradition he passes to the Middle Ages, from the Crusades to the Reformation, from the French Revolution to the Italian Risorgimento, considering the Greek Revolution and the other contemporary insurrections (European and American) as fundamental historical events whose purpose was to open a Mediterranean path to political modernity.

In 1868, Giuseppe Giarrizzo, who made important observations on Rapisardi's literary work, writes: "the time of 'revolutions' is over. But the dominant class sees doubts prevailing over generous illusions: if it doesn't want to be blamed … for recent disasters, it must take note of the imbalances of the building that has just been constructed, and get used to oppose every time this 'real Italy', which still needs to be discovered, to a still remote mirage of cohesion and national identity".[3]

In the delicate – and perhaps premature – attempt to narrate in less triumphalist terms the recent events of the Italian Risorgimento, Rapisardi acted as a forerunner of those revisionist works that, in the coming decades,

110 *Francesco Scalora*

would involve the political and cultural sensibility of numerous Italian personalities, who studied the Risorgimento in various capacities and from different ideological perspectives.[4] The young Rapisardi fully understands the extraordinary natural cycle of the revolutions that stirred the Mediterranean in the first half of the 19th century.[5] This is what seems to emerge from the verses extracts of Canto VIII of the poem: "Fra' bellici tumulti / De' *fluttuanti popoli risorti*, / quando serrati e forti / Di Libertate al grido / D' ogni lido sorgean gl' Itali inulti" (Between uproars of war / Of *fluctuating risen populations* / when quick and strong / And cry for Freedom / From every beach the unavenged Italians arose). And again: "Qual mai nove e sublime / *Turbine* di guerra in Europa io sento, / Che, de l'oppressa umanitade in nome / Corone infrange ed oppressori opprime?" (What a new and sublime / *Turmoil* of War I feel in Europe / That in the name of oppressed humanity / Breaks crowns and oppresses the oppressors?).[6]

Far from the widely depreciative historiographical readings of the following century, which would have judged the insurrections of 1820–1821 as the uncertain gasp of a generation of patriots who had already given their best on the national scene,[7] Rapisardi anticipates a transnational reading of a patriotism that would open new horizons to the politics of the early 19th century. After all, this interpretation would not seem to be too far from the one that in Italy, since a few decades ago, redefined some specific historiographical categories (including the one about exile) and put forward new ideological hypotheses and interpretative paradigms that offered an innovative revision of the historiography about the Risorgimento.[8]

However, by defining national movements also in terms of a more thorough ideological exchange, and insisting on the supranational dimension of events, Rapisardi seems to understand the new and important link between nation and statehood, along with the distinction between constitutional freedom, clearly of Spanish inspiration, and liberty, signifying independence from foreign occupation: "E libertate ha in petto, ira nel guardo. / ... E i conculcati antichi / Dritti gli chiede e l'abusata Carta, / E il tron gli scrolla e strappagli lo scettro" (And he has freedom in his chest and ire in his eyes / He asks him for the old trampled rights and the abused Charter / And takes his throne and snatches his sceptre away).[9]

As Antonino De Francesco rightly noted, it is perhaps worth emphasizing a point which has been somewhat discounted due to the transnational dimension of these developments, but which remains fundamental if one wishes to grasp how the 1820–1821 revolution was, in its Italian dimension, not only a constitutional revolution but also posed – from the outset – the question of the construction of a new concept of the state. The idea of the nation was, without any doubt, one of the key ideas of 19th-century history, especially in those areas which were yet to be politically unified and which aimed at becoming a nation, not only from a cultural and linguistic point of view but from a state perspective. Independence and constitutional freedom soon became the motto of the new state project. The production of a constitutional charter was supposed to be the outcome of a war of independence from the foreigner, whereas in Italy, up to that point, there was a misapprehension that the reverse sequence was possible.[10]

Therefore, the specifically Italian interest in the Greek revolutionary movement in the aftermath of 1821 must be viewed from this perspective, amongst others. This is perceived in all the triumphant rhetoric of the dualities oppressed/oppressor, Christian/infidel, and independence/slavery, and became at the same time the fulcrum of various confluent as well as mixed currents of thought: liberalism and nationalism, neo-Christianity, romanticism, as well as its opposite, the classical tradition.[11]

However, it is good to point out – as an additional note to what has been said so far – that the Greek revolution, as well as the different factors which gradually contributed to the success of that enterprise and to the formation of the Greek state, did not appear to Italian public opinion as an event that had developed in an unknown context. The definition of a patriotic movement also as an accurate ideological Italian-Greek exchange is rooted in Italy and relates to previous eras. These eras, although are not marked by exile – which undoubtedly contributed to giving a transnational dimension to the revolutionary events of the beginning of the 19th century – are characterised, for example, by the phenomenon of the Greek diaspora, which is not simply a movement of people, but it is concurrently an exchange of ideas and perceptions, which have traversed the entire Italian territory since the end of the 15th century.[12]

The vast literature regarding the appeals for Greece's liberation is a crucial example of a field that still requires careful investigation. In the aftermath of Constantinople's fall, it flourished in the various centres of the Greek diaspora that had been established a long time before in Italy and Europe.[13] Various traces of ethnicity-consciousness often emerge from this prosperous literary production. Over the centuries, this awareness seems to lead toward a national identity. It should be recalled that this old literary tradition had a great influence on 19th-century Philhellenic literature, at least the Italian one. In other words, as an example, the celebratory language of the vast literature that flourished in the aftermath of the naval battle of Lepanto (1571)[14] was reused, *mutatis mutandis*, on the occasion of the Chesme (1770)[15] and Navarino (1827) naval battles.[16] It is necessary to invest in these research fields, which can only briefly be mentioned in the context of this article, since a dialogue would have to be created between the most recent and innovative historiographical interpretations and the more old-fashioned historiographical categories, with the aim of "empirically verifying the interpretative hypotheses".[17]

Greece was therefore known, discussed and read of even before the revolutionary movement of 1821.[18] To mention a relative example, the interesting debate about the expedition of the Orlov brothers to the Peloponnese (1770) and the passage of the Russian fleet through the Italian ports of Venice, Trieste, Livorno, and Naples contributed over time to the

112 *Francesco Scalora*

creation of an ideology that associated the two political and cultural contexts and shed public light on the existence of a "Greek case". Indeed, premature Philhellenic propaganda messages circulated in these cities due to the presence of historical Greek communities and their activities. The news also reached Palermo and Sicilian cultural circles, attracting the interest of intellectuals from the Greek-Albanian communities in Sicily.[19] In practice, there was no basis for an actual collaboration between the two countries, but a new patriotic ideology emerged in Italy, and Italian society started developing a new interest in a little-known Greece.

The interest in the Greek world began as an admiration for the values, history, intellectual, literary, and artistic production of ancient and classical Greek civilization. From the second half of the 18th century, it took the form of ethical, political, and cultural solidarity with the struggles for freedom and national independence of a population rightly regarded as the natural (albeit dormant) heir to the past one. Within this pan-European phenomenon called Philhellenism, which resonated explosively throughout 19th century Italy, due to its history, geographical location, and political status, was prominent in a different way; it appears that the Greek phenomenon was perhaps more deeply felt and rooted.[20]

Sicilian autonomism and national identity

In Sicily, the interest in the Greek revolt acquired peculiar nuances from the beginning.

As the regional expression of a national phenomenon, Sicilian Philhellenism needs to be placed in the context of 19th-century Sicilian politics and culture and compared to similar cases in the rest of Italy. There are as many similarities as differences. For example, it is key for the purpose of this research to compare the birth and cultural-political evolution of the Sicilian Risorgimento with the broader national movement.[21] These are usually regarded as two separate phenomena,[22] especially as far as evident political autonomist instances are concerned.

After the Congress of Vienna, Ferdinand IV went back to Naples with the name of Ferdinand I as the king of a new unified state, the Kingdom of the Two Sicilies. Therefore, the last independent area of the island was no longer a separate territory.

Although the establishment of a central government in Naples was, at first, welcomed by Sicilian people, it soon caused misgivings and concerns. Palermo had lost its prestige and the baronial aristocratic class its privileges.[23]

Privileged classes started regarding independence from Naples as an urgent political issue. The old baronial class wished to break "the traditional political immobilism that had previously been its protection". The secessionist option represented the only chance to preserve feudal privileges and local interests. After the liberal threads and the French revolutionary principles disappeared, Sicilian barons put an end to the convenient alliance with the Bourbons, returned to their old attitude of enmity towards the king, and started contemplating a separation from Naples. The Sicilian aristocracy had "the opportunity to again become the guiding nation against an oppressive foreign domination and bring together the causes of anti-reformism, local patriotism and regional autonomy".[24]

The 1820 revolution, led by Palermo, had already shown that the Sicilian people had not resigned themselves to losing their independence. However, the absence of a political programme approved by the various social groups and the intention to maintain the old privileges gave a regional dimension to the insurrections of that year. There was not a national and unified view and the idea of an Italian nation was weak, provincial, and only linked to an anti-Bourbon sentiment.[25] That separatist attempt, albeit suppressed by the Bourbonic government, led to the creation of a national movement characterised by more exchanges. The outcomes of these exchanges seemed to be inconsistent. However, the ideology behind them contributed to the creation of new ideas. Greece was, more than anything else, at the centre of constant debates. Sicilian philhellene literature, published in the periodical press of the time, especially in the thirties, proves that Palermo and Sicily as a whole were not at all happy with the situation. Freedom from foreign domination, as the Greek example suggested, was still a goal to pursue.

From a cultural perspective, Sicilian political regionalism did not coincide with cultural regionalism. Sicilian autonomism, the relative closure of the island, and the rejection of any form of Italian penetration did not lead to a relative state of backwardness of Sicilian culture, compared to that of Italy and Europe.

"If Sicilian culture of the second half of the eighteenth century was, as Giovanni Gentile has written, inspired by the Enlightenment and by anti-metaphysical and anti-historical principles, the same applies to Italian culture in the same period".[26] This statement is by Caterina Mandalà, dating back to the years in which Sicilian autonomism was strong, and was supported by Eugenio Di Carlo and Giorgio Santangelo. On the other hand, Gaetano Falzone, in reference to a key issue of 19th-century Sicilian culture, such as the debate about romanticism and anti-romanticism, claimed that Sicilian culture was provincial and immature. According to Falzone, the innovations of contemporary Italian and European culture did reach Sicily, but they were filtered by the fear of novelty, "which has always been typical of islander".[27]

The lack of comprehensive studies about Sicilian culture in the two decades before the 1848 insurrections makes it difficult to contextualise this research about Sicilian philhellenic cultural phenomena[28]. Surely, these need to be placed in the context of a political-cultural milieu where the questionable cultural immaturity and alleged refractoriness of Sicilian society to continental penetrations combine their limits with an interest in renewal and experimentation. This approach led to the development of a moral and civic

114 *Francesco Scalora*

consciousness that looked at national unity. In other words, the island and its condition of isolation represented a solid perspective to analyse the outside.

If we abandon the identity stereotype and try to explain the complex relationship between literary culture and Sicilian identity, we should opt for a pre-Risorgimento Sicilian culture that has nothing to do with Romanticism.[29] The political and literary debate that animated local newspapers in those years included contributions "belonging to both tendencies and relating to both political and literary conceptions (Sicilian/Italian) and the economic ones (Protectionism/Liberalism".[30] Both approaches focused on the new needs of the time. On the one hand, for the Sicilian autonomists who claimed independence from Neapolitan centralism, the concept of homeland coincided with the "Sicilian nation". On the other hand, Liberal people on the island threw down a challenge in the name of a unified Italy and tried to make the most of what Sicily could offer to their political activism.

Reasonably, both tendencies lacked solid political deliberations.[31] However, a renewal was needed. The Italian sentiment, wishing for a future with fewer divisions between the states of the Italian mainland and unity against foreign domination, was a premature evolution of that Sicilian sentiment which was rooted in autonomist aspirations and fought the same oppression. This is why everybody in Sicily, from classicists to romantics, sympathised with the issue of modern Greece, a country that had been ruled by the Ottomans for centuries. Everybody was looking for freedom and a national identity.

Sicilian Philhellenism

If in the rest of the Italian peninsula there was an important debate about how the Greek revolutionary model could be a point of reference for the construction of a free and united Italy, in the Italian South, or *Mezzogiorno*, as we have seen, that debate was initially articulated along the lines of a Neapolitan nation and a Sicilian nation. This was certainly the case until the beginning of the second half of the 19th century, when it was considered appropriate to choose – at least conditionally (to free themselves from Naples) – in favour of Unity.

In the early 19th century the development of feelings of nationality in Sicily, Naples, and the rest of Europe, following the impact of the revolutionary discourse of France, had favoured a quick recourse to antiquity. This was considered a secure foothold for those who looked back over time and sought confirmations of the perennial nature of the nation. Under the shadow of the parallel triumphs of a narrative canon of the Risorgimento, the insistence on the specific Greek origin of the Southern populations, especially Sicilian, became functional in legitimizing the new state order in terms of a specific nationality.[32] The emphasis on the Greek origins of the

The Greek War of Independence 115

Sicilian population is evident from the rich editorial activity aimed at editing, translating, and commenting on texts of ancient texts of Greek literature written by authors living in the Sicilian Greek colonies. Therefore, a new editorial school within traditional classic philology developed in early 19th century Sicily, particularly between 1813 and 1834. This was based on the rediscovery of the prestige of ancient Greek tradition in Sicilian culture and history.[33]

The repeated and confident references to the historical-cultural link between Greek civilization, seen in its continuity, and Sicily, in addition to underwriting the construction of the new cultural (and soon political) sensibility regarding Italy in the early 19th century, provided fertile ground for the many expressions of philhellenic inspiration that became manifest on the island throughout the nineteenth century.

These were mostly manifestations of a philological and literary nature, which, because of the ideological dimension in which they were born and matured, allow us to clearly identify the existence of a specificity of Sicilian Philhellenism: a sort of Philhellenism within Philhellenism, so to speak – a regional appendix, but no less important or peripheral, of the contemporary Italian Philhellenism phenomenon.

The Sicilian scene was animated by an array of Sicilian poets, more or less known (or, to put it another way, major or minor), toward whom posterity has not always proved particularly generous. These come from the local ruling class and concern themselves with the historical facts of modern Greece and the protagonists of its Revolution. Almost all excellent connoisseurs of ancient Greece, passionate about Greek literature, these poets with their verses invigorated the literary mania that inspired the pen of Italian and European scholars and poets in the wake of the fortunes of the struggle in Greece.

The Italian Philhellenic literature is distinguished by its intensity, impact, and political repercussions for the process of forming the Italian state and its idea of a nation, even in a society that was still politically divided and not united but ideologically united by the convergence of liberal ideas and the hope of national redemption.[34] In this sense, the Greek laboratory was a space in which to experiment, after the first Piedmontese and Neapolitan failures, in a common struggle of a Risorgimental, national and notoriously anti-Austrian character.

The singularity of the Sicilian phenomenon is distinguished mainly by the specificity of the political condition of the island and by its generally anti-Bourbon and particularly anti-Parthenopean position. From this perspective, for example, the value of the homeland concept in early 19th-century Sicilian culture must be seen in terms of a quest for autonomy, not unity, and certainly not yet in the context of a national narrative. Therefore, when the terms "homeland" or "foreigner" occur in the Sicilian poetic production inspired by Philhellenism to voice the anti-Bourbon sentiment, they should be interpreted as elements of hatred of the Palermitan aristocracy. In point

116   *Francesco Scalora*

of fact, the majority of the philhellenic poets are noblemen who oppose Neapolitan centralism and authoritarianism. In those verses, therefore, the "Turkish foreigner" serves as a pretext for expressing the intolerance towards the Neapolitan interference in Sicilian political affairs, the aversion to attempts to crush the island's aspirations for autonomy, as well as the baronial privileges rooted in that reality. Reformulating the words of Guido Muoni, one of the first to mention the importance of Italian literary production of Philhellenic inspiration, it could be said that the Sicilian poet, "when cursing the Muslim, replaced him in his heart – or at least associated him – with his [Bourbon] master" (where the Italian associated "his Austrian master")[35] and with it the hated Neapolitan centralism and its intrusiveness in Sicilian affairs.

The Greek revolutionary experience thus became an example of rebellion to be followed. The Ottoman domination from which Greece had partially liberated itself symbolized the Bourbon domination from which Sicily had yet to free itself. The idea of homeland that appears in the verses of the Sicilian Philhellenes, which partially became a reality in the small Kingdom of Greece, therefore corresponds to the demand for regional autonomy so desired by the Sicilian ruling class. From this point of view, there is a certain divergence from the contemporary Italian Philhellenic literary production, where the binomial of Italy-Greece resonated from the beginning in its echo of national regeneration.

While in those years in which the autonomists were intent on claiming independence from Neapolitan centralism and equated the idea of homeland with the "Sicilian nation", the island's liberals launched a utopian challenge in the name of a united Italy. In this sense, within the articulated political, cultural, and economic context of Sicily, two different trends emerge, those of Palermo and those of Messina.

The centralism of Palermo, with its bond with feudal privileges, the baronial aspirations for regional autonomy, the strong anti-Bourbon and anti-Neapolitan sentiment were soon opposed by the fresh and vital cultural circles of Messina.

A link between Sicily and Italy, Messina, more bourgeois in its social appearance and more sensitive to European and Italian cultural styles, filters and elaborates the cultural innovations of the time with greater vivacity.[36] Messina opposes Palermo's centralism and responds with its own national impulses and aspirations.[37] Furthermore, in the Philhellene-inspired verses of Messinian scholars and notables, the idea of homeland, although always formulated in anti-Bourbon tones, also embraces Mazzinian republicanism and the idea of the Italian nation. The result is a more dynamic, concrete and lively poetry, which is in tune with the new romantic trend and far from classicism and the pedantic rhetoric of Palermo.[38]

Moreover, Messina, also strengthened by its status as a port and its centuries-old Greek presence[39] – with its overlap of the Byzantine, the medieval and modern Hellenism – follows and respects, perhaps in a more precise and coherent way than any other Sicilian reality, the cadenced pace of solidarity between the two realities, the Sicilian and the Greek, until the end of 19th century.

Sicilian-Albanian scholars and the Greek Revolution

Lastly, the role played by the cultivated circles of the Greek-Albanian colonies of Sicily[40] deserves special attention as they were decisive in shaping modern Albanian culture. Together, by virtue of the historical relationship with the Greek and Orthodox religion, they were able to act as intermediaries of knowledge, also thanks to the rise of figures engaged in studies of Greek. These figures were largely Sicilian-Albanian scholars of Greek studies, who followed the evolution of the Greek uprising with cautious interest. They did not hesitate to acknowledge on the conceptual level the notable relations between the Greek national movement and the formation of contemporary Albanian ideology, which was now confidently taking its first steps in Sicily. In this sense, the literary activity of Nicolò Chetta (1741–1803)[41] and Giuseppe Crispi (1781–1859)[42] constitutes the first testament to the genuine interest in contemporary Greek historical events, between the Hellenic revolts of 1770 and the ascension of Otto of Bavaria to the Greek throne (1833).

In the decades that followed, this feeling of "sympathy" towards the Greek revolutionary cause in Italy would take on different nuances, as it would in Sicily. The new philhellenic proposition would become functional with the founding moment of the Italian unitary state, replicating the enthusiasms of the early nineteenth century in an increasingly over-ambitious socio-political and diplomatic context, characterized by desires for territorial expansion and an increase in dynastic prestige. While the approach of many Sicilian and Italian personalities – who for various reasons continued to deal with modern Greece – could be roughly evaluated within these terms, for the Sicilian-Albanian scholars – who with a lively political sense never stopped looking towards the Orthodox East – the Greek issue would continue to offer the opportunity to broadcast the sorry political condition of the Albanian people, at the time still under Ottoman domination, to the educated world of their time. The prospect of a Greek-Albanian political union stimulated on several occasions the conscience of the Italian-Albanian patriots, in the hope that the resonance of the Greek insurrectionary fortunes could somehow affect the fate of the nearby Albanian people. The beginning of the Greek irredentist policies, known under the name of "Great Idea" (Μεγάλη Ιδέα), which pursued the redemption of all Greeks still under the Ottoman Empire within the confines of a unitary state, and the general enthusiasm with which that message permeated in the Greek and philhellenic consciousness, fed and justified such visions.[43]

118 *Francesco Scalora*

Conclusion

On 5 July 1860, on the occasion of Garibaldi's expedition to Sicily on the eve of the Italian unification, the Greek poet, Aristotelis Valaoritis (1824–1879), who passionately supported the cause of the annexation of the Ionian Islands by Greece, wrote

> It's been about forty years since then, and here is the Italian sister fighting this holy battle for independence. We should remember that we owe her blood in exchange for the blood shed a long time ago, sacrifices for the ones made a long time ago. Santarosa's soul requires intercession. It is time to offer to the tomb of that brave at least our obol rather than incense and vain prayers. Septinsula! Sicily, this real daughter of mother Greece, rises from the grave. Garibaldi, the hero, drew his sword and haughty and intrepid declares her free.[44]

The fight for Greek independence and the Italian Risorgimento are two phenomena with a nearly parallel evolution. Both countries fought for their independence and unification; Greece opposed the centuries-old Ottoman occupation, whereas Italy opposed the Austrian domination, and Sicily the Bourbonic one. The fact that these fights alternated at different phases meant that the two countries followed each other's example. Interest in the revolutionary cause of modern Greece did not seem to fade after the recognition of an independent state in 1830. The long tradition of exchanges between Italian and Greek revolutionaries, dating back to before 1821, was renewed in the most important phases of the independence fight of the two countries. Examples of this tradition are the presence of philhellene Italians in the Greek fields during the independence war and the warm welcome received by the Italian exiles in Greece on more than one occasion, especially in 1848–1849. On the eve of the Italian unification, this "brotherhood" sentiment between the two countries became stronger and offered new occasions for collaboration and solidarity. The new Philhellenic season, starting in 1859, would last for the entire second half of the 19th century. The most representative phases of this season were Garibaldi's expeditions in Greece on the occasion of Crete's insurrections of 1866 and 1896, the latter leading to the Greek-Ottoman conflict of 1897.

The Italian Philhellenic movement of the 19th century differs in both intensity and duration from the corresponding European movements. Obviously, the repercussions and the political and cultural consequences, in terms of a common national fight, had different impacts on the Italian and Greek independence fights. From this perspective, if we compare the origins and cultural-political evolution of the Sicilian Risorgimento with the national movement – two phenomena that used to be considered separate – we will have a valuable interpretative key to analyze the evolution of the relationship between Italy and Greece in 19th century.

The Greek War of Independence 119

Notes

1 M. Rapisardi, "Canto ottavo - Le Rivoluzioni", in Idem, *La Palingenesi. Canti dieci di Mario Rapisardi* (Florence, 1868), 183–202, 202. A second revised edition was published in Milan in 1878 (the canto VIII is on pages 195–214). On the literary production of Rapisardi inspired by Philhellenism see F. Scalora, *Sicilia e Grecia. La presenza della Grecia moderna nella cultura siciliana del XIX secolo* (Palermo, 2018), 229–230, 416–417. On Rapisardi's poetry more in general see S. Zappulla Muscarà, ed., *Mario Rapisardi*. Proceedings of the National Congress of Study organised on the occasion of the XVII Literary Price "Brancati – Zafferana", Zafferana Etnea, 20–22 December 1987 (Catania, 1991). In the text, the translations of the quotations from Italian and Greek into English are mine.

2 See https://rapiasrdi.altervista.org/palingenesi.htm (visited on 20.08.2020). On this topic see also: M. Rapisardi, "Prefazione", in idem, *La Palingenesi*, V-XIV, and idem, "Note al Canto ottavo", Ibid., 294–297.

3 G. Giarrizzo, "Il caso Rapisardi", in Zappulla Muscarà, ed., *Mario Rapisardi*, 7–25, especially 11.

4 An updated literature review about the methodology and the different interpretations within the historiography Risorgimento of the last decades can be found in P. Macry, "Masse, rivoluzione e Risorgimento. Appunti critici su alcune tendenze storiografiche", *Contemporanea* 27/4 (2014): 673–690.

5 On this topic see the publications mentioned in note 8 and A. M. Rao, "L'espace méditerranéen dans la pensée et les projets politiques des patrioties italiens. Matteo Galdi et la 'république du genre humain'", *Droit des gens et relations entre les peuples dans l'espace méditerranéen autour de la Révolution française*, eds. M. Dorigny and R. Tlili Sellaouti, Journées d'étude de Tunis, 6–7 mars 2002 (Paris, 2006), 115–137.

6 Rapisardi, "Canto ottavo", 185–187. The Italic in the quotation is mine.

7 This part of the literature according to which the 1820–1821 insurrections did not play an important role was highly influenced by Benedetto Croce. A re-evaluation of the historical events in question, whose unsuccessful outcomes contributed to opening new possibilities to nineteenth-century politics and re-defining the national movement in terms of more accurate exchanges can be found in A. Lepre, *La rivoluzione napoletana del 1820–1821* (Rome, 1967); F. Renda, *Risorgimento e classi popolari in Sicilia 1820–1821* (Milan, 1968), and R. Romeo, *Il Risorgimento in Sicilia* (Rome – Bari, 2015) (1st ed.: Naples, 1950). However, these publications do focus on the regressive and reactionary nature of the Palermo revolution.

8 Examples of the vast literature published in the last decades on this topic are: M. S. Miller, "A 'Liberal International'? Perspectives on Comparative Approaches to the Revolutions in Spain, Italy, and Greece in the 1820s", *Mediterranean Studies* 2 (1990): 61–67; M. Isabella, *Risorgimento in esilio. L'internazionale liberale e l'età delle rivoluzioni*, translation by D. Scaffei (Bari, 2011) (original ed.: Oxford – New York, 2009); A. Bistarelli, *Gli esuli del Risorgimento* (Bologna, 2011), and K. Zanou, *Transnational Patriotism in the Mediterranean, 1800–1850. Stammering the Nation* (New York, 2018). An evaluation of the of the Greek Revolution as a European event, analysed within the broader context of European and Ottoman historiography can be found in P. Pizanias, ed., *Η Ελληνική Επανάσταση του 1821. Ένα ευρωπαϊκό γεγονός* (Athens, 2009) (english ed.: Istanbul, 2011), and A. Karakatsouli, *Μαχητές της Ελευθερίας και 1821. Η ελληνική επανάσταση στη διεθνική της διάσταση* [Freedom fighters and 1821. The Greek Revolution in its Transnational Dimension] (Athens, 2016).

9 Rapisardi, "Canto ottavo", 194.

120   *Francesco Scalora*

10 See A. De Francesco, "Η ιταλική Χερσόνησος την εποχή των μεσογειακών επαναστάσεων του 1820–1821" [The Italian Peninsula during the Mediterranean Revolutions of 1820–1821], *Επαναστάσεις: κείμενα για τις επαναστάσεις σε Ευρώπη και Αμερική, τέλη 18ου– πρώτες δεκαετίες 19ουαιώνα*, eds Ch. Loukos, A. Sfoini and V. Sarafis, Athens (forthcoming: EMNE – Μνήμων, series Θεωρία και μελέτες). Special thanks to the editors who notified me of the paper by Prof. De Francesco before publication.

11 About the political and cultural relations between Greece and Italy as well as about the Italian philhellene movement in 1770–1844 see A. G. Noto, *La ricezione del Risorgimento greco in Italia (1770–1844). Tra idealità filelleniche, stereotipi e Realpolitik* (Rome, 2016). An updated bibliography about the Italian philhellene phenomenon from a cultural and literature perspectives in Nineteenth century can be found in Scalora, *Sicilia e Grecia*. The work of A. Liakos, *L'unificazione italiana e la Grande Idea. Ideologia e azione dei movimenti nazionali in Italia e in Grecia, 1859–1871*, Preface of S. Woolf, Translation by A. Giacumacatos (Florence, 1995) (original ed.: Athens, 1985), analyses from a political perspective the relationships between the two countries around the middle of Nineteenth century during their transformation into national States. The aforementioned work of Isabella, *Risorgimento*, 87–122, illustrates from a transnational perspective the exile and the main features of the Italian philhellene movement in relation to the corresponding European cases, particularly the English and French ones.

12 See M. Isabella and K. Zanou, eds, *Mediterranean Diaspora. Politics and Ideas in the Long nineteenth Century* (London and New York, 2016), and Zanou, *Transnational Patriotism*.

13 Useful analyses can be found in O. Katsiardi-Hering, "Έλληνες λόγιοι συνομιλούντες με τη Δύση, φωτίζοντες την Ανατολή: προς τον δρόμο της Παιδείας και της εθνικής συνείδησης. Λόγος Πανηγυρικός για την Εθνική Επέτειο της 25ης Μαρτίου 2017 στη Μεγάλη Αίθουσα του Εθνικού και Καποδιστριακού Πανεπιστημίου Αθηνών" [Greek Scholars Interacting with the West, Illuminate the East: on the Path of Education and National Consciousness …], in *Επίσημοι λόγοι στο Εθνικό και Καποδιστριακό Πανεπιστήμιο Αθηνών, επί Πρυτανείας Μελετίου Αθανασίου Δημόπουλου, 2015–2019*, vol. 37/2 (acad. year 2016–2017) (Athens, 2020), 23–71. On the tradition of the appeals (εκκλήσεις) for the liberation of Greece see M. I. Manoussakas, *Εκκλήσεις (1453–1535) τῶν Ἑλλήνων λογίων τῆς Ἀναγεννήσεως πρὸς τοὺς ἡγεμόνες τῆς Εὐρώπης γιὰ τὴν ἀπελευθέρωση τῆς Ἑλλάδος. Λόγος ἐκφωνηθεὶς τὴν 25ηνΜαρτίου 1963 εἰς τὴν μεγάλην αἴθουσαν τῶν τελετῶν τοῦ Ἀριστοτελείου Πανεπιστημίου Θεσσαλονίκης* [Appeals (1453–1535) of the Greek Scholars of the Renaissance to the European Sovereigns for the Liberation of Greece …] (Thessaloniki, 1965), relates to the appeals of the years 1453–1535; Idem, ""Εκκλήσεις τῶν Ἑλλήνων λογίων τῆς Ἀναγεννήσεως πρὸς τοὺς ἡγεμόνες τῆς Εὐρώπης γιὰ τὴν ἀπελευθέρωση τῆς Ἑλλάδος. Ὁμιλία τοῦ Ἀκαδημαϊκοῦ κ. Μ. Ἰ Μανούσακα. Πανηγυρικὴ Συνεδρία τῆς 24ης Μαρτίου 1984, Ἑορτασμὸς τῆς 25ης Μαρτίου 1821" [Appeals of the Greek Scholars of the Renaissance to the European Sovereigns for the Liberation of Greece …], *Πρακτικὰ τῆς Ἀκαδημίας Ἀθηνῶν* 59 (1984): 195–249, for the years 1535–1821; V. Rotolo, *Il carme «Hellas» di Leone Allacci* (Palermo, 1966), 1-47, and A. Pertusi, *Storiografia umanistica e mondo bizantino* (Palermo, 1967), 35–40.

14 See the rich bibliography in S. Kaklamanis, ed., *Andrea Cornaro. Historia Candiana. Μία ἀφήγηση τοῦ Δ΄ Βενετοτουρκικοῦ πολέμου (1570–1573). Κύπρος – Ναύπακτος, εἰσαγωγή, ἔκδοση κειμένου, ἀπόδοση στὰ ἑλληνικά, σημειώσεις & παράρτημα [Andrea Cornaro. Historia Candiana.* A Narrative of the 4th Venetian-Turkish War (1570–1573). Cyprus – Lepanto, Introduction, Edition, Greek Translation, Notes & Appendix] (Nicosia, 2017).

The Greek War of Independence   121

15 See, *infra*, notes 18–19.
16 See Scalora, *Sicilia e Grecia*, 238–251.
17 Macry, "Masse, rivoluzione e Risorgimento", 690.
18 See F. Venturi, *La Rivolta greca del 1770 e il patriottismo dell'età dei Lumi*, Introduction by O. Kresten (Rome, 1986).
19 See F. Scalora, "L'idea di Bisanzio nel pensiero dei dotti siculo-albanesi: il caso di Nicolò Chetta (1741–1803)", *Byzantino-Sicula VII. Giornate di studio sulla civiltà bizantina in Italia meridionale e nei Balcani dedicate alla memoria di André Guillou*. Proceedings of the International Congress *Ritrovare Bisanzio*, Palermo 26–28 May 2016, eds M. Re, C. Rognoni and F. P. Vuturo (Palermo, 2019), 291–318.
20 See, *supra*, note 11.
21 Apart from Romeo, *Il Risorgimento in Sicilia*; e G. Cingari, "Gli ultimi Borboni. Dalla restaurazione all'unità", in *Storia della Sicilia*, ed. R. Romeo, vol. VIII (Naples, 1977), 1–83, see L. Riall, *La Sicilia e l'unificazione italiana. Politica liberale e potere locale (1815-1866)*, translation by D. Scaffei (Torino, 2004) (original ed.: Oxford, 1998), 37-73; A. Spagnoletti, *Storia del Regno delle Due Sicilie* (Bologna, 1997), 44-55, and R. De Lorenzo, *Borbonia Felix. Il Regno delle due Sicilie alla vigilia del crollo* (Rome, 2013), 9–49. Another key publication is S. Lupo, *L'unificazione italiana. Mezzogiorno, rivoluzione, guerra civile* (Rome, 2011).
22 I am referring to the opinion of Giovanni Gentile, expressed in his work *Il tramonto della cultura siciliana* (Bologna, 1919).
23 See Spagnoletti, *Storia del Regno,* 12, 44–55.
24 D. Mack Smith, *Storia della Sicilia medievale e moderna*, translation by Biocca Marghieri (Rome – Bari, 2009) (original ed. in 2 vols.: London, 1968), 466.
25 For a reconstruction and evaluation of the historical events connected to the Sicilian insurrections of 1820 see Romeo, *Il Risorgimento in Sicilia*, 161–170, as well as the publications mentioned in note 7.
26 C. Mandalà, "La pubblicistica in Sicilia dal 1830 al 1835", *La Sicilia verso l'Unità d'Italia*. Memories and texts collected on the occasion of the 39° National Congress of the Institute (Palermo, 1960), 105–174, at pp. 105–106.
27 G. Falzone, *Battaglie romantiche e antiromantiche in Sicilia. La polemica de «La Ruota» di Palermo* (Bologna, 1965), 40.
28 At the moment there is no comprehensive and updated study of the island's literary culture of the first half of Nineteenth century. About see the bibliography in Scalora, *Sicilia e Grecia*, 123–134, at p. 126 note 13.
29 See M. Sacco Messineo, ed., *La Ruota (1840–1842)*, Preface of G. Santangelo (Rome, 1975), 17–68; and M. Di Gesù, *L'invenzione della Sicilia. Letteratura, mafia, modernità* (Rome, 2015), 2–21.
30 Mandalà, "La pubblicistica in Sicilia", 156.
31 See A. Sole, *Tre momenti della cultura sicilianistica dell'Ottocento (Alcozer, Perez, Buscaino Campo)* (Palermo, 1991), 74 *passim*; Sacco Messineo, ed., *La Ruota*, 24, 32, and Falzone, *Battaglie romantiche*, 70.
32 See A. De Francesco, "La nazione impossibile. Antiquaria e preromanità nella politica culturale delle Due Sicilie", *Mediterranea – ricerche storiche* 41 (2017): 479–498.
33 See E. Degani, "Domenico Scinà (1765–1837) e gli studi classici", *Eikasmòs* 5 (1994): 335–365, and Scalora, *Sicilia e Grecia*, 135–155, 284–315.
34 On this topic see the works of G. Muoni, *La letteratura filellenica nel Romanticismo Italiano* (Milan, 1907), and E. Persico, *La letteratura filellenica italiana (1787–1870)* (Milan, 1907).
35 Muoni, *La letteratura filellenica*, 2.
36 See Mandalà, "La pubblicistica in Sicilia", 108–137, and S. Bottari, "Stampa e opinione pubblica a Messina nell'Ottocento", *Messina 1860 e dintorni. Uomini, idee*

122 Francesco Scalora

e società tra Risorgimento e Unità, eds R. Battaglia, L. Caminiti and M. D'Angelo (Messina, 2011), 227–254.

37 On the peculiarity of the Messinese Risorgimento see N. Checco and E. Consolo, "Messina nei moti del 1847-48", *Rassegna storica del Risorgimento* 89/1 (2002): 1–41; e M. D'Angelo, "'Fatti precorredo e idee ... ' Messina tra Risorgimento e Unità d'Italia", *Messina 1860 e dintorni*, eds Battaglia, Caminiti, D'Angelo, 101–139.

38 See Scalora, *Sicilia e Grecia*, 331–437.

39 On the Greek presence in Messina, see Aa. Vv., *Immagine e scrittura. Presenza greca a Messina dal Medioevo all'età Moderna*. Exhibition Catalogue, Messina 23 March – 30 May 2013, Palermo 8 June – 24 August 2013, Curated by the Istituto Siciliano di Studi Bizantini e Neoellenici "B. Lavagnini", (Palermo, 2013).

40 An updated bibliography can be found in F. Scalora, "Ζητήματα ταυτότητας και προβλήματα ερμηνείας του όρου 'Graecus/Greco' στα καταστατικά ίδρυσης (Capitoli di fondazione) των ελληνο-αλβανικών κοινοτήτων της Σικελίας" [Identity and Interpretation Issues of the Term *Graecus/Greco* in the Statutes of Foundation (Capitoli di Fondazione) of the Greek-Albanian Communities of Sicily], *Έλλην, Ρωμηός, Γραικός: Συλλογικοί προσδιορισμοί και ταυτότητες*, eds O. Katsiardi-Hering, A. Papadia-Lala, K. Nikolaou and V. Karamanolakis (Athens, 2018), 363–378.

41 See Scalora, "L'idea di Bisanzio", 291–318.

42 See Scalora, *Sicilia e Grecia*, 284–315.

43 See Ibid., 315–329.

44 A. Valaoritis, *Βίος, ἐπιστολὲς καὶ πολιτικὰ κείμενα* [Life, Letters and Political Texts], Critical Edition by G. P. Savvidis and N. Lykourgou, vol. I (Athens, 1980), 63.

Part III

Reverberations of Revolution in Eastern and Southern Europe

9 Russia and Greece in the Age of Revolution

Simon Dixon

Posing variously as saviours of the Greeks, as their heirs, and, by contrast, as their guardian elder brothers, Russians have repeatedly drawn on the resources of a shared Orthodox faith. Since the "Greekness" of Rus' Christianity was, as Simon Franklin observes, "quite literally built in" from the start, showpiece churches echoing the architecture of Constantinople stand as monuments to this millennial legacy even today.[1] Nevertheless, it would be a mistake always to accept rhetoric at face value. President Putin's visit to Mount Athos in May 2016 – a gesture nominally intended to commemorate a thousand years of the presence there of Russian monks – reminds us of religion's uses as a cloak for *raison d'état*. Nowhere has it been more obvious than in the troubled history of the Holy Mountain, that a common faith, even (perhaps especially) at its most fervent and sincere, brings with it not only affinities but also animosities liable to erupt into open conflict. Though such tensions were exacerbated by the growth of modern nationalism, there was nothing new about the sense that Greeks were foreign to Russians. Dimitri Obolensky, the author of a much-cited study of "the Byzantine Commonwealth", was himself careful to quote an anonymous Russian traveller, who admired the "wise Greek language" he was studying in the 15th century but found the Greeks themselves "difficult people, un-friendly and unloving".[2]

Exemplified by, though not confined to, a contentious denominational bond, the relationship between Russians and Greeks was never more intense than in the Age of Revolution. Taking that period to extend from the 1760s to the 1840s, this chapter falls into three chronological sections with its fulcrum in the years around 1821.[3] By then, the Greek diaspora had reached northward into the expanding tsarist empire in a myriad of ways: through bands of sailors and Black Sea corsairs; through commercial networks with hubs first in Nezhin (present-day Nizhyn, in north-eastern Ukraine) then Odessa, named after Odysseus in 1794; and more ethereally in the Russian political imagination inspired, like the new city itself, by the celebrated "Greek Project" of Catherine II (r. 1762-96). In 1821, the Russians again turned southward to play a correspondingly kaleidoscopic role in the Greek struggle for independence; some joined the army of liberation led by

126　*Simon Dixon*

Alexandros Ypsilantis (1792–1828) on its march through Moldavia and Wallachia, others co-ordinated humanitarian relief for Greek refugees, still more yearned to realize the sorts of Philhellenic dream that inspired classically educated elites all over Europe and carried particularly plangent overtones for Russian liberals nervous of tsarist despotism. However, it was in the three decades after 1821 that the relationship between Greece and Russia was at its most complex and most significant. Alarmed by revolutionary challenges to Restoration monarchy, represented in Russia by the Decembrist movement (a partial and notably less successful parallel to the revolutionary *Philiki Etaireia*), the Russian autocracy nevertheless played a pivotal role in securing the international stability of the emergent Greek state and in settling its internal ecclesiastical establishment. Each of these moves was made under the umbrella of a mutual commitment to ecumenical Orthodoxy. Yet, to translate that commitment into readily compatible institutional terms proved to be a challenge beyond the diplomatic and intellectual resources of both governments and of both national churches.

By the end of the 17th century, a flourishing Balkan commercial network already extended, in vermicular fashion, in a line stretching north-eastward from Kastoria via Bucharest, Jassy, and Kiev to Moscow, where several wealthy merchants profited from the slave trades with Constantinople. The key link in the chain was Nezhin, where a "Brotherhood of the Greeks" was formally granted religious and trading privileges in either 1696 or 1697. Although the official language of the brotherhood's institutions was Greek, this was only the second tongue of many of its members, who styled themselves *Romioi*, or Orthodox Christians of the Ottoman Empire. References in Russian documents to Moldavian Greeks, Wallachian Greeks, Bulgarian Greeks, and occasionally simply "Serbs", suggest that "Greek" was a blanket term, conveniently encompassing all Orthodox merchants while revealing little about the ethnic origins which were probably not central to their identity.[4]

In much the same way that "Greek" merchants at the beginning of the 18th century were willing to accept whatever political protection might guarantee a profitable trade, it still made sense at the end of the century for a variety of multi-ethnic Mediterranean and Balkan intellectuals to seek the patronage of whichever powerful sovereign seemed most likely to fulfil their political ambitions. To a moderate liberal, such as the Corfiot Ioannis Capodistrias (1776–1831), an Italian-speaking Orthodox who learned modern Greek only in his twenties, it initially seemed plausible to trust that Alexander I (r. 1801–25) would prove not only a bastion against Jacobinism but a guarantor of evolutionary constitutionalism and even a degree of national self-determination. Working in St Petersburg alongside the Phanariot circle of the Moldavian Alexandre Stourdza (1791–1854), Capodistrias enjoyed a meteoric rise from the time of his first meeting with the tsar in 1813. Between 1815 and 1822, he served jointly with Karl Nesselrode (1780–1862) as Russia's foreign minister until Alexander's

Russia and Greece in the Age of Revolution   127

refusal to support the Greek Revolution effectively terminated his career. Having retired to Geneva to support the moderate Greek cause, Capodistrias was formally dismissed from Russian service only in 1827, when he declined an olive branch from Nicholas I (r. 1825–55) and instead became the inaugural president of the Greek republic.[5]

Although the Age of Revolution placed unprecedented pressure on dual loyalties in all Europe's multi-national empires – the relationship of the Hungarian Count Isztván Széchenyi to Austria is a signal case in point[6] – many of the conditions that shaped Greek attitudes to Russia were of comparatively recent vintage. Indeed, for Capodistrias and his generation, almost all the crucial developments were products of their own lifetime. Followed by the annexation of the Crimea in 1783 and a further triumph against the Ottomans in 1787–92, the treaty of Kuchuk-Kaindardji, which sealed Catherine's victory in the Russo-Turkish War of 1768–74, created a vast field of opportunity in New Russia, seized by the empress's mercurial viceroy and former lover, Prince G.A. Potemkin (1738–91). So desperate was Potemkin to populate the empty steppes that he would have founded a British penal colony there had he not been thwarted by Count S.R. Vorontsov (1744–1832), ambassador in London between 1785 and 1806. Instead, a variety of incentives attracted an improbable influx of Swedes, Moldavians, and Armenians, mostly from Bessarabia. "Albanians" and other Greeks flourished at Taganrog, to which some members of the Nezhin brotherhood were drawn as foreign trade expanded; the Crimean Greek community in the new town of Mariupol, on the northern shore of the Sea of Azov, still flourished at the end of the Russian old regime. In 1801, Greeks formed the vanguard of a further wave of settlers brought to Odessa and the former Turkish colony near Nikolaev under the auspices of the New Russian Guardianship Office established the year before.[7]

In keeping with the empress's pragmatic religious policy, two Corfiot Greeks were appointed to minister to their immigrant flock in a new diocese of Slaviansk and Kherson, founded in 1775. "With this name", Catherine declared, "we are also renewing those most famous designations that Russia conserves from the depths of antiquity, that our people is of one stock and a direct offshoot of the ancient Slavs, and that Kherson was the source of Christianity for Russia".[8] Four years later, Nikiphoros Theotokis (1731–1800), who dreamed of an "Orthodox commonwealth" in succession to Byzantium, was consecrated archbishop in succession to Evgenios Voulgaris (1716–1806), whose seat was originally at Poltava. Though both prelates risked the ire of the more ardent Greek patriots by preaching loyalty to Russia among restive Greek communities, Theotokis found Catherine's government predictably equivocal when he sought to resist the pretensions of the Armenian clergy following his translation to Astrakhan in 1787.[9] In Voulgaris, the empress discovered an inquiring mind, whose refined spirituality was formed, like that of her favourite prelate, Platon (Levshin) (1737–1812), in dialogue with the secular Enlightenment.[10] In return for her

128   *Simon Dixon*

patronage, Voulgaris offered unquestioning fealty and temptation on a larger scale. "It is the most precious moment of my life'" he assured Catherine when first presented to her in July 1771, "in which I am favoured to pay my most profound respect toward the devout, Christ-loving divinely invincible Great Empress of the Russians (would that Ye be also of the Greeks!)".[11]

In Greece itself, such developments served to strengthen what Paschalis Kitromilides has called "the Russian expectation" – the widespread conviction that Russia would rescue the Greeks from captivity by incorporating them into a revived and reconstituted Christian empire. Founded on an unstable amalgam of popular millenarianism and international power politics, "the Russian expectation" combined a demotic trust in the liberating potential of a fabled "blonde" people from the North with the growing realization that Russia had supplanted Austria and Venice as the power most likely to thwart the Ottomans. First expressed in oracular pronouncements in the 1750s, the notion reached its apogee in the work of Voulgaris, whose translation of Catherine II's *Instruction* portrayed the empress as a just and benevolent monarch whose methods could profitably be extended beyond Russia's borders.[12]

If such exaggerated expectations reached fantastic proportions, then the Russians had only themselves to blame. A network of agents across the Balkans – what the 19th century came to call "Russian propaganda" – persistently insinuated rumours of an invasion. Catherine II herself helped to stoke the flames as early as 1762, when, anxious to emphasize her Orthodox credentials in the wake of her coup, she told an Albanian Greek officer introduced to her shortly after her accession that she was keen "to attack the enemy of the Orthodox faith" and "to liberate the Greeks living under the Ottoman yoke".[13] When the opportunity came in 1768, with the onset of a Turkish war triggered by events in Poland,[14] she promptly dispatched a fleet under the command of Admiral G.A. Spiridov (1713–1790), acting as a proxy for her commander-in-chief, Count A.G. Orlov (1737–1808). Plausibly ranked as "one of the most spectacular events of the eighteenth century",[15] the appearance of three squadrons of Russian ships in the eastern Mediterranean soon generated equally audacious results. However, the destruction of the Turkish fleet at Chesme in July 1770 owed nothing to the Greeks, for despite Orlov's attempts to foment revolt in the Peloponnese as the prelude to a series of Russian landings, the result was an embarrassing squib, rapidly extinguished by Ottoman troops.

Mutual recriminations soon followed. The Greeks resented the puny Russian invasion force; Orlov in turn denounced them as greedy flatterers who paid only lip-service to their faith "and have no trace in their hearts of Christian virtue'"[16] The empress shared his sense of disillusion. Where once she had spoken of liberty (*volnost'*) for the Greeks – an aspiration that pleased Voltaire and excited the attention of the Italian press[17] – now these "unworthy" people merited only "possession" (*vladenie*) or "protection" *(pokrovitel'stvo)*. They received it, in return for taxes and supplies, in the form of an impromptu settlement, framed on the spot by Spiridov in characteristically paternalist terms. Spiridov's short-lived "Archipelago principality" bore scant resemblance to the dream of building in Greece "something like the Dutch states" expressed by Count N.I. Panin (1718–1783), foreign minister in all but name.[18] Yet, after its demise in 1775, it left in its wake a new generation of Greeks, experienced in Russian administration and keen to progress in tsarist service. Grigorios (Anton Konstantinovich) Psaro, a native of Mykonos presented to Catherine on her tour of New Russia in 1787, reached the rank of rear-admiral by combining naval and diplomatic expertise on Malta.[19] At a less exalted but equally important level, the recruitment of irregular Greek privateers raised questions about Russia's engagement with international maritime law, a secular discourse which arguably became as significant to the relationship between Russia and Greece in the nineteenth century as the framework of ecumenical Orthodoxy.[20]

In Russia, meanwhile, the cultural activity stimulated by Spiridov's naval expedition had taken on a life of its own. Long before Catherine set out her "Greek Project" to Joseph II in September 1782, poets had given literary expression to an idea heralded by the christening of her grandsons: Constantine (b. 1779), whose birth was commemorated by a medallion of Hagia Sophia, and before him Alexander (b. 1777), whose name combined echoes of the medieval warrior saint, Alexander Nevsky, with those of Alexander the Great, a convenient means of escape from classical Greece's republican associations. "In the 'Greek Project's' system of coordinates", as Andrei Zorin puts it, "religious succession was equated with the cultural, as if by default. Hence Constantinople and Athens were marked as equivalent and by definition Russia's role as the single heir to the Byzantine church also made her the only indisputably legitimate heir to classical Greek culture".[21]

Catherine's "Greek Project" envisaged not the fusion of Russia and Byzantium, but the creation of a new Greek empire ruled by her grandson Constantine, provided that he renounced any claim to the Russian throne. Nevertheless, the idea explicitly entailed the destruction of the Ottoman Empire. So it bears emphasis that Russia's next intervention in the Greek world was achieved under the terms of an improbable alliance with the Turks, concluded in 1799 by Catherine's son, Tsar Paul (r. 1796–1801). It is also worth stressing that, whereas Spiridov had made little impression on administrative practice in the Archipelago, and Alexander I's subsequent attempt to standardize the status of both Greek and Muslim elites in the Crimea similarly foundered on the resilience of established clan networks,[22] the Septinsular Republic was altogether more innovative. Notably more liberal than its aristocratic predecessor, the constitution introduced under Russian protection in 1803 inspired Capodistrias' admiration for Alexander I and led others to share his hope that Corfu might form the cradle of a Greek national renaissance. It was not to be. In 1806, Russia was obliged to

130   *Simon Dixon*

cede the Ionian Islands to France, thereby capitulating to the very power that the principal inspiration of the Republic's constitution, the tsar's Philhellenic 'young friend' Adam Czartoryski (1770–1861), had been determined to resist.[23]

With little to show for their investments in the Mediterranean since 1768, the Russians had neither motive nor opportunity to renew their interest until the defeat of Napoleon created conditions in which Greeks could again dream of independence. The bustling port of Odessa provided cover for a group of far from affluent diaspora merchants to germinate a secret Friendly Society, the *Philiki Etaireia*. Founded in 1814 to foment a Greek-led rising of all Balkan Christians, the society built a network as active in Russia as it was in the Danubian Principalities and the Peloponnese. By 1821, it claimed some 1,100 members, testing initiates with its own revolutionary catechism. But it failed to recruit Capodistrias, whose sympathies extended only as far as the philanthropic Society of Friends of the Muses (*Philomousos Etaireia*).[24] So instead, the conspirators turned to Ypsilantis, the Moldavian landowner who, in March 1821, led them over the River Pruth on their projected march to Athens, more than 650 miles away. Much as the Russians had done in the Peloponnese in 1770, so Ypsilantis now relied on spontaneous uprisings to ease his path. However, weakened by limited planning and by gratuitous anti-Turkish violence, his supporters were routed by Ottoman troops. Meanwhile, in the contemporaneous uprising among Greeks in the Peloponnese, atrocities on both sides threatened the start of a long and bloody conflict.[25] How would Russians react?

In revenge for these uprisings on the periphery of their empire, the Ottomans turned on the Phanariot elite at its heart.[26] When they condemned to death Mikhail Bazili, whose Albanian father had a history of anti-Ottoman agitation, the Russian ambassador in Constantinople, Count G.A. Stroganov (1770–1857), gave him sanctuary and eased his escape, first to Trieste and then to Odessa. Mikhail's son Konstantin (1809–84) went on to become Russia's leading diplomat in the Middle East as consul (from 1843, consul general) in Syria between 1838 and 1853.[27] Countless smaller fry benefited equally from Russian protection. The chief procurator of the Holy Synod and minister of education, Prince A.N. Golitsyn (1773–1844), mobilized both secular and ecclesiastical authorities to raise millions of roubles to ransom prisoners taken into Muslim slavery after the massacre at Chios and to relieve the Ottoman Christians who fled to Ukraine after the Turks hanged Patriarch Grigorios V at Easter 1821. Masterminded by the growing network of Russian consuls in the Ottoman Empire, many of them native Greeks, this operation has plausibly been classed as "one of the first state-driven humanitarian interventions of the nineteenth century".[28]

The Decembrists, the Russian secret society which developed in parallel to the *Philiki Etaireia*, remained socially narrower in its membership and ideologically divided in its aims. Nevertheless, its leaders included several committed Philhellenes, of whom none was more fervent than Kondratii

Ryleev (1795–1826), a constitutional monarchist who sanctioned regicide. In 1821, Ryleev urged General A.P. Ermolov to order his men to "rush to save the sons of Hellas". That same year, the poem "Desert" (*Pustynia*) expressed Ryleev's own frustrated longing to join the campaign. "War seethes! In the Morea a flame blazes! Raising the banner of freedom, the Greek seeks revenge against the Ottoman. But I have not the power to fly as an arrow where my soul flies." The political views of Aleksandr Pushkin (1799–1837), who was not a Decembrist but who had met Ypsilantis and other members of the *Philiki Etaireia* in Kishinev, defy easy summary because they were never systematically expressed. However, as he told his Philhellenic friend Vasilii Davydov in March 1821, the "big question" was, "What is Russia going to do? Shall we seize Moldavia and Wallachia under the guise of peace-loving mediators? Shall we cross beyond the Danube as allies of the Greeks and as enemies of their enemies?"[29]

Sensing a greater threat to peace than at any time since 1815, much of Europe anticipated a Russian invasion of which some would certainly have approved. As London's *Morning Chronicle* complained in November 1821, "The language now is – Russia must have this, Russia must have that – it is better for the world, for civilisation, and for Greece itself, Russia should possess it."[30] This, the paper warned, was a "specious argument", and suspicions of Russian motives merely intensified when, against all odds, no invasion came. As Lord Byron inimitably put it in *The Age of Bronze* (1823):

> These, these shall tell the tale, and Greece can shew
> The false friend worse than the infuriate foe.
> But this is well: Greeks only should free Greece,
> Not the barbarian, with his mask of peace.
> How should the Autocrat of Bondage be
> The king of serfs, and set the nations free?
> Better still serve the haughty Mussulman,
> Than swell the Cossaque's prowling caravan;
> Better still toil for masters, than await,
> The slave of slaves before a Russian gate, –[31]

It was not that Russia lacked a 'war party'. On the contrary, hawks almost certainly dominated the elite. Capodistrias, their leading spokesman, was backed in St Petersburg by Stourdza. At the Constantinople embassy, Stroganov scarcely sought to conceal his sympathies for the Greeks; neither did several army generals.[32] In the event, however, their hopes foundered on the stubborn resistance of Alexander I. No matter how stoutly Stourdza argued that it was wrong to equate Greek rebels with other revolutionaries because that would place Christian monarchs on the same level as the sultan, Alexander, egged on by Metternich, continued to regard Ypsilantis's insurrection as part of a broader conspiracy, which he imagined to be centrally directed from Paris. In a letter brimming with what his latest biographer

132 *Simon Dixon*

calls "paranoid overtones", the tsar complained to his friend Golitsyn that the plotters must deliberately have intended "to create a diversion for the benefit of Naples and to prevent us from destroying one of the synagogues of Satan, established for the sole purpose of preaching and diffusing his anti-Christian teaching".[33]

At a more positive level, Alexander refused to act unilaterally because he was determined to uphold the collective approach to European affairs he had done so much to inspire at the Congress of Vienna.[34] Whatever loyalty he may have owed to Russian Orthodoxy was overshadowed by the supranational mysticism that underpinned his Holy Alliance, an international coalition under the ultimate sovereignty of the one true Christ. Only belatedly did it dawn on the tsar that his self-restraint had played into rival hands. While others intrigued, Alexander reportedly told Nesselrode in a fit of self-righteousness tinged with bitterness about Metternich, he alone had remained pure. "I have pushed scruples so far as not to have a single wretched agent in Greece, not an intelligence agent even, and I have to be content with the scraps that fall from the table of my Allies."[35] Meanwhile, Alexander's failure to support the Greeks not only spelled the end of Capodistrias' Russian career but also heralded Stourdza's resignation in 1823. As a modern historian has remarked, to one who had seen the Holy Alliance as a means of promoting Christian political ideals, "abandoning Christians to the vengeance of infidels in the name of legitimism and the balance of power was the *reductio ad absurdum* of this conception".[36]

In the aftermath of the failed Decembrist Revolt, it rapidly emerged that Nicholas I cared even less for the rebellious Greeks than had his elder brother. However, the new tsar's priority was to undermine rather than destroy the Turks. And since it was compatible with Nesselrode's "weak neighbour" policy to see a small Christian polity harry the western fringe of the Ottoman Empire, Russia, having secured Britain's compliance through the St Petersburg Protocol of 4 April 1826, eventually sanctioned the creation of an independent Greek state.[37] Managing Russia's future relations with that state proved more difficult, with religion at the heart of the matter.[38] Across the Balkans, separatist political nationalism challenged the universalist values of the ecumenical Patriarchate in Constantinople.[39] The Russians, too, faced a growing dilemma. By mid-century, they were torn in Serbia and Bulgaria between loyalties to pan-Orthodoxy and pan-Slavism. In Greece, the problem was institutional rather than ethnic. Even though the national ecclesiastical establishment proclaimed in 1833 closely resembled the Russian Holy Synod, Russian diplomats and the Greek politicians who supported them found themselves paradoxically opposed to it because it was bound to undermine the fraternal pan-Orthodox framework in which all their wider aspirations were couched. Russia subsequently put pressure on the Bavarian King Othon to convert to Orthodoxy.[40] Neither campaign succeeded. Othon remained resolutely Roman Catholic and the Russian-backed Patriarchate proved unable to reverse the unilateral declaration of

Greek autocephaly. Even when Constantinople finally agreed a compromise that returned the schismatic Greek Church to the ecumenical fold in 1850, it remained an integral part of the state's apparatus.[41]

For a more effective assertion of Russian interests, we must move beyond the borders of the nascent Greek state to Mount Athos, which remained a key marker of the Greek diaspora and became an increasingly volatile flashpoint in the relationship between Russians and Greeks. Many a 19th-century traveller noticed on the hillside above Vatopedi monastery "the extensive and picturesque ruins of a college, now deserted, but which in the last century, when protected by Russia, and under the learned Eugenius Bulgari [Voulgaris] of Corfu, attained such reputation that more scholars resorted to it from all parts of the East than the building could lodge".[42] Much, indeed, had changed since the 1750s, an era of relative harmony between Russia and the patriarchate, when an academy directed by Voulgaris had briefly opened up the Holy Mountain to the ideas of Descartes, Leibniz, Wolff and John Locke.[43] Later in the 18th century, Athos became associated instead with the heyschastic tradition of the *Philokalia*, published in Russia in Slavonic translation in 1793, and diffused across the Slav world in the 19th century. Though the *Philokalia* has recently been portrayed as "an alternative 'Enlightenment'", Athos became increasingly identified with anti-intellectualism, and the primary focus of its relations with Russia turned to matters of money.[44]

Although the question of Russian financial support for the Athonite monasteries understandably figured during Spiridov's archipelago expedition,[45] it became particularly acute after 1821 thanks to the vengeance wreaked by Ottoman troops on monks who had abandoned the peninsula to support the Greek Revolution or remained there to tend to displaced refugees.[46] Though precise numbers were elusive, it seemed clear to travellers by the mid-1830s that physical damage had been accompanied by demographic depletion.[47] All the more reason for fund-raising abbots to welcome the appearance of the monk Anikita, formerly Prince S.A. Shirinskii-Shikhmatov (1783–1837), whose residence on the Holy Mountain in 1835 marked a significant moment in Russia's re-engagement with Athos.[48] Following the Russian occupation of Moldavia and Wallachia in 1828, the abbots' reliance on Russian protection intensified as they sought to secure their income from the Dedicated Monasteries. In this case, however, the reforming tsarist government proved more sympathetic to the Romanians than to the monks. In 1851, the Russian consul in Bucharest recommended the Greek clergy to take guard not against the government of the Principalities, "but against the *hegumens*, against that crowd of greedy people who live at the expense of the church and are interested in perpetuating the abuses".[49]

The advance of Russian interests on Athos, therefore, depended on less formal influences, notably in the person of the former Synodal official, A.N. Murav'ev (1806–74), who had awakened public interest the Orthodox East

134 *Simon Dixon*

with a repeatedly reprinted account of his *Journey to the Holy Places in 1830*.[50] Murav'ev's visit to Athos in 1849 came four years after a tour by the tsar's second son, Grand Duke Konstantin Nikolaevich (1827–92).[51] Both men sought to increase Russia's profile on the peninsula, if necessary at the expense of the Greeks, whose version of Orthodoxy seemed especially alien to the grand duke. After his first taste of it at the Greek churches of Constantinople, he reported to his father:

> The singing is inexpressibly awful. There is no regular chant at all. The choir, which is made up of boys, drawl and shout through the nose, so that to listen is simply dreadful. Not even in the lowest of our parish churches do they sing worse than in the metropolitan's church here. And the people stand in church even more appallingly: not one of them removes his red fez or black turban, and they all crowd around near the altar gates, paying no attention at all to this holy place. In the service itself, there were even some things completely contrary to our own ecclesiastical rite.

On Athos, it was a relief to retreat to the St Elijah skete, where "they say the service and sing completely like us", whereas at Bulgarian Zograph and Serbian Hilandar "they sing the intolerable Greek chant even though they serve the liturgy in Slavonic".[52]

Konstantin's visit to Athos prompted a flurry of diplomatic activity in 1845–46 when the Ionian monks of the monastery of St Paul complained to the British of a Russian-inspired intrigue.[53] Though some of the keener Greek patriots among them resented the fact that the Ionian Islands had been governed by Britain since 1815, the monks nevertheless recognized the benefits to be gained from British protection in the formidable person of Sir Stratford Canning, ambassador at Constantinople between 1842 and 1858. While their abbot paid court to Canning en route to the monastery's estates in Moldavia, the ambassador himself surprised his Russian counterpart by visiting Athos in 1850, when his wife offended traditional sensibilities by stepping onto the hallowed male preserve. Still shrouded in mystery, the episode exemplifies Canning's love of conspiracy. Its connection with mounting Anglo-Russian tensions is less clear, not least because the British Foreign Office regarded religion as an irritant rather than an inspiration in the formulation of policy.[54]

Greeks tempted to look northward between 1760 and 1850 saw Russia not only as a potential liberator but as a source of seemingly infinite financial largesse. It was also a land of commercial opportunity. For their part, Russians keen to populate New Russia and export its abundant grain regarded Greeks as promising colonists and essential Black Sea traders. To Catherine II and Potemkin, however, culture was as important as economics. Anxious to emphasize Russia's common European roots in ancient civilization, they carved out a distinctive role for their empire by claiming a unique

Russia and Greece in the Age of Revolution 135

line of descent from both classical Athens and Christian Byzantium. Whereas their "Greek Project" envisaged the ultimate destruction of the Ottoman empire, it proved both more practical and more advantageous to Russia to preserve it in a weakened form. So Greek independence ultimately resulted not from a Russian conquest of Constantinople, but from diplomatic negotiations between powers who each had something different to gain from the creation of a small Christian state in the Eastern Mediterranean. A shared commitment to Orthodoxy continued to provide the justification for all manner of collaborative ventures between Russia and Greece. However, religion proved an equally fertile source of disagreement, and while Alexander I initially seemed a plausible political patron for moderates such as Ioannis Capodistrias, the legitimist autocracy of Nicholas I could never guarantee autonomy for Greek liberals in the Age of Revolution.

Notes

1 Simon Franklin, "Identity and Religion", in *National Identity in Russian Culture: An Introduction*, eds Simon Franklin and Emma Widdis (Cambridge, 2004), 98.
2 Dimitri Obolensky, *The Byzantine Commonwealth: Eastern Europe, 500–1453* (London, 1974), 345.
3 For a survey distilling the scholarship of a lifetime, see G.L. Arsh, *Rossiia i bor'ba Gretsii za osvobozhdenie ot Ekateriny II do Nikolaia I* (Moscow, 2013). O.E. Petrunina, *Grecheskaia natsiia i gosudarstvo v XVIII-XIX v- Ocherki politicheskogo razvitiia* (Moscow, 2010), exemplifies the work of a later generation.
4 Iannis Carras, "Community for Commerce: An Introduction to the Nezhin Greek Brotherhood Focusing on its Establishment as a Formal Institution in the Years Between 1692 and 1710", in *Merchant Colonies in the Early Modern Period*, eds. Victor N. Zakharov, Gelina Harlaftis, and Olga Katsiardi-Hering (London, 2012), 141–156, 220–230. See also idem, "Connecting Migration and Identities: Godparenthood, Surety and Greeks in the Russian Empire (18th – Early 19th Centuries)", in *Across the Danube: Southeastern Europeans and Their Travelling Identities* (17th–19th C.), eds Olga Katsiardi-Hering and Maria A. Stassinopoulou (Leiden, 2017), 65–109.
5 On Capodistrias and Stourdza, start from Konstantina Zanou, *Transnational Patriotism in the Mediterranean, 1800–1850: Stammering the Nation* (Oxford, 2018), 94–97.
6 R. J. W. Evans, "Széchenyi and Austria", in *History and Biography: Essays in Honor of Derek Beales*, eds T. C. W. Blanning and David Cannadine (Cambridge, 1996), 113–141.
7 Roger P. Bartlett, *Human Capital: The Settlement of Foreigners in Russia 1762–1804* (Cambridge, 1979), 124–142, 205–212.
8 Andrei Zorin, *By Fables Alone: Literature and State Ideology in Late-Eighteenth-Early-Nineteenth Century Russia*, transl. Marcus C. Levitt (Boston, 2014), 102. Of the two projected new towns, only Kherson was built.
9 Stephen K. Batalden, *Catherine II's Greek Prelate: Eugenios Voulgaris in Russia, 1771–1806* (Boulder, CO, 1982), 65–71; Gregory L. Bruess, *Religion, Identity and Empire: A Greek Archbishop in the Russia of Catherine the Great* (Boulder, CO, 1997), 194–197.
10 See Iannis Carras, "Understanding God and Tolerating Humankind: Orthodoxy and Enlightenment in Evgenios Voulgaris and Platon Levshin", in *Enlightenment*

136 *Simon Dixon*

and Religion in the Orthodox World, ed. Paschalis M. Kitromilides, Oxford University Studies in the Enlightenment, 2016:02 (Oxford, 2016), 73–139.

11 Batalden, *Catherine II's Greek Prelate*, 22–23.

12 Paschalis M. Kitromilides, *Enlightenment and Revolution: The Making of Modern Greece* (Cambridge, MA, 2013), 120–133. On the earlier period, see Nikolas Pissis, *Russland in den politischen Vorstellungen der griechischen Kulturwelt 1645–1725* (Berlin, 2020).

13 Elena Smilianskaia, "Catherine's Liberation of the Greeks: High-Minded Discourse and Everyday Realities", in *Word and Image in Russian History: Essays in Honour of Gary Marker*, eds Maria Di Salvo, Daniel H. Kaiser, and Valerie A. Kivelson (Boston, MA, 2015), 71–89, quoted at page 74, distills some of the conclusions of the massive I. M. Smilianskaia, M. B. Velizhev, E. B. Smilianskaia, *Rossiia v Sredizemnomor'e: Arkhipelagskaia Ekspeditsiia Ekateriny Velikoi* (Moscow, 2011).

14 As David Abulafia notes, 'a consistent feature' of Russia's Mediterranean projects between 1768 and 1806 'was the way they originated beyond the Mediterranean': *The Great Sea: A Human History of the Mediterranean* (London, 2011), 503–523, quoted at page 509.

15 M. S. Anderson, 'Great Britain and the Russo-Turkish War of 1768–1774', *English Historical Review* 69 (1954): 44.

16 Isabel de Madariaga, *Russia in the Age of Catherine the Great* (London, 1981), 210.

17 See Franco Venturi, *La rivolta greca dei 1770 e il patriottismo dell'età dei lumi* (Rome, 1986), and idem, *The End of the Old Regime in Europe, 1768–1776* (Princeton, NJ, 1989).

18 Smilianskaia, Velizhev, and Smilianskaia, *Rossiia v Sredizemnomor'e*, 148–161.

19 I.M. Zakharova, "Anton Konstantinovich Psaro", *Voprosy istorii* (2015), no. 11: 19–33.

20 Julia Leikin, "'The Prostitution of the Russian Flag': Privateers in Russian Admiralty Courts, 1787–1798', *Law and History Review* 35 (2017): 1049–1079, heralds her major re-assessment of the significance of international law in Russia.

21 Zorin, *By Fables Alone*, ch. 1, quoted at pp. 27–28.

22 Kelly O'Neill, *Claiming Crimea: A History of Catherine the Great's Southern Empire* (New Haven, CT, 2017), 107–109.

23 A. M. Stanislavskaia, *Rossiia i Gretsiia v kontse XVIII-nachale XIX veka. Politika Rossiia v Ionicheskoi respublike 1798–1807 gg.* (Moscow, 1976); W. H. Zawadzki, *A Man of Honour: Adam Czartoryski as a Statesman of Russia and Poland 1795–1831* (Oxford, 1993), 75–77, 95–98; Zanou, *Transnational Patriotism*, 75–82.

24 Since this was a fruitful subject for a Soviet historian, G. L. Arsh, *Eteristskoe dvizhenie v Rossii* (Moscow, 1970), remains fundamental. See also Richard Stites, *The Four Horsemen: Riding to Liberty in Post-Napoleonic Europe* (Oxford and New York, 2014), 192–197.

25 Stites, *Four Horsemen*, 197–222, is a brilliantly evocative account.

26 Christine M. Philliou, *Biography of an Empire: Governing Ottomans in an Age of Revolution* (Berkeley, CA, 2011), 65–74.

27 See K.M. Bazili, *Siriia i Palestina pod turetskim pravitel'stvom* (Jerusalem and Moscow, 2007), 8–10, Preface by I. M. Smilianskaia.

28 Theophilus C. Prousis, *Russian Society and the Greek Revolution* (DeKalb, IL, 1994), 55–83; Lucien J. Frary, "Slaves of the Sultan: Russian Ransoming of Christian Captives during the Greek Revolution, 1821–1830", in *Russian-Ottoman Borderlands: The Eastern Question Reconsidered*, eds Lucien J. Frary and Mara Kozelsky (Madison, WI, 2014), 101–130, quoted at page 103.

Russia and Greece in the Age of Revolution   137

29 Prousis, *Russian Society*, 111–112, 141. On Ryleev's civic poetry, see Patrick O'Meara, *K. F. Ryleev: A Political Biography of the Decembrist Poet* (Princeton, NJ, 1984), ch. 5.

30 *Morning Chronicle*, 2 November 1821, p. 2.

31 [George Gordon Byron, 6th Baron Byron] *The Age of Bronze* (London, 1823), 17, lines 296–305. I owe this reference to my colleague, Dr. Thomas Lorman.

32 Prousis, *Russian Society*, 32–54. On the army, see Alexander Bitis, *Russia and the Eastern Question: Army, Government and Society, 1815–1833* (Oxford, 2006).

33 Marie-Pierre Rey, *Alexander I: The Tsar who Defeated Napoleon*, transl. Susan Imanuel (DeKalb, IL, 2012), 343.

34 Paul W. Schroeder, *The Transformation of European Politics 1763–1848* (Oxford, 1994), 619–621.

35 Janet M. Hartley, *Alexander I* (Harlow, 1994), 160.

36 Alexander M. Martin, *Romantics, Reformers, Reactionaries: Russian Conservative Thought and Politics in the Reign of Alexander I* (DeKalb, IL, 1997), 196.

37 Schroeder, *Transformation*, 642–664.

38 Lucian J. Frary, *Russia and the Making of Modern Greek Identity, 1821–1844* (Oxford, 2015), is exceptionally well documented.

39 For a penetrating analysis, sympathetic to the Patriarchate, see Paschalis M. Kitromilides, *Religion and Politics in the Orthodox World: The Ecumenical Patriarchate and the Challenges of Modernity* (London, 2019), 6, 34–35.

40 Dimitris Stamatopoulos, "The Orthodox Church of Greece", in *Orthodox Christianity and Nationalism in Nineteenth-Century Southeastern Europe*, ed. Lucian N. Leustean (New York, 2014), 37–47.

41 Yanni Kotsonis, 'Russia and the Greek Revolution', *Kritika: Explorations in Russian and Eurasian History* 19 (2018): 666.

42 George Ferguson Bowen, *Mount Athos, Thessaly, and Epirus: Diary of a Journey from Constantinople to Corfu* (London, 1852), 64. Bowen was president of the Greek University of Corfu (1847–51) and returned there as chief secretary to the government of the Ionian Islands in 1854.

43 Paschalis M. Kitromilides, "Athos and the Enlightenment", in *Mount Athos and Byzantine Monasticism*, eds A. A. M. Bryer and Mary Cunningham (Aldershot, 1996), 257–272.

44 Compare John Anthony McGuckin, "The Making of the *Philokalia*: A Tale of Monks and Manuscripts", in *The* Philokalia*: A Classic Text of Orthodox Spirituality*, eds. Brock Bingaman and Bradley Nassif (New York, 2012), 36–49, and Andrew Louth, "The Influence of the *Philokalia* in the Orthodox World", ibid., 50–60 with Dimitrios Moschos, "An Alternative 'Enlightenment': The *Philokalia*", in *Enlightenment and Religion*, ed. Kitromilides, 63–72.

45 E. B. Smilianskaia, "Afonskie kontakty Pervoi arkhipelagskoi ekspeditsii 1769–1775 gg. i delo stranstvuiushchego inoka greka Nikolaia Mikhailova", in *Rossiia i Khristianskii Vostok, vyp. IV–V* (Moscow, 2015), 474–488.

46 Charles A. Frazee, *The Orthodox Church and Independent Greece 1821–1852* (Cambridge, 1969), 40–41. For a contemporary "Narrative of the Capture of the Holy Mount Athos by the Ottomans in 1821", see Tendrafil Krastanov, "From the History of the Athonite Monasteries in 1821", *Bulgarian Historical Review* 22 (1994): 96–100.

47 Lieut. Webber Smith, "On Mount Athos and its Monasteries; with Notes on the route from Constantinople to Saloniki, in June 1836", *Journal of the Royal Geographical Society* 7 (1837), 72. See also, *Description du Mont Athos, par Minoïde Mynas (1842)*, ed. Henry Omont (Paris, 1917), 8–9.

138   *Simon Dixon*

48 *Puteshestvie Ieromonakha Anikity po sviatym mestam Vostoka v 1834–1836 godakh*, ed. G. A. Shpet (Moscow, 2009). In 1836, Anikita served briefly as chaplain to the Russian embassy at Athens.
49 Barbara Jelavich, *Russia and the Romanian National State* (Cambridge, 1984), 132–133.
50 [A.N. Murav'ev], *Puteshestvie ko Sviatym mestam v 1830 godu*, 4th ed., (St Petersburg, 1840).
51 See *Andrei Nikolaevich Murav'ev i rossiiskaia diplomatiia na Pravoslavnom Vostoke: Diplomaticheskie zapiski i perepiska*, ed. I.Iu. Smirnova (Moscow, 2019), 82–87. Dr. Smirnova's study of Murav'ev's engagement with Mount Athos is eagerly awaited.
52 Quoted in Vsevolod Voronin, "Velikii kniaz' Konstantin Nikolaevich na pravoslavnom Vostoke i arabskom Zapade v seredine 1840-kh gg", *Rossiiskaia istoriia* no. 2 (2019): 85, 92.
53 See reports to the British embassy in Constantinople between 12 February 1845 and 28 December 1846 by Charles Blunt, British consul at Thessaloniki, The National Archives, London, FO 195/240, fols. 265, 358, 426, 523, 714.
54 I.Iu. Smirnova, *Rossiia i Angliia v Sviatoi Zemle v kanun Krymskoi voiny* (Moscow, 2015), 299–312, leans toward a more sinister interpretation.

10 The decade prior to the Greek Revolution: A black hole in Ottoman history

H. Şükrü Ilıcak

From an Ottomanist's perspective, the decade preceding the Greek Revolution constitutes a black hole. Although full to the brim with events bringing about momentous changes in the fabric of the Ottoman polity, this is one of the most understudied periods of Ottoman history. What marked this decade was the reframing of the boundaries between the Ottoman central state and its provinces in the aftermath of the Russo-Ottoman War of 1806–1812. The shift in the balance of power from the provinces to the imperial center did not only prove devastating to large sections of the empire but also had immediate consequences for the fate of the Greek Revolution. A brief examination of the history of the Ottoman central state's turbulent relations with its provincial power brokers is necessary in order to have a better understanding of this decade.[1]

In the second half of the 18th century, the Ottoman central state's survival strategies against Russian expansion came to determine virtually all aspects of its political, military, administrative, and financial choices and practices. Since 1677, there had been seven Russo-Ottoman wars, the last three of which led to the Ottoman Empire's loss of strategic territories (northern Caucasus, northern shore of the Black Sea, and eastern part of Moldavia), significant resources, manpower, and – perhaps more importantly – its standing with its non-Muslim subjects.

It was in the Russo-Ottoman War of 1768–1774 that the Sublime Porte's military and financial dependence on Muslim provincial power brokers (who will be subsumed under the umbrella term *ayan*) became established. The war with Russia and the ensuing Treaty of Küçük Kaynarca were arguably the most catastrophic events that had befallen the Ottoman Empire in the last centuries, turning the question of its disintegration from a European fantasy into a realizable prospect. With this war, the Russian Empire had not only fundamentally changed the European balance of power but had also become the gravest danger to the abode of Islam, the nightmare of the Sublime Porte and the empire of the rhyming *"Rūs-u menhūs"* (the accursed Russian) of Ottoman chroniclers, threatening the very existence of the Ottoman Empire.

In the following half-century, arguably all operations of the Ottoman state to regulate the *ayanlık* (*ayan*hood) were done and then undone due to the Russian wars, which were increasingly fought by the soldiers recruited by the *ayans*.[2] It had become a matter of life or death for the central state to mobilize the *ayans*' resources whenever the need arose. Yet, not every *ayan* had the same level of allegiance to the imperial center or the same level of interest in tapping his resources for the protection of "religion and state (*din ü devlet*)", the most conclusive argument advanced by the Sublime Porte to keep the *ayans* within the imperial framework. Responding to the Sublime Porte's calls for help was costly and, as many official documents attest, was avoided by the *ayans* to the best of their abilities.

It seems that by 1798, when the Sublime Porte proved unable to suppress Pazvandoğlu Osman, the insurgent *ayan* of Vidin, despite an eight-month siege laid by 80,000 men, and was finally humbled into granting him the title of pasha the following year, the Ottoman Empire had practically become a confederation of the Ottoman central state with provincial magnates. It can also be argued that the *Sened-i İttifak* of 1808 – which is called the Ottoman Magna Carta by many historians and came into force in the midst of yet another war with Russia (of 1806–1812) – was designed to give this confederation a legal basis, indicating to each actor in Ottoman politics his due place.[3]

The Russian war of 1806–1812 began when French victories over the Russian and Austrian empires fueled revanchist Ottoman aspirations. Until the fourth year of the war, the *ayans* mobilized considerable resources. However, heavy defeats inflicted on the Ottoman armies made the *ayans* ever more independent and less responsive to the Sublime Porte's demands. There is enough evidence to suggest that the *ayans* gave the Ottoman central state little chance of surviving the war with Russia. Especially after 1808, the magnates' actions reflected their outlook, namely, that they were free agents in a dissolving empire, and that they could not and did not wish to rely upon, nor lend their military and financial support to the Sublime Porte. Not only did very few *ayans* briefly engage themselves with the *Sened-i İttifak* regime; during the six years of intermittent warfare, even minor *ayans* constructed castles and fortifications, acquired canons, ignored the Sublime Porte's orders to join the imperial army, built private armies by attracting vagabond elements, and ventured to extend their influence over the neighboring territories.

The Treaty of Bucharest (May 1812), which ended the war with Russia and Russia's revised nonaggressive imperial agenda in the post-Napoleonic world order brought about the favourable conditions for a certain clique at the Sublime Porte to set out to redefine its boundaries with the *ayans*. In order to establish a capable defense system, the Sublime Porte endeavored to save itself from being at the mercy of the *ayans* by uniting its borderlands under a central authority and by establishing a new provincial army under the command of imperial viziers, whose soldiers would not turn tail and flee when they faced the disciplined and bayonet-using Russian *soldats* and light artillery.

Hence, in February 1813, the Ottoman central state embarked upon a military and administrative project to reassert itself in the provinces. I suggest the term *de-ayanization* instead of centralization for this proceeding, because, while what was destroyed and dismantled is apparent (e.g. the elimination of an *ayan* or of his entire family and retinue), what exactly replaced the old structures appears to have varied according to the particular conditions in each province and did not necessarily result in establishing the authority of the central state. Besides, not every *ayan* was subdued, and not every subdued *ayan* was executed or exiled. "Re-imperialization" of local authority in the provinces was a gradual and complex nonlinear progression, which continued well into the 20th century. Thus, contrary to the Turkish statist historians' panegyric accounts, it is not possible to construct a narrative of linear centralization of provincial administration.[4]

The apparent head of the *de-ayanizing* clique at the Sublime Porte was Sultan Mahmud II's advisor, Halet Efendi, and, according to a well-informed contemporary, Marc-Philippe Zallony, the mastermind behind the project was Michail Soutsos, a young member of a prominent Fanariot dynasty.[5] The testimony of Zallony is the only piece of information linking *de-ayanization* to Soutsos, but it is well known in both Greek and Ottoman historiographies that Halet Efendi had close ties with him.

The *de-ayanization* project would be brought about through the re-allocation of the tax farms and various state revenues (*mukataas*) from the *ayans* to imperial viziers. With these revenues, the imperial viziers were to keep their retinues in good order, recruit soldiers, and head for their posts without delay.[6] Zallony provided a unique and more detailed account of Halet Efendi's vision; according to the plan, the territories that had hitherto been ruled by the *ayans* would be converted into 50 *pashaliks* of three horsetails. The imperial viziers would each raise at least 50,000 men with the immense wealth they would accumulate, put an end to the desolating battles amongst the "suzerain princes" [i.e. *ayans*], and most importantly, "in case of war, would raise an army of more than two million men for the state's disposal, which might give law to Europe and Asia."[7]

As of February 1813, only imperial governors and sub-governors (*sancak mutasarrıfı*) were allowed to bid in auctions for the *mukataas* in their appointed domains.[8] In theory, this revolutionary measure did not stipulate an overall overthrow of local power structures. In practice, however, transferring the *mukataa* revenues (in other words, the *ayans*' main source of financial, and thus, military and political power) from the magnates to imperial viziers, in most cases could only be carried out through force. The backbone of the imperial viziers' military man-power in most cases consisted of Albanian mercenaries. The project brought imperial viziers in direct confrontation with the provincial magnates and allowed the viziers to subject the locals to additional extortionary practices. This was the declared cause of many uprisings and complaints brought to the Sublime Porte in the following period.

142   *H. Şükrü Ilıcak*

What followed was, for all intents and purposes, a civil war between the Ottoman central state and a myriad of provincial power brokers of varying calibers, religions, ethnicities, and levels of popular support. Official Ottoman documents and chronicles allow us to trace dozens of urban and rural uprisings led by provincial power brokers throughout the empire, from Yemen to Wallachia, from Caucasia to Serbia, which ruined large sections of the empire. The extensive intra-magnate struggles only added to the anarchy that prevailed even in the provinces closest to the imperial capital.

Yet, this crucial decade has not attracted its due scholarly attention. While historians of several ex-Ottoman nationalities, especially the Serbs, Greeks, and Romanians, have dealt with this period from the perspective of their national narratives, there is not a single monograph, or even a comprehensive article, examining the concomitant empire-wide events and developments. Studies investigating the *ayan*s limit themselves to the death of the first and the last grand vizier of *ayan* origins, Alemdar Mustafa Pasha, and the subsequent end of the *Sened-i İttifak* regime in November 1808. Ottomanists have contributed mostly recycled remarks with minor modifications about the following decade, basing their works almost exclusively on the *History* of Cevdet, whose main source for the period was Şanizade's teleological (yet incomplete) account of the fate of the treacherous and rebellious *ayan*s. Thus, secondary sources briefly mention the period and cast the events within Mahmud II's recentralization efforts in the relative international peace atmosphere following the Treaty of Bucharest. Given that the Serbian *knez*es, the Greek *kapetanaioi* and *kotzabasi*s, the Kurdish *mir*s, the Moldowallachian *boyar*s, the Bosnian *kaptan*s, the Arab sheikhs and *emir*s, the Mamluks of Baghdad, the *ashraf* in Aleppo, the Wahhabis of the Arabian peninsula, numerous Arab, Laz, Caucasian and Albanian tribal chieftains, and all other provincial power-brokers who governed over non-Turkish peoples are not considered an essential part of the "imperial narrative", their resistance against the Ottoman central state's enterprise is either ignored or treated as isolated events of mere banditry. Thus, apart from brief passing remarks by Ariel Salzmann, this period has not been viewed as a civil war.[9]

The whole extent of the *de-ayanization* project and the exact number of its victims requires extensive research. To begin with, if we make an estimate based on the 153 ethnic-Turkish *ayan*s from Anatolia alone who were ordered to join the imperial army for the summer campaign of 1811 in the lower Danube region, the total number of provincial power brokers throughout the empire before the commencement of the project must have approached a four-digit figure.[10] Hence, it is impossible to follow the Sublime Porte's dealings with the provincial power brokers to the full extent. What is important to understand is the striking contrast between 1811 and 1823; for the first planned and somewhat coordinated military expedition of the Sublime Porte for the suppression of the Greek uprising in 1823, there was not a single Anatolian *ayan* in the Ottoman army encampment in

A black hole in Ottoman history   143

Larisa, and a mere 12,000 out of 50,000 soldiers had been recruited by the *ayans* of Rumelia. The only Anatolians in the encampment comprised freelance mercenary troops, totaling around 3,000 soldiers, and the rest were Albanian mercenaries.[11] Although the absence of the Anatolian *ayans* in the army does not mean that all of them had been exterminated in the preceding decade – as we still trace them in official documents – the figures are very telling about the consequences of the project.

"The *ayans*' tyranny" was central to the discourse in the official documents legitimating their elimination. Numerous mandates and decrees underscored that the common folk had been suffering at the hands of the usurpers (*mütegallibe*, i.e. the *ayans*) and would be salvaged by the re-establishment of imperial governors in the provinces. The voices of the suppressed provincial power brokers cannot be traced in the available sources; however, with the hindsight of several popular uprisings in their support, and the firmans issued to the imperial governors after 1815 to stop oppressing the people and focus on punishing the usurpers, we can talk about a discourse of "contested tyrannies" between the central state and the provincial power brokers.

The *de-ayanization* process gained impetus after the Congress of Vienna due to the Sublime Porte's conviction that Russia would not bring its issues with the Ottoman state to the point of aggression in the new order of international relations. Since the imperial center could not and did not pursue an all-out extermination campaign against the *ayans*, the transition took many shapes and forms over the course of the following decades. While the Sublime Porte managed to subdue some provinces, it simultaneously lost complete control over others.

It is not possible to follow every mutiny in detail. We learn about the uprisings of most minor provincial power brokers only when their severed heads made it to Istanbul or through the orders for the confiscation of their patrimony. Popular support to the provincial power brokers' resistance varied. In several provinces, the events were probably limited to the mutiny of the warlords and their men, and either eventually died away or were suppressed by the Sublime Porte. It seems that in some provinces the common folk were mere observers of the fight between the central state and the power brokers, whereas in others, especially in the non-Turkish provinces, the magnates found substantial popular support for their resistance against the Sublime Porte.[12]

Curiously, the most powerful *ayan* dynasties in Anatolia, the Cabbarzades and the Karaosmanzades, did not put up armed resistance when the Sublime Porte replaced their patriarchs and prominent figures with imperial agents and confiscated their *mukataa*s. Thanks to their compliance they were not fully eliminated. When the patriarch of the Cabbarzade dynasty, Süleyman Bey, passed away in December 1813, his domains were divided into two *sancak*s administered by imperial viziers.[13] At the death of the patriarch of the Karaosmanzades, Hacı Ömer Agha, the Superintendent of Timber in

İzmit, Osman Efendi took over the administration in the region. Their domains were fragmented into smaller parts and some were repurchased by family members.[14]

Several revolts that had their origins in the period before the beginning of the *de-ayanization* project flared up again in this period. The tribes of Kurdistan revolted in 1812, once again under the leadership of Babanzade Abdurrahman Pasha. In April 1815, the Second Serbian Uprising began against the rule of the Governor of Belgrade Maraşlı Ali Pasha and lasted for two years. In Arabia, the Wahhabis took up arms against the Sublime Porte several times between 1811 and 1818, and each time they were quelled by the Governor of Egypt.

The revolt of the Tuzcuoğlus – *ayan*s of the Laz regions, Rize and Hopa – began in 1814 and lasted for seven years, wreaking havoc to the Eastern Black Sea region. The uprising evolved into an all-out war, in which many imperial viziers and the Ottoman navy were also involved. Tuzcuoğlu Memiş Agha died in the meantime and the leadership of the revolt was taken up by his son-in-law until its suppression in 1821.[15]

The Nusayri tribes in the mountains of Lazkiye revolted several times in 1816 against the governor of Sidon, Süleyman Pasha. The mutiny ended abruptly with the execution of forty-nine Nusayri chieftains.[16]

In the summer of 1816, Khimshiashvili (Hamşizade) Ahmed Bey, the son of the ex-governor of Çıldır, Selim Sabit Pasha, making use of the ongoing strife in the south-western Caucasus since the Russian war, rallied the Muslim Georgian tribes of Adjara and also found collaborators in Ahıska (Akhaltsikhe) for his revolt. The Sublime Porte could not quell Ahmed Bey's revolt for several years and was obliged to pardon him due to his domain's proximity to the Russian border. By October 1821, Ahmed Bey was once again serving in the Ottoman army.[17]

A Greek provincial power broker, whose increasing influence and acts of disobedience in the Volos-Argalasti region that attracted the Sublime Porte's attention, was the Kapetan of Makrinitsa, Tanaş/Thanasis Basdekis.[18] Kapetan Basdekis had constructed castle-like stone towers in his domain and extended protection to the minor warlords and bandits in the region, threatening the security of the mountain defiles which were under Tepedelenli Ali Pasha's control. The Sublime Porte hastened to issue an order for the Kapetan's execution in the autumn of 1818, before Tepedelenli's possible occupation of the region. The order was carried out by local officials in December and Kapetan Basdekis's towers in Makrinitsa were demolished.[19]

In 1818, the locals of Sivas revolted against the governor Hacı Ali Pasha under the leadership of two city notables, Kenanoğlu Ahmed and Mütevellioğlu Mahmud. The rebels besieged the palace of the governor and the courthouse for 45 days. The revolt was quelled by Lütfullah Pasha, *mutasarrıf* of Karahisar, and the leaders of the rebellion were exiled to Cyprus, where they were executed.[20]

Between 1818 and 1820, three full-scale revolts broke out on the eastern fringes of the empire against the new governors sent to the provinces. The first rebellion took place in late 1818 by Derviş Mehmed Pasha, castellan of Van, whose authority relied on the Kurdish tribes of the region. After two years of verbal strife and correspondence geared to convince him to end his encroachments on rival Kurdish tribes, which eventually sought refuge in Iran, the Sublime Porte finally embarked on a punitive expedition. All imperial agents from Diyarbekir to Trabzon were mobilized against Mehmed Pasha and managed to quell his uprising in a matter of months.[21]

The second mass revolt broke out in Diyarbekir in the summer of 1819 against the new governor of the province, Behram Pasha, who reportedly announced to the city notables and the leader of the dominant clan, Şeyhzadeoğlu İbrahim, that "he was sent [by the state] to destroy them, to scatter their belongings [to the wind] and to burn their houses [to the ground]".[22] The town surrendered after a three-month siege, during which the entire city folk mobilized themselves to defend their town.

In October 1819, a revolt led by the notables of Aleppo (the *ashraf*) broke out against the extortions of the governor Hurşid Ahmed Pasha, who had been recently sent there to put the Kurdish, Bedouin, and Turcoman tribes of the region in order. The siege of Aleppo lasted for 101 days, leaving behind yet another scorched town and many executed local notables.[23] Upon his success against the locals of Aleppo, who, in the words of the Sultan, "had long got used to banditry",[24] Hurşid Pasha received orders to leave the region immediately and take charge of quelling the Tepedelenli Ali Pasha rebellion in Albania.

The Sublime Porte sent out two punitive expeditions against the dissident Greek power brokers of Mani in summer 1815 and autumn 1820. On both occasions, the main target was the Koumoundouraki clan and on both occasions, the rebellions were put down by the joint forces of the Chief-Kapetans of Mani and the Ottoman navy. The second expedition was triggered by the assassination of the uncle of Petros Mavromichalis, Bey of Mani, by the Koumoundourakis and the ensuing warfare among the rival clans. According to Petro Bey, the Koumoundourakis were in cahoots with Tepedelenli Ali Pasha and dared to revolt based on the latter's support.[25] Eventually, the patriarch of the Koumoundouraki clan, Thodoraki, was executed, the defensive towers in the region were demolished and the *kapetan*s of Mani tendered their allegiance to the Sublime Porte in writing. In less than a year, the clans of the peninsula would unite and rise up against the Sublime Porte and the *kapetan*s who were defined as bandits in Ottoman official documents would become prominent heroes of the Greek War of Independence.[26]

De-ayanization on the eve of the Greek Revolution: The Ali Pasha Revolt

In January 1820, Halet Efendi brought his associate Seyyid Ali Pasha to the grand vizierate and unleashed the most crucial stage of the

146   *H. Şükrü Ilıcak*

de-ayanization project, suppression of the legendary *mutasarrıf* of Ioannina, Tepedelenli Ali Pasha. In a smooth progression reminiscent of the establishment of the Ottoman state, Ali Pasha, a Tosk Albanian himself, had conquered the territories of the neighboring Albanian magnates one after another and carved out a state for his dynasty. He acquired Gjirokastër (Gr. Αργυρόκαστρο) and Libohovë (Gr. Λιμπόχοβο), through intermarriages of his family with the local magnates.[27] Taking advantage of the pandemonium of the Russian war, he captured Berat (Gr. Μπεράτι), Vlorë (Gr. Αυλώνας), Kardhiq (Gr. Γαρδίκι), Peqin (Gr. Πεκίν) from their *ayan*s and became the master of the entire Toskëria (i.e. the land of Tosk Albanians. Turk. *Toskalık*) by 1812.[28]

By capturing Tirana, Ohrid (Gr. Αχρίδα) and Elbasan (Gr. Ελμπασάν) between 1815 and 1817, Ali Pasha made himself a bold encroacher on the Gegëria (i.e. the land of Geg Albanians. Turk. Gegalık) and utterly annoyed both the Geg magnates and the Sublime Porte. The possibility of an all-out fight between the Tosks and the Gegs – which had been barely prevented in 1812 – became too great to ignore, when, in 1818, Tepedelenli embarked on a new aggrandizement project in the Gegëria. Bushati Mustafa Pasha, *mutasarrıf* of Shkodra and the patriarch of the predominant dynasty of the *Geg* Albanians, petitioned the Sublime Porte in panic and united most Geg tribes in an alliance for the suppression of Ali Pasha.[29]

The first reports from the Ottoman viziers on the battlefield against Tepedelenli attest to the fact that the Greek insurrection in the Morea began as an extension of the Tepedelenli revolt. In other words, to the Ottoman central state, the Greek uprising was initially one out of the many abovementioned provincial revolts. As early as January 1821, Hurşid Ahmed Pasha reported that the Tosk Albanians had revolted and their goal was to unite with the Greeks and march onto Ioannina in order to save Tepedelenli.[30] By 6 March 1821, Hurşid Ahmed Pasha had no doubt that the sedition of the Greeks in Mani was the work of Tepedelenli and there were signs of uprisings among the Greeks of the Morea.[31]

Conclusion

De-ayanization had a double effect on the Greek Revolution. First, the attempts at reasserting Ottoman imperialism provoked rebellions on the part of the provincial power brokers across religion and ethnicity. Can the Greek Revolution be considered as a link in the chain of ongoing uprisings throughout the Ottoman Empire? Mainstream historiography of the Greek Revolution is already a panegyric account of the deeds of the Greek magnates-*cum*-warlords. Although more recent Greek historiography tends to give more credit to the enlightened and politicized radical Greeks who shared the sparks of Enlightenment with the Greek magnates, it requires extensive research to assess how apprehensive were the *kotzabasis* and *kapetan*s of the Morea and Rumelia – namely the Greek provincial power

A *black hole in Ottoman history* 147

brokers who were the actual driving force of the Greek Revolution by providing the bulk of the fighting power – of the Sublime Porte's boundary shifting enterprise in the provinces, and whether they were waiting for their turn to come.

Secondly, *de-ayanization* had serious implications for troop recruitment. By 1821, the *de-ayanization* of Anatolia was almost complete and terminated in Rumelia due to the commencement of the Greek Revolution. The elimination of some of the most powerful provincial political and military brokers and their networks reduced the Sublime Porte's means of military recruitment. Provincial magnates were toppled hastily without replacing their networks and infrastructures with effective alternatives. Consequently, the imperial viziers who replaced the provincial magnates found it extremely difficult to recruit and mobilize soldiers against the Greek insurgents. Military human resources of Anatolia were so depleted that when war with Iran broke out in September 1821, the Sublime Porte sought to dispatch mercenaries from Rumelia to fight the Iranians; yet, it proved incapable of organizing this venture.[32] The Sublime Porte was obliged to resort to the Ottoman "violence market", whose most important providers at the time were Muslim Albanian *ayans*-cum-warlords. In other words, the Ottoman state had little to no army when the Greek Revolution broke out and was at the mercy of Albanian warlords and mercenaries until the advent of the Egyptian forces in 1825. However, the Albanians had their own agenda, and their averseness to put on a united Muslim front against the Greeks proved to be another failure of the Sublime Porte's already crumbling system of imperial allegiances.

Abbreviations:

BOA: Başbakanlık Osmanlı Arşivi [Ottoman State Archives, Istanbul]
C.ZB: Cevdet Zaptiye
HAT: Hatt-ı Hümayun [Imperial Rescripts]

Notes

1 For the most up-to-date literature review and elaborate theoretical framework regarding the Ottoman state's relations with its provincial power brokers until 1808, see A. Yaycıoğlu, *Partners of the Empire*: *The Crisis of the Ottoman Order in the Age of Revolutions* (California, 2016).
2 For details about the Russian wars being the driving force in the making of *ayan*hood see H.Ş. Ilıcak, "A Radical Rethinking of Empire: Ottoman State and Society during the Greek War of Independence, 1821–1826" (Ph.D. diss., Harvard University, 2011), chapter 1.
3 Sened-i İttifak: "Deed of Agreement" between the Ottoman central state and several Muslim provincial magnates in October 1808. With this Deed, the *ayans* pledged to protect the Ottoman crown and respect its authority as long as the Ottoman central state respected their authority in their respective domains. For an English translation of the document, see A. Akyıldız and M.Ş. Hanioğlu,

148   H. Şükrü Ilıcak

"Negotiating the Power of the Sultan: the Ottoman Sened-i İttifak (Deed of Agreement), 1808", in *The Modern Middle East: a Sourcebook for History*, eds. C. M. Amin, B.C. Fortna, and E. Frierson (London, 2006), 22–30.

4   See, for example, Ö. Mert, "II. Mahmut Döneminde Taşradaki Merkeziyetçilik Politikası" [Policy of Centralization during the Reign of Mahmud II], *Osmanlı*, ed. K. Çiçek (Ankara, 1999), 720–729.

5   M. P. Zallony, *Essai sur les Fanariotes, où l'on voit les causes primitives de leur élévation aux hospodariats de la Valachie et de la Moldovie, leur mode d'administration, et les causes principales de leur chute* (Marseille, 1824), 271. Zallony was the physician of Grand Vizier Koca Yusuf Pasha.

6   Şanizade Mehmed Ataullah Efendi, "İhale-i idare-i iltizamat ve mukataat ba-vüzera" [The transfer and administration of the tax-farms and state revenues by the viziers], *Şanizade Tarihi (1808–1821)* [History of Şanizade (1808–1821)], ed. Ziya Yılmazer (Istanbul, 2008), 1, 627.

7   Zallony, *Essai*, 271.

8   Mandate to the Chief Accountant, 9 February 1813, BOA/C.ML 4819, in Y. Cezar, *Osmanlı Maliyesinde Bunalım ve Değişim Dönemi* [The Period of Crisis and Change in the Ottoman Fisc] (Istanbul, 1986), 242.

9   A. Salzmann, *Tocqueville in the Ottoman Empire: Rival Paths to the Modern State* (Leiden & Boston, 2004), 187.

10   Register of the Anatolian *ayan*s ordered to dispatch troops, 11 March 1811, BOA/HAT 41621-A.

11   Register of Soldiers Employed in the Morea and its Environs, 18 January 1823, BOA/HAT 39969.

12   For a list of the subdued, exiled, or executed *ayan*s, see H.Ş. Ilıcak, "A Radical Rethinking", 59.

13   See İ. H. Uzunçarşılı, "Çapan Oğulları [The Çapanoğlus]", *Belleten* 150 (1974): 249–251.

14   R. W. Zens, "Ayanlık and Pasvanoğlu Osman Paşa of Vidin in the Age of Ottoman Social Change, 1791–1815" (Ph.D. diss., University of Wisconsin-Madison, 2004), 216–217.

15   M. M. Aktepe, "Tuzcu Oğulları İsyanı" [The Revolt of the Tuzcuoğlus], *İstanbul Üniversitesi Edebiyat Fakültesi Tarih Dergisi* 3 (1953): 21–52.

16   Süleyman Pasha (Governor of Sidon) to Sublime Porte, 3 August 1816, BOA/HAT 24372.

17   Mehmed Ragıb (Kadi of Erzurum) to Sublime Porte, 13 June 1816, BOA/HAT 47906-F.

18   For Basdekis see, A. Politis, "Η 'μορφή' του καπετάν Μπασδέκη", *Mnimon* 11 (1987): 1–31.

19   Derviş Mehmed Pasha (Grand Vizier) to Mahmud II, undated, BOA/HAT 21281; Tepedelenli Ali Pasha to Sublime Porte, undated, BOA/HAT 21281-A.

20   BOA/C.ZB 1313, 28 October 1818.

21   El-Hac Ali Pasha to Sublime Porte, 16 October 1817, BOA/HAT 22390; Şanizade, 2/921.

22   Salzmann, *Tocqueville*, 192.

23   Hurşid Ahmed Pasha (Governor of Aleppo) to Sublime Porte, 27 January 1820, BOA/HAT 59091.

24   Mahmud II's imperial rescript, 6 February 1820, BOA/HAT 34722.

25   Petro Bey Mavromichali (Bey of Mani) to Sublime Porte, 14 October 1820, BOA/HAT 39698-i.

26   Petro Bey Mavromichali (Bey of Mani) to Sublime Porte, undated, BOA/HAT 39698.

27   W. M. Leake, *Travels in Northern Greece* (London, 1835), 1, 40–41.

A *black hole in Ottoman history*   149

28 There were two major ethno-cultural Albanian groups, the Tosks and the Gegs, the former inhabiting areas south of the Shkumbin River [i.e. Toskëria] and the latter the northern regions [i.e. Gegëria]. They spoke mutually unintelligible dialects and had different customs and ways of life. They also had a long history of frequent mutual strife.
29 Mustafa Pasha Bushati (Mutasarrıf of Shkodra) to Sublime Porte, 28 April 1819, BOA/HAT 21000-H.
30 Hurşid Ahmed Pasha (Commander-in-chief of the Morea) to Sublime Porte, 9 January 1821, BOA/HAT 20928.
31 Hurşid Ahmed Pasha (Governor of Rumelia) to Sublime Porte, 6 March 1821, BOA/HAT 38866.
32 Salih Pasha (Mutasarrıf of Ormenio) to Sublime Porte, undated, BOA/HAT 37321.

11 The Serbian, Greek, and Romanian Revolutions in comparison

Harald Heppner

Introduction

When we focus on revolutions, we have to take into consideration the following aspect, revolutions are less coincidence and more deliberate actions. The main element is neither the visions nor the concepts nor the results, but the people involved. Who is at the forefront of groups of people and tries to change the relationship to these others? Who understands the violent acts as *rebellion* and who understands them as *resistance*? Who participates in the actions and who does not? Does the intention to change the life circumstances fundamentally since the outbreak of a hot phase exist or does it follow a period of longer escalation? What is the main element of a revolution – the *change in power* which allows new rulers to manage the fate of a large collectivity of people, or the *change in the system*, that is, the way of forming the life conditions of this collectivity?

In a limited way, studies of *history* can be titled as *studies of the future* because historians know which future visions existed at an earlier time and which were their results at a later time. Therefore, studies of revolution processes allow us to point out what the anterior perspectives were and what the posterior retrospectives were. With such a comparison, we can find out how many revolution programmes aimed to change a concrete situation and which consequences concerned later generations. In addition, reflecting on the history of revolutions, we have to distinguish several perceptions, the perception of the leaders involved as well as of the population involved, and the perception of the contemporary external observers as well as of later generations who were using the impact of the revolution for their own needs, perhaps as a measure for identity building or for legitimizing a political system.

For people, life normally consists of daily needs, and all extraordinary events (such as wars, revolutions, coups d'état) represent something exceptional which do not have any continuity from generation to generation. All happenings, which contain uncertainty, violence, and a loss of order, cannot be controlled and create a mixture of fear and hope. Therefore, revolutions are not a category of love, and willing and planning revolutionary activities

The Serbian, Greek, and Romanian Revolutions 151

are not the permanent aim of a people but sometimes become an inevitable reaction to political pressure and social need.

Retrospectively, the revolutionary processes do not seem to be as important as their results, the change from one political status to another. Therefore, historians risk interpreting all acts of resistance before a revolution had started as preliminary phenomena and invent a "revolutionary tradition", as Dimitrije Djordjević and Stephen Fischer-Galati did some decades ago.[1] In this case, all kinds of coincidences during a longer or shorter period of resistance are underrated, and the logic of the process depends only on the final effects. When we look at the Serbian, Greek, and Romanian revolutions[2] at the beginning of the 19th century, the comparison reveals several diversities, some similarities and some uniformities.

Divergencies

The divergencies consist of the period of time, the event profile, the circumstances of collaboration, and the results of the revolutionary processes.

In the case of the Serbs, resistance to Ottoman rule broke out in the province of Belgrade in 1804 as a reaction to some cruel acts by the local Turks. After several negotiations between the Serbian and Ottoman leaders, which did not bring a satisfactory result, the resistance started again. The military success of the Serbs, as well as the defeats of the Sublime Porte, allowed the establishment of a provisional political system with its seat in Belgrade (December 1806). After the peace treaty of Bucharest (1812), the situation changed again and new attacks by the Ottoman army quelled the first Serbian Uprising in 1813. After a two year break, the second Serbian Uprising took place in 1815, and the main Serbian leader, Miloš Obrenović, and the Ottomans quickly stopped the reactivated conflict. The Serbs achieved in bilateral negotiations with the representatives of the Ottoman government a moderate autonomy in the province (except the city of Belgrade itself). Two years later, Miloš Obrenović was elected as the first "prince" by the delegates of the Serbian population living in this new and still small "principality". Therefore, when the Greek Revolution broke out, this part of the Serbs had completed its "revolution" six years earlier. As we know, the Greek resistance acts against the Turks started in 1821 in many parts of Southern and Central Greece and led to a series of battles and skirmishes. Following the Greek defeats, Great Britain, France, and Russia came with their navies in 1827 and stopped the aggression of the Turkish army against the Greeks. The most important result of this cooperation was that the Sublime Porte accepted the creation of an independent Greek state (1830).

By comparison to these two revolutionary processes, which unfolded over several years, the Romanian case took only a short time. The revolutionary events in the Romanian lands consisted on the one hand of the operations of Alexander Ypsilantis who led the forces of the Philiki Etairia and on the other hand of the activities of Tudor Vladimirescu leading local people in

152   *Harald Heppner*

Wallachia. By June 1821, the Turkish troops occupied both capital cities (Bucharest and Jassy) and suppressed the revolutionary movements that had started the previous winter. The further steps in favour of a new political system were not the direct result of these short military actions but rather the result of the negotiations of some Romanian nobles with the Sublime Porte. This meant the end of Phanariote dominance in the principalities and the enlargement of economic and financial liberty (1822).

As it is well known, the Greeks enjoyed the best chance to get help from the outside based on three main factors. The first one was the interest of the Sea Powers (France, Great Britain, and Russia) in the Mediterranean Sea concerning their own roles against the Ottomans. The second one was the sympathy for Greek affairs reflected in Philhellenism, which existed in the higher social groups of the Western public. Therefore, the *Greek Question* preoccupied not only politicians, but a wider social horizon in the Occident. The third factor was the efforts of the Greeks in the diaspora in favour of the fate of their home areas. The Serbs did not have a comparable background because they lived in continental and not maritime regions. The single great power that was willing to favour the Serbian efforts at this time was Russia, but the collaboration with this "Nordic Empire" remained limited and depended on the variable relationship between Tsar Alexander and Emperor Napoleon. Therefore, the Serbs got some diplomatic help from the Russians who were operating in Wallachia between 1806 and 1812. Help from Austria, in the immediate neighbourhood, was only a half-hearted one and stayed at a low level. The Romanians in Wallachia in 1821 did not receive any substantial help from outside, neither from the Moldavians nor from a great power. The Austrians (including the Transylvanian Romanians) behind the Carpathians did observe the events but did not intervene in favour of the Wallachians. Only in the second half of the 1820s (in the background of the Greek emancipation process) the great powers influenced also the Ottoman position vis-à-vis the Romanians.

The results show that these three revolutionary processes opened quite different perspectives. Founded on the Protocol of London (1830), the Greeks got an independent state with their own political system, but the territory of this state did not include all territories settled by Greeks. At this time the Serbs did not have an independent state, but a small principality with moderate autonomy which was the result of negotiations with the Sublime Porte, without any military or diplomatic help from the outside. Following this, the Serbs had the chance to develop a new political system as their own responsibility. The Romanians in the Danubian principalities, who had their territories since the Middle ages, received a deeper system change only with Russian initiative after the peace treaty of Adrianople (1829), as the so-called *Regulamentul organic* was implemented. The Serbs in Serbia and the Romanians in Moldo-Wallachia had, at this time, some kind of advantage; they could note an option of organizing their future in their immediate neighbourhood. This was supplied by the model of progress of many Serbs and Romanians who were living in the Eastern provinces of the Austrian Empire and their different path of development than "at home". The Greeks did

The Serbian, Greek, and Romanian Revolutions 153

not have a similar option because the British protectorate in the Ionian Islands did not furnish a model similar to the transformation processes within the Habsburg Monarchy since the middle of the 18th century.

Similarities

Similarities between the three revolutionary movements concern the memory profile of the ethnic collectivities before the outbreak of revolutionary action, revolutionary leadership, and coordination problems during the revolutionary period.

When we look at the Serbian case, some older and newer elements of the memory of resistance come into focus. The oldest went back to the memory of the battles in 1389 and 1448 when the Serbian armies had fought on the Kosovo plain with the help of other armies against the Ottomans. It is quite difficult to have an opinion as to the weight of this memory, which was kept alive by the Orthodox Church and popular songs. At the beginning of the 19th century, the temporal distance of more than 400 years could not preserve more than a mythical character. A second older memory was connected with the existence of the Serbian Orthodox patriarchate, which was founded in 1557 and did not only express the political identity of the Serbian community but also their resistance to the Greek dominance within the Orthodox millet. Also the younger memory elements consisted of two factors. The first factor was the memory of the immigration of a great number of Serbs from the Ottoman to the Austrian Empire accompanied by their patriarchs in 1690 and 1737, which opened a new option for the future; the other factor was the repeated instances of collaboration of the Serbs with the Austrian armies in the Balkans from the end of the seventeenth till the end of the 18th century, always combined with the perspective to create a territory with Serbian responsibility (either being integrated in the Habsburg Monarchy or half-depending on it). The memory of resistance among the Greeks takes shape on three different pillars. The first one was the Klephts movement, corresponding to the Hajduk movement in other Balkan regions and the Pandur movement in the Danubian Principalities, which had a long tradition. The second was the Greek diaspora, which may be interpreted not only as the option of exile for oppressed persons but also as an initiative for developing alternative perspectives for the future of the Greeks; and the third pillar was the memory of collaboration with the Russians during the so-called "Orlov expedition" in the 1770s. On the basis of these three pillars of resistance, the conspiratorial project under the name Philiki Etairia was built.

The situation of the Romanians in the Danubian Principalities in the year 1821 shows that there was no active resistance memory at their disposal comparable with that of Serbs and Greeks. When we look at the relations between the vassal principalities to the Sublime Porte in Constantinople the chances to realise relevant resistance against the Ottomans appear quite limited. The attempt of Michael the Brave (1558–1601)[3] to leave the vassal platform and to unite Wallachia, Moldavia, and Transylvania in 1600 was

154   *Harald Heppner*

more than two centuries earlier and was not more than a short episode; the liberation ambition of prince Constantin Brâncoveanu (1654–1714)[4] cost him his head in 1714 and stimulated the establishment of a Greek Phanariot on the throne in Bucharest. The intention to realize a status change with the use of force in 1821 – without any doubt influenced by the Greeks – was something new and unusual.

When we look at the leaders of the Serbs, Greeks, and Romanians, we can also observe certain similarities. These consist of the intellectual work in favour of future visions, that is, after the overthrow of the dominance of the Ottoman Sultans. Among the Greeks, there were scholars, merchants, publishers, and clergymen, who, in the late 18th and at the beginning of the 19th century, reflected on the further prospects of the Greeks (Adamantios Korais, Rhigas Velestinlis, and many others).[5] Among the Romanians within the Danubian Principalities, the equivalent social element was the educated representatives of the younger noble generation, who were observing Western progress and had the willingness to implement it "at home" (Dinicu Golescu, Barbu Ştirbei, and others).[6] Among the Serbs, the representatives of the progressive ideas were found mostly among soldiers who had some experience with the Austrian army and the Austrian authorities in the province of Belgrade (for instance, Karadjordje, Aleksa Nenadović) some years before. These Serbs and Romanians were in contact with some of their fellow national scholars behind the border (in Hungary and Transylvania) where the officially initiated reform generated the first enlightened models of nation-building (e.g., Dositej Obradović for the Serbs, the so-called Transylvanian school for the Romanians).[7]

Another kind of similarity was the coordination problems among the warlords. One of the reasons for the defeat of the revolutionary movement in Wallachia was the difference in opinions between Alexander Ypislantis (who had to escape from Wallachia to Austria) and Tudor Vlădimirescu (who was killed) to find a common strategy.[8] Also, the limited success of the Serbs during the first Uprising was influenced by the differences of opinion among military and civil leaders, especially between the hardliners and the compromisers.[9] Additionally, the Greek War of Independence and its immediate aftermath were characterised by rivalries and disagreements among the different groups and personalities with divergent interests.[10]

Uniformities

The uniformities marking the three revolutions consist in their limited validity for the national communities, of the relevance of the economic situation, and of the new uncertainties after the end of the revolutions.

As we know, the Serbs, Greeks, and Romanians[11] were not settled in closed areas but were dispersed in different regions. The Serbs lived in the Balkan hinterland as well as in some parts of the Adriatic coast, in Hungary, and in Southern Russia. Also, the Greeks lived in what is now Greece and also in Western Minor Asia, in Constantinople, in many Balkan destinations, in the

The Serbian, Greek, and Romanian Revolutions 155

Danubian principalities, in Odessa, in Southern and Central Hungary, in Trieste, and in Vienna. The Romanians were not only the majority of the population in Wallachia and Moldavia, but also they lived in Transylvania and in the Bucovina, as well as in the Banat and in the area south of the Iron Gates of the Danube. All these groups did not live in the same state or under the same rulers; they had neither the same education and knowledge nor the same social position and political ambition. Based on these facts, they could not have a unified identity; not all of them could get the same information about the revolutionary events; not all of them could support the fighting people, and not all of them could have the same emotional approach to the revolutionary events. Therefore, it is necessary to underline the fact that as the revolutions were taking place primarily in the province of Belgrade, in Greece, and in Wallachia, only some minorities were involved in the hot phases of revolutionary action, while a significant part of co-nationals remained uninvolved.

It is astonishing that these three revolutions at the beginning of the 19th century have been interpreted mostly in their political dimension, but only rarely in their economic concomitant.[12] Revolutionary activities mean a loss of human capital, time, and resources; this loss always has deep relevance for life circumstances during and after the revolutionary period. The occupation of men with military operations instead of agrarian or other forms of everyday work, the death of ruling and working people, the lack of sowing and reaping, all these factors influence the normal food supply, the additional need of food (including the used animals), or the robbery or destruction of resources made by the enemies. All of this symbolizes an exceptional circumstance. When a revolution had finished successfully and allowed the establishment of their own state by the people involved, new economic uncertainty begins. Where does the financial base for paying the administration, the army, the residence costs of a dynasty, the liabilities towards foreign sponsors, *et al.* come from?

The third element of uniformity marking these three cases was the lack of experience in managing further political courses after the hot revolutionary phases. The management of a state is based on two areas of responsibility, the work inside the organism –that is, all kinds of domestic politics – and the work outside – that is, the foreign politics. This work needs some ruling elements who have experience in their respective functions, a legal basis accepted more or less by the entire population, and a lot of luck, which helps to keep stability in the new political community. If these preconditions do not exist, the start of a new state is a quite complicated and risky procedure, because the development of a state organism needs time, discipline, and patience by the new citizens, as well as by the neighbouring entities. The Greeks, the Serbs, and the Romanians never had these preconditions at their disposal; when the first chances for self-management were opened, they had not had any real opportunity to collect higher management practice, and they were depending on private and official help from outside and had to defend their acquired positions against external and internal enemies from the beginning. Therefore, organizing the future of a state   and

156 Harald Heppner

a collective of citizens was a big task, for which they were not really prepared. In all three cases, the revolutions opened, on the one hand, the future in freedom, but included, on the other hand, an existence with drastic compulsions which limited the imagined liberty.

Notes

1 D. Djordjevic and St. Fischer-Galati, *The Balkan Revolutionary Tradition* (New York, 1981).
2 Charles and Barbara Jelavich, *The Establishment of the Balkan National States, 1804–1920* (Seattle and London, 1977), 26–37, 38–52, 84–98. A large overview was has been given by O. Katsiardi-Hering, "Von den Aufständen zu den Revolutionen christlicher Untertanen des Osmanischen Reiches in Südosteuropa (1530–1821)", *Südostforschungen* 68 (2009): 96–137. See also the comparison by M.-J. Calic, *Südosteuropa. Weltgeschichte einer Region* (Munich, 2016), 229–251. As examples for the revolution history studies see: P. M. Kitromilides, *Enlightenment and Revolution. The Making of Modern Greece* (Cambridge, MA, 2013); S. Rudić, ed., *Srpska revolucija i obnova državnosti Srbije dvesta godina od drugog srpskog ustanka* [The Serbian revolution and the renewal of the Serbian State after the second Serbian Uprising] (Belgrade, 2016); D. Berindei, "Revoluţia din 1821 in Pricipatele Române" [The revolution of 1821 in the Romanian Principalities], in idem, ed., *Istoria Românilor* VII/1: *Constituirea României moderne (1821–1878)* [History of the Romanians. The Constituion of Modern Romania] (Bucharest, 2003), 21–54.
3 "Mihai Viteazul." Wikipedia. Last modified 11 December 2003. https://ro.wikipedia.org/wiki/Mihai_Viteazul. Accessed 24 July 2020).
4 "Constantin Brâncoveanu." Wikipedia. Last modified 16 May 2004. https://ro.wikipedia.org/wiki/Constantin_Brâncoveanu. Accessed 24 July 2020).
5 O. Katsiardi-Hering, "Politische und ökonomische Regionen in der Peripherie: Der Weg zu den Revolutionen in Südosteuropa zu Beginn des 19. Jahrhunderts", in *Provincial Turn. Verhältnis zwischen Staat und Provinz im südöstlichen Europa vom letzten Drittel des 17. bis ins 21. Jahrhundert*, eds. U. Tischler-Hofer and K. Kaser (Frankfurt/Main, 2017), 91–109.
6 E. Turczynski, *Von der Aufklärung zum Frühliberalismus. Politische Trägergruppen und deren Forderungskatalog in Rumänien* (Munich, 1985), 70–97.
7 N. Bocşan, "Luminile şi paşoptismul" [The Enlightenment and the 48-Mouvement], in *Istoria Transilvaniei* vol. III (*de la 1711 pană la 1848*) [History of Transylvania. From 1711 to 1848], eds I.-A. Pop, Th. Nägler and A. Magyari (Cluj-Napoca, 2008), 119–127.
8 A. Oţetea, *Tudor Vladimirescu '821* (Bucharest, 1971), 142–158.
9 H. Sundhaussen, *Geschichte Serbiens 19.–21. Jahrhundert* (Wien-Köln-Weimar, 2007), 65–75.
10 Katsiardi-Hering, "Politische und ökonomische Regionen", 108.
11 H. Sundhaussen, "Südosteuropäische Gesellschaft und Kultur vom Beginn des 19. bis zur Mitte des 20. Jahrhunderts", in *Geschichte Südosteuropas. Vom frühen Mittelalter bis zur Gegenwart*, eds K. Clewing and O. J. Schmitt (Regensburg, 2011), 345–355.
12 For instance D. Milić, "Ekonomski potencijal ustaničke Srbije" [The economic potential of Serbia in resistance], in *Istorijski značaj srpske revolucije 1804. godine* [L'importance historique de la révolution serbe de 1804], ed. V. Čubrilović (Belgrade, 1983), 161–174; the same, "Oporabak privrede u sloboðenoj Srbiji 1804–1813" [Economic recovery in the liberated Serbia in 1804–1813], in *Srbija i osloboðenje srpskog naroda u Turskoj 1804–1812* [Serbia and the liberation of Serbian people in Turkey 1804–1812], ed. V. Stojanevi (Belgrade, 2003), 79–90.

Part IV

Revolutionary Waves in the Greek World I

12 From the revolts to the Greek Revolution: Economic-political realities and ideological visions among the Greeks (end of the 18th C.–1821)

Olga Katsiardi-Hering

On 6 July 1797, Pier Antonio Pittoni, the police director of Trieste, informed Conte Pompeo de Brigido, the Governor of the city, about a revolutionary plan which was supposedly going to be organised in the Morea (Peloponnese) "che la Morea tutta di revoluzionarsi intenda, e che a tal effetto per proceder con sicurezza, conveniva che la Francia prendesse l'Isole Venete dal Levante: che scosso il giogo della Porta, sarrebbe facile anzi quasi sicuro che la Morea tutta si dasse sotto la protezione Francese".[1] The plan was communicated to the French consul in Trieste by a certain Andrea from the Peloponnese and a Greek named Palatino, a former Russian official. It was supposed that "the French consul had given them letters for Bonaparte". Bonaparte had just occupied the northern part of the Italian peninsula and on 12 May 1797, the French had taken over the administration of Venice. The city was ceded to the Austrians after the Treaty of Campo Formio (6/17 October 1797), while the Ionian Islands were turned over to France. Five months after the receipt of this information, on 16 December, and due to a betrayal on the part of a Greek merchant (an Austrian subject himself), the police of Trieste arrested Rhigas Velestinlis,[2] the Greek intellectual who had written and published secretly at the Greek printing house of the Markides-Poulios brothers in Vienna his political texts (*Declaration of Rights, New Political Administration, Constitution for the "Hellenic Republic", Thourios* (Revolutionary Hymn).[3] He probably planned to travel to the Ionian Islands, which had only just come under French rule,[4] and also to the adjacent Ottoman provinces inhabited by Greeks, as well, and to distribute his pamphlets for the revolution to come. His efforts to communicate with the French consul in Trieste did not bear fruit; he was taken to Vienna and, after a lengthy police investigation, the Austrian authorities handed him and seven of his Greek followers, as Ottoman subjects, over to the Ottomans. All of them were executed in Belgrade.[5] In the following years, Rhigas became the incarnation of the revolutionary tradition for the Greeks but also for the rest of Southeastern European peoples.

Many of the terms and connotations (plan of revolution, Peloponnese, Trieste, Venice, Ionian Islands, Austria, Russian officer, French, Bonaparte,

160   Olga Katsiardi-Hering

diaspora) included in this somewhat unorthodox introduction will be at the centre of our argumentation in the analysis that follows.

The 50 years following the *Orlofika* (1770) revolt, which took place in the Peloponnese in the context of the Russo-Ottoman war (1768–1774) were a period of uprisings among the Christian and Muslim subjects of the Ottoman Empire, most of them due to the tax increases and interventions by foreign powers. As it is well known, most of the uprisings during the era after 1453 took place in the context of the Ottomans' conflicts with the Venetians and other European powers, and most were prepared or took place in the Peloponnese and in Epirus.[6] The long 18th century was a critical period in the history of the Ottoman Empire and was marked by unstable relations with the European powers;[7] these political conditions gave rise to the so-called *Eastern Question*. The Austro-Russo-Ottoman war of 1787–1792, the outbreak of the French Revolution in 1789, the intense competition and military rivalries among the European powers on land and at sea, and the weakened position of the Ottoman Empire all fed into political and economic changes which included a destabilization in Southeastern Europe. On the one hand, rebel movements led by powerful Muslim *ayans,* such as Ali pasha of Ioannina, Mehmet pasha of Shkodra, and Osman Pasvandoglu of Vidin, challenged central Ottoman power in the Balkans;[8] on the other hand, the increasing economic strength of Greek Orthodox individuals – in particular Greeks – in maritime and overland commerce was another new reality. This economic development can also be explained in terms of the European powers' growing commercial interest in the Levant and the special commercial policy of many of them (e.g., the Habsburgs after 1717). This new situation had an indirect result of the economic and commercial strengthening of the Jewish and Christian subjects of the Sublime Porte.[9] Merchant networks extended throughout the Southeastern European Ottoman provinces connecting the Diaspora of Greek Orthodox commercial communities established in Central and Western Europe and Russia.[10] Education centres flourished in these communities; scientific books, newspapers and journals were published in the Greek (and Serbian) language in the printing houses of Venice, Vienna, Pest, and elsewhere. This was followed by an ideological osmosis of modern political ideas.[11] It was through this osmosis, and through the political interactions among the European powers, that various projects on the part of the Greeks seeking liberation with European assistance (French or Russian) emerged. The fall of Venice and its impact on the Ionian Islands at the turn of the 18th into the 19th century led to the establishment of the first semi-autonomous Greek republic (the *Repubblica Settinsulare,* 1800–1807) and the establishment of new sovereignties (Russian, French, English) on the Ionian Islands. The impact of these successive political sovereignties would be seen also during the decade of the Greek revolution. The first decade of the 19th century saw the emergence of a, more or less, mature political ideology of change of economic and political status, or liberation wrought

From the revolts to the Greek Revolution   161

without external assistance among the Serbs and Greeks. Political visions of nation, fatherland, and liberty[12] spread through various social strata and prepared the way for the outbreak of the Revolution in 1821.

The title of this article includes two terms: Revolts and Revolution. A semantic differentiation is already found in the *Encyclopédie* of Diderot et D'Alembert (1765). "*Rebellion*: les ordonnances mettent ce crime au nombre des cas royaux", "*Révolte*: Soulevement du people contre le souverain", "*Révolution*: signifie en terme de politique, un changement considérable arrivé dans le gouvernement d'un état".[13] This differentiation would crystallise during the French Revolution and its legacy.[14] In the following argumentation, we will use terms such as *insurrection, rebels, rebellions, revolts, upheavals, uprisings,* and *revolution* (in Greek, *εξέγερση, σηκωμός/σηκώνονταν, ταραχές, αντίσταση, επανάσταση*).[15]

As a turning point for the initiation of our discussion, I begin with the revolt of *Orlofika* (1770).[16] It was an insurrection – although there were uprisings in some parts of Sterea Hellas (Rumeli), Thessaly, and on Crete (Daskalogiannis uprising)[17] – that was organized in the Peloponnese, which had enjoyed a privileged administrative status after its reoccupation by the Ottomans on 1715.[18] The revolt was prepared by Russian military officials under the Brothers Orlov. Oracular texts and popular prophecies about Russian aid helped in the ideological preparation of the revolt.[19] Agents from Russia or Greeks in its services came in contact with Greeks in Epirus, in Peloponnese, and in the Diaspora; in Trieste, such as Georgios Papazolis, who published his political text, *Διδασκαλία* (Teaching), in Venice on 1765,[20] in which he stressed the relationship between religion, community, and patria (it is from this point on that religion and revolution and nationalism are almost always intertwined);[21] in Venice, Panos Maroutsis, the rich Epirot merchant and Venetian noble, served as a Russian consul in Venice since 1768,[22] through whom Catherine the Great tried to come in contact with Montenegro; as well as Demetrios Motzenigos, a Zantiot noble in Venice, who helped the Orlovs in Tuscany[23] in connection with Aggelis Adamopoulos and Ioannis Palatinos;[24] an extraordinary personality was Loudovikos Sotiris[25] a doctor from Naples who acted to prepare the revolt in Ioannina, Epirus. These and other Russian agents[26] formed relationships with prominent Christian leaders in the Peloponnese (e.g., Panagiotis Benakis in Calamata) on Zante and Cephalonia,[27] and other people on the Balkan peninsula. Bourgeois and merchant networks – not only in the Ottoman provinces – became a common feature in the planning of subsequent uprisings and they certainly found their best incarnation in the *Philiki Etaireia* (Society of Friends) of 1814, which prepared the Greek Revolution. Promises made by Catherine II about liberation from the Ottomans and the offers of protection by a Christian Orthodox power fell on many eager ears. The Russian fleet passed through the ports of Livorno, Naples, Venice, and Trieste (all "historic headquarters of the Greek communities in Italy, as well as places for the political-cultural mediations

162 *Olga Katsiardi-Hering*

between Italy and Greece"[28]), but did not arrive in the Peloponnese as the major and well-organized campaign for which the Greeks hoped. The details are well-researched in the literature.[29] In the case of *Orlofika,* the historian encounters continuous abuse and antagonisms among the Christian *koca-başis* as well as towards the provincial Ottoman authorities in the Peloponnese, primarily because of tax increases (a *zülüm/tyragnia/*tyranny),[30] in particular in the decade before 1770.

I would agree with V. Molos, that "The Orlov movement was one that opened a new horizon of political possibility, as the idea of self-determination raised the possibility of Greeks assuming some degree of autonomy over their own political affairs...".[31] The Proclamation of Catherine in 1770,[32] in which she promised to provide protection for the religion of the Greeks and other Balkan people and to liberate them from "the Ottoman yoke"[33] – promises which would be renewed in the next war (1787–1792) with her so-called "Greek project"[34] – the *Ικετηρία*[35] attributed to Evgenios Voulgaris (who in 1771 accepted Catherine's invitation to come to Russia and to offer his future ecclesiastical services in Kherson[36]), all led to a new political understanding. As Molos notes, the Russians contributed to conveying the "political understanding of Greekness into the Greek world, and the forging of an insurrectionist network effectively reconstituted the disparate groups of insurgents into a political community capable of advancing political claims".[37] The Russian propaganda "politicized" religion, propagated the meaning of freedom and the revising of relations between an Orthodox sovereign (e.g., the Russian Tsarina) and their subjects;[38] Voltaire was one of the defenders of the Greek cause. The Greeks could be included among the European states. The *Orlofika* can be seen from an international point of view. For the first time, a Russian fleet, having received British permission to cross the Channel and through the Straits of Gibraltar, appeared in the Mediterranean in 1768, and defeated the Ottomans in 1770 at a naval battle near Chesme in Asia Minor. The history of the war was written in Italian as a contemporary, current, serious historical event.[39] A similar project was realized by Agapios Loverdos for the first two years (1787, 1788) of the subsequent Austro-Russo-Ottoman war (1787–1792). This awareness of recording important contemporary historical events was in line with the dictates of the Enlightenment.[40]

The Treaty of Küçük Kaynarca (1774) upset the Mediterranean and European balance of powers, strengthening the Russian role in the area, but also positively impacting the development of Greek commercial shipping and mercantile expansion.[41] The ships, having been forced – either by the presence of piracy in the Mediterranean sea or by their obligation to participate in the Ottoman navy – to be armed, became the most powerful force in the Greek Revolution. After 1770, the nine-years-long *Arvanitokratia* in the Peloponnese, an anarchic and oppressive period for both the Greeks and the Ottomans when the Muslim Albanians seized power after helping the Ottomans suppress the revolt,[42] caused migratory waves in the interior of the Empire as well as an expansion of the Greek Diaspora,[43] which also contributed considerably to the War of Independence. In the subsequent Austro-Russo-Ottoman war (1787–1792), instead of a Russian fleet, Lampros Katsonis[44] and other corsairs crossed the Levant in the service of Russia, under a new military and ideological mantle. New promises of revolts by Catherine had not made so much an impact on the Greeks,[45] despite some petitions for liberation (authentic or not) addressed to her. However, during this war, too, Greeks acted as Russian agents (these included Georgios Palatinos) all over the Balkan peninsula and in the Aegean.[46] In the context of the growing controversy over Ali Pasha of Ioannina, *klephtes* and *martoloz* (local warrior groups) were strengthened, in particular in Epirus, Thessaly, and Sterea Hellas.[47] Their war experience was useful during the Greek Revolution. The Russian fleet appeared in subsequent years and wars and played a significant role in the Mediterranean conflicts.[48]

The geographical area where Greeks lived permanently or in the Diaspora, the socioeconomic and political relations they had with the authorities, and the coexistence with other Balkan peoples within the Ottoman empire and in the Diaspora could be some of the factors that explain the dynamic of the insurrections or the projects that formed. Most of the projects for uprisings originated from merchants or with the aid of intellectuals in the Diaspora. Living in the era of Enlightenment, coming into direct or indirect contact (through books, press, etc.) with the new revolutionary ideas[49] but also through the widening of the education possibilities in the Diaspora and the Ottoman Empire, as well as through the ways of dissemination of the ideas of the intellectuals living on the Ionian Islands who were in contact with the Italian, French, and Austrian/ German scholarship, these people were the bridge for the propagation of the idea of liberation.[50] The weak position of the Ottoman empire had also led some of the Greeks to draw up "utopian" projects of liberation. The Greek businessman, Anastasios Paraskevas, originally from Ioannina in Epirus but a resident in Vienna, submitted a memorandum to the emperor Joseph II on 17 July 1783.[51]

At a time when the Habsburg empire had to tread delicately in its policy towards Russia and the Ottoman Empire, Paraskevas proposed the organisation of a Pan-Balkan military campaign led by the emperor himself. After offering a detailed economic and political description of the lands and peoples of Southeastern Europe, he stressed the miserable situation of the Greeks and all the Christians ruled by the Sultan. He invoked Joseph II's right to the throne of Constantinople as a *Römischer Kayser* and a successor to *Constantini des Grossen* and to *Constantini Paleologi.*[52] He pointed out the danger posed for the Habsburg Empire by the possibility of the Russians crossing the Dniester, Pruth, and Danube to fight the Ottomans. It seems that Paraskevas was well informed about the critical nature of the Habsburgs' political relations in terms of Russian rivalry with regard to the Ottomans.[53] He stressed the danger of a future war leaving the French,

164   *Olga Katsiardi-Hering*

Venetians, and others occupying some of "the most beautiful provinces of Greece".[54] He proposed that Joseph could undertake two secret campaigns, one from Fiume towards Epirus (Arta), and the other from Livorno into the Morea (*Modon und Koron*).[55] He also proposed to lead the first campaign himself, as he alone knew the province and he could come into contact with the inhabitants of Chimara[56] and other Epirot settlements with promises of protection from the side of the emperor Joseph. He explained the course of his war in great detail as it moved through various cities in Epirus, Macedonia, and Thessaly with the aid of the Greeks and against the Turks and Albanians (meaning the Muslim Albanians).[57] Then, as they moved through Thebes and Corinth, he would try to contact the other campaign group in the Morea. In the meantime, the main expedition with the soldiers of emperor Joseph would be in Thessaloniki, and Paraskevas would march on Constantinople "um mich mit der großen Armee zu vereinigen und mit allgemeiner Stimme der Griechischen Völcker aufzurüffen, es lebe Joseph der Zweyte." Although this was a utopian plan, his proposal could be examined within the framework of the old traditional *militia Christiana* projects;[58] it could also be considered as a vision for the liberation of Greece with many elements in common with military actions that we encounter later during the Greek Revolution of 1821 (e.g., it focuses on Epirus, Sterea Hellas and the Peloponnese as revolutionary areas). Paraskevas's memorandum emerged at a time when certain circles in the Habsburg empire were discussing a possible division of the Ottoman Empire.[59]

In the years that followed, more projects (e.g., those of Dimo e Nicolò Stefanopoli in connection with Tzanetbey Grigorakis in Mani / Smolenitz in Hungary / Constantinos Stamatis in Paris,[60] etc.) were planned for future revolts. Until the 1790s, the projects were oriented toward the expectation of Russian aid. After that, the French Revolution and especially Bonaparte's policy towards Italy, the Adriatic, the Ionian Islands, and the Levant, in general, fed into new visions for liberation. Bonaparte wrote in his memoirs that "La Grèce attend un libérateur...ce serait une belle couronne de gloire!...Quand, dans ma campagne d'Italie, j'arrivai sur les bords de l'Adriatique, j'avais sous mes yeux le royaume d'Alexandre!".[61] Despite the opposition of the established authorities of the *ancien régime*, new ideas about freedom and political rights circulated all over Europe. Most of the projects for the liberation of the Greeks were envisioned in or around the centres of the Greek Diaspora. Trieste, Venice, Ancona, Vienna, Livorno, Budapest, Komárom were places that hosted agents or visionaries of liberation with the support of the French.[62] Merchants or agents from the Peloponnese and other parts of South-eastern Europe tried to come into contact with French consuls or agents or with Bonaparte. The best known of all these visions is that of Rhigas Velestinlis, who formulated a comprehensive political program for the liberation of the Balkan peoples from the Ottoman Porte. His *Χάρτα της Ελλάδος* (Map of Greece])[63] from 1797 was the geographical incarnation of his *Hellenic Republic,* as he proposed it in the "Constitution", on the basis of which all the peoples of Southeastern Europe would be politically reorganized.[64]

Even Ali Pasha of Ioannina tried to establish diplomatic contact with Bonaparte. A lot of local wars were fought in the vast area of his pashalik during his efforts to expand it.[65] These battles had as a consequence the strengthening of armed bands, the *klephts,* the *martoloz,* all over its area. The *klephts* (bandits) and *hajduks* as a social phenomenon,[66] or as a rebellious one, have been an object of fervent historiographic discussion in relation to the *reayas* within the Ottoman Empire. *Klephts* and *hajduks* were a manifestation of agrarian unrest; they were protests and, as such, were different forms than the *peasant rebellions* of Central and Western Europe.[67] In traditional Balkan historiography, the terms *klephts, hajduks,* and *martorloz* have become synonymous with hero-warriors; it was their role in the Serbian revolt[68] and in the Greek War of Independence that ideologised them in this way.

The new era of antagonistic relations in the Eastern Mediterranean at the turn of the 18th into the 19th century, and in particular after the Congress of Vienna of 1814–1815,[69] led the Greeks, among the Balkan people, to projects of resistance based on their own resources. The anonymous political text of *Rossoanglogallos,* as well as that of *Hellenic Nomarchy* (*Ελληνική Νομαρχία,* 1806), can be seen as "the vision of freedom embodied in a return to nomarchy" (the rule of law in opposition to *monarchy*).[70] Among intellectuals, the turn towards political emancipation stemmed from a stance taken by Adamantios Korais, especially after 1805, and his disappointment with the French position on the Greek vision for freedom. His enthusiasm for a strong French-Greek friendship, as expounded in his *Asma polemistirion* (1800) and *Salpisma polemistirion* (1801),[71] was replaced by his orientation towards the formation of "an infrastructure of freedom created by cultural reconstruction". "…The nation should attain maturity through appropriate cultural preparation".[72]

This idea of "maturity" was not, perhaps, taken to heart by those middle-class merchants who founded the revolutionary *Philiki Etaireia* (Society of Friends, 1814)[73] in Odessa, home to a flourishing Greek commercial community, which had established itself within the framework of the Russian economic policy.[74] The Society had the goal of preparing a Greek Revolution within the framework of the secret societies of the time. The Greeks of the Diaspora, and many others in urban centres within the Ottoman Empire (e.g., Smyrna) or on the Ionian Islands (e.g., Zante), participated in masonic lodges and in secret societies,[75] with some also taking part in revolutionary processes. According to George Frangos,[76] the majority of the members of the *Philiki Etaireia* belonged to the wider bourgeois strata, most of them being merchants (51.5%, followed by intellectuals but also political community elders in the Peloponnese, as well as clergymen, et al.). Knowing the socioeconomic plurality of these strata (in particular in the Ottoman provinces), our aim is to identify the broader

166 *Olga Katsiardi-Hering*

ideological context of the revolutionaries, as well as of those who were attracted by political discussions and responded to revolutionary stimuli. That the majority of the members of the *Philiki Etaireia* originated from the Peloponnese (37.2%), followed by the Aegean and Ionian Islands and Epirus (14.6%, 12.3%, and 10.5%, respectively), could be seen as additional support for the argument that the networks and social conditions of the provinces in which earlier revolutionary activities had taken place or been planned were those in which eventually the revolution took place. Although under English administration, the Ionian Islanders – and particularly those on Zante – had shown strong connections to the Greek revolutionary cause. The most obvious example is that of the poet Dionysios Solomos. Others, such as Andreas Moustoxydis, also had manifested an interest in a national idea in a more "transnational patriotism".[77]

This short presentation does not seek to provide a monolithic image of the attitude of the Greeks on the eve of the Revolution. There was certainly a plurality of tensions and visions. However, the economic crisis after 1814, the end of the Napoleonic wars, the return of "normality" in the Levantine sea trade, and the crisis in the Ottoman Empire produced the conditions under which broader population strata would tend to espouse the cause of revolution.[78]

In the urban centres, the echoes of the French Revolution were more intense, but then the philosophical and ideological exhortations to fight for one's religion and patria, for freedom and nation were more powerfully accepted; the texts of political and military "catechisms" propagating the new "virtues" (*Glaube, Vaterland, Freiheit*) of the people (*Volk*) circulated during the Napoleonic wars, particularly among the Germans.[79] The proclamations of the Greek Revolution were drafted in a similar vein; "*Μάχου υπέρ Πίστεως και Πατρίδος*" (Fight for the Faith and the Patria)[80] was the repeated motto of every revolutionary proclamation before and during the Greek War of Independence. In the spring of 1821, merchants, clergymen, community elders, ship owners, and seamen from the islands, *klephts, martoloz*, and the common people would react positively to these proclamations, making the Revolution – in particular in the Peloponnese, Sterea Hellas and most of the Aegean Islands – generally accepted.

The Greek War of Independence was a national Revolution. If the Orlofika can be described as an insurrection that had taken place in some Greek locations, though without the aim of establishing an actual independent state, the Greek Revolution of 1821 was the project of modernity. The Revolution broke out in an era in which the anti-revolutionary European empires were striving to reconstruct and stabilise themselves after the Napoleonic wars. The timing was not favourable for a revolution fomented by the subjects of an empire, even if the empire in question had not been officially invited to attend the Congress of Vienna. The Greeks began fighting with their own forces; they wished that their new state could be included, under its new Constitution (1822) among the Christian, "well-governed" European powers.[81]

From the revolts to the Greek Revolution 167

Notes

1 O. Katsiardi-Hering, "Ελληνικά διαβήματα στον Βοναπάρτη. Η περίπτωση του Γεωργίου Παλατίνου" [Greek petitions to Bonaparte. The Case of George Palatinos], *O Eranistis* 14 (1977): 36–68, here: p. 40.

2 O. Katsiardi-Hering, "Ο Ρήγας Φεραίος. Νέα Στοιχεία από τα αρχεία της Τεργέστης" [Rhigas Pheraios. New material from the Archives of Trieste], *Mnimon* 7 (1979): 150–174; Eadem, "L'impresa al di sopra di tutto: parametri economici del martirio di Rigas", *Rigas Fereos, la rivoluzione, la Grecia, i Balcani. Atti del Convegno Internazionale "Rigas Fereos – Bicentenario della morte"*, ed. L. Marcheselli-Loukas, Trieste, 4–5 dicembre 1997, (Trieste 1999), 59–81.

3 P. M. Kitromilides, ed., *Ρήγα Βελεστινλή, Άπαντα τα σωζόμενα* [Rhigas Velestinlis, Complete Surviving Works], vol. 5 (Athens, 2002), 33–45, 45–71, 73–77.

4 D. Arvanitakis, *Η αγωγή του πολίτη. Η γαλλική παρουσία στο Ιόνιο (1797–1799) και το έθνος των Ελλήνων* [Educating citizens. The French presence on the Ionian Islands (1797–1799) and the nation of Greeks] (Athens, 2020).

5 https://kulanebojsa.rs/изложбена-поставка/?lang=el (access on 1.8.2020) an exhibition about the martyrdom of Rhigas Velestinlis organised by Greeks and Serbs at the Nebojša castle in Belgrade.

6 O. Katsiardi-Hering, "Von den Aufständen zu den Revolutionen christlicher Untertanen des osmanischen Reiches in Südosteuropa (ca. 1530–1821). Ein Typologisierungsversuch", *Südost-Forschungen* 68 (2009): 96–137; A. Anastasopoulos and E. Kolovos, eds, *Ottoman Rule and the Balkans, 1760–1850: Conflict, Transformation, Adaptation*. Proceedings of an International Conference, Rethymnon, Greece, 13–14 Dec. 2003 (Rethymno, 2007); B. Gundoglu, "Ottoman Constructions of the Morea Rebellion, 1770s: A Comprehensive Study of Ottoman Attitudes to the Greek Uprising" (PhD diss., University of Toronto, 2012), 7; A. Yaycıoğlu, *Partners of the Empire: The Crisis of the Ottoman Order in the Age of Revolutions* (Stanford, 2016), but see also the critical book review by E. Gara, in *Istorein* 18/2 (2019): https://doi.org/10.12681/historein.18635

7 O. Katsiardi-Hering, "The Habsburg Empire and the Ottoman Empire in the Long Eighteenth Century: A Recalcitrant but a Positive Vicinity", in *L'Avenir des Lumières. The Future of Enlightenment*, eds. L. Andries and M.-A. Bernier (Paris, 2019), pp. 253–280; V. Aksan, *Ottoman Wars 1700–1870. An Empire Besieged* (New York, 2007).

8 St. Shaw, *Between Old and New. The Ottoman Empire under Sultan Selim III 1789–1807* (Cambridge, MA, 1971); Fr. Anscombe, ed., *The Ottoman Balkans, 1750–1830* (Princeton, 2006).

9 O. Katsiardi-Hering, "Christian and Jewish Ottoman Subjects: Family, Inheritance and Commercial Networks between East and West (17th–18th C.)", *The Economic Role of the Family in the European Economy from the 13th to the 18th Centuries*, Atti della Quarantesima Settimana di Studi, 6–10 Aprile 2008, Istituto Internazionale di Storia Economica F. Datini, Serie II, Atti delle *Settimane di Studi*, ed. S. Cavaciocchi, (Florence, 2009), vol. 40, 409–440.

10 O. Katsiardi-Hering, M. Stassinopoulou, eds., *Across the Danube: Southeastern Europeans and Their Travelling Identities (17th–19th C.)* (Leiden, 2017).

11 P. M. Kitromilides, *Enlightenment and Revolution. The Making of Modern Greece* (Cambridge, MA and London, 2013).

12 P. M. Kitromilides, "The Vision of Freedom in Greek Society", *Journal of the Hellenic Diaspora* 19 (1993): 5–29.

13 *Encyclopédie ou dictionnaire raisonné des Sciences, des Arts et des Métiers*, par une Société de Gens de Lettres, mis en ordre et publié par Mr. *** Neufchastel (1765), vol. 13, p. 840, Rébellion; vol. 14, p. 237, Révolte and Révolution.

168   Olga Katsiardi-Hering

14 A historical controversy arose around the French Revolution and its legacies, M. Vovelle, *La Bataille du bicentenaire de la Révolution française* (Paris, 2017).

15 On the use of these terms in their historical context in particular in Southeastern Europe s. Katsiardi-Hering, "Von den Aufständen zu den Revolutionen", 96–102, 108, with literature; E. Gara, "Prophecy, Rebellion, Suppression: Revisiting the Revolt of Dionysios the Philosopher in 1611", in *Paradigmes rebelles. Pratiques et cultures de la désobéissance à l'époque moderne*, eds Gr. Salinero, M.-Á. Darcía Garrido and R. Păun (Brussels, 2018), 335–363.

16 From the rich literature see M. Sakellariou, *Η Πελοπόννησος κατά την δευτέραν Τουρκοκρατίαν (1715–1821)* [The Peloponnese during the second period of Ottoman occupation (1715–1821)] (Athens, 1978²), 131–192; Fr. Venturi, *La Rivolta greca del 1770 e il patriotismo dell'età dei lumi*, Rome, 1986; a rich Ottoman source has been published by N. Sarris, *Προεπαναστατική Ελλάδα και Οσμανικό κράτος. Από το χειρόγραφο του Σουλεϋμάν Πενάχ Εφέντη του Μοραΐτη (1785)* [Prerevolutionary Greece and the Ottoman State. From the manuscript of Suleÿman Penach Effendi of Morea (1785)] (Athens, 1993).

17 Ap. Vakalopoulos, *Ιστορία του Νέου Ελληνισμού*, vol. 4, *Τουρκοκρατία 1669–1812. Η οικονομική άνοδος και ο Φωτισμός του Γένους* [History of Modern Hellenism, v. 4, Period of Ottoman rule 1669–1812. The economic development and the Enlightenment of the Nation] (Thessaloniki, 1973), 397–430.

18 Sakellariou, *Η Πελοπόννησος*, 162–192.

19 M. Hatzopoulos, "Ancient Prophecies, Modern Predictions: Myths and Symbols of Greek Nationalism" (Ph.D. thesis, University of London, 2005); Idem, "Oracular Prophecy and the Politics of Toppling Ottoman Rule in South-East Europe", *The Historical Review/La Revue Historique* 8 (2011): 95–116.

20 Georgios Papazolis, *Διδασκαλία ήγουν Ερμηνεία της Πολεμικής Τάξεως και Τέχνης…* [Teaching namely an interpretation of war order and art…] (Venice, 1765).

21 V. Molos, "Nationness in the Absence of Nation: Narrating the Prehistory of the Greek National Movement" (Ph.D. diss., New York City University, 2014), 147–151; I would like to thank Dr. Molos for our thorough scholarly discussion. M. Isabella, "Religion, Revolution, and Popular Movement", in *Re-imagining Democracy in the Mediterranean, 1780–1860*, eds J. Innes and M. Philip (Oxford, 2013), 231–249; I. Kyriakantonakis, "Nationalism and Religion: Historical Aspects of the Relationship", *The Historical Review/La Revue Historique* 16 (2018): 188–210.

22 Molos, "Nationness in the Absence of Nation", 158–162; about Maroutsis see V. Kollios, "Ο Πάνος Μαρούτσης και η συμβολή του στα Ορλωφικά (1768–1774)" [Panos Maroutsis and his role in the Orlofika (1768–1774)] (Ph.D. diss., University of Ioannina, 1994).

23 Molos, op. cit., 162–167.

24 Ibid., 155, 163.

25 Ibid., 156–157, 186.

26 N. C. Pappas, *Greeks in Russian Military Service in the Late Eighteenth and Early Nineteenth Centuries*, Thessaloniki 1991; G. Ars, ed., *Η Ρωσία και τα πασαλίκια Αλβανίας και Ηπείρου, 1759–1831. Έγγραφα ρωσσικών αρχείων* [Russia and the pashaliks of Albania and Epirus, 1759–1831. Documents from the Russian archives] (Athens, 2007).

27 D. Vlassi, "Η συμμετοχή των Επτανησίων στα Ορλωφικά (1770) και η αντίδραση της Βενετίας" [The Participation of the Ionians at the Orlofika (1770) and the Reaction of Venice], *Mnimon* 8 (1980–1982): 64–84; N. Kapodistrias, "Στάσεις και μορφές αρχοντικής εξουσίας στη βενετική Ζάκυνθο. Η οικογένεια Μακρή και τα Ορλωφικά" [Attitudes and Forms of Noble Power in Venetian Zante. The Makris

From the revolts to the Greek Revolution 169

Family and the Orlov Revolt] (Ph.D. diss., National and Kapodistrian University of Athens, 2020).

28 Fr. Scalora, "L'idea di Bisanzio nel pensiero dei dotti Siculo-Albanesi: il caso di Nicolò Chetta (1741–1803)", in *Ritrovare Bisanzio. Atti delle Giornate di Studio sulla civiltà in Italia meridionale e nei Balcani dedicate alla memoria di André Guillou (Palermo, 26–28 Maggio 2016)*, eds M. Re, Cr. Rognoni and Fr.-P. Vuturo, Byzantino – Sicula VII (Palermo, 2019), 297–318, here p. 307.

29 For a historiographic review, see N. Rotzokos, *Εθναφύπνιση και εθνογένεση. Ορλωφικά και ελληνική ιστοριογραφία* [National Awakening and Ethnogenesis. Orlofika and the Greek Historiography] (Athens, 2007); Molos, "Nationness in the Absence of Nation", offers a very good critical analysis also from the ideological point of view of this revolt; A. Vlachopoulou, *Revolution auf der Morea. Die Peloponnes während der zweiten Turkokratie (1715–1821)* (Munich, 2017), 127–163 does not offer new material from Ottoman sources. Eleni Gara, "Writing Contemporary History: Ottoman Turkish and Greek Narrations of the Morean Rebellion in the late 18th century", in *Writing History in Ottoman Europe (15th–18th century)*, ed. by Ovidiu- Victor Olar and Konrad Petrovszky, in press. Gundoglu, "Ottoman Constructions of the Morea Rebellion", is based on Ottoman sources (some of them, such as Penah effendi, better known in the literature than he seems to assume), but focusing on writings from the nineteenth century and, not having access to the broader Greek and international bibliography on the subject, proceeds to unusual generalizations and misinterpretations.

30 Sarris, *Προεπαναστατική Ελλάδα*, 34, 37, 400; for a very good analysis of this period see J. Alexander, *Brigandage and Public Order in the Morea, 1685–1806* (Athens, 1985); D. Papastamatiou, "Οικονομικοκοινωνικοί μηχανισμοί και το προυχοντικό φαινόμενο στην οθωμανική Πελοπόννησο του 18ου αιώνα: Η περίπτωση του Παναγιώτη Μπενάκη" [Socioeconomic mechanisms and the elders phenomenon in the Ottoman Peloponnese of the eighteenth century: the case of Panagiotis Benakis], (Ph.D. diss., Aristotelian University of Thessaloniki, 2009); Idem, "Οθωμανικές στρατιωτικές προετοιμασίες και ο αφοπλισμός της Πελοποννήσου κατά τα έτη 1768–1769" [Ottoman military preparation and the disarmament of the Peloponnese in the years 1768–1769], in *Τουρκολογικά* [Turkologika], ed. G. Salakides (Thessaloniki, 2011), 395–422.

31 Molos, 41.

32 K. Palaiologos, "Ρωσικά περί Ελλάδος έγγραφα, νυν το πρώτον εις την ελληνικήν μεθερμηνευόμενα" [Russian documents about Greece, now translated into the Greek language for the first time], *Parnassos* 5 (1881): 147–148; Molos, op. cit. 168–172.

33 E. Gara, "Conceptualizing Interreligious Relations in the Ottoman Empire: the Early Modern Centuries", *Acta Poloniae Historica* 116 (2017): 57–91, here 61–66.

34 E. Hösch, "Das sogenannte, 'griechische Projekt' Katharinas II: Ideologie und Wirklichkeit der russischen Orientpolitik in der 2. Hälfte des 18. Jahrhunderts", *Jahrbücher für Geschichte Osteuropas*, N.F., 12/2 (1964): 168–206.

35 Molos, 114–117, 185; Evgenios Voulgaris, *Ικετηρία του Γένους των Γραικών προς πάσαν την χριστιανικήν Ευρώπην* [Petition of the Nation of Greeks to all of Christian Europe], [Petersburg] 1771; P. Kanellopoulos, "Ποιος συνέγραψε την *Ικετηρίαν του Γένους των Γραικών προς πάσαν την χριστιανικήν Ευρώπην;*" [Who wrote the Petition of the Nation of Greeks to all of Christian Europe?], *Nea Estia* 106 (1979): 908–916.

36 S. K. Batalden, *Catherine II's Greek Prelate. Eugenios Voulgaris in Russia, 1771–1806* (New York, 1982); from the rich literature on Voulgaris, see most recently: Ch. Karanasios, ed., *Ευγένιος Βούλγαρης: o homo universalis του Νέου Ελληνισμού: 300 χρόνια από τη γέννησή του (1716–2016)* [Evgenios Voulgaris: the

170   Olga Katsiardi-Hering

homo universalis of Modern Hellenism: 300 years since his birth (1716–2016)] (Athens, 2018).
37 Molos, 186.
38 For a political ideological analysis of Russian policy see Rotzokos, *Εθναφύπνιση*, 180–185, 221–249.
39 P. M. Kitromilides, "Ιδεολογικές επιλογές και ιστοριογραφική πράξη: Σπυρίδων Παπαδόπουλος και Domenico Caminer" [Ideological choices and historiographical practice: Spyridon Papadopoulos and Domenico Caminer], *Thesaurismata* 20 (1990): 500–517.
40 P. M. Kitromilides, "The Identity of a Book. European Power Politics and Ideological Motivations in Agapios Loverdos's *Ιστορία των δύο Ετών (Venice 1791)*", *Thesaurismata* 28 (1998): 433–449.
41 G. Harlafti, K. Papakonstantinou, eds, *Ναυτιλία των Ελλήνων, 1700–1821. Ο αιώνας της ακμής πριν από την Επανάσταση* [Greek shipping 1700–1821. The century of thriving before the Revolution] (Athens, 2013).
42 Sakellariou, *Η Πελοπόννησος*, 193–203.
43 O. Katsiardi-Hering, "Migrationen von Bevölkerungsgruppen in Südosteuropa vom 15. Jahrhundert bis zum Beginn des 19. Jahrhunderts", *Südost-Forschungen* 59/60 (2001): 125–148.
44 O. Katsiardi-Hering, "Μύθος και Ιστορία. Ο Λάμπρος Κατσώνης, οι χρηματοδότες του και η πολιτική τακτική" [Myth and History. Lampros Katsonis, his financiers and the political practice], in *Rodonia.* Honour to M. I. Manoussacas, vol. 1 (Rethymno, 1994), 195–214.
45 G. Kollias, *Οι Έλληνες κατά τον ρωσοτουρκικόν πόλεμον (1787–1792)* [The Greeks during the Russo-Turkish war (1787–1792)] (Athens, 1940). For a broader view of the war see Franco Venturi, *Settecento Riformatore*, vol. IV/2, *Il patriotismo repubblicano e gli imperi dell'Est* (Milano, 1984), 780–969.
46 Katsiardi-Hering, "Ελληνικά διαβήματα στον Βοναπάρτη".
47 Vakalopoulos, *Ιστορία του Νέου Ελληνισμού, ibid.*, 548–590; about these groups as local warriors see Alexander, *Brigandage*; D. Skiotis, "Mountain warriors and the Greek Revolution", *Technology and Society in the Middle East*, eds. V. J. Parry and M. E. Yapp (Oxford, 1975), 308–329; F. Adanır, "Heiduckentum und osmanische Herrschaft. Sozialgeschichtliche Aspekte der Diskussion um das frühneuzeitliche Räuberwesen in Südosteuropa", *Südost-Forschungen* 41 (1982): 43–116.
48 N. Saul, *Russia and the Mediterranean, 1797–1807* (Chicago, 1970); D. Tzakis, "Η ρωσική παρουσία στο Αιγαίο. Από τα Ορλωφικά στο Λάμπρο Κατσώνη" [The Russian presence in the Aegean. From the Orlofika to Lampros Katsonis], in *Ιστορία του Νέου Ελληνισμού, 1770–2000* [History of Modern Hellenism, 1770–2000], vol. 1, ed. V. Panagiotopoulos (Athens, 2003), 115–149; see also the vol. 2 of: O. Katsiardi-Hering, A. Kolia-Dermitzaki, and K. Gardika, eds, *Ρωσία και Μεσόγειος. Πρακτικά Α΄ Διεθνούς Συνεδρίου (Αθήνα, 19–22 Μαιου 2005)* [Russia and the Mediterranean. Proceedings of the 1st International Conference (Athens, 19–22 Mai 2005)] (Athens, 2011).
49 A. Sfoini, "Transfert des idées par la voie de la traduction pendant l'ère révolutionnaire grecque (1797–1832)", *The Historical Review/La Revue Historique* 12 (2015): 47–74.
50 O. Katsiardi-Hering, "Il mondo europeo degli intelletuali greci della Diaspora (sec. XVIII ex.-XIX in.)", in *Niccolò Tommaseo: popolo e nazioni. Italiani, Corsi, Greci, Illirici. Atti del Convegno internazionale di Studi nel bicentenario della nascita di Niccolò Tommaseo, Venezia 23-25.1.2003*, ed. Fr. Bruni (Roma-Padova 2004), 69–85.
51 Österreichisches Staatsarchiv, Kriegsarchiv, Kartensammlung [ÖStA, KA, Kartensammlung], KIa, 9F, Memorandum of Anastasios Paraskevas, 1783, f.

From the revolts to the Greek Revolution   171

1–27, to the emperor Joseph II; s. G. Loukas, "Ευρωπαϊκές δυνάμεις και βαλκανικοί λαοί. Σχέδια για απελευθερωτικά κινήματα. Προσδοκίες και προοπτικές. Το 'όραμα' του Αναστάσιου Παρασκευά (1783)" [European powers and Balkan peoples. Plans for liberation movements. Expectations and prospects. The "vision" of Anastasios Paraskevas (1783)] (Master's Thesis, National and Kapodistrian University of Athens, 2009).

52 ÖStA, ibid., f. 13v–15r.
53 K. Roider, *Austria's Eastern Question, 1700–1790* (Princeton University Press, 1982), 151–168.
54 ÖStA, ibid., f. 17v–18r.
55 Ibid., f. 19r.
56 Chimara was a central place for the revolts also in previous centuries. On the literature see Katsiardi-Hering, "Von den Aufständen", 120–121; in 1785 Chimariots would appeal to Joseph II with the request to join his military service, Haus-, Hof- und Staatsarchiv, Türkei III, Karton 11, Grenzangelegenheiten (Chimarioten, 1785–1788).
57 ÖStA, KA, ibid., f. 25v–26r.
58 R. Păun, "Enemies Within. Networks of Influence and the Military Revolts Against the Ottoman Power (Moldavia and Wallachia, Sixteenth-Seventeenth Centuries)", in *The European Tributary States of the Ottoman Empire in the Sixteenth and Seventeenth Centuries*, eds G. Kármán and L. Kunčević (Leiden, 2013), 209–249.
59 B. Bronza, "The Habsburg Monarchy and the Projects for Division of the Ottoman Balkans", in *Empires and Peninsulas. Southeastern Europe between Karlowitz and the Peace of Adrianople, 1699–1829*, eds P. Mitev, I. Parvev, M. Baramova and V. Racheva (Berlin, 2010), 51–62.
60 Aik. Koumarianou, "Ενέργειες του Κωνσταντίνου Σταμάτη για την απελευθέρωση της Ελλάδος (1798-1799)" [Energies of Constantine Stamatis for the liberation of Greece (1798–1799)], *Proceedings of the Third Panionian Congress* (in Greek), vol. 1, (Athens, 1967), 154–174.
61 Las Casas, *Le Mémorial de Sainte-Hélène*, vol. 1 (Paris, 1935), 415–416.
62 See literature in: O. Katsiardi-Hering, "L'idée de la Révolution dans l'horizon politique des Grecs de Hongrie (fin XVIIIe siècle)", *La Révolution Française et l'Hellénisme Moderne*, Actes du IIIe colloque d'histoire (Athènes, 14–17 Oct. 1987) (Athens, 1989), 87–118.
63 http://www.e-perimetron.org/Vol_3_3/Livieratos_b.pdf (access on 20.8.2020).
64 Kitromilides, ed., *Ρήγας Βελεστινλής, Άπαντα τα σωζόμενα*, vol. 5 (Athens, 2000), 45–71.
65 K. E. Fleming, *The Muslim Bonaparte: Diplomacy and Orientalism in Ali Pasha's Greece* (Princeton, 1999).
66 E. Hobsbawm, "Social Bandits: Reply", in *Comparative Studies in Society and History* 14/4 (1972), 503–505, his response to the criticism of his books: *Primitive rebels: Studies in Archaic Forms of Social Movement in the 19th and 20th Centuries* (Manchester, 1959) and *Bandits* (London, 1969).
67 Adanır, "Heiduckentum", 115; B. Cvetkova, "The Bulgarian Haiduk Movement in the 15th-18th Centuries", in *East Central European Society and War in the Pre-Revolutionary Eighteenth Century*, eds G. E. Rothenberg, B. K. Király, and P. F. Sugar (New York, 1982), 301–338; K. Barkey, *Bandits and Bureaucrats. The Ottoman Route to State Centralization* (Ithaca-London, 1997), 176–185.
68 From the rich bibliography on the Serbian revolt see: D. Friesel-Kopecki, "Die Serbische Nationalbewegung", in *Nationalbewegungen auf dem Balkan*, ed. N. Reiter (Berlin, 1983), 177–279.
69 M. Jarrett, *The Congress of Vienna and Its Legacy. War and Great Power after Napoleon* (London-New York, 2013).

172　*Olga Katsiardi-Hering*

70 Kitromilides, *Enlightenment*, 230–250, at 249; A. Sfoini, "Loyaume and Nomarchie: Keywords of the French Revolution in the Greek Vocabulary", *The Historical Review/La Revue Historique* 11 (2014): 127–138.
71 Kitromilides, 394.
72 Ibid., 260–290, here 268, 269.
73 O. Katsiardi-Hering, ed., *Οι πόλεις των Φιλικών: οι αστικές διαδρομές ενός επαναστατικού φαινομένου. Πρακτικά ημερίδας* [The cities of the Philikoi: the urban routes of a revolutionary phenomenon. Proceedings of a conference] (Athens, 2018).
74 Ev. Sifnaios, *Imperial Odessa: Peoples, Spaces, Identities*, (Leiden, 2017).
75 I. Chatzipanagioti-Sangmeister, *Ο Τεκτονισμός στην ελληνική κοινωνία και γραμματεία του 18ου αιώνα: οι γερμανόφωνες μαρτυρίες* [Freemasonry in Greek society and scholarship in the eighteenth century: the German testimonies] (Athens, 2010).
76 G. D. Frangos, *The Philike Etaireia, 1814–1821. A Social and Historical Analysis*, (PhD, Columbia University 1971); O. Katsiardi-Hering, "Politische und ökonomische Regionen in der Peripherie: Der Weg zu den Revolutionen in Südosteuropa zu Beginn des 19. Jahrhunderts", in *Provincial Turn. Verhältnis zwischen Staat und Provinz im südöstlichen Europa vom letzten Drittel des 17. bis ins 21. Jahrhundert*, eds U. Tischler-Hofer and K. Kaser (Frankfurt, 2017), 91–112, for an analysis of the political-economical networks on the eve of the Greek Revolution.
77 K. Zanou, *Transnational Patriotism in the Mediterranean, 1800–1850. Stammering the Nation* (Oxford, 2018).
78 G. Hering, "Zum Problem der Ursachen revolutionärer Erhebungen am Anfang des 19. Jahrhunderts", in *Nationalrevolutionäre Bewegungen in Südosteuropa im 19. Jahrhundert*, eds Chr. Choliolčev, K. Mack and A. Suppan (Vienna-Munich, 1992), 17–30.
79 Katsiardi-Hering, "Introduction", in Eadem, *Οι πόλεις των Φιλικών*, 19.
80 I. Philimon, *Δοκίμιον Ιστορικόν περί της Ελληνικής Επαναστάσεως* [Historical Essay about the Greek Revolution], (Athens, 1859), vol. 2, 79–80.
81 O. Katsiardi-Hering, "Die Europaidee in den Texten des griechischen Unabhängigkeitskrieges (1821–1829)", in *Südosteuropa. Von moderner Vielfalt und nationalstaatlicher Vereinheitlichung*, Festschrift für Edgar Hösch, eds K. Clewing and O. Jens Schmitt (Munich, 2005), 237–252.

13 The vigilant eye of the Revolution: Public security and police in revolutionary Greece

Vaso Seirinidou

Introduction

Revolutions are not doing well with the police. From the tsarist *Okhrana* to Ceausesku's *Securitate*, and from the paramilitary *garde mobile* in the streets of revolutionary Paris in 1848 to the riot police forces of modern liberal democracies, the history of revolutions has endowed the police with the quality of the most potent metonymy for counter-revolution. For, what else, apart from constitutionally opposed, could be two concepts, one referring to the overthrow of the order and the second to its maintenance?

Nevertheless, the police are, to a great extent, a product of the revolution. We do not mean here only the dialectics of uprising and repression, inherent in almost every revolutionary condition. We are referring, instead, to that global historical experience of the late 18th and the first half of the 19th century, known as the Age of Revolutions, during which the police began to acquire their modern meaning as a publicly constituted agency empowered to use force to impose public order and security and to prevent crime. Namely, a meaning much narrower than the early modern notions of the "gute Polizey" as a set of administrative practices, mostly in the form of prohibitions and decrees, covering a wide range of everyday life, aimed at the well-ordered society and the general (state's and subject's) welfare.[1]

Indeed, the advancement of security to a political key notion was not a novelty of the revolutionary age. Linked to the emergence of the princely territorial states in seventeenth-century Europe and the consequent conceptual distinction between internal and external security, the idea of domestic security became, under the influence of the 18th-century cameralist administration science (Policeywissenschaft), a leading principle of governance, replacing or supplementing the older state objective of welfare.[2] At the theoretical level, the Austrian statesman, Joseph von Sonnefels, was the first who "relieved" the police of the ambitious task of promoting the collective well-being, defining it as "the science that teaches us how to create and cater to the domestic security of the state".[3] In the last quarter of the 18th century, surveillance of marginalized groups, the regulation of immigrant and transient population as well as the employment of informants

174 *Vaso Seirinidou*

to monitor social and political activities were established policing practices throughout Europe, with the capital cities being the prime sites for the implementation of the public security objective.[4]

Although not breaking with pre-existing concepts and practices on matters of public security and policing, the French Revolution and its worldwide political upheavals generated new international security and conspiracy dispositive that advanced political crime to a primary public security threat and called for the intensification of monitoring population mobility and political policing.[5] Strict border control and elaborated passport techniques, that had developed during the French Revolution and the Napoleonic era, continued in the following period, with new passport laws being issued throughout Europe.[6] On the other hand, new legal notions of political crime as an offense against public security emerged along with the establishment of political police institutions that became integral parts of the modern state apparatus.[7] Moreover, the impact of the French Revolution as a cross-border security threat promoted an increasing internationalization of security and policing discourses and practices.[8] In the international system of interlocking power relations created after 1815, security at home became increasingly a matter of international concern, making the police "as indispensable for the functioning of the international state system as the standing armies and navies and as necessary as the permanent diplomatic missions in all the capitals of Europe".[9] Related to this context was the increasing professionalization, bureaucratization, and specialization of the police as a state institution endowed with the monopoly on the use of legitimate force.

This article attempts to approach the Greek Revolution from the perspective of the public security dispositive, namely the set of practices, discourses, legal categories, and institutions put in place to respond and to interact with new doctrines, emergencies, and threats that configured the public security landscape in Europe and the world in the Age of Revolutions. In particular, it focuses on police formation in revolutionary Greece and on their role as a securitizing agent in an emergency situation. Based on the voluminous archival records of the Ministry of Police in the timespan between 1822 and 1826, we will argue that the turbulent revolutionary period was crucial for the accumulation of knowledge and the implementation of practices and techniques of territory and population control and that despite their organizational weakness the police were a constituent part of the "governmental rationalities" of the revolutionary state.

From policing to the police: The establishment of police institutions in revolutionary Greece

A real child of its age, the Greek Revolution included security and the formation of police institutions among its political priorities. Immediately after the outbreak of the Revolution, the care for safeguarding internal security and order had been assigned to the various regional governments (*Τοπικές Διοικήσεις*) that had been founded by regional assemblies as provisional administrative bodies to respond to the organizational needs of the struggle. The *police* (*αστυνομία*), as a term referring to a distinct administrative authority, appeared for the first time in the constitutional chart of the Samos island (*Στρατοπολιτικόν Σύστημα Σάμου*), issued in May 1821, and six months later in the Legal Ordinance of Eastern Continental Greece (*Νομική Διάταξις της Ανατολικής Χέρσου Ελλάδος*), the most sophisticated, and mostly inapplicable, regional constitutional text that bored the imprint of its author's, Theodoros Negris, legal expertise.

Some months before the issuance of the Legal Order, and in a less sophisticated manner, 44 masters from Ydra island petitioned the island's communal authorities to set up "a police post, or what the Italians call executive police" charged with the task of controlling incoming and outgoing individuals, ships and letters, and informing the local authorities. In their response, issued on the same day (24 June 1821), the community's notables authorized the masters to appoint a police officer and a secretary, and, in this way, Ydra became the first place in revolutionary Greece to have police.[10]

Despite the innovation in the administrative vocabulary, both the constitutional charts of Samos and eastern continental Greece and the police office of Ydra did not introduce completely unknown experiences in the Greek world. Responsibilities related to law enforcement maintenance of order, and the common peace, as well as to market operation and public health, were exercised by various actors, from state officials and armed bodies to the local Muslim and Christian landlords and the communities' and neighbourhood's heads.[11] Above all, however, policing, as was the case in the early modern world, was integrated into everyday social interaction, and social control was not a domain of a particular institution, but it was exercised daily through the vertical and horizontal structures of the community.[12] Especially in the Ottoman Empire, it was the principle of the collective responsibility that through the imposition of fines and the obligation for monetary guarantees encouraged collective bodies, such as communities and *mahalles* (neighbourhoods), to carry out policing function within their boundaries. Access to a different neighbourhood was not a simple matter, and there is evidence that no one could even visit a *mahalle* without giving the name of at least one resident as a guarantor.[13]

Consequently, it was the assignment of all police competencies to a single authority, as it was provided by the Legal Order, which constituted the main shift from the pre-revolutionary reality.

In any case, except Ydra, police authorities were not set up in Greece during the first months of the Revolution. The first step in establishing police institutions was taken with the Provisional Constitution of Greece (*Προσωρινόν Πολίτευμα της Ελλάδος*) of January 1822. The Constitution recognized the life, property, and honour of every Greek citizen as legally

176 Vaso Seirinidou

protected goods and ordered the establishment of the Ministry of Police as one of the eight ministries of the Provisional Administration.[14] The Law of Epidaurus (Νόμος της Επιδαύρου) in April 1823 went a step further, by distinguishing between the general (pubic) and the partial (private) security of the nation and placing both of them among the key duties of the Executive.[15] In the same month, the Organizational Law of the Greek Provinces (Οργανισμός των ελληνικών επαρχιών) provided in each province a post of a general police officer, apparently following the French model of the *commissaires de police* in cities with over 5,000 population, appointed and salaried by the Ministry of Police, to which he was accountable.[16] By the summer of 1823, police authorities had been established in each Greek province.

Despite its implementation throughout the revolutionary territory, the scheme of the General Police (Γενικαί Αστυνομίαι) was far from constituting a coherent system, as the degree of institutional formation of police authorities in each province and of course the size of their archival footprint, was proportional to their importance in the military and political conjuncture. In conditions of war, the importance of the island and coastal areas as entrance gates for ships, foreigners, and epidemic diseases was upgraded. At the same time, the political organization of the Revolution formed a new hierarchy of space that followed the tense and geographically differentiated processes of state formation. Therefore, the police existed primarily in the headquarters of the Administration.[17]

Regarding its institutional organization, the police during the Revolution has the inherently incomplete character of an institution in the making. We propose, instead, to shift our focus from the organizational structure to the competencies and practices of the police as it is in this field where some major "events" of the state formation process were produced.[18]

Producing a territory: Mobility control and identification practices

A general operating regulation did not accompany the establishment of police institutions in revolutionary Greece. The first text of this kind, entitled, Provisional Duties of the General Police Officers (Προσωρινά Καθήκοντα των Γενικών Αστυνόμων) was issued in September 1825. It included 15 articles, five of which were related to the administrative obligations of police officers towards the Ministry of Police. Of the remaining ten articles, one was about vigilance for public order and security of life, property, and honour of the citizens, one about the duty of the police to arrest and imprison proven criminals, two about public health, two about market matters, while the remaining six articles were related to issues of state security and population control. Specifically, the duties of the general policemen included informing the Ministry of Police about the obedience or disobedience of the population of their province to the Administration's orders, arresting spies, recording incoming and outgoing individuals to and from their provinces, and issuing passports, as well as the censorship of suspicious letters.[19]

Issued at a time when the conflict, known as the "second civil war", between the Administration and the Peloponnesian notables and chieftains was at its height, and Ibrahim's military operations threatened the very survival of the Revolution, the ordinance of 1825 confirmed the predominant role the protection of internal security acquired among the duties of the police, as well as the highly political nature of the latter.

The engagement of the police in state security protection unfolded through systematic activity in the fields of mobility control, identification of individuals, and intelligence matters that left an impressive archival imprint. The control of population movement was among the first domains where the revolutionary state manifested its sovereignty over individuals and a territory. It is not coincidental that the Ministry of Police launched its administrative communication with the local police offices with documents concerning the regulation of movement and the issuance of passports. According to them, every person entering the province had to report to the local police and hand over their passports to obtain a residence permit for a certain period. No one could leave the province without a passport, issued by the police. Particular emphasis was placed on the control of incoming ships and boats, the crew and passengers of which had to carry passports and be quarantined.[20] These commands were set in practice through an intense activity of recording and identification of individuals that extended to the non-mobile population and peaked in the population census of Nafplion in November 1825, where 2,311 individuals were registered.[21] Although mobility control with emphasis on the capital and other cities was practiced in the Ottoman Empire and Ottoman subjects were regularly registered for taxation and other purposes,[22] there are reasons to believe that the Revolution introduced a new experience in population and territory control.

The first element that differentiated the control of movement during the Revolution was its overall strong ideological connotation. In a conspiracy imagery full of "spies", "traitors", and "suspect individuals", identification and registering of the transient population was a means of safeguarding the dignity of the Revolution. The embodiment of major public security threats in the person of the "foreigner" and the intensification of foreigners' control was a common characteristic of European state policies from the last quarter of the 18th century onwards, expressed, among other things, through the creation of police branches specialized in the monitoring of foreigners.[23] But who was the "foreigner" in a revolutionary state coming into being with a vague political and territorial sovereignty? In the police registering and identification practice, we can discern two notions of the "foreigner". The first one referred to those who were not natives of the province, namely, it was close to the pre-revolutionary, locality-based concept of belonging.[24]

178 *Vaso Seirinidou*

The second one referred to those originating in areas where no revolutionary authorities had been established, and it was closer to the spirit of the Epidaurus Constitution, which defined as Greek citizens "all the indigenous inhabitants of the Greek territory who believe in Christ".[25] Although all transient populations had to be registered, particular attention was directed to the second category of "foreigners", which included both subjects of foreign states and Greek Orthodox folks from Ottoman provinces.

Through practices of identification and monitoring of those coming from "abroad", the police substantiated the rather vague notion of the *Greek territory*. The same practices produced a range of discourses and events that affirmed and manifested the sovereignty of the revolutionary state. The refusal, for instance, of some captains of European-flagged vessels to undergo passport control while mooring in the Greek ports was the cause of incidents between the consuls and the local police, in which issues of territorial sovereignty came to the fore.[26] In July 1825, a serious diplomatic incident erupted when, on the occasion of the inspection of the documents of the French ship, *Amirante,* by the police of Syros, the French consul in Smyrna accused the island's authorities of insulting the French state. As a result, a French squadron under Admiral De Rigny blocked the port of Syros. The Ministry of Police reacted immediately, urging the French consul "not to interfere in cases involving the identification of traitors against an entire nation" and he defended the right of every government "to examine and prevent any individual from resisting when the case concerns the security of its territory".[27] Meanwhile, the Police Committee of the Aegean Sea, set up in the summer of 1825 to investigate a network of Greek merchants, suspects of espionage in favour of Ibrahim, added another dimension to the incident.

> The Administration loves and encourages trade … But it can no longer tolerate the subjects of any power to load from its sacred ground and export food and ammunition to hostile destinations … Those who want to help their collaborations who die in their minds and souls as Turks, have to go to hostile and neutral places and supply the enemy as they wish.[28]

Apart from the new discourse invested in the control of movement, the Revolution brought increased centralization of information management. From the first months of the operation of police institutions, there had been a systematic communication and information exchange between the Ministry of Police and the local police offices on issues of espionage and identification of suspects. As early as the summer of 1822, the Ydra police wrote to the Ministry to notify all local border police of the large number of spies scattered across Greece and gave information for a suspicious monk who had passed through Ydra in the Peloponnese without a passport.[29] In turn, the Ministry gave the news about the monk to the police of Tripolitsa and Nafplion and notified the police of Ydra, Syros, and Naxos of

The vigilant eye of the Revolution   179

"someone Ioannis Kokkinis, marked by smallpox, solidly-built, of Western doctrine, speaking vernacular Greek, at first dressed in European clothes and now Greek, is suspect of working for Ibrahim".[30]

This "institutional" circulation of information throughout the territory created a sense of bureaucratic community, but also the need for standardization of written procedures in matters of travel control and personal identification. Police officers often reported their inability to verify the authenticity of travel documents of those entering their provinces and asked for instructions. The Ministry responded in July 1823 with a document, entitled "Police duties, or provisionary interpretation of them" (*Χρέη αστυνομίας, ήτοι προσωριναί αιρμινίαι αυτής*), which, among others, contained directions for issuing of passports, focusing on technicalities such as passport numbering, the location of the stamp and the police officer's signature, and the uniform recording of the incoming and outgoing individuals by name, age, place of origin, and occupation.[31] The document did not have the status of a passport regulation like the one issued by Capodistrias in August 1828.[32] Although handwritten passport templates are available in the sources,[33] we do not know to what extent there have been standardized methods and documents of personal identification during the Revolution. Nevertheless, what we can observe, albeit faintly, is that the control of mobility and the identification of persons was tending to be assigned to a more "specialized" staff. From the summer of 1823 "passport police" (*αστυνόμοι διαβατηρίων*) were appointed in cities and ports, charged with the registration of the transient population and financed by the fees for the issuance and validation of passports. If we add to them the "secret individuals" (*μυστικά υποκείμενα*), who were paid to monitor foreigners and other suspicious persons,[34] then assuming some kind of "specialization" in matters of mobility control is not entirely unfounded. Besides, it was the general police commissioner of Tripolitsa who, albeit on an unfortunate occasion, acknowledged that the work of personal identification involved bureaucratic tools and secret police methods.

> Carrying out your orders and after having searched all over the province, I could not find out anything about the spies, because, apart from the fact that there is no document of their name, homeland or any specific personal mark, the police are deprived of the necessary eavesdroppers (*ωτακουστών*) needed for the discovery of these individuals.[35]

The enemy within

Most of all, the Revolution brought about the emergence of new legal conceptualization of political crime. At the end of the 18th century, a variety of terms was already in use throughout Europe and in the Ottoman Empire to describe and punish political crime.[36] Nevertheless, it was the French revolutionary penal codes (1791, 1795), and especially the Napoleonic penal

180 *Vaso Seirinidou*

code of 1810 that established the modern concept of political crime as a crime against the state and advanced polity and public security to legally protected goods.[37] A template for almost every European penal code in the 19th century, the Napoleonic code of 1810, found its resonance in revolutionary Greece in the Compilation of Criminal Laws (*Απάνθισμα των Εγκληματικών*), a precursor form of penal law issued by the Second National Assembly in July 1824. This was a blend of Byzantine and modern European criminal laws, blamed for its sloppiness, its shortcomings in determining offenses and penalties, and especially its leniency.[38] If the latter applies to the section on crimes against personal security, the same does not apply to the section on crimes against public security. On the contrary, this was a short and simplified version of the third book, title I, of the Napoleonic code, adapted to domestic conditions. It distinguished between crimes against the external and the internal security and differentiated between plots and factions against the nation's polity, as well as armed assaults against public property, seizure of fortresses and towns against the Administration's command, the incitement of civil war, and the violation of public health orders. For these crimes, the Compilation provided for capital punishment, while threatening with two to five years of imprisonment those who would not reveal to the authorities conspiracies against state security.[39]

The Compilation of Criminal Laws and its equivalent at the executive level, the police ordinance of 1825, reflected security threats as prioritized by the Administration in conditions of war and political unrest. From 1824, and under the weight of the civil war and the political conflict that followed the Act of Submission in Britain (July 1825), political policing gained prominence over other police duties. Most of the police activity involved monitoring the Administration's opponents and sending relevant reports to the Ministry, while among the qualifications of candidate police officers was their proven pro-government stance.[40] In the conspiracy discourse of the period, terms such as "anti-patriots" (*αντιπατριώται*), "anti-national thinking individuals" (*αντεθνικώς σκεπτόμενα υποκείμενα*), "enemies of the Revolution" (*εχθροί της Επαναστάσεως*), "counter-administratives" (*αντιδιοικητικοί*) were appearing more and more next to the old known "rebels", "conspirators", and "factionists" to designate those threatening the internal security of the state. As armed conflicts, involving trials, imprisonment, and amnesty for the political opponents, the civil wars (1823–1825) have been decisive in the formation of the security dispositive in revolutionary Greece, both at the practical and the ideological level, and have been thoroughly studied.[41] The interest, as expected, has been focused on the protagonists of the conflict, and to a lesser extent on its social accommodation. Surviving police records offer insight into the latter, and especially the denunciation letters sent by individuals to the police to report actions against public security.

The practice of denunciation had a long tradition under the Old Regime, but it was again in the context of the French Revolution that it was radically reconceptualized from a synonym of the arbitrariness and secretiveness of monarchical justice, into a public act of civic virtue, political action for defending the Revolution.[42] Following the Napoleonic penal code, the Compilation of Criminal Laws promoted the non-disclosure of crimes against the security of the state as a criminal offense. From our research so far in the archives of the Ministry of Police and the Executive, we have identified 24 denunciations filed between April 1823 and March 1825. Of these, three were related to espionage in favour of Mehmet Ali, five to spreading of defeatism among the population, seven to factionalism against the Administration, and nine to actions endangering the common peace. Six of them had the form of a collective denunciation signed by more than one person. The denunciators disclaimed any personal interest, invoking patriotism, and awareness for the common good as the motive of their action. Next to these "pure" denunciations, there are several complaints about private disputes involving accusations of anti-patriotic attitude and factionalism. Regardless of the real motives of the authors, invoking public security as a patriotic duty, or engaging it as a means against the opponent – often a neighbour – in private disputes allow us to assume a degree of penetration of the state security ideology in the society.[43] In any case, these reports remained an important source of information for the police. After all, it was the denunciation letter by the citizen Dimitrios Hoidas that revealed the largest espionage network on behalf of Mehmet Ali in Greece, that of the trade representatives of the Alexandrine merchant house Tositsa. Again, it was a private complaint about an unpaid debt that provided information for the arrest of a small anti-government faction in Athens.[44]

The "dangerous classes"

Following the political and philosophical thought of their time, the penal codes of the 19th century made an axiomatic distinction between crimes against public and private security, reserving different legal treatment in each category. In reality, however, the lines between them were more fluid than liberal ideology claimed. Studies on policing and criminal justice have shown how private security fears of the proprietied classes in the 19th century were transformed into public security threats and led to the criminalization of social groups, such as the poor, vagrants, beggars, and prostitutes.[45] In the Napoleonic penal code, vagrancy and mendicancy appeared as delicts against the public peace and vagabonds, or unowned people, were punished with imprisonment or deportation.[46]

Despite the strong influences from the Napoleonic penal code, the idea of "dangerous classes" was absent from the Greek normative texts of the revolutionary period, which were more concerned with "spies" and "conspirators" than with "vagabonds" and "beggars". Nevertheless, many complaints from individuals and collective bodies to the authorities about assaults against their private security indicated a new public threat, personified in the irregular soldiers, who, under the command of various

182 *Vaso Seirinidou*

chieftains, formed the military arm of the Greek Revolution. As early as May 1823, the Minister of the Interior and Police informed the Executive about the popular discontent caused by the violent actions of the soldiers and called for the exemplary punishment of the latter, acknowledging them as a threat to public order and security.[47] A year later, residents and communal authorities in Argos would make dramatic calls to protect themselves from the brutal actions of soldiers who had gathered in the city in support of the government against its Moreot opponents. Residents of Argos went so far as to protest outside the police station and threatened to leave the city with their families, no longer suffering the daily attacks on their lives, honour, and property.[48] Similar complaints reached the police authorities in other parts of continental Greece (especially in Athens), while in the Peloponnese there was discontent not only about the Roumeliot "invaders" but also about soldiers of the local chiefs.[49] In coastal areas, piracy and robbery by armed refugees on some islands constituted a significant security threat for the local population and foreign fleets, undermining the legitimacy claims of the revolutionary state.[50] To the extent that the boundaries between piracy and corsairing were fluid and, in the absence of sufficient squadrons, raid licenses to vessels were employed against the enemy fleet, the Administration did not intervene officially, leaving the responsibility of the prosecution to the local authorities.[51] It was after the naval battle of Navarino (October 1827) that a repressive policy was initiated, and piracy was conceptualized as an "abominable" crime.[52]

Things turned out differently with armed groups in the continental territory. The Executive saw them primarily as a threat to state security rather than a public order problem. During the civil war, its primary concern was to record all irregular soldiers, to identify and disarm those who belonged to the anti-government forces.[53] In the same direction, a "Secret Police Officer" (*Μυστικός Αστυνόμος*) was appointed at the General Camp of the Peloponnese, in July 1825, with a mission to monitor and report to the Ministry of Police suspected of spying for Ibrahim within the army.[54] The burden of dealing with public order incidents involving irregular soldiers in the towns fell on the local police, whose effectiveness was doubtful. Instead, police reports attest to the inability to enforce public order and are full of examples of police officers returning to their posts beaten and scorned.[55] However, the intensity of the daily violence associated with, among other things, the presence of armed groups in the cities created new areas of police intervention. Thus, on the grounds that drunkenness triggers violent behaviour, the police of Nafplion banned the public use of alcohol and allowed its sale only for home use. They ordered the sealing of the taverns where gambling and music were played and went so far as to propose a ban on the use of sweets and products containing butter for being harmful to physical and spiritual health.[56] Above all, the demand for security of life and property in conditions of generalized violence and insecurity created spaces for the presence and the legitimization

The vigilant eye of the Revolution 183

of the state in the local population. In the climate of war and political turmoil, the traditional mechanisms of social pacification (community, church) seemed to be reaching their limits and the state, in the person of the general police officer, began to emerge as a new agent in the management of violence.

Despite the documented readiness of citizens to appeal to the police on issues of their private security, we could hardly speak of wide social acceptance of it in revolutionary Greece. They were not only the representatives of the traditional world of arms who undermined the claim of the monopoly of violence by the police. The Lieutenant of Nafplion describes his sufferings when, at the behest of the Administration, he attempted to evacuate a house intended for General Plapoutas, but was occupied by soldiers and refugee families.

> The people who live there, some soldiers with their wives, some women from Chios and other trashy ones, every time I go there, they curse me. Today, when I went there a skivvy said to me 'what do you want here and you come every day? Go away, go away', while the other women advised her to push me. Shortly after I left this house, I met some soldiers of Photomara and the soldiers who live there, and when they saw me, they started insulting me with obscene words and threatening me not to step on the house again, otherwise, they will tear me in pieces.[57]

Apparently, for those who did not have anything private to protect, the police were on the opposite bank.

Conclusion -and a desideratum

An era of worldwide revolutionary upheavals and violent political overthrows, the sixty years between the French Revolution and the Revolutions of 1848, was also the period in which the modern notions and practices of public security and policing took shape. The Revolution of 1821, intense in war and political events, was a defining moment in the inclusion of the Greek experience in the new public security paradigm of the revolutionary age. The police played a key role in this process. In the previous pages, we followed the emergence of the police into a multi-purpose tool of governance. More than an organizational structure, we saw them as a set of practices through which key concepts of state formation, such as sovereignty, territory, and population, were substantiated and visions of social disciplining were articulated.

Examining here the various imprints of the 19th-century public security regime in revolutionary Greece, we left out the other half of the picture, that is, the ways in which the Greek Revolution affected the security dispositive of its time. It is well known that as a threat to the international monarchical

184 *Vaso Seirinidou*

balance of power, the Greek uprising activated conspiracy theories and repressive mechanisms at the interstate level. As for its impact on the internal security policies of the European monarchies, the most studied case is that of Austria, in which the outbreak of the Greek Revolution intensified press censorship and political policing.[58] Of particular interest is the impact of the Revolution on the security policy in the Ottoman Empire, which since the time of Selim III was increasingly focused on population control and social regulation.[59] We know, for instance, that apart from the traditional repressive measures, the "Rum Riots" triggered the systematization of the Ottoman travel documents, at a time when official passport regulations were still absent.[60] Embedding the Greek Revolution in the security and policing environment of the Ottoman Empire could shed more light on the turbulent Balkan paths to modernity, as well as to the role of the former as a founding experience in this process.

Notes

1 On this development, see Roland Axtmann, "'Police' and the Formation of the Modern State. Legal and Ideological Assumptions on State Capacity in the Austrian Lands of the Habsburg Empire, 1500–1800", *German History* 10 (1990): 39–61.

2 See Werner Conze's entry "Sicherheit, Schutz", in *Geschichtliche Grundbegriffe: Historisches Lexikon zur politisch-sozialen Sprache in Deutschland*, v. 5, eds, O. Brunner, R. Koselleck (Stuttgart, 1984), 831–862. For a thorough account see, Giuseppe Campesi, *The Genealogy of Public Security: The Theory and History of Modern Police Powers* (New York, 2017). See also, Karl Härter, "Security and 'Gute Polizey' in Early Modern Europe: Concepts, Laws, and Instruments", in *The Production of Human Security in Premodern and Contemporary History* [= *Historical Social Research/Historische Sozialforschung* 35 (2010)], eds C. Zwierlein, R. Graf and M. Ressel, 41–65.

3 As quoted in Hsi-Huey Liang, *The Rise of Modern Police and the European State System from Metternich to the Second World War* (Cambridge, 1992), 1.

4 See, for instance, Robert M. Schwartz, *Policing the Poor in Eighteenth-Century France* (Chapel Hill & London, 1988); Vincent Denis and Vincent Milliot, "Police et identification dans la France des Lumières", *Genèses* 54 (2004): 4–27; Betül Başaran, *Selim III, Social Control and Policing in Istanbul at the End of the Eighteenth Century* (Leiden, 2014).

5 Cornel Zwierlein and Beatrice de Graaf, eds., "Security and Conspiracy in Modern History", in *Security and Conspiracy in History, Sixteenth to Twenty-First Century* [*Historical Social Research/Historische Sozialforschung* 38 (2013)], 16–18. On the Foucauldian notion of security dispositive, see Sverre Raffnsøe, Marius Gudmand-Høyer, Morten S. Thaning, "What is a dispositive? Foucault's Historical Mappings of the Networks of Social Reality", *Organization* 21 (2014): 1–27.

6 John C. Torpey, *The Invention of the Passport: Surveillance, Citizenship and the State*, 2nd edition (Cambridge, 2018), 26–91.

7 For an overview, see Clive Emsley, "Introduction: Political Police and the European Nation-State in the Nineteenth Century", in *The Policing of Politics in the Twentieth Century. Historical Perspectives*, ed. M. Mazower (Providence, 1997), 3–9. On the German case, see Wolfram Siemann, *Deutschlands Ruhe,*

The vigilant eye of the Revolution 185

Sicherheit und Ordnung. Die Anfänge der politischen Polizei in Deutschland,
1806–1866 (Tübingen, 1985), 41–59.

8 Karl Härter, "Security and Cross-Border Political Crime: the Formation of Transnational Security Regimes in Eighteenth and Nineteenth-Century Europe", in *Security and Conspiracy in History*, eds Zwierlein and Graaf, 96–106; Ido de Haan, Jeroen van Zanten, "Constructing an International Conspiracy: Revolutionary Concertation and Police Networks in the European Restoration", in *Securing Europe after Napoleon. 1815 and the New European Security Culture*, eds B. de Graaf, I. de Haan and B. Vick (Cambridge, 2019), 171–192.

9 Liang, *The Rise of Modern Police*, 8.

10 Ioannis Papageorgiou, *"Η αστυνομία της Ύδρας κατά τον αγώνα του 1821"* [The police of Hydra during the struggle of 1821], *Αστυνομικά Χρονικά* 431 [*Police chronicles*] (1972): 215.

11 On the full range of tasks and agents that formed the concept of police in the Ottoman Empire before the Tanzimat, see, Ferdan Ergut, "State and Social Control: The Police in the Late Ottoman Empire and Early Republican Turkey, 1839–1939" (unpublished Ph.D. thesis, New School for Social Research, New York, 2000), chapter 1. Especially for the policing of Istanbul, see Fariba Zarinebaf, *Crime and Punishment in Istanbul, 1700–1800* (Berkeley, 2010), 125–140; Başaran, *Selim III*, 40–54. On the management of public order in the Peloponnese, see John Alexander, *Brigandage and Public Order in the Morea (1685–1806)* (Athens, 1985). On the public order system in the Greek mountainous countryside, see Panagiotis Stathis, "From Klefts and Armatoloi to Revolutionaries", in *Ottoman Rule and the Balkans, 1760–1850: Conflict, Transformation, Adaptation*, eds A. Anastassopoulos and E. Kolovos (Rethymno, 2007), 167–179.

12 For a brief account, see Gerhard Sälter, "Early Modern Police and Policing", *Encyclopedia of Criminology and Criminal Justice*, eds G. Bruinsma and D. Weisburd (New York, 2014), 1243–1256.

13 Ferdan Ergan, "Surveillance and the Transformation of the Public Sphere in the Ottoman Empire", *METU Studies in Development* 34 (2007): 176–178; Başaran, *Selim III*, 53–54.

14 *Προσωρινόν Πολίτευμα της Ελλάδος* [Provisional Constitution of Greece], Epidaurus 1822, §7 and §22.

15 *Νόμος της Επιδαύρου* [Law of Epidaurus] (Astros, 1823), §51.

16 Georgios D. Dimakopoulos, *"Ο κώδιξ των νόμων της ελληνικής Επαναστάσεως, 1822–1828: η νομοθετική διαδικασία, τα κείμενα των νόμων"* [The code of the laws of the Greek Revolution, 1822–1828: the legislative procedure, the texts of the laws], *Επετηρίς Κέντρου Ερεύνης της Ιστορίας του Ελληνικού Δικαίου* [Annals of the research centre for the history of Greek law] 10–11 (1963): 107, 109.

17 See the list of the various headquarters of the Administration between 1822–1827 in Georgios D. Dimakopoulos, *Η διοικητική οργάνωσις κατά την Ελληνικήν Επανάστασιν, 1821–1827: συμβολή εις την ιστορίαν της ελληνικής διοικήσεως* [The administrative organization during the Greek Revolution, 1822–1827: A contribution to the history of the Greek administration] (Athens, 1966), 247–249.

18 On the strong empirical and practical dimension of the police, see Paolo Napoli, *La naissance de la police moderne. Pouvoir, normes, societé* (Paris, 2003).

19 General State Archives [=GSA], Archive of the Ministry of Police [=AMP], fol. 38 (24.09.1825). The text is published by Christos K. Reppas, *"Αστυνομικά της επαρχίας Πραστού κατά την Επανάσταση του '21"* [The police in the province of Prastos during the Revolution of 1821], *Χρονικά των Τσακώνων* [Tsakonian Chronicles] 18 (2004–2005): 118–120.

186 *Vaso Seirinidou*

20 GSA, AMP, fol. 1 (03.10.1822), (07.11.1822). Also, AGR, op. cit., 390–391 (27.03.1822).

21 GSA, AMP, fol. 44, f. 77–126 (17.11.1925). See, also, Christos K. Reppas, *"Γενική απογραφή του πληθυσμού του Ναυπλίου κατά το* 1825" [General census of the population of Nafplion in 1825], *Μνημοσύνη* 9 (1982–1984): 261–348. Census data are available at http://cities.ims.forth.gr/search_results.phpsearch_type=census&search_term=&search_year=1825 (accessed: 18.06.2020).

22 Suraiya Faroqhi, *Travel and Artisans in the Ottoman Empire: Employment and Mobility in the Early Modern Er*a (London and New York, 2014), 156–163.

23 See, for instance, Michel Pertué, "La police des étrangers sous la révolution française", *Police et migrants. France 1667–1939*, (dir.) Marie-Claude Blanc-Chaléard et al. (Rennes, 2001), 63–741; Friedrich Wilhelm Schembor, "Der Zustrom der Fremden nach Wien vor 200 Jahren. Polizeimassnahmen gegen die Niederlassung unliebsamer Ausländer", *SIAK-Journal. Zeitschrift für Polizeiwissenschaft un polizeiliche Praxis* 2 (2016), 81–95.

24 See, for instance, the list of foreigners registered by the police of Hydra island published by Ioannis Papageorgiou, *"Η αστυνομία της Ύδρας κατά τον αγώνα του* 1821" [The police of Hydra during the struggle of 1821, *Αστυνομικά Χρονικά* [Police chronicles] 431 (1972), 216–217.

25 *Νόμος της Επιδαύρου* [Law of Epidaurus], §2. On the definition of the Greek citizen during the Revolution, see Elpida K. Vogli, *Έλληνες το γένος. Η ιθαγένεια και η ταυτότητα στο εθνικό κράτος των Ελλήνων (1821–1844)* [Greek by descent: Identity and Citizenship in Modern Greece], (Herakleion, 2012), Part one.

26 See, for instance, the reports of the general police of Kalamata in GSA, AMP, fol. 6 (04.06.1823), fol. 21 (06.04.1825).

27 GSA, AMP, fol. 29 (20.07.1825).

28 GSA, AMP, fol. 30 (27.07.1825).

29 GSA, AMP, fol. 1 (07.11.1822).

30 GSA, AMP, fol. 1 (15.12.1822).

31 GSA, AMP, fol. 7 (26.07.1823).

32 AGR, vol. 4, Athens 1973, 371–374, 382 (20.08.1828).

33 The passport contained the following information: name, age, stature, height, nose, eyes, mouth, specific marks. See GSA, AMP, fol. 1.

34 See, for instance, the "Salaries and expenses of secret individuals employed by the Ministry", in GSA, fol. 54 (15.04.1826). Published by Christos K. Reppas, *Υποθέσεις κατασκοπίας κατά την Επανάσταση του* 1821. *Αρχειακά κείμενα* [Espionage cases during the Revolution of 1821. Archival texts] (Athens, 2012), 430–433.

35 GSA, AMP, fol. 21 (03.04.1825) and op. cit., 177.

36 For the Ottoman concepts, see Maurus Reinkowski, "The State's Security and the Subject's Prosperity: Notions of Order in Ottoman Bureaucreatic Correspondance (Nineteenth Century)", in H. T. Karateke, ed., *Legitimizing the Order: The Ottoman Rhetoric of State Power* (Leiden, 2005), 195–212.

37 Karl Härter, "Legal Responses to Violent Political Crimes in 19th-Century Central Europe", *Vom Majestätsverbrechen zum Terrorismus: Politische Kriminalität, Recht, Justiz und Polizei zwischen Früher Neuzeit und 20. Jahrhundert*, Beatrice de Graaf, ed. (Frankfurt, 2012), 164–168.

38 Dimosthenis Mirasjetzis, *Η ελληνική ποινική νομοθεσία κατά τα έτη 1822–1832* [The Greek criminal law during the years 1822–1834] (Athens, 1934), 10–17.

39 The text of Compilation is published by Dimakopoulos, "The code of the laws of the Greek Revolution", op.cit., 129–140.

40 GSA, AMP, fol. 14, (28.06.1824), fol. 20 (18.01.1825).

The vigilant eye of the Revolution 187

41 See, characteristically, Nikos V. Rotzokos, *Επανάσταση και εμφύλιος πόλεμος στο εικοσιένα* [Revolution and civil war in 1821] (Athens, 1997).

42 Sheila Fitzpatrich, Robert Gellately, "Introduction to the Practices of Denunciation in Modern European History", *The Journal of Modern History* 68 (1996): 747–767; Colin Lucas, "The Theory and Practice of Denunciation in the French Revolution", *The Journal of Modern History* 68 (1996): 768–785.

43 For the politicization of private disputes in revolutionary France, see Christiane Kohser-Spohn, "Das Privat wird politisch. Denunziationen in Strassburg in der Frühphase der Französischen Revolution", in *Der Staatsbürger als Spitzel. Denunziation während des 18. und 19. Jh. aus europäischer Perspektive*, M. Hohkamp, C. Ulbrich, eds (Leipzig, 2001), 213–270.

44 GSA, AMP, fol. 26 (24.06.1825); fol. 36 (15.09.1825).

45 See, characteristically, Douglas Hay, "Crime and Justice in Eighteenth- and Nineteenth-Century England", *Crime and Justice* 2 (1980): 45–84.

46 *Code Pénal de 1810*, Livre III, Chapitre III, Section V, Articles 269–282.

47 GSA, AMP, fol. 4 (12.05.1823).

48 GSA, AMP, fol. 16 (28.10.1824), fol. 20 (04.03.1825, 05.03.1825).

49 GSA, AMP, fol. 12 (04.11.1823).

50 Dimitris Dimitropoulos, "*Πειρατές στη στεριά; Πρόσφυγες, καταδρομείς και καθημερινότητα των παράκτιων οικισμών στα χρόνια του Αγώνα* [Pirates ashore? Refugees, cruisers and daily life of coastal settlements during the Greek Revolution]", *Όψεις της Επανάστασης του 1821* [Aspects of the Revolution of 1821], Conference Proceedings, eds Ch. Loukos and P. Mihailaris (Athens, 2018), 87–105.

51 Despoina Themeli-Katifori, "*Καταδρομή και πειρατεία κατά την Επανάσταση του 1821:φαινόμενα οικονομικών και κοινωνικών μετασχηματισμών* [Privateering and piracy during the Revolution of 1821: phenomena of economic and social transformations", *Parousia* 5 (1987): 239–254; Dimitris Dimitropoulos, "Pirates during a Revolution: The Many Faces of Piracy and the Reactions of Local Communities", in *Corsairs and Pirates in the Eastern Mediterranean, Fifteenth – Nineteenth Centuries*, eds G. Harlaftis and D. J. Starkey (Athens, 2016), 37–38.

52 Dimitropoulos, op. cit., 30.

53 GSA, AMP, fol. 14 (16.03.1824).

54 Reppas, *Υποθέσεις κατασκοπίας* [Espionage cases], 58–66, 140–156.

55 See, for instance, GSA, AMP, fol. 6 (09.06.1823), fol. 7 (02.07.1823).

56 GSA, AMP, fol. 26 (19.06.1825).

57 GSA, AMP, fol. 35, (12.11.1825).

58 See, for instance, Donald E. Emerson, *Metternich and the Political Police: Security and Subversion in the Hapsburg Monarchy, 1815–1830* (The Hague, 1968), 144–145.

59 Başaran, *Selim III*, 72–105.

60 Burak Eryılmaz, "Unearthing the Past: Passport Regulations in the Ottoman Empire", *History Studies* 11 (2019): 6–7.

Part V

Revolutionary Waves in the Greek World II

14 Internal conflicts and civil strife in the Serbian and the Greek Revolutions: A comparison[*]

Maria Efthymiou

The Serbian and the Greek Revolutions occurred in Ottoman-held Southeastern Europe in the first quarter of the 19th century; one happened in a period during which Europe was ablaze from the impact of the Napoleonic Wars, the other after the Congress of Vienna and the imposition of "supervised peace" in Europe[1]. Both belong to the constellation of upheavals which, under the influence of the American and the French Revolutions, were triggered by the age of nationalism,[2] and are offshoots of the Balkan peoples' tradition of resistance,[3] in which the Greeks could boast, for centuries, "the largest number of anti-Turkish actions".[4]

The Serbian Revolution[5] began as an uprising that built up into a revolution.[6] Its first phase lasted some nine years (1804–1813), under the leadership of Djordje Petrovich Karadjordje and, in its second phase, of Milosh Obrenovich. 17 years later, the Greek Revolution[7] started as such from the outset, with the action of a patriotic secret society, the Philiki Etaireia. Thus, it became "the first truly 'national' war of independence in the Balkans and the Near East"[8] and, like its Serbian counterpart, lasted for about nine years (1821–1830).

In a clime of fondness for Russia, the fellow Orthodox Christian power that was battling vigorously against the Ottoman Empire, the two revolutions were succoured by prophecies and millennialist visions.[9] Nonetheless, they quickly took on the character of a struggle for national liberation. When their fight was over, the Serbs had won extensive autonomy, and the Greeks had succeeded in creating an independent state, the first independent state to arise from the disintegrating Ottoman Empire. The decisive involvement of the Great Powers in these revolutions – of Russia, mainly, in the Serbian and of Great Britain, mainly, but also France and Russia, in the Greek – was instrumental in achieving this outcome, to the extent that it could be said that "although the Balkan revolts were commenced by the Christian people, the great powers made the final decisions over the establishment of the new states, their boundaries and their forms of government".[10]

The two revolutions took place at different geographical areas of Southeastern Europe and were waged by, apparently, different peoples. The Serbs, at the time of their insurrection, were living in and around the

192 *Maria Efthymiou*

sanjak of Belgrade, an inland plain, wooded and punctuated by hills. Concurrently, a significant number of Serbs resided in the neighbouring Austrian Empire, with many of them serving in Austrian military units guarding the frontiers, the *Freikorps*.[11] Enjoying a regime of privileges, granted to them by the Sublime Porte in 1792, at the end of the Turkish-Austrian Wars, the overwhelming majority of Serbs in that period were illiterate, Orthodox Christian, Slavic-speaking peasants, some of whom were involved in transporting and trading pigs to the Austrian Empire, which was also home to the Serbian intelligentsia, such as it was, that had developed in those years.[12] Serbian society was based on the traditional communal extended family, the *zadruga*, whose members lived under the same roof and held property in common, with the singular structures of kinship-based and wider administration that this institution had.[13]

By contrast, Greek society at the time of its revolution was complex, multi-faceted, and diffused throughout the Greek peninsula, the Balkans, and Asia Minor.[14] The rural element was dominant in the plains and in the high, rugged, semi-autonomous mountains that were administered, on behalf of the Porte, by local armed men, the *armatoloi*. The situation was analogous for the communities of maritime Greeks on the extensive coasts and hundreds of islands, many of which functioned semi-autonomously under the administration of local councils of primates or elders, the *demogeronties*. Strange as it may seem, this was, in a way, also the case for the large "island" of the Peloponnese, due to the political sway of the Greek primates there. Greek craftsmen, artisans, muleteers, porters, book-keepers, middlemen, merchants, entrepreneurs, sailors, captains, and ship-owners, were active on land, rivers, and sea, and settled in dozens of towns and cities in the Ottoman Empire, all over the Balkans and Asia Minor. Merchants and entrepreneurs had created numerous émigré communities in Italy, Austria, Hungary, Russia, and Western Europe, with their own Orthodox churches and priests, as well as Greek schools, teachers, and scholars. Moreover, from the mid-17th century, and particularly during the 18th and 19th centuries, scores of schools of high standard were operating in the Greek mainland and islands, the Balkans, and Asia Minor. In fact, because of the special importance of the Greek language for trade and Orthodoxy, these schools were attended by non-Greek pupils, too. So great was the economic, social, educational, religious, and cultural influence of the Greeks in the Balkans during the eighteenth and nineteenth centuries[15] that the Turkish historian Kemal Karpat stresses, with reference to the Greek Revolution, that "The rise of the national state of Greece and of its nationalism effectively undermined the hellenization of the Balkans by further strengthening the determination of the non-Greeks to maintain their own linguistic and ethnic identity"[16]. At the same time, Charles and Barbara Jelavich, comparing the situation of Serbs and Greeks on the eve of their respective revolution, emphasize that at the end of the eighteenth century, among the Balkan peoples the Greeks "occupied the most favourable place

Internal conflicts and civil strife 193

... were certainly the best educated of the Christian people ... together with the Jews and the Armenians, held the principal commercial positions in the Empire ... the sea trade was dominated by them ... were the first to establish a system of secular education based on western models ... because of their maritime interests and their geographical position some elements of the Greek population had always been in close touch with European intellectual developments", whereas the Serbs were "a primarily peasant people living in impoverished circumstances".[17]

Ostensibly, the two models of revolution are divergent. However, if we take into account that, in the end, the Greek Revolution was stabilized in a finite region of the south of the Greek peninsula (Central Greece, Peloponnese, islands of the Argosaronic Gulf and the Cyclades, Samos), many traits would seem to be convergent. Firstly, the fact that in both re-volutions there was a phenomenon that is observable more generally in the Ottoman Empire at the period, namely that privileged regions, social strata, and groups – independently of religion – such as janissaries, armatoloi, primates, Phanariots, ayans, merchants, clerics, pashas, led the field in ac-tions against the Porte.[18] Secondly, as regards the education and the en-trepreneurial activity of the two regions, although these seem to diverge, in the end, to a degree, they converge; since the burgeoning of Greek en-trepreneurialism concerned regions to the north of today's Central Greece, the fact that the Greek Revolution was confined actually to the south, shifted the centre of gravity of events to the humble, almost illiterate pea-sants of these regions. Entrepreneurial activity here was proportionately limited and concentrated in a few urban centres – those mainly associated with the sea, with which the Greeks, in contrast to the Serbs, had deep-rooted ties, with hundreds of ships sailing in the Black Sea and throughout the Mediterranean, West, and East.[19] Correspondingly, a number of Serbian leaders had been merchants before the Revolution.

The robust and hardened workforce of the countryside, together with the klephts in the mountains, bore the brunt of both the Serbian and the Greek Revolution, two revolutions that ushered in wider developments: the Serbian revolution intensified the dissolution of the Ottoman Empire, created diffi-culties for the sultan and weakened his position,[20] at the same moment as it boosted the aspirations of Balkan national-patriotic circles for liberation. In the view of Djordjevic and Fischer-Galati, "The true significance of the Serbian insurrection can best be understood in terms of its impact on the history of the Balkan Peninsula. The uprising put in motion the process of seeking solutions to Balkan problems through national-revolutionary manifestations".[21] For its part, the Greek Revolution exacerbated even more decisively the internal problems of the Ottoman Empire[22] and played a role in ideological and political equilibria of Europe and America in a critical phase of the Eastern Question,[23] at the same time as it created the ideological basis for the liberation movements in the Balkans during the second half of the 19th century. Neither the one nor the other revolution succeeded in

194 *Maria Efthymiou*

igniting a pan-Balkan uprising, as had been envisioned in the late 18th century by the pioneering Greek revolutionary Rhigas Velestinlis,[24] Nevertheless, as Djordjevic and Fischer-Galati point out, "The Greek revolution of 1821 was clearly more significant than the Serbian uprising, in that the realization of Greek independence was an achievement which profoundly affected the course of Balkan, Mediterranean, and European politics in the nineteenth century",[25] while S. Pavlovitch underlines that, "it was Greek intellectuals who introduced the European concept of nationalism to the Balkans. The First Serbian Rising notwithstanding, it was the Greek War of Independence which brought the Balkans to the attention of Europe".[26]

The political environment in which the Serbian Revolution took place was given, as the motive force of Serbian society was, for centuries, the local meetings of its *kmets* and *knezes* which functioned as representatives of the communities and their constituent families, on the basis of the *zadruga*. In 14 such wide-scale meetings, the *skupština*, in a strongly confrontational climate between ambitious Serb leaders divided into "Russophiles", "Austrophiles", "Turcophiles" and "Independents",[27] the burning issues of the moment were debated during the Revolution and a central Council was set up. Since the Serb revolutionaries were "more warriors than politicians and more national revolutionaries than statesmen",[28] this Council "was never recognized as the supreme authority; its existence conflicted with Karadjeordje's desire to be supreme ruler; as an organ of central power, it clashed with the desires of local and district leaders to retain as much power as possible".[29] With Karadjordje and, later Obrenovich playing a principal role in the effort to gain the greatest possible power and become hereditary rulers, Serbia moved in a traditional political direction, even though a constitution of Russian inspiration was drafted by the Greek Phanariot Constantinos Rhodophoinikis, whom Russia sent as an emissary to the Serbs in the period of their alliance.[30]

In contrast to the Serbs, the Greeks, in their revolution, adopted from the outset political and governmental schemes taken from the Western Enlightenment, as well as radical constitutions aligned with those of the American and the French Revolution. Thus, under the influence of the western-oriented Greek intelligentsia, the revolution espoused and instituted the separation of powers, creation of a Parliament and an Executive, independent Judiciary, freedom of the Press, protection of citizens' property and safety, abolition of slavery, universal access to offices on the sole criterion of personal merit, and so on.[31] Nonetheless, it is noteworthy that in both the Serbian and the Greek case, internal political fomentations were branded by assassinations of political leaders, cases in point being the murder of G. Karadjordje by M. Obrenovich in 1817 and that of the Greek Governor Ioannis Capodistrias in 1831.

In the case of the Greek Revolution, which has been judged as "the bloodiest of all Balkan uprisings" against the Turks[32], the disputes came to a head in a civil war, which was fuelled by many antagonisms. The most

Internal conflicts and civil strife 195

significant were those between the "military men" (armatoloi, klephts, kapoi) and the "politicians" (primates of rural, maritime and urban areas), even though the armatoloi were simultaneously political chiefs of their highland domains. The antagonism was latent prior to the revolution, but it became manifest with its outbreak. A contributing factor to this was the fact that many primates, particularly those in the Peloponnese, turned simultaneously into "military men", forming, with the help of armed mercenaries, their own armed corps, which enabled them to claim a manifold role in the Struggle. This fluidity, combined with the ability of the most political of the "politicians", the Phanariot volunteers from Constantinople[33] – some of whom actually took part in fighting as well – played a role by heightening dissensions and clashes which led to the civil war.[34]

The civil war began in the second half of 1823, after the Second National Assembly of the Greeks (March 1823), at which Theodoros Kolokotronis – the most important Peloponnesian guerrilla leader who, eight months earlier, had vanquished a mighty Ottoman army at Dervenakia – sought to control the political affairs of the revolution. By mustering a broad-based faction, he collaborated with a section of the "military men", as well as with a section of the Peloponnesian leading primates with whom until then he had been viciously at loggerheads, and tried to secure crucial offices for himself and for members of his faction. The reaction to his moves was swift and vehement, resulting in the creation of two governments: one under the control of Kolokotronis, and the other, the "legitimate government". In this conflict, the Peloponnese found itself divided, with one section of its primates and military men aligning with Kolokotronis, and others with the government based at Kranidi. In this round, Kolokotronis and his henchmen were defeated, but they quickly bounced back, this time reinforced, as almost all the "military men" and "politicians" of the Peloponnese now closed ranks. The Kranidi, under the leadership of the Hydriots, hired troops from Central Greece, in order to invade the Peloponnese and conquer it. Kolokotronis and the Peloponnese were defeated, and, at the beginning of 1825, the "antipatriotic" ring-leaders of the "mutiny" were imprisoned for several months in a monastery on Hydra.

Underlying this conflict were pre-revolutionary political and social equilibria and the reversals that the revolution caused to them. In the Peloponnese before the Revolution, the main role in local affairs among the Christians was played by their local leaders, but the outbreak of the revolution and the removal of the Turks overturned the status quo and novel agents of power emerged, such as independent guerrilla chiefs, as well as recently-arrived Phanariot volunteers. The same happened, on a smaller scale, in Central Greece, where, before the Revolution, dominant among the Christians were the armatoloi in the mountains, and the primates – here, proportionately less powerful than their Peloponnesian counterparts – in the towns of the plains. With the outbreak of the Revolution, primates and clerics of the Peloponnese set up the Peloponnesian Senate, in the footsteps

196 *Maria Efthymiou*

of a corresponding pre-revolutionary administrative body in which they participated. Thanks to its members' experience in administration, the Peloponnesian Senate succeeded – despite internal oppositions – in becoming a strong administrative body, even though the First National Assembly (December 1821–January 1822) had, meanwhile, elected a Central Government. Before the National Assembly was convened and in parallel to the operation of the Peloponnesian Senate, East and Central Greece too had acquired forms of administrative control, in which the local guerrilla chiefs played, to their chagrin, a secondary role, for here also the Phanariots had the upper hand.

This situation, together with the fact that the First National Assembly, which was dominated by primates and Phanariots, did not disband the local administrative bodies, heightened the tension between "politicians" and "military men". This tension poisoned the course of the revolution and led to civil war. It is not fortuitous that this erupted after the Second National Assembly (March 1823), at which it was decided to abolish the local administrative bodies, thus depriving the traditional forces of the Peloponnese of their safety net, at the same time as the Hydriots – with their powerful fleet, their wealth, and their international experiences, as well as the politically highly-experienced, polyglot and well-educated Phanariots – considered it self-evident that they should have the main say in all matters. Victory leaned towards the side of Hydra and the islanders – with the help of the most brutal "military men", those of Central Greece – leading to an unstable political landscape that would have generated in the future new unrest and upheavals. Because, as Peter Sugar remarks,

> while the Greek movement started among the merchants and other middle-class elements, this group lacked leadership, was dispersed all over Europe, and was unable to shape events during Greece's war of independence. The civil war that paralleled this event also proved that no other element of the population was able to impose its views on the rest. Greek factionalism remained a serious problem, making united action difficult even after Greece had gained her independence following the intervention of the Great Powers[35].

As it is already clear, in both revolutions a dynamic role was played by individuals who came from other places in order to participate on their compatriots' side, in the regions where the Struggle was in full swing. These individuals frequently found themselves at the eye of the storm, even though they invariably had extensive political abilities and international experience, good education, and linguistic skills. Both in the Serbian and the Greek case, the "locals" treated them with caution, dislike, and suspicion, no matter that they were compatriots, scholars, physicians, teachers, merchants, or statesmen. For the local Serbs, they were always "foreigners" or "German", whereas they themselves were "old Serbs", while for the "indigenous"

Internal conflicts and civil strife   197

Greeks they were Greeks from another land, "incomers". Among the "incomers", especially in the Greek case, the Phanariots were the most characteristic element, as this particular echelon of Greek Orthodox patricians in Constantinople, which, from the 17th into the 19th century was a source from which the Porte drew part of its senior administrative personnel,[36] proved to be ready for anti-Ottoman actions during the 18th and mainly the 19th century, being often prone to anti-Ottoman appeals of Russia.[37] If the Phanariot C. Rhodophoinikis, as envoy of the tsar, played a role in political matters during the Serbian Revolution, the contribution of the Phanariots to the Greek Revolution was considerably bigger. Among the protagonists were Alexandros Ypsilantis, leader of the Revolution at its very beginning in February 1821; Alexandros Mavrokordatos, the most important and most capable statesman of the Struggle; Dimitrios Ypsilantis, an officer in the Russian Army and devoted freedom-fighter throughout the Revolution; the politicians Theodoros Negris, Constantinos Karatzas, and others.

With so many politicians, merchants, and scholars, as well as Philhellenes who came from the West to fight on the battlefields[38] – something that did not happen in the Serbian Revolution – we would expect the Greek Revolution to have created a stable political front that would allow it to conduct a more systematic war, avoiding divisive internal clashes and fronts. Instead, however, it was the Greek Revolution that had the most serious internal strife, devolving into civil war, by contrast to the Serbian, which, notwithstanding "the widespread dissent and disunity in the Serbian lands",[39] avoided civil war by presenting commensurately greater military and political orderliness than the Greeks. We could assume that contributory factors to this were:

a. what Peter Sugar points out, namely the fact that the Greek merchants who started the revolution were dispersed throughout Europe and did not manage to form a cohesive and effective core in administrating the Greek Struggle;[40]

b. the fact that whereas the traditional leaders of the Greeks (primates, armatoloi, clergy) enjoyed local status, political authority, and networks of power, they were highly fragmented and internally antagonistic, as a result of which the "incomer" scholars and Phanariots were enhanced as more efficacious handlers of affairs, for they had knowledge, experience, a modernist vision and relations with the West – with which, in the end, the Greek Revolution was structurally connected. However, the Phanariots did not have access to local networks and communities, which the traditional powers had, as a result of which their possibility of controlling power was finite. Of the non-'incomers', those who had a broader spectrum of experience were the islanders, and especially the Hydriots. But again, they did not have a panhellenic ambit and networks, so as to be able to hold on to authority, even though they were victorious in the civil war;

198 *Maria Efthymiou*

c. the fact that, in contrast to the Serbs who presented, in their simplicity, uniformity of familial and social articulation in a finite and almost uniform geomorphological space, the Greeks – due to the varied nature of their terrain, their dispersion, the range of their occupations and the complexity of their society – presented diverse forms of social structure, attitudes, experiences and mindsets, something that nurtured conflicts and deviations;

d. precisely because of the relative uniformity and simplicity of Serbian society, the traditional, assimilated and tried-and-tested institutions of the *zadruga* and of the representative assemblies, the *skupština*, provided safeguards averting uncontrolled internal violence. Quite the opposite was the case with the Greeks. Before the Revolution, in some regions (such as the Peloponnese or Zagori in Epirus) they too had the experience of representative bodies and meetings at the regional level, nonetheless, as a rule, their experiences of self-government concerned their local microcosm, and in the mountains, local self-government was suffocated by the presence of the armatoloi;

e. the *skupština* of the Serbs, underpinned by the traditional organizational scheme of Serbian society, presented relative flexibility of action and facility of convergence, in contrast to the National Assemblies of the Greeks, which were a novel and unassimilated institution in Greek society. They were complicated too, which is why they could not be held frequently;

f. thanks to the above, the Serbs managed to operate their irregular forces with greater cohesion and control, even though there, too, as in the Greek case, most of the freedom-fighters were peasants and former brigands.[41] The greater orderliness of the Serbian army could be attributed to the fact that a number of Serb freedom-fighters had military experience in a constituted European corps since they had served in the Austrian *Freikorps* – something that the Greeks did not have, with very few exceptions;

g. on the contrary, the Greek side, after failed attempts to create a regular national army – mainly, due to reaction of the traditional forces of 'military men'– conducted the war with militias, hardly controlled or not at all by the serving 'Minister of War'.[42] The fact that the navy presented, thanks to the undeniable nautical superiority and predominance of Hydra and Spetses at sea, more 'regular' characteristics than those of the land forces, explains moreover, to a degree, the final prevailing of Hydra in the civil wars;

h. because of the aforesaid, the Greeks, despite the numerous able individuals, did not manage to acquire an effective central administration under a strong leader, in contrast to the Serbs, who in both phases of their Struggle possessed firm leadership;

i. in the Greek case, the lack of an acknowledged head favoured the emergence of indiscipline and even vagarious forces, resulting not only

Internal conflicts and civil strife   199

in anarchy but also in squandering the resources of the Revolution. This, in its turn, brought a tendency for looting, which fired atrocities and corrupted morals, in this way honing the knife of civil war;

j. an important factor in the smoother course of events in the Serbian Revolution was Karadjordje's timely decision to share out the land which, due to the realignments of the war, was 'bereft' of its Muslim ex-owners, among the Serbian peasants, locals, and "foreigners". This meant that the Serbian Revolution "resolved two fundamental issues: the liberation from Ottoman Rule and the destruction of the Ottoman feudal order",[43] as "the peasant in Serbia was the first in Europe to obtain land in hereditary ownership without any feudal encumbrances, and with the full right to dispose of his land as he wished".[44] In the Greek case, to the contrary, the sequestrated large and wealthy ex-Muslim estates of the Peloponnese, which were judiciously bound as "national land", were dealt with awkwardly in the long run, without a clear and final solution. This whetted the appetite of avaricious individuals and groups, so worsening the climate of conflict and weighing down political developments.[45]

Greeks and Serbs took their revolution along different trajectories, with different political and statehood results. The Serbs achieved widened autonomy, at the same time keeping many Ottoman features in their political system;[46] the Greeks achieved independence, having introduced into their system many Western features novel to the region. With the Church severed from the Patriarchate of Constantinople, in both cases, Serbs and Greeks stressed their intention of serving the national imperative of their age.[47] Although the Serbs did not become entangled in a civil war, the strong sentiments that were generated in the two revolutions were by no means smoothed over quickly but, quite the opposite envenomed the life of the two countries for decades. So, the rivalry between the Karadjordje and Obrenovich families was destined to characterize Serbian political life in the 19th century, just like the enmity between the inhabitants of the Peloponnese and of Central Greece, which is related to events of the civil war. This was the price paid by many of the Revolutions that had gone before – such as the American and the French, in which too many antagonisms and clashes were recorded, to a greater or lesser degree[48] – within the cycle of transition of power and overthrowing the societal status quo, which are the sine qua non of every Revolution.[49] In any case, as Annie Jourdan comments in her book, "every revolution is also a civil war".[50] In this perspective, the experience of civil war made the War of Independence of the Greeks more revolutionary, since this society, through complex courses of action, bypassing the popular perception of Russia and the religious element, was joined firmly to the heterodox West by adopting, albeit unassimilated, ground-breaking policies and radical constitutions.

200   *Maria Efthymiou*

Notes

* For this study, thanks are due to the Seeger Centre for Hellenic Studies of Princeton University and to its Director D. Gondikas for awarding the author a bursary, and facilitating a productive stay during the academic year 2006–2007.

1 H. G. Nicolson, *The Congress of Vienna: a Study in Allied Unity, 1812–1822* (London, 1946).

2 On the rise of nationalism and the revolutions in the 19th century Balkans -the ones of the Greeks' and Serbs' included- see L. Stavrianos, *The Balkans since 1453* (New York, 1958); D. Djordjevic, *Révolutions nationales des peuples balkaniques, 1804–1914* (Belgrade, 1965); St. Xydis, "Modern Greek Nationalism", in *Nationalism in Eastern Europe*, eds P. Sugar and I. Lederer (Seattle, 1969), 207–258; R. Viers Paxton, "Nationalism and Revolution: A Re-examination of the Origins of the First Serbian Insurrection 1804–1807", *East European Quarterly* 6 (1972), 337–362; K. Karpat, *An Inquiry into the Social Foundations of Nationalism in the Ottoman State: From Social Estates to Classes. From Millet to Nations*, Research Monograph no 39 (Princeton University, 1973); D. Djordjevic and St. Fischer-Galati, *The Balkan Revolutionary Tradition* (New York, 1981); P. M. Kitromilides, "Imagined Communities and the Origins of the National Question in the Balkans", *European History Quarterly* 19 (1989): 149–192; Charles Jelavich and Barbara Jelavich, *The Establishment of the Balkan National States, 1804–1920* (London, 1993); St. Pavlowitch, *A History of the Balkans 1804–1945* (London, 1999); P. Lekas, "Nationalism qua Modernization: The Greek War of Independence", in *Η Ελληνική Επανάσταση του 1821. Ένα ευρωπαϊκό γεγονός*, ed. P. Pizanias (Athens, 2009), 267–277; D. Stamatopoulos, ed., *Balkan Nationalism(s) and the Ottoman Empire* (Istanbul, 2015).

3 Olga Katsiardi-Hering, "Von den Aufständen zu den Revolutionen christlicher Untertanen des Osmanischen Reiches in Südosteuropa (ca. 1530–1821). Ein Typologisierungsversuch", *Südost-Forschungen* 68 (2009): 96–137.

4 Djordjevic and Fischer-Galati, *The Balkan*: 24.

5 For the history of the Serbian Revolution, see L. von Ranke, *The History of Servia and the Servian Revolution* (London, 1853); M. Boro Petrovich, *A History of Modern Serbia 1804–1918* (New York, 1976); W. Vucinich, ed., *The First Serbian Uprising, 1804–1813* (New York, 1982).

6 D. Batakovič, "A Balkan Style French Revolution? The 1804 Serbian Uprising in European Perspective", *Balcanica* 36 (2005): 113–128.

7 For the history of the Greek Revolution see Thomas Gordon, *History of the Greek Revolution*, Edinburgh, 1832; D. Dakin, *The Greek Struggle for Independence 1821–1833*, London, 1973. The 3,500 or so pages of volumes V–VIII of the opus magnum by Ap. Vacalopoulos, *Ιστορία του Νέου Ελληνισμού* [History of Modern Hellenism], Thessaloniki 1974–1988 are the fullest history of the Greek Revolution yet compiled.

8 P. Lekas, "The Greek War of Independence from the Perspective of Historical Sociology", *The Historical Review / La Revue Historique* 2 (2005): 161.

9 M. Hatzopoulos, "Prophetic Structures of the Ottomans -ruled Orthodox Community in Comparative Perspective: Some Preliminary Observations", in *Greek-Serbian Relations in the Age of Nation-Building*, ed., P. Kitromilides and S. Matthaious (Athens, 2016), 121–147.

10 Jelavich and Jelavich, *The Establishment*, 25.

11 G. Rothenberg, *The Military Border in Croatia, 1740–1882: A Study of an Imperial Institution* (Chicago, 1966).

12 St. Pavlowitch, "Society in Serbia, 1791–1830", in *Balkan Society in the Age of Greek Independence*, ed. R. Clogg (London, 1981), 137–156.

Internal conflicts and civil strife   201

13 J. M. Halpern, *A Serbian Village* (New York, 1958); G. Castellan, *La vie quoti-dienne en Serbie au seuil de l'indépendence 1815–1839* (Paris, 1967), 121–169; R. F. Byrnes, ed., *Communal Families in the Balkans: The Zadruga* (London, 1976).

14 Y. Yannoulopoulos, "Greek Society on the Eve of Independence", in *Balkan Society*, 18–39.

15 P. Mackridge, "The Greek Intelligentsia 1780–1830: a Balkan perspective", Ibid, pp. 6–84. For the role of Greek men of letters and the movement of the Enlightenment in the Greek Revolution see D. Geanakoplos, "The Diaspora Greeks: The Genesis of Modern Greek National Consciousness", in *Hellenism and the First Greek War of Liberation (1821–1830): Continuity and Change*, eds N. Diamandouros et al. (Thessaloniki, 1976), 59–77; P. Kitromilides, *Enlightenment and Revolution: the making of Modern Greece* (Cambridge Mass, 2013), 43–62.

16 Karpat, *An Inquiry*: 78.

17 Jelavich and Jelavich, *The Establishment*, 9, 10, 11, 13, 14; W. Puchner, "Griechische Hegemonialkultur im Östlichen Balkanraum zur Zeit der Aufklärung und der nationalen 'Wiedergeburt'. Beispiele und Tendenzen", in *Griechische Dimensionen südosteuropäischer Kultur seit dem 18. Jahrhundert. Verortung, Bewegung, Grenzüberschreitung*, eds Maria Oikonomou et al. (Frankfurt, 2011), 17–25.

18 For the phenomenon see the deliberations in M. Efthymiou, "Call in and keep out: Local communities and Ottoman rule in the privileged-status islands of Hydra and Samos", in *I Turchi, il Mediterraneo e l' Europa*, ed. G. Motta (Milano, 1998), 429–443; D. Tzakis, "Intégration et révolte: élites chrétiennes et musulmanes dans le Peloponnèse sous la domination ottomane (XVIIIe -début du XIXe siècle)", in *La Société grecque sous la domination ottomane. Economie, identité, structure sociale et conflits*, ed. M. Efthymiou (Athens, 2010), 171–200. See also endnotes 20 and 22 in the present chapter.

19 Sp. Asdrachas et al., eds, *Ελληνική Οικονομική Ιστορία, ΙΕ', ΙΘ' αιώνας* [Greek Economic History XV-XIX centuries] (Αθήνα, 2003); G. Harlaftis, "The 'eastern invasion'. Greeks in the Mediterranean trade and shipping in the eighteenth and early nineteenth centuries", in *Trade and Cultural Exchange in the Early Modern Mediterranean: Braudel's Maritime Legacy*, eds M. Fusaro et al. (London, 2010), 223–252.

20 For the Ottoman Empire in that period, its challenges and dysfunctions, see A. Yaycioglu, *Partners of the Empire. The Crisis of the Ottoman Order in the Age of Revolutions* (Stanford, 2016). F. Anscombe considers that the troubles in the Balkans—and the Serbian and the Greek Revolutions— are linked not so much to the nationalist movement as to the economic pressures exerted on the popu-lation by the Porte, so as to finance the reforms it was attempting to implement, Fr. Anscombe, "The Balkan Revolutionary Age", *Journal of Modern History* 84 (2012): 572.

21 Djordjevic and Fischer-Galati, *The Balkan*, 76. See also, D. Djordjevic, "The Impact of the First Serbian Uprising on the Balkan Peoples", *The First Serbian Uprising*, ed. Vucinich, 361-389; B. Jelavich, "The Balkan Nations and the Greek War of Independence", *Hellenism and the First Greek War of Liberation (1821–1830)*, 157–169.

22 Y. Hakan Erdem, "The Greek Revolt and the End of the Old Ottoman Order", in *Η Ελληνική Επανάσταση*, ed. Pizanias, 281–288; H. Sukru Ilicak, "A Radical Rethinking of Empire: Ottoman State and Society during the Greek War of Independence (1821–1826) (Ph.D. thesis, Harvard University, 2011).

23 M. A. Anderson, *The Eastern Question, 1774–1923: A Study in International Relations* (New York, 1966).

202   *Maria Efthymiou*

24 P. M. Kitromilides, *Ρήγας Βελεστινλής. Θεωρία και πράξη* [Rhigas Velestinlis. Theory and Practice] (Athens, 1998).
25 Djordjevic and Fischer-Galati, *The Balkan*, 77.
26 Pavlowitch, *A History*, 333.
27 W. Vucinich, "Russia and the First Serbian Uprising 1807–1809", *The First Serbian Uprising*, 122.
28 W. Vucinich, "Introductory remarks: Genesis and Essence of the First Serbian Uprising", *The First Serbian Uprising*, p. 8.
29 Al. Dragnich, "Political Organization of Karadjordje's Serbia", *The First Serbian Uprising*, 346.
30 R. V. Paxton, "Russian Foreign Policy and the First Serbian Uprising. Alliances, Apprehensions, and Autonomy, 1804–1807", *The First Serbian Uprising*, 41–70.
31 N. Diamandouros, *Οι απαρχές της συγκρότησης σύγχρονου κράτους στην Ελλάδα 1821–1828* [The beginnings of modern state-building in Greece, 1821–1828] (Athens, 2002).
32 Djordjevic and Fischer-Galati, *The Balkan*, 84.
33 See also endnote 36 in the present study.
34 J. Petropulos, *Politics and Statecraft in the Kingdom of Greece, 1833–1843* (Princeton 1968), chapters I, II.
35 Sugar, "External and Domestic Roots of Eastern European Nationalism", in *Nationalism in Eastern Europe*, 51.
36 A. Pallis, *The Phanariots: A Greek Aristocracy under Turkish Rule* (London 1951); C. Mango, "The Phanariots and the Byzantine Tradition", in *The Struggle for Greek Independence: Essays to Mark the 150th Anniversary of Greek War of Independence*, ed. R. Clogg (Hamden, 1973), 41–66.
37 Karpat, *An Inquiry*, 53, 54, 57, 70, 72, 74.
38 W. St Clair, *'That Greece might still be free'. The Philhellenes in the War of Independence* (Oxford, 1972).
39 Em. Turczynski, "Austro- Serbian relations", in *The First*, 197.
40 See endnote 35 in the present study.
41 G. Škrivanič, "The Armed Forces in Karadjordje's Serbia", in *The First*, 303 ff.
42 Ap. Vakalopoulos, *Τα ελληνικά στρατεύματα του 1821* [The Greek armed forces of 1821], Thessaloniki, 1991.
43 Vucinich, "Introductory remarks", in idem, ed., *The First*, 10.
44 Vl. Stojančevic, "Karadjordje and Serbia in his time", in *Ibid.*, 34.
45 W. Mc Grew, "The Land Issue in the Greek War of Independence", in *Hellenism*, 111–130.
46 Č. Antič, "The formative years of the Principality of Serbia (1804–1856): Ottoman influences", *Ottoman Rule and the Balkans, 1760–1850. Conflict, Transformation, Adaptation*, eds A. Anastasopoulos and El. Kolovoss (Rethymno, 2007), 243–248.
47 M. Petrovich, "The Role of the Serbian Orthodox Church in the First Serbian Uprising 1804–1813", in *The First*, 259–302; Ch. Frazee, *The Orthodox Church and Independent Greece, 1821–1852* (Cambridge, 1969).
48 Fr. Cogliano, *Revolutionary America, 1763–1815. A Political History* (London, 2008); A. Jourdan, *Nouvelle Histoire de la Revolution* (Paris, 2018).
49 J. M. Gates, "Toward a History of Revolution", *Comparative Studies in Society and History* 28 (1986): 535–544.
50 A. Jourdan, *Nouvelle Histoire*, 10.

15 The sea and nation-building: Between a privately-owned merchant fleet and a revolutionary National Navy, 1821-1827[1]

Gelina Harlaftis and Katerina Galani

Shipping proved pivotal for the outcome of the Greek War of Independence, one of the important pillars of the rebellious Greeks on a military, economic, and political front. It was the most important concentrated military weapon that spread and withheld the Revolution in the Archipelago and the Ionian Seas. At the same time, it remained the most productive force of the rebels bringing income to the State and the local communities through commerce, privateering, and piracy. Despite its importance, minimal research has been undertaken on the subject, and the literature about the history of war at sea during the Greek Revolution limits itself to a narrow event-based narrative, focusing on military actions and the three-island fleet of Hydra, Spetses, and Psara disregarding the fleet of hundreds of vessels from the other islands and coastal towns of the revolted areas.[2]

Greeks, subjects of the Ottoman Sultan, when they revolted had a comparative advantage over their rulers. On the eve of Greek Independence, they owned the largest merchant sailing ship fleet of the eastern Mediterranean and the Black Sea carrying mainly grain from the East to West. The deep-sea-going merchant fleet of the Greeks, Ottoman, and Ionian subjects, was composed of 1,000 cargo sailing ships of an average tonnage of 125 tons, which belonged to about 1,800 shipping families established in 40 maritime communities, *nautotopoi*, of the Aegean and Ionian seas, with about 17,000 seamen. With the exception of the Ionian islands and a few Aegean islands, about 25 *nautotopoi* took part in the Revolution that owned more than 700 large sailing ships with about 13,000 sailors.[3]

The merchant captains who took part in the War of Independence were highly experienced seamen who had ploughed the troubled Mediterranean Sea for decades during the Napoleonic wars. They sailed on a dangerous sea where they had to confront Barbary corsairs, north European privateers, and often the British, French, or American Navies. Their ships sailed mainly under the Ottoman flag, a neutral flag among the western European belligerents, and supplied the West with grain from the East. At sea, the law of the powerful prevails. Greek merchant ships were equipped with cannons while their crews were armed with pistols, carabines, rifles, and knives, as the Ottoman Archives prove.[4] The success of the Greeks as seafarers of the

204 *Gelina Harlaftis and Katerina Galani*

Ottoman Empire backfired as they put their large fleet to the service of the War of Greek Independence. This put the Ottoman Imperial Navy in a weak position, as the first years of the Revolution indicate.[5] The Revolution disorganized and created huge problems in the operation of the Ottoman Imperial Fleet as the Ottoman documents show.

The aim of this chapter is to examine the three ways shipping owned by Greeks contributed to the Greek War of Independence from 1821 to 1827. Firstly, it formed the Revolutionary naval fleet; secondly, it formed the privateering fleet that complemented the Navy; and thirdly, it formed the merchant fleet that provided a constant flow of supplies and cargoes.[6]

A privately owned Navy

The first way that shipping contributed to the national cause was by forming the first Greek Revolutionary Navy. The Revolution broke out in March 1821 in the Peloponnese, in Roumeli and it spread gradually across the maritime space of the Aegean Sea, the Corinthian bay, and the Ionian Sea. Apart from the Ionian fleet, which belonged to the British jurisdiction, almost all of the prosperous *nautotopoi* of the Ottoman dominion joined the Revolution.

The fleet of more than 700 cargo merchant sailing ships of the *nautotopoi* that took part in the revolution is distributed as follows: in the Ottoman territory of the Ionian Sea and the Corinthian Gulf the most important *nautotopos* was Galaxidi (101 sailing ships), followed by the fleets of Messolonghi and Aetoliko; in the region of the Western Aegean Hydra (112) and Spetses (56) led the way, followed by the fleet of Kranidi, Aigina, and Poros, as well as that of the Sporades (mainly Skopelos and Trikeri); in the Central Aegean, the most important fleet was that of Santorini (35 ships) followed by Mykonos, Andros, Tinos, and Crete; in the Eastern Aegean Psara (78 ships) had the largest fleet followed by Kasos, Patmos, Samos, and Kastellorizo, along with the important fleets of the coastal towns of Ainos (Thrace), and Kydonies and Chesme on the coasts of Asia Minor.[7] Moreover, there were approximately another 300 merchant vessels owned by the shipowners of the Ionian islands, which were under British jurisdiction. The tacit contribution of the Ionian shipping in the national cause has not yet been analysed or even mentioned.

It is no coincidence, therefore, that the first Greek Revolutionary Navy was formed by the fleets of the largest maritime centres the Ottoman dominion: Galaxidi in the Corinthian bay, Hydra and Spetses in the Western Aegean, and Psara and Kasos in the Eastern Aegean. During the struggle for Independence, Hydra, Spetses, and Psara took the lead on a political, economic, and military level. It is this "three-island fleet" that has remained in the national historic memory as the only one that participated in the Revolution. Greek historiography has neglected Galaxidi, which was destroyed in September 1821 at the very beginning of the Revolution, but its seafarers continued their activities throughout the war; Kydonies, a maritime centre, was also destroyed in June 1821, and Kasos was destroyed in June 1824 along with Psara. In reality, however, the three so-called "Nautical Islands" together accounted only for one-third of the total merchant fleet of the revolutionaries. They had the full support of the fleets of all the other *nautotopoi*, of the western, central, and eastern Aegean and Ottoman Ionian. Albeit overlooked by the historiography, these *nautotopoi* contributed taxes and capital through fundraising but also human capital, seamen, ships as fireships – which proved to be the main weapon of the Greek Navy – auxiliary vessels in naval expeditions, privateering fleet for blockades, as well as hundreds of small and large vessels that ensured the flow of supplies and communication and raided Ottoman non-revolutionary ships that weakened the enemy's shipping force.

In naval operations, the Greek Navy could not confront directly the Ottoman Imperial Navy at any major naval battle. The Ottoman Navy was a regular fleet with officers trained according to Western European standards consisting, in March 1821, of 81 warships, of which 30 were ships of the line. More precisely, the Ottoman fleet was composed of 4 three-decker ships, that is, with three rows of cannons carrying a total of 120 cannons; 3 two-decker ships carrying 80 cannons; 12 frigates with 74 cannons, and ten frigates with 50 cannons.[8] These ships were designed for a naval tactic known as the "line of battle", by which two columns of each fleet, one behind the other, were attacking each other from the canons of their broadside. The Ottoman ships of the Imperial Navy were high "as mountains" next to the small brigs.[9] In fact, if they confronted the Ottoman ships on an opposite column the range of the canons of the brigs could not even touch those giants. As they reported to Austrian captains "we can't lunge at the Imperial fleet, since our cannonballs can't reach their ships, while they can hit us".

So, they followed a different tactic. The Greek Navy was an irregular fleet composed annually by an average of 40 privately owned "grain" merchant vessels, carrying from 4 to 20 cannons each and an average of 7 fireships (Table 15.1). Due to the inferiority of their vessels, they resorted to a war of attrition; they harassed and attacked parts of the Ottoman fleet in various maritime regions.[10] Thus, the "naval battles" mentioned in Greek historiography are essentially small-scale conflicts, rather than full-fledged battles between two equal opponents with ships-of-the-line. Nevertheless, the successful hit-and-run tactics of the Greeks forced the Ottoman Navy to form supply convoys accompanied by a naval escort.[11] The main service of the Greek naval and privateering fleets was the interception of the Ottoman supply lines (e.g., to castles in the Peloponnese like Nafplion in 1822), the supply of towns under Ottoman siege-like Messolonghi (1823–1826), the support of the revolts of the islands like Crete (Souda 1822), the protection of islands from an Ottoman siege, such as the case of Samos (battle of Geronta in 1824) and Hydra (battle of Cavo d'Oro in 1825), or the disruption of the enemy fleet in their home waters (Alexandria 1825,1827).

206 Gelina Harlaftis and Katerina Galani

Table 15.1 Main naval expeditions, 1821–1827

Year	Number of main expeditions	Annual average of number of vessels per expedition	Annual average of number of fireships per expedition	Duration of expeditions (months)
1821	3	88	6	2
1822	5	44	6	6
1823	5	23	4	6
1824	4	33	8	6
1825	7	32	7	6
1826	3	31	12	4
1827	3	25	5	7
Total	30	40	7	5

Source: Appendix 1, Katerina Galani and Gelina Harlaftis (eds.), *Greek shipping during the War of Independence: naval and merchant ships 1821–1831* (Crete University Press, 2021).

The biggest fear of the Ottomans at sea was Greek fireships. "Our fireships is our most important weapon against the enemy," G. Sachtouris wrote in the diary of the brigantine *Athina*.[12] It has been estimated that from 1821–1827 in all expeditions 112 fireships were used out of which 96 were consumed during the expeditions. Of these 65 were from Hydra, Spetses and Psara. The other 36 were from Kasos, Lemnos, Lesvos, Chios, Samothrace, Skopelos, Santorini, Kastellorizo, Syros, Aegina, and Cephalonia, which shows the extent of participation of all of the *nautotopoi* in the common cause. The rest were ships that were seized or captured from the Ottomans and/or Austrians and transformed into fireships.

As Table 15.1 indicates, there were 30 main naval expeditions that took place from 1821–1827. The Greek Navy targeted its activities to disrupt and harass the main routes of the Ottoman Imperial Navy that, from 1822 onward, was joined by the Egyptian Navy which integrated Algerian and Tunisian fleets. The main routes of the Ottoman-Egyptian Navy were on the axis of Istanbul-Alexandria to cover the large eastern Aegean islands from Lesbos to Rhodes and that of Crete; to supply the castles and towns of Euboia and eastern Peloponnese; and the western coast of Peloponnese to the bay of Patras with a long-term siege of Messolonghi.

The aim of the Provisionary Government was to keep in service a fleet of 60–65 vessels, but this did not prove possible but only in certain periods of time and in few expeditions. The average fleet per expedition during the seven years between 1821 and 1827 was 40 vessels. What is also remarkable to note is the increasing number of fireships that were used in each expedition culminating in 1826 to 12 per expedition. Naval expeditions were formed *ad hoc* according to the demand of the war in both the Aegean the Ionian seas and the southeastern Mediterranean. The average time at sea was five months annually. Expeditions took usually place during the summer between May and September and very few during the winter months, mainly to supply Messolonghi.

It is evident that it was privately-owned ships from the Aegean islands, designated for grain trade and armed with several canons, that acted as warships in the uprising. However, the main corpus of the Greek Navy formed by vessels of Hydra, Spetses, and Psara consisted of an average of 40 privately-owned vessels chartered by the central Government. This was a small portion, about 6%, of the 700 merchant sailing ships owned by Greeks, which were deployed as naval ships for a limited time and for specific expeditions. The question that arises, here, is what did the unaccountable vessels do? The answer indicated in the next two sections was that they were involved either in privateering or trade.

A privateering fleet

The second way shipping contributed to the national cause is through the privateering fleet. This was a "private Navy" that was used to blockade the supply of castles and towns, to attack the flow of commerce, and weaken the enemy by taking cargoes and prizes. In this way, it complemented the Navy, a well-known practice of European fleets throughout the early modern period to the first half of the nineteenth century.[13]

Greeks were highly experienced seamen in the Mediterranean and had confronted western European privateering but also Barbary corsairing. Some Greeks had been predators, acting as privateers for the English, the French, or the Austrians, and encountered prize courts but also preys, as the pre-revolutionary archives of Hydra reveal.[14] It is no coincidence that the Provisionary Greek Government early on followed the western practices to impose blockades and issue privateering passports. It imposed blockades in 1822 to embargo the supplies of Ottoman castles, but blockades raise the demand for supplies and freight rates. Thus, tens of Austrian and other western European captains tried to break the embargoes and bring supplies to the Ottomans. When attacked by Greek privateers, they disregarded them as pirates and demanded indemnities. One has to understand that the Greek Revolution was not recognized as a legitimate uprise by westerners and particularly by the Holy Alliance during the first years of war. The recognition of the Greeks as belligerents by the British on 25 March 1823 was a turning point and was followed tacitly by other European nations. However, the French, the Austrians, and the Russians did not acknowledge the legitimacy of Greek privateers and treated them as pirates.[15]

So Greek privateers were licensed by the Provisionary Government either to blockade a particular maritime region or attack the enemy anywhere within the Aegean and Mediterranean seas; that is Ottoman or neutral ships that "smuggled" goods for the enemy. They were allowed to take cargoes and ships as prizes and to profit from part of the booty. The aim from a

208 *Gelina Harlaftis and Katerina Galani*

military scope was fourfold: 1) to guard or blockade maritime regions by preventing the smuggling of food and ammunition for the enemy, 2) to decimate the enemy by capturing its merchant fleet, necessary for the flow of supplies, 3) to strengthen the navy since part of the prizes were used for fireships and auxiliary vessels for the navy, and 4) to form a fleet that proved a constant and sudden threat to the merchant ships and supply vessels of the enemy. It seems that after the July Treaty of 1827, Edward Codrington, head of the British Naval Squadron in the Mediterranean, urged the Greek central administration (Αντικυβερνητικήν Επιτροπήν) to issue privateering licenses *en masse* as "privateering is one of the most powerful weapons against the enemy".[16]

In Greek historiography, anything that was not considered naval has been described as piratical and the actions of Greek privateers and corsairs were indiscriminately equated with piracy. It is true that along with privateering, piracy flourished. The line between privateering and piracy was quite thin. The Provisionary Government right from the beginning established jury committees as prize courts to try cases of misuse of privateering licenses, piracy, and smuggling.[17] In April 1827, a five-member committee made up the Maritime Court (Αντι Θαλασσίου Δικαστηρίου Επιτροπή), which was under the Ministry of Shipping (την επι των Ναυτικών Γραμματείαν).[18] By 28 January 1828, Capodistrias made it the Prize Court of the government, still known as the "Maritime Court".[19]

Piracy exploded in 1827 and 1828, but it is impossible to estimate to what extent prizes were legitimate or not. After 1827 piratical dens were formed in Sporades, in Gramvousa in Crete, and in Mani.[20] Mani had a centuries-long tradition of flotillas of small coastal vessels that plundered any ship under any flag that passed through their routes, killed the crews, and sunk the boats. The participation of the Maniots in the Revolution of 1821 and their bravery overshadowed their piratical activities and turned them into "social robbers", as Hobsbawm has written, and heroes of the liberation from the tyrant. The people of Mani continued intensively during this turbulent era their piratical actions, almost legal now, as they acquired privateering licenses.[21] Through the papers of the Court, the Mavromichali stand out as leaders of a piratical fleet of coastal and some large vessels. A seminal case brought to the Maritime Court was that of the ship *Constanta* with Sardinian flag that carried cargo from Herakleion, Crete to Trieste, and belonged to the French merchant Louis Godebout. The Maritime Court, fully supported by the Governor Ioannis Capodistrias, decided that "the 'denudation of most of the cargo of the Sardinian ship in the port of Vitellon [Oitylon]'" was true and held responsible "for all the damage caused to Godebout", Messrs. Ioannis and Elias Mavromichalis, while it considered Constantinos Mavromichalis as "irresponsible" of this deed.[22] The Mavromichalis were found guilty had to pay the enormous amount of 50,000 francs to Godebout under a state order on 25 October 1829.[23] In Mani, a land where revenge and vendettas were part of people's tradition such a verdict was perceived as a direct insult. Compliance with the rules of a new state that tried to enforce the law, modernize its institutions, and control the insubordinate local leaders meant that a price had to be paid. The tragic assassination of Ioannis Capodistrias on Sunday 27 September 1831 at the Church of Ayios Spyridon in Nafplion by Georgios and Constantinos Mavromichalis is partly owed to the Governor's tenacity to end piracy, source of wealth, and power.[24] The blood that was shed by Governor Capodistria sealed the Maniot piracy that was brought to an end.

Merchant shipping

The third way shipping contributed to the Greek cause was through merchant shipping that on the one hand continued the transport of goods and supplies to the belligerents and on the other provided the means of survival to the local maritime communities. How did the outbreak of war affect Greek shipping and trade in the Mediterranean? Was it annihilated or reconfigured under the pressure of war? In order to trace Greek shipping, we used as a benchmark the western ports mostly frequented by Greek vessels during the golden 18th century as well as ports of the Black Sea with significant Greek mercantile communities to examine continuity or change. A systematic survey of the port records of Livorno, Trieste, Genoa, Malta, and Marseilles corroborate without doubt the withdrawal of Greek ships from the Western-Mediterranean ports in the years of war.[25] Meanwhile, in the pre-revolutionary years, several hundreds of vessels arrived in the western ports, the traffic was dramatically reduced in the following decade.

While traffic in the Italian Peninsula was frail, one cannot fail to notice the emergence of two new poles of maritime activity, the Ionian islands and the Black Sea, that seem to concentrate Greek shipping. Discontinuous data from the ports of Odessa and Taganrog record several hundreds of Greek-owned ships sailing the Black Sea during the years of war.[26] In practice, Greeks and predominantly Ionians continued to sail in the Black Sea protected by the Russian, Austrian, or British flag. The continuation of the Black Sea trade, despite the ongoing war, was crucial for the Ottomans to secure food supplies for the capital of the Empire, and for the Russians to sustain their economic activity in the Mediterranean and Western Europe.

From the daily port traffic in the Ionian islands, captured in the newspaper *Gazzetta Degli Stati Uniti Delle Isole Jonie,* almost 300 Ionian ships per year connected the islands with the opposite coast, the Peloponnese and the Aegean islands between 1822 and 1826. Due to their neutral position Ionian ships transported in reality goods for both of the belligerents. As a consequence, several times they would fall prey to Greek privateers, who would seize the cargo destined, for example, for the Ottoman fortresses but not the vessel that was protected from seizure or molestation.

210   *Gelina Harlaftis and Katerina Galani*

The war brought about the restructuring of the trade routes and the reconfiguration of shipping and trade in the Aegean. The systematic study of port traffic in the coastal towns and islands of the Aegean reveals a brisk short-distance trade and shipping activity that connected the rebel areas.[27] This was carried by smaller vessels with a Greek flag that traded mostly local produce and other foodstuffs. After all, the prolonged duration of the war dictated the necessity to sustain a local economic activity and trade for the subsistence of the population. Furthermore, the lack of an official naval fleet and the constant need for warships granted individual shipowners the bargaining power to decide upon their discretion and self-interest to place their vessels in the service of the central government, as an alternative to trade. The proper conditions of war and the inflated demand for sea transport to carry provisions, soldiers, and ammunitions across the theatre of war induced a second, shipping market, that is, the transport service. Ships could be placed in the service of the Provisional Government for a steady hire, which varied greatly according to the dangers of transport.[28] For example, the transportation of food and ammunition ranged between 400 and 7,000 piasters/month, while the monthly hire for the participation in a siege was estimated between 3,500 and 10,000 piasters.

Greek shipping and nation-building

The revolutionaries aspired to a western model of governing that would include the new state in the circle of the "civilized" western European nations, as opposed to the Eastern "barbarian" state of the Ottomans.[29] The Organic Law of the State was passed by the National Assembly in January 1822.[30] The Revolution declared its political autonomy and ministries were created, one of the first of which was the Ministry of the Navy. Laws were issued, the Navy was formed, privateering licenses were granted, a Prize Court was set up to combat piracy, and arrangements were made for war at sea and for the protection of seamen.[31] Until the official acknowledgment of the Greek Revolution by the various European states in 1823, the Greek ships – whether part of the revolutionary Naval fleet, the privateering fleet, or just the merchant fleet that sailed the independent revolutionary flag – were considered as pirate ships by the Western European powers. Britain recognized the Greeks as a nation at war on March 25, 1823, followed by France that began to tacitly accept Greek naval blockades.[32]

With the establishment of the Ministry of the Navy, a Commission formed by the three islands was responsible for the naval logistics, in consultation with the fleet commander and the squadron commanders.[33] In 1821, the local commanders of the fleets, called under various names "commanders" (στόλαρχοι), "admirals", "amiraglios" (αμιράλιοι), or "commanders" (κομαντάντες), were Yakoumakis Tombazis in Hydra, Georgios Androutsos in Spetses, and Nikolas Apostolis in Psara; soon, however, Andreas (Vokos) Miaoulis was de facto recognized as the *primus inter pares* commander. All naval expeditions were organized by the island communities that provided ships and crews. Besides, the three islands, exceptionally, maintained their existing self-government system under the elites (πρόκριτους) of each island who were accountable directly to the Provisional Administration. The three islands undertook the ship-repairs, the supply of stores (sail, ropes, iron rods, nails, tow, timber, tar, fat), the provision of ammunition (cannonballs, gunpowder, bullets), and of ignitable material (sulphur, turpentine, resin, tar, nitro), as well as, of course, food supplies and provisions for the population of the islands and for the crews.

The maintenance of a Naval fleet was extremely expensive. While in the first year of the Revolution, the communities carried the financial burden of the first expeditions, from the second year onward the Navy was financed by the Provisional Government. In practice, the Administration chartered merchant vessels that carried between 10–20 canons for certain expeditions and a limited time. Based on the state budget of 1823 a ship of 16 canons and 108 men needed 14,250 pastiers per month for wages, food, ammunition, and repairs.[34] The preparation and expedition of a Navy was thus of high cost and was estimated at about 7.5 million grossia per year, for a fleet of 60 ships that would serve for six months.[35] Recent research by Dimitris Dimitropoulos on the expenditures of six Koundouriotis vessels that took part in the Navy estimates the cost at 17,800 grossia, quite near to that of the central administration whereas yet another analysis brings this to 10,000 grossia, but for a smaller vessel.[36] One needs also to take into account the high cost of fireships. Fireships bought and prepared with explosives between 1825 to mid-1826, had an estimated average price of 30,000 piasters.

From an economic point of view privateering counterbalanced the cost of the Navy. It provided a constant flow of money for the National Fund and at the same time prosperity to the local maritime communities. Captains with privateering licenses blockaded maritime regions and would stop and control by-passing non-revolutionary vessels, while their remuneration came from the seizure of cargo and ships destined for Ottoman castles or Ottoman territory.[37] Rules for the distribution of the booty were set right from the beginning of the Revolution according to which third of the prizes went to the ships and shipowners involved in the expedition, one third to the seamen, and one third to the National Treasury.[38] According to a rough calculation by Simos Bozikis, the number of legal prizes before distribution was about 3.5 to 4 million piasters for the period 1824–1827.[39]

Shipping played a central role in the unification of the rebellious regions and the interconnection of the different battlefronts into one cause. Furthermore, it assisted the establishment of a central administration, through the collection of taxes and donations from the Aegean islands or prizes from privateering. What is more, the importance of the formation of a modern Navy was manifested in the first foreign loans, that were directed to the purchase of battleships of the latest technology, frigates, and steamships.

212 *Gelina Harlaftis and Katerina Galani*

In this way, the finances of shipping during the Revolution were directly connected with the establishment of national Administration and national dominion.

In April 1827, the Third National Assembly decided to form a National Fleet, that is, the formation of a fleet owned by the state with specific ships available for war expedition throughout the year. On March 16, 1827, Thomas Cochrane, was appointed Commander-in-Chief of all naval forces, with the task to organize a regular navy. Cochran demanded that the new Navy should consist of steam-powered ships, which was the new technology. With the first national loans, six steamships were ordered, of which only three arrived in Greece at the end of the war or in the aftermath; the most famous of them is the *Karteria,* commanded by F. Hastings. *Karteria* and the frigate *Hellas*, a beautiful sailing ship of 64 guns, built in New York on behalf of the Greek provisionary administration, took part in the expeditions during the summer of 1827, but this was the beginning of the Greek Navy organized according to the international military standards of the time.[40]

Conclusions

The fleet contributed to the war in three ways: with ships that formed its Navy involved in the war at sea, with privateering ships, and with merchant ships. Shipping proved to be one of the pillars of the Greek War of Independence and contributed decisively to the final outcome. The ultimate success was written to a great extent by thousands of sailors, from dozens of Aegean and Ionian islands and seaports; hundreds of merchant ships that, from time to time, became warships; privateers or remained merchantmen ensuring the communication with the Provisionary Governments and central administration; the flow of supplies of war zones; and, ultimately, its cohesion. Shipping spread the Revolution in the Aegean and the Ionian to the most remote islands and coasts. It controlled and blocked sea routes. It prevented the transport and supply of Ottoman troops and broke their siege. It participated by sea in the blockade of the castles controlled by the Turks. It connected the island and mainland with the national Administration. It gathered financial resources, mainly from the islands and the expeditions securing financial gains and the financing of the common cause. Ultimately, it was at sea that the fate of the Greek Revolution was decided at the Battle of Navarino.

Notes

1 This study is based on the Research Programme "Greek Shipping in the Age of Revolution: Naval and Merchant Ships, 1821–1831" funded by the Stavros Niarchos Foundation, 2016–2019, Ionian University, led by Gelina Harlaftis and the post-doc researcher Dr. Katerina Galani. The outcome of this project is

The sea and nation-building 213

contained in the volume K. Galani and G. Harlaftis, eds, *Ο εμπορικός και πολεμικός στόλος κατά την Ελληνική Επανάσταση* (1821–1831) [Greek shipping during the War of Independence: naval and merchant ships (1821–1831)] (Herakleion, 2021). We would like to thank Dr. Şükrü Ilicak for providing us the Ottoman documents and their translation.

2 From the plethora of publications that followed, the works of T. Konstantinidis, *Καράβια, Καπετάνιοι και Συντροφοναύται* (1800–1830) [Ships, Captains and sailors (1800–1830)] (Athens, 1954); C. Varfis, *Το Ελληνικό Ναυτικό κατά την Καποδιστριακή περίοδο. Τα χρόνια της προσαρμογής* [The Hellenic Navy during the Period of Kapodistria. The Years of Adjustment] (Athens, 1994) and K. Metallinos, *Ο Ναυτικός Πόλεμος κατά την Ελληνική Επανάσταση* [Naval War during the Greek Revolution 1821–1829] 2 vols. (Athens, 2016), stand out due to their diligence, detailed analysis, and the use of primary and secondary sources.

3 We use the term *nautotopos* for the islands and coastal towns that provided the largest number of ships and seamen in the maritime regions of the Ionian and Aegean seas. See Gelina Harlaftis, Helen Beneki and Manos Haritatos, *Ploto, Greek shipowners from the late eighteenth century to the eve of WWII* (ELIA/ Niarchos Foundation, 2003), 16, and G. Harlaftis and K. Papakonstantinou, eds, *Η ναυτιλία των Ελλήνων*, 1700–1821 [Greek Shipping, 1700–1821. The Heyday before the Greek Revolution] (Athens, 2013), chapter 1.

4 G. Harlaftis, "The 'eastern invasion'. Greeks in the Mediterranean trade and shipping in the eighteenth and early nineteenth centuries", in *Trade and Cultural Exchange in the Early Modern Mediterranean: Braudel's Maritime Legacy*, eds M. Fusaro, C. Heywood and Mohamed-Salah Omri (London, 2010), 223–252.

5 V. Sfyroeras, *Τα ελληνικά πληρώματα του τουρκικού στόλου* [The Greek crews of the Turkish fleet] (Athens, 1968).

6 G. Harlaftis, *"Που πάτε να πολεμήσετε με σιτοκάραβα βατσέλα;"* ['Where are you going to fight with grain-cargo vessels?.]" in *Ο εμπορικός και πολεμικός στόλος κατά την Ελληνική Επανάσταση* (1821–1831) [Greek shipping during the War of Independence: naval and merchant ships (1821–1831)], eds Galani and G. Harlaftis (Herakleion, 2021).

7 We talk about sailing ships of an average size of 125 tons that were engaged in the long-haul trade; there were a few thousand more small coastal vessels in the islands and seaside towns. See G. Harlaftis, "Η 'ναυτική πολιτεία' του Ιονίου και του Αιγαίου. Στόλος και ανταγωνιστικότητα" [The 'maritime city' of the Ionian and Aegean seas. Fleet and competitiveness], in *Greek Shipping*, Table 9.4.

8 E. Mahmuzlu, "Ottoman Empire Strikes Back: Naval Reforms as a Response to Greek Revolution (1822–1827)", in *Greek Shipping during the War of Independence*, 2021.

9 «État de la marine militaire dans l'Empire Ottoman, tel qu'il a été présenté en janvier 1820», Januray 1821, Archives du Ministère Des Affaires Étrangères, Turquie 233.

10 Metallinos, *Naval War*, vol. 1, 353.

11 E. Mahmuzlu, "Ottoman Empire Strikes Back: Naval Reforms as a Response to Greek Revolution (1822–1827)", in *Greek Shipping*, 2021.

12 G. Sachtouris, *Ημερολόγιο του υδραίικου βριγαντίνου Αθηνά* [Logbook of the Hydriot brigantine *Athina*], *Ιστορικά Ημερολόγια του Ναυτικού Αγώνα του* 1821 [Historical Logbooks of the naval struggle of 1821] (Athens, 1890), 54.

13 Thomson, *Mercenaries, Pirates and Sovereigns*, 24–27. See also N. A. M. Rodger, *The Command of the Ocean. A Naval History of Britain, 1649–1815* (London, 2004), 177; J. S. Bromley, *Corsairs and Navies 1660–1760* (London, 1987), 213–241. D. J. Starkey, E. S. Eyck van Heslinga and J.A. de Moor, *Pirates and*

214   *Gelina Harlaftis and Katerina Galani*

Pirvateers. New Perspectives on the War on Trade in the Eighteenth and Nineteenth Centuries (Exeter, 1997), Introduction.

14 About the difference of privateers, corsairs and pirates see G. Harlaftis, "Η αρπαγή και οι κίνδυνοι στη θάλασσα: Πόλεμοι, κούρσος και πειρατεία στη Μεσόγειο του 18ου αιώνα [Plunder and risks at sea: Wars, corso and piracy in the Mediterranean of the eighteenth century], in *Greek Shipping*, 145–206. See also Despoina Themeli-Katifori, "Η λειτουργία λειοδικείων στο Μεσολόγγι στην περίοδο της επαναστάσεως (1821–1826) [The operation of Prize Courts in Messolonghi during the time of the Revolution (1821–1826)], *Parousia* 2 (1984): 329–350.

15 D. Katifori-Themeli, *Η Δίωξις της Πειρατείας και το Θαλάσσιο Δικαστήριο κατά την πρώτην καποδιστριακήν περίοδο* [The Prosecution of Piracy and the Maritime Court during the first kapodistrian period 1828–1829], vol. 1 (Athens, 1973), 6–8.

16 Katifori-Themeli, ibid., 15.

17 Katifori-Themeli, "The operation of Prize Courts".

18 Katifori-Themeli, *Η Δίωξις της Πειρατείας*, vol. 2, 11.

19 Ibid., 22–23.

20 Ibid., vol. 1, 25.

21 J. M. Wagstaff, "The Economy of the Mani Peninsula (Greece) in the eighteenth Century", *Balkan Studies* 6 (1965), 293–303.

22 "η γενόμενη γύμνωσις εις τον λιμένα Βίτελον του μεγαλυτέρου μέρους του φορτίου της σαρδικής νηός", Katifori-Themeli, *Η Δίωξις της Πειρατείας*, 249–255.

23 Katifori-Themeli, *Η Δίωξις της Πειρατείας*, vol. 2, 88–94.

24 Ibid., Katifori has proposed remarkably early this interpretation in a footnote.

25 See Table 1 in K. Galani, "The multiple uses of the ship during the Greek Revolution", in *Greek Shipping*. Malta and Marseilles are not included in the table as there is no record of Greek ships entering these ports during the period under consideration.

26 Ibid.

27 Fragmented and discontinuous data from the customs of the ports of Nafplion, Vostizza, Syros, Tinos between 1823 and 1829. See Galani "The multiple uses of the ship during the Greek Revolution".

28 ΓΑΚ, *Πρωτόκολλα της περιόδου Αγώνος και Καποδιστρίου* 1821–1833, Κατάστιχο 512 [άτιτλο], 1824–1825.

29 D. Tzakis, "Τα πολεμικά γεγονότα. Οι εξελίξεις στα μέτωπα του πολέμου (1822–1824) [The military events. The developments from the war front (1822–1824)]", in *Ιστορία Νέου Ελληνισμού*, 1770–2000 [History of Modern Hellenism, 1770–2000], ed. by V. Panayotopoulos, vol. 3 (Athens, 2003), 73–102; G. K. Theodoridis, "Ένα σύγχρονο κράτος. Η πολιτική οργάνωση του Αγώνα, 1822–1827" [A modern state. The political organization of the Struggle, 1822–1827], Ibid., 125–142.

30 G. D. Dimakopoulos, "Ο κώδιξ των νόμων της Ελληνικής Επαναστάσεως 1822–1828" [The Codex of the laws of the Greek Revolution, 1822–1828], *Epetiris tou Kentrou tis Istorias tou Ellinikou Dikaiou* 10–11 (1963–1964), 40-234.

31 Themeli-Katifori, "The operation of the Prize Courts".

32 Ibid.

33 Dionysis Tzakis, "Η στρατιωτική και πολιτική ενοποίηση των επαναστατημένων Ελλήνων και το ζήτημα του εθνικού στόλου" [The military and political unification of the revolutionized Greeks and the issue of the national fleet], in *Greek Shipping during the War of Independence*.

34 Simos Bozikis, "'Τα καράβια εστάθησαν γεννητικά, επροξένησαν διάφορον εις την επικράτειαν'. Ναυτικός αγώνας, δημόσια οικονομία και εθνική κυριαρχία το

Εικοσιένα" ['The ships were productive and 'made the difference in the domain'. The Naval War, public economy and national dominion during the War of Independence], in *Greek Shipping during the War of Independence*.

35 Ibid.

36 For a detailed analysis of the activity of the 6 ships of Lazaros Koundouriotis, see Dimitris Dimitropoulos, "Η άλλη πλευρά του πολέμου στη θάλασσα. Κόστος λειτουργίας των πλοίων στα χρόνια του Αγώνα" [The other side of the war at sea. Cost of operation of ships during the years of the Struggle], in *Ο εμπορικός και πολεμικός στόλος κατά την Ελληνική Επανάσταση* (1821–1831) [The merchant and military fleet during the Greek Revolution (1821–1831)], eds Galani and Harlaftis (Herakleion, 2021). Eftychia Liata dealt with the case of the Hydriot sailing ship *Timoleon*. Eftychia D. Liata, *Εκ του υστερήματος αρμάτωσαν... Η φρεγάτα «Τιμολέων» στην Επανάσταση του 1821* [They armed the ships from the savings... The frigate "Timoleon" in the Revolution of 1821] (Athens, 2020), 61–62.

37 Hundreds of such privateering licenses are in the Greek General State Archives. See General State Archives, Κεντρική Υπηρεσία, Αρχείο Μινιστέριου/ Γραμματείας/Υπουργείου των Ναυτικών, files 006, 007, 008, 010, 014, 021, 031, 041, 042, 044, 045, 051, 054, 056, 059.

38 On 22 April 1821 an order was published on the distribution of prizes, *Διάταξις περί διανομής των λειών*. See Petros Skylitzis Omiridis, *Συνοπτική ιστορία των τριών ναυτικών νήσων Ύδρας, Πετσών και Ψαρών καθ' όσον συνέπραξαν υπέρ της ελευθερίας της αναγεννηθείσης Ελλάδος το 1821 και πρώτον έτος της ελληνικής αυτονομίας. Μετά παραρτήματος διαφόρων επιστολών και άλλων επισήμων εγγράφων προς απόδειξιν της αληθείας* [Concise History of the three maritime islands Hydra, Spetses and Psara and all they did for the freedom of reborn Greece in 1821 and the first year of the Greek autonomy. With an appendix of various letters and other official documents for the proof of the truth] (Nafplion, 1831).

39 Bozikis, "The ships were productive".

40 Metallinos, *Naval War*, vol. 1, 257–296.

16 Economy and politics in the correspondence of the Neapolitan consuls in Greece[*]

Anna Maria Rao

Consular correspondence has increasingly attracted the attention of scholars, who regard consuls as intermediaries in the circulation of news. The consuls were not diplomatic agents; their main function was to protect the legal rights of their country's subjects and to collect information that could facilitate trade. Often, however, they were also valuable sources of information from a political point of view. Required to identify and distinguish the subjects of their sovereign from others, they could participate in the process of construction of national belonging.[1]

The Kingdom of Naples, from the middle of the 18th century, had an increasingly wide consular network. Having recovered its independence with Charles of Bourbon (1734), it immediately started an autonomous foreign policy, stipulating trade treaties with the powers of Northern Europe, with the Barbarian regencies, with the Ottoman Empire. Consuls and vice-consuls were sent in the Mediterranean, particularly in the Levant, in Corfu, Thessaloniki, and Smyrna. They had to report to the ministers in Naples, in particular to the Secretariat of Foreign Affairs, but also to the diplomatic representatives of the Sicilies in Constantinople.

Naples had a long tradition of economic and cultural relations with the Greeks. Imbued with ancient culture, the Enlightenment reformers of the second half of the 18th century considered indelible the Greek-Roman imprint at the origins of Italian history;[2] many believed that the relationship between southern Italy and the ancient Greek world had been a relationship of mutual cultural exchange, and sometimes of the supremacy of Magna Graecia over Greece itself. Ancient Greece was for them a model of democracy and military organization.[3]

Different were the current judgments about the modern Greeks. In Naples, the Greeks for centuries had their own church, around whose government there had been conflicts between the "Venetian" Greeks (coming from areas under Venetian rule) and the "Ottoman" ones (subject to the Turks).[4] Negative comments ran in consular circles, for both religious and commercial reasons: identified as "schismatic" for their Orthodox religion, the "Greeks" were also designated as the least reliable among the "Turkish" merchants. For this reason, in 1784, their request to have their

Economy and politics in Greece 217

own consul in Naples was rejected, thanks to the opinion expressed by Guglielmo Ludolf, minister plenipotentiary of the King of Naples in Constantinople, on the "character of the nation" that made "the Greek presumptuous, arrogant and insolent".[5] According to Gian Vincenzo Meola, author of a history of the Greek church in Naples (1790), the Bourbon government had to take measures to prevent the Greeks arriving on the coasts of the Kingdom from being insulted by the people, "used to confuse their national dress with the Turkish".[6]

The Russo-Ottoman wars had a strong impact in Naples and contributed to the construction of new images of "Greekness". Greece was increasingly considered not only and not so much for what it had been in antiquity but for what it was, with its faults and its aspirations.[7] Soon, with the French Revolution, the democracy of the moderns broke in, nourished, of course, by ancient culture, but to build a new future.

In the years of the revolution and of the Italian republican triennium (1796–1799) important reflections emerged on the geopolitical structure of the Mediterranean, linked to the ongoing struggles between France and England for control of the market, particularly in the Levant. A considerable influence exercised *La liberté des mers* by Bertrand Barère; against the English monopoly, Barère hoped for a European pact to ensure the maritime rights of all nations, a general navigation act based on natural law, on the law of nations, and European public law.[8] Among the most important contributions to this debate are the writings of Matteo Galdi, a Neapolitan patriot who was the ambassador of the Cisalpine Republic in the Batavian Republic.[9] Galdi published in Milan in 1796 the pamphlet, *Necessity of establishing a Republic,* in Italian, also translated into French. It was one of the first projects of unification of the Italian peninsula in a unitary and indivisible democratic republic. Not only, but the creation of an Italian Republic, sister and faithful ally of the French Republic, was part of a more general project of revision of the balance between Northern Europe and Mediterranean Europe, which belied the intention attributed to Russia to free the Greeks from the Ottoman yoke. In the Mediterranean, regenerated by the liberating France, "the liberty of Greece, long announced, would not be the work of Russian despotism, which would only change and aggravate its chains, but it would be the work of a generous and powerful people who, along with freedom, would bring back the love of science and fine arts".[10] In 1798, in another of his writings, dedicated to the new international relations that needed to be established in Europe, Galdi hoped for a general alliance of the peoples of the South against the two "terrible powers of the North", Russia and Germany. The spirit of conquest of the "barbarians of the North" had led to the destruction of Greek and Roman civilization and now threatened the Mediterranean peoples again, Germany aspiring to the possession of Italy and Russia to that of Greece.[11] Galdi's was an interesting attempt to substract the eastern Mediterranean from the politics of power, in the belief of an imminent disintegration of the Ottoman Empire. In

218   *Anna Maria Rao*

another of his memoirs of 1801, he wrote: "Who knows how long this decrepit Empire will last!".[12] In this conviction he believed he had to consider what advantages Italy, and particularly Naples, could gain with the support of France. In 1806, he suggested a series of measures to exclude the English and the Russians from the Mediterranean, to develop the Neapolitan trade with the Levant, to play a "civilizing" function on the North African coast.[13] It should be remembered that the Russians, in Greece considered as potential liberators, in Naples in 1799 had been on the side of the Turks, the British, and the Austrians against the Republic and for the return of the Bourbons.

The "trienio liberal", an expression used for Spain during the constitutional struggles of 1820–1821, was a liberal triennium in most of Mediterranean Europe, from Spain to Italy to Greece, during which "an international network of exile" was intertwined with "an international network of voluntary militancy.[14] Italians also participated in international philhellenism, and among them the Neapolitan patriots, albeit in an isolated and episodic manner.[15] Many of these patriots (as they liked to call themselves) had lived through the years of the French Revolution and voluntary or forced exile in France after the fall of the Neapolitan Republic in 1799. Already heirs of Enlightenment thought, the revolutionary experience had nourished projects of independence and national unity and constitutional aspirations that were partly sacrificed during the new French government of 1806–1815, but not forgotten. Exile had already proved the importance of mutual support among peoples fighting for their freedom.[16]

Even in the correspondence of the Neapolitan consuls in the Levant, it is possible to see how the French revolution had provided a new language and new political categories, in the light of which to interpret local events. Raffaele Graziani, consul in Thessaloniki, on 15 May 1795 observed, "in all scales of the Levant the French have formed two parties. One Royalist, and the other Jacobin".[17] In Thessaloniki, since the beginning of 1785, as vice-consul and then as consul until 1818, Graziani, writing from Constantinople on 19 January 1816, called "barbarians" these countries where he had been consul for so long.[18] In 1820, during the brief period of parliamentary monarchy in Naples, he published an essay on the trade of the Levant, in which he declared that he had now spent 42 years of consular service between Thessaloniki and Smyrna "in support of the glory of the Prince and the splendor of the nation".[19] He complained that the Sicilies had neglected the trade with the Levant and indicated some measures to remedy, first of all, the creation of lazarettos in some crucial ports. He also provided a series of reports containing information that he considered necessary for merchants and captains who intended to go to the main ports in the Levant, in particular Smyrna, Thessaloniki, Constantinople, and Alexandria.

Mainly dealing with commercial matters, as Graziani reiterated, the consuls did not neglect to provide information on the more general political situation. Giorgio Balsamo, the Neapolitan consul in Corfu since 1820, gave

Economy and politics in Greece 219

information on the situation in the United States of the Ionian Islands, established in 1817 under as a British protectorate, and on the consequences of the "various insurrections" that had broken out in the Morea in 1821. On 10 April 1821, he sent the Neapolitan Foreign Minister a copy of the Proclamation of 9 April in which the Senate of the Ionian Islands informed its subjects living in the Morea that they would lose any right to protection if they took part in the uprisings.[20] Subsequent measures by the same Senate required ships flying the Ionian flag to respect the blockade of Morea's ports decided by the Sublime Porte.[21] On 7 May, Balsamo wrote of the widespread enthusiasm for the struggle of the Greeks but also of the conviction, equally widespread, that it could not have had a happy outcome:

> It is certain that the greatest enthusiasm reigns among the Greeks, of whatever class or condition they may be; but wise people ... believe that the violent attempt made by the Greeks to escape from their slavery cannot have a happy result, that they must necessarily succumb.[22]

In the following days, he emphasized, on the one hand, the "enthusiasm and ardour" of the Greeks fighting against the Turkish troups[23] and, on the other hand, the harshness of the repression against the Greeks in Constantinople.[24] The Ionian Islands, he wrote on 27 March 1823, had only to show loyalty and obedience, if they did not want to lose English protection. Almost without comment, finally, on 2 August 1827, he sent to Naples a copy of the Treaty of London that decided "the fate of the Greeks" and, immediately afterward, on 20 October, he informed of the destruction of the Turkish-Egyptian fleet at Navarino.[25] A few years later, it was from the consul in Cyprus that news reached Naples about the theaters of war and the disastrous consequences on trade,

> The Trade of the Europeans is almost annihilated and the Manufactures in general do not find new locations, given the misery of the inhabitants. The European Navigation is then for the most part in disarmament; finally everything is in such a state of violence that there is to fear ... to see new disasters.[26]

Little other information could be sent to Naples about the revolution in the absence of a consul general.[27] Only in the new Greek state did the Sicilies finally have a consul general, first in Nafplio, then in Athens.

Rocco Martuscelli was the first consul general of the King of the Two Sicilies in the Kingdom of Greece. Decisive for his formation had been the father figure, Domenico Martuscelli, a lawyer, who had participated in the Neapolitan Republic of 1799, in which he was Secretary of the Court of Admiralty. In this capacity, on 20 February 1799, he addressed a proclamation to the officers of the Navy, significant of the intertwining of political culture and religious faith that characterized many patriots.

220 *Anna Maria Rao*

He attributed to the "provident hand of God" the restitution to the country of its ancient freedom. Always thanks to God, merit could triumph against the whims "of a malignantly imbecile court" and everyone could contribute to the common good. Only the law now directed their steps, assuring freedom and equality; only the love of justice was the basis of republican government. These principles were to inspire their action, in the name of brotherhood.[28] After the fall of the Republic, he was condemned to exile; in a list of Neapolitans who landed in Marseille on 29 January 1800, he was 39 years old and was said to be teaching Latin in France.[29] Already a widower, in exile he married Silvia Ternoire, with whom he had Rocco in 1802. Returned to Naples, he collaborated until December 1814 to the drafting of *Biographies of illustrious men*, great publishing enterprise started in 1813 and ended in 1830. His introduction, addressed "to the lovers of patriotic glory", was a sort of summa of the key ideas of the political culture fed by the Enlightenment and the French Revolution. The differences between nations, he asserted quoting Helvétius, depended not on climate or other physical causes, but on education. For this reason, all nations were proud of their past and of the virtues of their ancestors. Italy could boast of merits in the sciences and the arts, which were also recognized by the *Encyclopédie*. Neapolitan culture, in particular, had distinguished itself in the fields of philosophy, of arts and fine letters since the time of Magna Graecia. Even in the general decadence of science that occurred in the Middle Ages, southern Italy had kept alive the sciences, thanks to the contribution of the Arabs. From the mid-15th century, then, a fundamental contribution had come from the "many distinguished Greeks", fleeing from Constantinople occupied by the Turks, who had taken refuge in Naples, where many of them taught.[30] After becoming a judge of the Grand Criminal Court, Domenico Martuscelli continued to cultivate his interests in history; in 1817, he published in six volumes the French translation of *Rudiments de l'histoire* by Louis Domairon (Paris 1801), former professor of Napoleon Bonaparte at the École Militaire, and since 1802 Inspector General of Public Education. The *Rudiments of history*, extensive reconstruction of universal history from antiquity to the end of the eighteenth century, was adopted by ministerial decree as textbooks in high schools and military colleges in the Kingdom of the Two Sicilies, and had numerous editions and reprints.[31]

With a French mother and a father patriot, jurist, historian, and man of letters, Rocco Martuscelli had a cosmopolitan education, entrusted first to the Bishop of Pozzuoli Monsignor Rosini, a great scholar and connoisseur of antiquity, with whom he studied Latin, Greek, Hebrew, and philosophy. He then studied law and learned modern languages, French, English, Spanish, and German. At the age of only 23 years, in 1825, he had the chair of Hebrew language at the University of Naples, which he left to move to a diplomatic career. So his biographer narrated his activities as a consul in Greece:

Economy and politics in Greece 221

Meanwhile Greece with blood sacrifices, with heroisms recorded by contemporary history, departed from Ottoman slavery. Raised to the rank of nations, risen to new hopes saw in Rocco Martuscelli the first consul general sent by the King of the Two Sicilies. First in Nafplio, then in Athens ... he held the consulship for five years, and he deserved the recognition of that young king and of his nation.

He took advantage of his stay in Greece for educational trips. Back in Naples, after a brief period as secretary of legation in Vienna, he became the first consul of the Kingdom of the Two Sicilies in New York and then chargé d'affaires in Washington. Member of the Academy of Philadelphia, participated in the VI Congress of Italian scientists held in Naples in 1845.[32] In Washington in June 1850, he became the diplomatic representative of the Duchy of Parma.[33]

As his biographer remarked, Rocco Martuscelli, born in France for "the sad events of the times", was "the first consul that Naples sent to Greece after its political regeneration".[34] His biographical story makes particularly interesting his testimony on the Mediterranean liberalism of the early nineteenth century.

As soon as he arrived in Nafplio, on 19 May 1833, he wrote to Foreign Minister Antonio Statella, Prince of Cassero, informing him of the logistical difficulties: the house rents were expensive, water was scarce. He certainly did not intend to compete with the splendour that could afford the residents of France, England, Russia, and Sweden, but its resources just allowed him to have "a living room, a bedroom, a study, and a kitchen with some other small indispensable convenience".[35] There was nothing new in these complaints: almost always the Neapolitan consuls complained about the scarcity of resources, making it a matter not only and not so much of personal decorum but of the prestige of the nation they had to represent.

On 18 October, the minister replied that it was not possible to sustain the expenses, and therefore he would be replaced by someone local or a foreign merchant established in Nafplio, who would have the task of consul general "without money", with only "consular rights". But Martuscelli remained in his post for five years, although forced (at least at the beginning), to draw on family assets to provide for his maintenance.[36]

He returned on matters of representation on 4 July. The local political situation appeared to him to be far from stabilized with the birth of the Kingdom entrusted to Otto of Bavaria. The "palicari" – the Greek and Albanian soldiers fighting against the Turks – were about to lay down their arms in exchange for amnesty, but he believed that they would remain enemies of the government and of the "good men". Greece's seemed to him an unfinished "Risorgimento", much remained to be done for the islands that remained outside the borders of the Kingdom, which despite their contribution were still subjected "to the rule that they wanted to shake, and that cost them so much blood". He was skeptical about the willingness of the powers involved to revise the terms of the London agreements, he feared that they would reconsider it only when the "gale would have almost sunk the ship already broken". Relations between Bavaria and Greece also seemed to him to be anything but easy. Certainly, the king of Bavaria had been generous by lending soldiers and funds to Greece, as well as his own son, but he could only look out for his own interests and those of his subjects. Some discontent was raised by the decision to replace the traditional uniforms of the Greeks, civilian and military, with those in use in Bavaria. He enclosed the drawings of the new Greek flag and recalled that on the occasion of solemnities there was "the custom for each Foreign Representative to fly the flag of his own Government", but that he had not been able to do so because "he was not appropriately housed to fly the Royal Coat of Arms"; "I care too much about the honour of my office to make it appear less in front of others".[37]

Martuscelli frequently returned to the subject of relations between Bavaria and Greece. He could not fail to show a particular sensitivity to an issue that had affected and in part continued to affect the Two Sicilies, poised between France and England. The relationship between the new laws introduced by the French "liberators" and local traditions during the so-called Decade 1806–1815 had been and continued to be an important topic of political reflection. Still, in 1820–1821, the recent constitutional uprisings in Naples had failed because of the decisive intervention of an external force, Austria, wanted by Ferdinand I.

On 22 July 1833, he described the difficult situation of public order; the provinces were "infested with Masnadieri", often their victims were precisely the diplomatic agents. He returned to some aspects of the difficult coexistence between Greeks and Bavarians, adding further details on the inconveniences arising from different lifestyles, including food. Bavarian garrisons were affected by fevers and intestinal diseases related to the abuse of wine, watermelons, wild fruits, from which Bavarian doctors could not cure them because they claimed to apply in the warm climate of Greece the same drugs considered excellent in cold Bavaria. The government should have been more attentive to the differences between the two peoples and "should not have been dominated in its operations by that impossible and constant phlegm of the North, which does not go well with the Greeks who are active and impatient".[38]

Nor was it just a matter of different "national characters". Greece was treated as an occupied country; jobs in the gendarmerie or in the navy were reserved for the Bavarians and denied to the locals, citing as a reason the ignorance of the German language "almost as if they, in expelling the Turks from their country, had to fight with the saber in their right hand, and hold the Alemannic grammar with the other to enjoy the fruits of their repeated and too costly victories". Therefore, brigandage grew in the provinces, while at sea piracy of "Ionian" boats raged.[39]

In other letters, Martuscelli informed of particular issues that he had to deal with. Who was to be considered a subject of the King of the Two

Economy and politics in Greece   223

Sicilies and therefore fall under the jurisdiction of the consul and enjoy his help in case of need? On 19 September 1833, he communicated that he had given aid to a Neapolitan woman, widow of a Greek soldier who had been in the service of France, who had been left destitute with her children. He apologized for not having asked for prior royal authorization. "Hunger does not allow for reasons, and the lack of regularity of this mail would perhaps have caused me before the remorse of not having been able to help a wretched family in time". On 20 November, his decision was disavowed by the Minister, who reminded him that according to royal instructions the consuls were authorized to "provide aid in a very small amount to ship-wrecked seamen and some indigent Royal Subject to repatriate"; the widow and her children had to be considered Greek subjects, they could expect help not from Naples but from the Greek government, or from the French, under whose colours her husband had served.[40]

A rather unprecedented issue among those that the consuls had to deal with was the request addressed to the Athenian government by the then young musician Ferdinando Taglioni (he was born in 1810) to organize a Conservatory of music on the Italian taste, and to direct the military music. Martuscelli was sorry to have to reject this request, not only for lack of financial resources but also because the court music master, who was a Bavarian, would certainly not have agreed to let others direct such an in-stitute, while the direction of military music was already entrusted to a captain who did it for free.[41]

The long transmission time of the letters made it difficult to make quick decisions if it was necessary to ask and receive instructions from Naples. The letter of 4 July was examined by the minister in Naples only in early October; only the problem of the flag seemed to attract his interest, while the observations on the political situation seemed to find little or no audience. From December 1833, the consul's letters informed mainly about economic matters, the possibilities of exchange with Naples, and the opportunities that might arise from the port that would be established in Nafplio. Martuscelli stated that he wanted to explore the various provinces and islands, to in-vestigate their commercial potential, before leaving.[42] He urged the Bourbon government to strengthen commercial relations with Greece by means of facilitation, as France, Austria, and the Papal Government had already done, otherwise he would have been cut off from the market of Greek products, in particular wines, which the French were taking over.[43] The Consul General of the Kingdom of Greece at the Kingdom of the Two Sicilies, Gaetano Bellotti, wrote on 12 and 13 February 1835 to the President of the Bourbon Council of Ministers requesting from the Sicilies a treatment similar to the one that the Austrian, Tuscan, and Papal governments had granted to some Greek entrepreneurs: sanitary facilities and exemption from the payment of navigation rights.[44]

Martuscelli's financial situation remained suspended for a long time, de-spite his heartfelt requests for help. Still, on 27 March 1834, he wrote about

224 *Anna Maria Rao*

the expenses incurred for his accommodation. On 24 November 1834 the Bourbon Council of State decided to transfer him to Athens, the new seat of the Greek government, leaving a vice-consul in Nafplio. In the correspondence from Athens in the following months, the consul general repeatedly returned to the subject that was closest to his heart, the relationship between the Bavarian government and Greece.[45] Martuscelli said he was convinced that Bavaria could only think of its own interests and not those of the Greeks. The trip to Greece by the King of Bavaria with his son on 7 December 1835, appeared to him to be dictated by "a simple desire to look around at antiquities", although he did not exclude that he also wanted to think about the welfare of the country. In the Peloponnese, there was persistent "discontent", due to the fear of new taxes. Even the project to establish a bank seemed to him "the safest way to extract from Greece the little money that there is replacing it with paper".[46] Since Greece had escaped from Turkish rule, the tax burden had only increased.[47] The bank should have ensured "prosperity in the country ... feed trade, help the arts to flourish, encourage agriculture, double the treasures of the capitalist, and extinguish the idea of the fixed disconsolate misery at all", but could ensure these objectives only if entrusted to the Greeks and not to "foreigners", who would think only of their own interests.[48]

Quite pessimistic was the picture drawn at the beginning of 1836. The frontiers of the Kingdom were infested with gangs, the Bavarian troops were not suited to fight between cliffs and fortresses, where they were constantly ambushed, but the government did not trust the Greek troops. On the other hand, the news that the foreign press published on the instability of the situation was also due to the calculations of "wily speculators":

> That the country is not at peace, that its foundations are not yet consolidated, that the shortage of money is great, that the mood is also general, there is unfortunately no one who can contradict it, but that the picture is then such as it is described to us, I can assure Your Excellency that the frame is much larger than the canvas itself.[49]

For three years, the government "did not seem to have found the best way to operate". In short, if on the one hand he considered the problems of public order and the tensions between rulers and ruled undeniable, on the other hand, he was convinced that the news about factional struggles, banditry, and endemic rebellions only made things worse, slowing down or preventing trade essential for the survival of the country.

> The alarming rumors that spread throughout Europe on such occasions greatly contribute to extinguish or at least slow down the commercial operations ... and the capital ... will be employed elsewhere; so that, if measures are not taken terminating the causes of discontent, the misery into which the country will fall will precede its total ruin.[50]

It seemed, however, that the government had offered various facilities in order to attract "wealthy and solid commercial houses".[51]

The task of a consul, as has been said, was primarily to protect the trade and merchants of his own country and to inform them of the economic opportunities offered in the host country. A man of notable culture, Martuscelli clearly grasped the connections between economic opportunities and the political climate, and not only that, but between economic opportunities, the political climate, and the information system, and he underlined the dangers that could derive both on the economic and political levels from the manipulation of news. He also pointed out the censorial interventions on the internal press, for example, the arrest of the director of the opposition newspaper, which took place without any particular reaction from the "public".[52]

He believed that periods of apparent tranquility should be mistrusted. The visit of the king, in the spring of 1836, had been an opportunity to meet the population. The Greeks had welcomed him "cheerful and animated with good hopes", but then, disappointed, they had seen him leave "taciturn, and I would say almost with marked indifference". Waiting for his return, foreseen for October, it almost seemed that all that was left to do was to talk about the climate, postponing the discussion of more important topics until autumn.[53]

In reality, the rebellion in the Peloponnese was not completely quelled, but he hoped to see "this wretched country resurrected and deserving the confidence of those who would like to come here from abroad to employ conspicuous capital". Unity was lacking, the country was dominated by discord and uncertainty.[54]

The apparent quiet was interrupted by the appearance of English and French boats near Piraeus, while rumours were circulating that were not even worth reporting, since he could not yet "know the direction that the pens of the cabinets of Europe give to these cannons". Martuscelli hoped that Bavaria would consider Greece "as an ally, and not as its province", since "the Allied Powers had wanted to make a monarchy of Greece". The economic conditions remained disastrous, the population was in misery, trade was insignificant. Only the decisive support by those same powers could resolve the situation.[55]

Nor was it only the British and French, even Russian warships, Austrians, and Americans did not disdain to "visit" Greece, leaving the field open to speculation: but "nothing can be said about the political motive behind their operations".[56]

Equally acute were Rocco Martuscelli's considerations regarding religion. On 5 November after having communicated that the king was expected with the new queen, he commented on the conditions in which many religious buildings were abandoned to neglect.

> The people murmur about it ... A people that does not see its religion respected by its leaders, will never be able to remain faithful ... Since the Government does not respect the natural sentiment of Religion that

preserves every Greek unharmed and that makes him submissive and animated by filial obedience, with the passage of time it will accustom him to neglect his duties and will find him reluctant and insubordinate to its commands. The civilization of a country must not be procured by destroying religion, but rather by making its duties known to it. A people guided by religious sentiments will always be the most peaceful and devoted to its true well-being, preserving tranquility, and seeking only the placid amelioration of its industry.[57]

In these observations, we can perceive the echo of experiences that the Sicilies, too, had lived through during the revolutionary and Napoleonic ages, when populations had risen up under the impulse of ecclesiastical propaganda that portrayed the French as deniers of God. Equally to the history of the Sicilies could fit the considerations that the consul frequently made on the distance between dynastic needs and needs of the country, between countries governed "as province" – even the Sicilies had been such under the Spanish and Austrians, before the advent of Charles of Bourbon in 1734 – and countries as "allies".

At the end of 1836, while still awaiting the arrival of the king, perhaps prevented by cholera in Bavaria,[58] he expressed concern that this could encourage the Bavarians who had come in Greece to exercise a craft, to return home. He believed that those engaged in manufacturing trades could contribute to the development of the country, spreading technical and practical knowledge which the Greeks lacked.[59] He remained very pessimistic, all were discontented, no one excluded; "there is no class ... that does not show discontent: owners, shopkeepers, artisans, civil and military employees, villagers and foreigners, all find that their interests do not go on a par with the contributions they make to see them prosper". Instead of increasing, the resources decreased, and instead of facilitating trade, agriculture, and industry, unnecessary expenses were made. He hoped that the king, until then "ill-advised", would return accompanied by wise counsellors who would help him provide for the public good. Bavaria had to stop considering Greece as its province, a source of capital to be taken away.[60]

On 7 January 1837, he announced that he had received news of the departure from Munich of King Otto and his wife, news that had immediately created a climate of optimism about the future of the Kingdom.[61] However, things did not change.

It would be too long and repetitive to go through Martuscelli's letters in the following months, which continue to describe a situation of permanent economic difficulty and widespread discontent. The consul himself was well aware of this and almost regretted that his reports always had to have an alarmist tone.[62] It is worth noting his attention to the many and very concrete aspects of this crisis, not only poverty but also the many obstacles that some fiscal measures placed in the way of the economy. He pointed out the resentment of the "merchant class" for the obligation to use stamped paper and for the 5% tax

Economy and politics in Greece 227

on the earnings of their stores, which forced them to keep an "exact register" of their daily operations, which, according to them, undermined confidence in their good faith, "the main basis of a House of commerce". In Patras, these measures had raised vigorous protests, the stores had been closed for several days. The government proceeded without caution, enacting measures that had not been adequately examined, short-sightedly adopting styles of government that might have been appropriate in Bavaria, not in Greece. "The more they would like and desire a Greek administration in the country, the more they seem to want to consolidate that subject to Bavaria". To worsen things, there were also the forces of nature, an earthquake on 20 March; the island of Hydra, already reduced to poverty by lack of trade, was particularly affected and was likely to be completely abandoned by its inhabitants.[63]

On 26 May 1837, he sent to Naples a long report, which presented a reflection firmly anchored in historical and philosophical considerations on the meaning of "colonization". If Bavaria had used for the advantage of Greece half of the effort it had expended on harming her, "the prosperity of this realm would be far advanced, and safer prognostications of well being could now be formed on its bleak future." He added,

> The talent of colonization does not seem to be a virtue of Bavaria, and the colonies, whatever they are, cost at the beginning unspeakable sums, hard work, and considerable sacrifices for the country from which they derive; but here, instead, what is wanted is for the weak and poor son to provide for the sustenance of the Father, without the latter having provided the means.

He presented a concept of colonies and colonization which was quite different from the one that was emerging from the facts, disproving that the term "colonies" was not "very common in the Italian language", if not in the ancient meaning of a people "sent to inhabit a country with the same laws of the city that sent them".[64] Being a man of the 19th century with a wide 18th-century culture, Martuscelli had an idea of a colony that was very reminiscent of the colonization of the 18th century in Spain or in the Sicilies, movements of the population to poor and uninhabited areas to start a process of economic development and learning of agricultural and manufacturing techniques. It was not a matter of taking money, but of investing it. Instead, he continued, in Greece there were only costs; the cost of Bavarian troops exceeded that of the rest of the army, without a particular effectiveness in putting down the riots and maintaining public order. The insurrection in Macedonia, which seemed to find sympathy in Greek territory, had aroused all the vigilance of the government, which had sent numerous troops to the border. Meanwhile, the treasury decreased, the discontent grew, nothing positive was decided "for the relief of this small unfortunate Kingdom, where the apple of discord seems to be more disputed than it was by the Graces in the hands of Paris".

228   *Anna Maria Rao*

Even the solemn inauguration of the new University in the presence of the king gave Martuscelli the cue for a series of reflections on the relationship between ancient and modern and on the problem of communication between philosophers and the masses. These topics were unusual in consular correspondence, which was more at ease with calculations of port arrivals and departures and commercial exchanges. The University, he observed, wanted to emulate the "Academy where Plato, Thucydides, Xenophon, Aeschylus, Sophocles, Euripides, Aristophanes, and Demosthenes, like large rivers irrigated with their doctrines the then barbaric lands of Europe". Yet, without adequate preparation, these remained empty proclamations. It was necessary to start gradually, in order to be able to "accustom the soul to culture, to imbue the mind with firm and regular principles, and thus put it within reach of grazing on such sciences". The myth and the model of antiquity found all their strength in the reflection on the reforms that had to be carried out in the new Greece, together with the dramatic teaching derived from the experience of the Neapolitan Republic of 1799 and the distance between the Republicans and the masses. Before thinking about university studies, it was necessary to educate young people in schools, high schools, colleges. "The ancient philosophers used a language understood by the masses, and they educated them ... they taught morals, they spoke to the heart". University professors risked having to "dust the benches" with no one to lend "an ear to their beautiful and erudite lectures". The Greeks had lived in the grossest ignorance; only a few, endowed with considerable fortune, had provided for their education in different parts of Europe and now, made men, they asked to be able to use their talents, certainly not to go to university.[65]

Martuscelli's reflections must have appeared to the Neapolitan ministry as vain disquisitions. A note on his report urged him to give more information about the insurrection in Macedonia in the future.[66] Not surprisingly, the correspondence becomes poorer on the ground of political testimony, and more attentive to economic aspects.

Back in Naples, Martuscelli, after a short period in Vienna, went to the United States. The new Consul General of the Sicilies in Athens, Domenico Morelli, also wrote during 1841 about the difficult political situation in Greece and the precarious international balance that conditioned it. The dramatic revolt of Candia had attracted English and French vessels against the Ottoman frigates, but the rebels aspired to their independence, did not want to join Greece, or place themselves under the protectorate of any power. Various "disorders" had arisen on the borders, especially in Thessaly, Russia fomented "these turmoil with dexterity".[67]

It is not difficult to think of a parallel reflection between the Italian Risorgimento and the Greek Risorgimento. In both cases, much, if not everything, depended on the international equilibrium and the positions assumed by the great European powers. Placed at the centre of the great land and sea manoeuvers, among various insurrections and repressive

Economy and politics in Greece 229

interventions, the Neapolitan consuls read the Greek events in the mirror of past experiences and those in progress in Italy itself. Yet, stronger and more direct appeared to them in Greece the "fomenting sparks of foreign Cabinets", as Morelli wrote on 27 May 1841. The forecasts of a dismemberment of the Ottoman Empire suggested the birth of a new state of "7 million people, which would embrace Moldavia, Wallachia, Bulgaria, Serbia, and Bosnia", bordering the Hellenic Kingdom. The latter would in turn have hinged the whole of Albania, Thessaly, Macedonia, and Rumelia, while Constantinople would have ended up as a Hanseatic city. Asia Minor, the "apple of discord", seemed destined to satisfy the aims of the British and Russia, while Egypt and the other Regencies were to satisfy the interests of France, Austria, Prussia, Sweden, and Denmark. The Consul alerted the King of the Two Sicilies so that, like the others, he, too would think of his own interests. "The future destiny of Asia calling upon itself the calculation of European Politics, it seems convenient that the Royal Government monitors them in the same way as the other Courts, and explains among them that interest to which it is called by nature and by the geographic position of the Kingdom". Morelli concluded his report stating that he had probably exceeded the boundaries of his functions.[68] Yet still, on 27 September 1841, he sent a disenchanted diagnosis on the various movements taking place: "the present governmental system tries to bring this people back to the state in which it was at the time of the battle of Navarino. Such is the political state of this country today".[69]

The relationship between local cultural traditions and the contributions of the European Enlightenment and the French Revolution to the Greek national movement and liberalism has been and is much discussed[70], as it is for Italy, particularly for Naples. In the ways of looking at Greece by 'our' consuls, we witness an extraordinary tangle of cultural suggestions deriving at the same time from the knowledge and the myths of the ancient world and from the experience of the Enlightenment and revolutionary movement, from the new languages of the nation elaborated between the 18th and the 19th century, which fed aspirations to independence and reflections on what a "Risorgimento" and a "war of liberation" really were and should be.

Notes

* This article is part of the Research Project on "Revolutionary genealogies: historical discourses, construction of experience and political choices in the revolutions of the Modern Age" (PRIN 2017), Research Unit of Naples University "Federico II", Principal Investigator prof. Antonino De Francesco.

1 For an updated bibliography, see M. Aglietti, M. Grenet, and F. Jesné, *Consoli e consolati italiani dagli Stati preunitari al fascismo (1802–1945)* (Rome, 2020), 369–403.

2 G. Ceserani, *Italy's Lost Greece* (Oxford, 2012); A. De Francesco, *The Antiquity of the Italian Nation. The Cultural Origin of a Political Myth in Modern Italy, 1796–1943* (Oxford, 2013).

230 *Anna Maria Rao*

3 A. M. Rao, "Tra Illuminismo e Restaurazione: caratteri nazionali e costituzione nell'opera di Onofrio Fiani", in O. Fiani, *Carattere de' Napolitani. Quadro istorico-politico, scritto in Francia dopo la Controrivoluzione*, eds A. M. Rao and L. Membrini (Napoli, 2005), vii–li.

4 G. V. Meola, *Delle istorie della Chiesa greca in Napoli esistente* (Napoli, 1790), 148. On the Greek presence in Naples see also G. Varriale, "Exiliados griegos en una capital de la frontera mediterránea", in *Los exiliados del rey de España*, eds J. J. Ruiz Ibáñez and I. Pérez Tostado (Madrid, 2015), 185–206.

5 Quoted in A. M. Rao, "Napoli e il Mediterraneo nel Settecento: frontiera d'Europa?", in *Il Mediterraneo delle città. Scambi, confronti, culture, rappresentazioni*, ed. F. Salvatori (Roma, 2008), 15–53, especially at page 28.

6 Meola, *Delle istorie della Chiesa greca in Napoli*, 25.

7 F. Venturi, *Settecento riformatore*, III, *La prima crisi dell'Antico Regime (1768–1776)* (Torino, 1979), 111–153. On Greekness see M. Grenet, *La fabrique communautaire: les Grecs à Venise, Livourne et Marseille 1770–1840* (Rome-Athens, 2016); M. Sotiropulos and A. Hadjikyriacou, "Patris, Ethnos, and Demos. Representation and Political Participation in the Greek World", in *Reimagining Democracy in the Mediterranean, 1780–1860*, eds J. Innes and M. Philp (Oxford, 2018), 99–104.

8 Bertrand Barère de Vieuzac, *La liberté des mers ou le gouvernement anglais dévoilé*, Imprimé en France, Ventôse, an VI de la République, 2 vols.

9 A. M. Rao, "L'espace méditerranéen dans la pensée et les projets politiques des patriotes italiens: Matteo Galdi et la 'république du genre humain'", in *Droit des gens & relations entre les peuples dans l'espace méditerranéen autour de la Révolution française*, eds M. Dorigny and R. Tlili Sellaouti (Paris, 2007), 115–137; Matteo Galdi, *Memorie diplomatiche*, ed. A. Tuccillo (Napoli, 2008).

10 *De la nécessité d'établir une République en Italie*, A Milan, De l'Imprimerie de Louis Veladini. L'An IVe de la République Française, 73.

11 *Discorso sui rapporti politico-economici dell'Italia libera con la Francia e col resto dell'Europa*, Milano, Villetard et C., anno I della Libertà Italiana; *Discours sur les rapports politiques-économiques de l'Italie libre avec la France et les autres États de l'Europe*, à Paris, Baudouin, 15 pluviôse an VI, 17–18.

12 Galdi, *Memorie diplomatiche*, 110.

13 Ibid., 119–156.

14 A. Arisi Rota, *Risorgimento. Un viaggio politico e sentimentale* (Bologna, 2019), 121.

15 P.-M. Delpu, *Un autre Risorgimento. La formation du monde libéral dans le royaume des Deux-Siciles (1815–1856)* (Rome, 2019), 173–175.

16 A.M. Rao, *Esuli. L'emigrazione politica italiana in Francia (1792–1802)* (Napoli, 1992).

17 Archivio di Stato di Napoli (=ASNa), Esteri, 2521.

18 Ibid.

19 *Saggio sul commercio di tutto il Levante di Raffaele Graziani Console di S. M. Il Re Del Regno delle Due Sicilie in Salonicco* (Napoli, 1820), 4.

20 ASNa, Esteri, 2542.

21 Ibid., 9 May 1821.

22 Ibid., 7 May 1821.

23 Ibid., 9 July 1821.

24 Ibid., 28 July 1821.

25 Ibid.

26 Console Callimery, Cipro 15 February 1829, ASNa, Esteri, 2673.

27 But see in this regard the old contribution of A. Nuzzo, *La rivoluzione greca e la questione d'Oriente nella corrispondenza dei diplomatici napoletani (1820–1830)* (Salerno, 1934).

Economy and politics in Greece   231

28 *Proclama del cittadino Domenico Martuscelli, Segretario del Tribbunale dell'Ammiragliato e Consolato ai Vice Ammiragli nella Marina della Repubblica napoletana. Napoli, 20 febbraio 1799*, in M. Battaglini and A. Placanica, *Leggi, atti, proclami ed altri documenti della Repubblica napoletana 1798–1799*, vol. I (Cava e' Tirreni, Salerno, 2000), 397–398.

29 Archives du Ministère des Affaires Etrangères, Paris, Mémoires et documents, *Italie*, 13, *pièce* 49, lista del 10 piovoso VIII/29 gennaio 1800.

30 *Biografia degli uomini illustri del Regno di Napoli ornata de loro rispettivi ritratti compilata dal sig.r Domenico Martuscelli socio delle Accademie di Marsiglia e di Livorno*, tomo I (Napoli, Nicola Gervasi, 1813), 3–10.

31 L. Domairon, *Les rudimens de l'histoire, ou idée générale et précise des peuples les plus célèbres, tant anciens, que modernes, pour servir d'introduction a leur histoire*, 4 vols. (Paris 1801); *Rudimenti di storia tradotti dal francese da Domenico Martuscelli*, 6 vols. (Napoli, 1817).

32 *Degli scienziati italiani formanti parte del VII congresso di Napoli nell'autunno del MDCCCXLV Notizie biografiche raccolte da Gaetano Giucci* (Napoli, 1845), 500–501.

33 H.R. Marraro, *Diplomatic Relations between the United States and the Kingdom of the Two Sicilies*, vol. I, 1816–1850 (New York, 1951), 35–37.

34 *Degli scienziati italiani*, 501.

35 ASNa, Esteri, 2660.

36 Ibid., 28 October 1833.

37 Ibid., 4 July 1833.

38 22 July 1833.

39 5 and 9 September 1833.

40 19 September 1833

41 9 and 23 December 1833.

42 9 and 23 December 1833.

43 7 April 1834.

44 Ibid.

45 18 July 1835.

46 18 December 1835.

47 18 June 1836.

48 6 August 1836.

49 19 January 1836.

50 5 April 1836.

51 5 November 1836.

52 5 September 1836.

53 5 April 1836.

54 18 July 1836.

55 6 August 1836.

56 5 September 1836.

57 5 November 1836.

58 24 December 1836.

59 7 December 1836.

60 24 December 1836.

61 7 January 1837.

62 26 May 1737.

63 8 April 1837.

64 *Dizionario della lingua italiana* of Tommaseo and Bellini (1861–1978) quoted by Aglietti and Jesné, "Introduzione", in *Consoli e consolati italiani*, 14.

65 26 May 1837.

66 Ibid.

232 *Anna Maria Rao*

67 27 April 1841.
68 27 May 1841.
69 Ibid.
70 I will just mention, *Hellenism and the first Greek war of liberation (1821–1830): Continuity and change*, with an Introduction by J. A. Petropulos, eds N. P. Diamandouros, J. P. Anton, J. A. Petropulos, and P. Topping (Thessaloniki, 1976), in particular D. Geanakoplos, "The Diaspora Greeks: The Genesis of modern Greek national consciousness", 59–77; more recently K. Zanou, "Imperial Nationalism and Orthodox Enlightenment: A diasporic story between the Ionian Islands, Russia and Greece, ca. 1800–30", in *Mediterranean Diasporas. Politics and Ideas in the Long nineteenth Century*, eds M. Isabella and K. Zanou (London and New York, 2016), 117–134.

Part VI

Aspirations of Freedom in the Greek World

17 The vision of the rebellious Greeks for a democratic and liberal state: The constitutions of the Greek Revolution

Spyros Vlachopoulos

The general constitutional and political framework of the revolutionary constitutions

The "Constitutions of the Revolution" or "Constitutions of the Struggle" are three (Epidaurus 1822,[1] Astros 1823, Troezen 1827) and are named after the places where the National Assemblies that voted them met. They were preceded by the so-called "local" regimes (the "Organization of the Senate of Western Greece", the "Legal Ordinance of Eastern Greece" and the "Organization of the Peloponnesian Senate"), as well as the three Constitutions of the Ionian Islands (1800, 1803, 1817) that were then under foreign occupation. Although they were not fully implemented (more precisely, they were applied to a very limited extent), due mainly to the critical war situations and civil conflicts between the Greeks, they are of great significance not only because they form the beginning of modern Greek constitutional and political history, but also because they exercised a decisive influence on it.[2]

The Constitutions of the Struggle are part of a more general constitutional and political framework. First of all, the revolutionary constitutions were influenced both by the Draft Constitution of Rhigas Velestinlis in which it was stipulated that all powers come from the "Emperor people", and by the *Hellenic Nomarchy* of the Anonymous Author, who called on the Greeks to rise up and restore the "Nomarchia", a regime where laws will prevail and not arbitrariness. Also, mention should be made of the influence of the three Constitutions of the Ionian Islands (1800, 1803, and 1817), which were aristocratic in character, but at the same time (especially that of 1803) contained many liberal elements and enshrined the most important individual rights. Furthermore, the content of the constitutions of the Revolution was shaped by the decisive influence of the ideas of the Enlightenment, and inspired by national aspirations and the ideals of constitutionalism. This influence is to be seen in the guarantee of fundamental rights and the organization of state power through a written constitution with superior legal effect.

In this context, the contribution of foreign constitutions and declarations for the protection of rights, which were permeated by the same principles, was also important. Thus, the provisions of the Greek constitutions of the

236 *Spyros Vlachopoulos*

Revolution largely reflect the content of the French Declaration of the Rights of Man and Citizen of 1789, the three French Constitutions of 1791, 1793, and 1795, and the Constitution of the United States of America of 1787. It is characteristic that the Italian liberal Carbonaro Vincenzo Gallina (a lawyer from Ravenna and a friend of Lord Byron), who participated in the First National Assembly of Epidaurus, acting as a kind of expert, brought to the attention of the members of the National Assembly the main constitutional texts of that time.

The democratic character of the revolutionary constitutions

a. Popular sovereignty as the source of all powers. With regard to the organizational bases of a constitution, all the revolutionary constitutions affirm unconditionally the principle of popular sovereignty which at the time appeared under the term "national sovereignty". The Constitution of Troezen stipulated (Article 5) that "sovereignty is inherent in the nation; all power comes from it, and exists for it". The similarity with the wording of Article 1, paragraph 3 of the 1975 Constitution in force in the Hellenic Republic today ("all powers emanate from the people, exist in favour of them and the nation, and are exercised as prescribed by the Constitution"), is obvious. Also in the other revolutionary constitutions, the principle of popular sovereignty was enshrined through the provision of elections at regular intervals.
b. The drawing up of the revolutionary constitutions by elected National Assemblies.

The constitutions of the Revolution are still impressive regarding the democratic way in which they were drafted. Although the assemblies that drafted them were not fully representative because of the state of war in which Greece was, all three constitutions, though, were drawn up by a process that not only ensured the free expression of the various opinions but was also distinguished for its rational character. Key features of this process were the drawing of a draft by small committees and the passage of the final text by the plenary of the assemblies with free debate.

Thus, the Regulation of the National Legislative Assembly of Epidaurus of 20 December 1821 defined specific operating rules concerning, among others, the quorum, the election of a president, and the required majority for decision-making:

> when two-thirds of the assembly's plenary session are present, the assembly is considered to be complete ... the decisions of the Assembly shall be made by the vote of the majority; and when the votes are also divided in equal parts, the party in which the vote of the president is found shall prevail; and after the decision has been legally made, no objection to it is admitted ...

The provisions of the Regulation guaranteed the full freedom of speech for members of the National Assembly. Their remarks had to be marked with their name in the Minutes in order to undertake the responsibility for their words: "Every one of the members has the right to speak at the assembly on the specific case ... the president may not cut anyone off ... In the assemblies, anyone who says or puts something forward, shall be noted in the minutes with their name". At the same time, rules were established, which ensure the orderly and rational discussion and conduct of the meetings:

> Members of the National Assembly should, however, beforehand ask to take the floor from the president after the cessation of the previous speaker; ... Each of the members shall have the right to declare what they approve, but only when the examination of another case shall cease ... the Assembly shall keep the required respect both during the speech and while seated, and so on; and if any man errs in these, the president shall call them to order ... Each of the members ought to be careful in the course of speaking, and not to speak particularly in a manner troublesome to the Assembly ... None of the members may interrupt the speech of another, even if it appears uncontrolled; only the president overlooks the speaker regarding mischief or lack of control.

The establishment of individual rights: The revolutionary constitutions as a model of liberal constitutionalism

The *Provisional Constitution of Greece* voted at Epidaurus enshrined individual rights, such as those of religious freedom (with simultaneous establishment as the prevailing religion that of the Eastern Orthodox Church of Christ[3]), property (with a ban on the retroactivity of tax laws), honour and security,[4] the prohibition of torture and general confiscation[5] and the protection of the citizen by independent courts.

The protection of fundamental rights is enriched in the Astros Constitution. Thus, slavery is forbidden, and it is emphatically stated (par. θ′) that

> in the Greek territory a human being is neither sold, nor bought; a slave of any race and of any religion, when he has trodden the Greek soil, is free, and cannot be claimed by his tyrant.

Further guarantees of the personal safety of citizens are provided, while freedom of the press is guaranteed for the first time, as well as the principle of proper trial at an impartial court, and the right of petition to Parliament. The Astros Constitution also lays down the state's obligation to protect and enhance public education, commerce, and agriculture.[6] This is perhaps the first guarantee of social rights in Greek constitutional history, albeit in an imperfect form.

238 *Spyros Vlachopoulos*

The most innovative provisions for the protection of fundamental rights are found in the Constitution of Troezen, which, as will be analyzed below, enshrines the most up to date list of individual rights, with most typical examples the presumption of innocence of the accused and the prohibition of imposing a double penalty for the same offense.

Yet, freedom is "the one side of the coin". The other side is the principle of equality, similarly enshrined in the revolutionary constitutions in its various manifestations (e.g., general equality before the law, justice in the distribution of public revenues, equality in the exercise of civil rights, equal access to public office, the principle of meritocracy).[7] In this way, it is once again confirmed that the relationship between freedom and equality is complementary and not antithetical.

Differences between the Constitutions of Epidaurus and Astros on the one hand, and of Troezen, on the other

The fatigue of the Greeks from civil strife is clearly discernible in the Constitution of Troezen. Constitutions (as well as all legal norms, in general) are the reflection of a certain historical conjuncture and are influenced both by the dominant ideological currents and by the prevailing political, economic, social reality. The Greek revolutionary constitutions, which left their imprint on Greek history during the early post-revolutionary years, can be subsumed under this general rule.

Thus, discord and civil strife among the Greeks exerted a decisive influence on the content of the first two revolutionary constitutions (of Epidaurus and Astros), which establish the duality of the "parliamentary body" (the Parliament) and the "executive body" (the Government). One body depends on the other, and neither can act independently. In this context, the Epidaurus Constitution established complex and impracticable procedures in order not to disturb the delicate balance between the parliamentary and the executive body.[8] The mutual distrust between the parliamentary and the executive body is particularly evident in the following regulation (par. με′) of the Constitution of Epidaurus:

> It is absolutely forbidden for the parliamentary body to consent to any treaty, the purpose of which is to abolish the political existence of the nation; if indeed it is evident, that the executive body was involved in such illegal treaties, the parliamentary body is obliged to indict the president, and after his investigation, his office shall be declared revoked before the nation.

The situation remained essentially the same with the Constitution of Astros, which maintained the confusion of powers between the executive and the parliamentary body by merely strengthening the position of the second over the first.

The constitutions of the Greek Revolution 239

The fatigue from the repeated outbursts of civil strife among the Greeks and the awareness of the need for a strong and single-faced central power was reflected a few years later in the Constitution of Troezen, which stipulated (Article 41) that "The executive [power] belongs to only one, named Governor, having various Secretaries of State under him". The Governor, whose person was inviolable (article 103) and immune "for his public acts" (Article 104), was elected for a long period of seven years (Article 121) and ratified (Article 73) the bills passed by the House.

The desire for a strong ruler after the discord and the polyarchy of the first revolutionary years is reflected with particular clarity in the report dated 16 March 1827 by Theodoros Kolokotronis to the third National Assembly of the Greeks (of Troezen):[9]

> It is undeniable that the plethora of members of the law executive power hurt us a lot and hindered the progress of our nation, and it is a wise opinion, of both ancient and modern men, that "there is no good in polyarchy". One, then, must be our ruler, the executor of the laws, and a man skilled in the politics of the enlightened world. Such a man, and indeed a Greek man, experienced, [...] we have the famous Ioannis Capodistrias, whose noble virtues no one ignores; we must therefore make the most of him for this endeavour. Behold my opinion!

The one revolutionary constitution which stands out for its excellence is undoubtedly the Constitution of Troezen. Without underestimating the importance of the first two constitutions of the Struggle, the Constitution of 1827, very strongly influenced by the American Constitution of 1787, is the fullest and most innovative.

With regard to fundamental rights, the Constitution of Troezen enshrines extensive guarantees of personal security and safeguards in the context of criminal proceedings,[10] the presumption of innocence of the accused,[11] the publicity of court meetings[12] and the public recitation of their decisions,[13] the prohibition of imposing a double penalty for the same offense,[14] the protection of property with the possibility of expropriation with prior compensation "for public benefit, sufficiently proven",[15] the economic freedom and the freedom of education,[16] the prohibition of preventive censorship[17] and the non-retroactive application of laws in general (and not only criminal laws).[18]

In general, however, the Constitution of Troezen impresses with its groundbreaking provisions, even for the present time. Indicatively, mention should be made of the rule of the partial renewal of the composition of Parliament[19] and the prohibition of the election of the same person for a second term in a row as a Representative (Member of Parliament),[20] while it should not escape our attention that already by 1827, the Constitution of Troezen established a process that could be characterized as a precursor to parliamentary control. "Each of the Representatives has the right to seek

240　*Spyros Vlachopoulos*

and receive the necessary information from the Secretariats (the ministries) on anything, debated in the House" (article 83).

The end of the revolutionary constitutions

The history of the revolutionary constitutions ends with the Resolution of the Parliament of 18 January 1828, which decides the suspension of the Constitution of Troezen of 1827 on the basis of the principle "the salvation of the motherland is the supreme law" (*salus populi suprema lex esto*).

The suspension of the Constitution of Troezen is justified by the following phrases of the Resolution:

> Because the noble lord Ioannis A. Capodistrias, trusted with the reins of the government by the Greek Nation, arrived in Greece. Because the suffering circumstances of the homeland and the duration of the war did not allow, nor do they allow the application of the Political Constitution ratified at Troezen throughout its extent. Because the salvation of the nation is the supreme of all laws, and because the Parliament has been entrusted by the people with the providence of their salvation. The Parliament's sole purpose is to save Greece, and as its most sacred duty considers this and the bliss of the Greek nation, with whose care it is entrusted.

The years that followed after the suspension of the Constitution of Troezen proved even more difficult; the murder of Capodistrias, a renewed wave of civil strife, the advent of Regency and King Otto and governance without a Constitution (absolute monarchy), until the introduction of the Constitution of 1844, which marked the transition to constitutional monarchy.

Evaluation of the constitutions of the Greek Revolution

The influence of the revolutionary constitutions of modern and contemporary Greek history and practice has been decisive for several reasons.

First, the revolutionary constitutions were liberal constitutions, which enshrined many individual rights and recorded the desire of the Greek people in revolt for democracy. Although these constitutions were largely not implemented due to prevailing war conditions, nevertheless through them the Greek people were educated in a liberal and democratic spirit, proving at the same time the pedagogical character of the constitutional texts. It is no coincidence that Greece was a pioneer in securing universal suffrage with the Constitution of 1844 (if only for men according to the standards of that period of time), when in the same period, only one in twelve citizens had the right to vote in Great Britain (the cradle of parliamentarism).[21]

Second, the Constitutions of the Struggle reveal to us the faith of the Greek people that there can be no Greek state without a constitution. The

The constitutions of the Greek Revolution   241

constitution was, in other words, a constituent element of the independence of the rebellious nation and there is perhaps no better proof of this than the Preamble of the Constitution of Epidaurus:

> the Greek Nation, which, under the horrible Ottoman despotism, unable to bear any longer the heavy and inexplicable yoke of tyranny, overthrew it with great sacrifices, proclaims today through its legal representatives in a National Assembly, before God and people, its political existence and independence.

Third (and particularly important for the history of constitutional law), at a time when the meaning of the Constitution with a superior legal effect compared to ordinary laws was not at all self-evident, the constitutions of the Struggle claimed their supremacy over ordinary laws and expressed the perception of the rebel nation that there are some immutable and timeless principles of the organization of governance, which are not permitted to be revised by coincidental majorities in the legislature. The first explicit expression of the supremacy of the Constitution is found in the Resolution of 15 April 1823 of the Second National Assembly, which, at the same time as the adoption of the Constitution of Astros, solemnly declared: "under no excuses and circumstances can the administration legislate against the present Constitution". The supremacy of the Constitution over the common laws is clearly stated as well in the Constitution of Troezen, which states that "the present constitutional laws prevail over all others" (Article 143).[22]

Fourth, the revolutionary constitutions proved that rebellious Greece was a very important "workshop of ideas". The Revolution of the Greeks from 1821 onward was not conducted only on the battlefields. It was conducted both in the National Assemblies and in the field of constitutional ideas. The Greeks at that time, although they fought, did not cease to reflect on the constitution, the organization of the state, and on fundamental freedoms, influenced by the great ideological currents and liberal constitutions of the Age of revolutions. Their "thirst" for constitutionalism and liberal and democratic organization of their state, within the framework of the great ideological and constitutional currents of that time, is reflected in the Declaration of independence issued by the First National Assembly on 15 January 1822:

> Descendants of the wise and philanthropic nation of the Greeks, and contemporaries with the now enlightened and well-governed peoples of Europe, and spectators of the good, which they enjoy under the unshatterable rule of the laws, it was impossible to suffer anymore ..., the scourge of Ottoman power ...
>
> The war, a war sacred, a war, whose only cause is the recovery of the rights of our personal freedom, property and honour, which, while

242 *Spyros Vlachopoulos*

today all the well-governed and neighbouring peoples of Europe enjoy, only the cruel tyranny of the Ottomans tried by force to take away from us ... is our word less important than that of other nations so that we deprive ourselves of those rights ...? Impelled by these principles of natural laws and wanting to be treated like the rest of our fellow European Christians, we started the war against the Turks ...

Notes

1 The first Constitution of Epidaurus (1822) was called "Provisional Constitution" in order not to provoke the conservative powers of Europe because of its republican and liberal character. This invocation of the temporary character was abandoned in the following year (1823), when the Constitution of Astros was called the "Law of Epidaurus".

2 On the constitutions of the Greek Revolution see, among others, Nikos Alivizatos, *Το Σύνταγμα και οι εχθροί του στη νεοελληνική ιστορία* 1800–2010 [The Constitution and its enemies in modern Greek history 1800–2010] (Athens, 2011), 33–73; Giorgos Daskalakis, *Ελληνική συνταγματική ιστορία* 1821–1935 [Greek constitutional history 1821–1935], 3rd ed. (Athens, 1952), 21–38; Nicholas Kaltchas, *Introduction to the Constitutional History of Modern Greece* (New York, 1940), 34–57; Antonis Pantelis, *Εγχειρίδιο συνταγματικού δικαίου* [Handbook of constitutional law], 3rd ed. (Athens, 2016), 189–196; Antonis Pantelis, Stephanos Koutsobinas and Triantaphyllos Gerozisis, eds., *Κείμενα συνταγματικής ιστορίας* [Texts of constitutional history], vol. 1 (1821–1923) (Athens-Komotini, 1993), 28–75; Katerina Sakellaropoulou, "Τα Συντάγματα του Αγώνα: Το δίκαιο της ελευθερίας" [The Constitutions of the Struggle: the law of freedom], *Δημόσιο Δίκαιο* (Ηλεκτρονικό Περιοδικό Ένωσης Ελλήνων Δημοσιολόγων), 2 (2017), no. 2, 3 (April–September). www.publiclawjournal.com/imdex_6_7.html; Alexandros Svolos "Η συνταγματική ιστορία της Ελλάδος" [The constitutional history of Greece], in *Τα ελληνικά συντάγματα 1822–1975/1986*, foreword-introduction Evangelos Venizelos 2nd ed. (Athens, 1998), 57–70; Spyros Vlachopoulos, "Τα Συντάγματα του Αγώνα" [The Constitutions of the Struggle], in *Οι φιλελεύθεροι θεσμοί του Αγώνος της Ελληνικής Επαναστάσεως* (Πρακτικά του Ζ΄ Συνεδρίου της Ιεράς Συνόδου της Εκκλησίας της Ελλάδος) (Athens, 2019), 139–144 with further references. On Greek constitutionalism of the revolutionary period, see also Paschalis M. Kitromilides, "Οι καταβολές του ελληνικού συνταγματισμού" [The origins of Greek constitutionalism], in *30 χρόνια από το Σύνταγμα του 1975. Τα Ελληνικά Συντάγματα από το Ρήγα έως σήμερα* (Athens: Hellenic Parliament Foundation, 2004), 15–24; Paschalis M. Kitromilides, "Ο Αδαμάντιος Κοραής και ο φιλελεύθερος συνταγματισμός στην ελληνική πολιτική σκέψη" [Adamantios Korais and liberal constitutionalism in Greek political thought], in *Αδαμάντιος Κοραής, Σημειώσεις εις το Προσωρινόν Πολίτευμα της Ελλάδος* (Athens: Hellenic Parliament Foundation, 2018), 11–60; Apostolos Papatolias, "Η συνταγματική ιδεολογία του 1821. Παράδοση και Νεωτερικότητα στον πρώιμο ελληνικό συνταγματισμό" [The constitutional ideology of 1821. Tradition and modernity in early Greek constitutionalism]. www.constitutionalism.gr.

3 par. α΄: "The prevailing religion in the Greek territory is that of the Eastern Orthodox Church of Christ; but the administration of Greece tolerates all other religions, and the rites and ceremonies of each of them are performed without fail".

4 par. ζ΄: "The property, honour, and security of each of the Greeks, is under the protection of the laws" and par. η΄: "All collections must be distributed rightfully to all classes and ranks of the inhabitants, throughout the whole area of the Greek territory; no collection is made without a pre-issued Law".

The constitutions of the Greek Revolution 243

5 par. κθ´: "Torture shall be abolished forever, as shall be the penalty of confiscation".

6 par. λζ´: "Public education is under the protection of the parliamentary body", par. πζ´: "The administration will systematically organize the education of youth and introduce throughout the territory the mutual teaching method" and par. πη´: "The administration owes active measures, with the aim of encouraging the trade and agriculture in Greece, taking care, among other things, to establish companies, agricultural and commercial, and a commercial court".

7 The Constitution of Epidaurus stipulated: par. β´: "Those indigenous inhabitants of the Greek territory who believe in Christ, are Greeks, and enjoy without any difference all civil rights", par. γ´: "All Greeks are equal before the laws without any exception or rank, or class, or office", par. δ´: "Those who come from outside to live or sojourn in the territory of Greece, are equal to the indigenous inhabitants before the Laws" and par. ς´: "All Greeks, in all offices and honours have the same right; and the giver of these can only be each one's value". Similar provisions are found in the Constitutions of Astros and Troezen.

8 See in particular, par. ι´: "These two bodies counterbalance with their equal contribution to the construction of the Laws; because neither the decisions of the Parliamentary body have the status of Law without the ratification by the Executive body, nor the bills presented by the Executive body to the Parliamentary have certification, if they are not approved by the Parliamentary body" and par. λδ´ of the Constitution of Epidaurus: "If the Executive body shall deny the ratification, or proceed to additions and deductions, after they explain the reasons for the refusal, or for the additions and deductions, the case is again brought before the Parliamentary Body after the comments of the Executive, and it is disputed again; and the final refusal, or the additions and deductions of the Executive body are approved, or, if the Parliamentary body insists on the same, the case is directed for the second time to the Executive body, which, if does not give in again, the law is annulled in that circumstance".

9 See Antonis Pantelis, Stephanos Koutsobinas, and Triantaphyllos Gerozisis, eds, *Κείμενα συνταγματικής ιστορίας* [Texts of constitutional history], vol. 1 (1821–1923) (Athens-Komotini, 1993), 58–61.

10 Articles 13 and 14: "No order concerning the examination and arrest of any person or thing may be issued, without relying on competent evidence, and describing the place of the examination, and the person and thing to be arrested [...] in all criminal proceedings everyone has the right to ask the cause and nature of the charge brought against him, to be cross-examined before the accusers and the witnesses, to bear testimony for him, to take counsel, and seek a speedy decision from the court".

11 Article 15: "Any person shall not be deemed guilty before his conviction".

12 Article 140: "Judgments shall be made in public, except when the publicity is contrary to the principles of morality; and then the court shall decide it".

13 Article 141: "Decisions of courts shall always be made in public".

14 Article 16: "No one is judged twice for one and the same offence, and is not condemned or temporarily deprived of his possessions, without prior procedure. And any case, once finally tried, shall not be reviewed".

15 Article 17: "The government may require the sacrifice of one's estates for a public benefit, which is sufficiently proven, but by prior compensation".

16 Article 20: "The Greeks have the right to set up shops of all kinds, education, charity, industry, and Arts, and to elect teachers for their education".

244 *Spyros Vlachopoulos*

17 Article 26: "The Greeks have the right, without any pretension to write and publish freely through the press or otherwise their thoughts and opinions, keeping the following terms: [...]".
18 Article 19: "The law cannot have a retrospective application".
19 Article 57: "Representatives shall be elected for three years; one-third of them shall be changed annually; during the first and second year they shall be changed by lot".
20 Article 58: "The same person may not be elected as a representative for two consecutive periods".
21 The Constitution of 1844 is a milestone in Greek constitutional history because on the same day as this (18 March 1844) the electoral law that recognized the right to vote to all Greeks who had been born in the kingdom, had reached the 25th year of age and had "property within the province", was passed. But because property did not have to be immovable and because, even without property, one could vote if he exercised "any profession or independent skill" (essentially only domestic servants and artisan apprentices were excluded), the electoral law essentially established universal suffrage. Even if the right to vote was limited only to males (which was self-evident for the conceptions of that time), the electoral law of 1844, by substantially recognizing the universality of voting, was "revolutionary" for its time, proving that early Greek constitutionalism not only followed the liberal and democratic currents of its time, but also in many cases was placed in the vanguard. Comparisons with other European countries "speak for themselves". As Nikos Alivizatos notes, *To Σύνταγμα και οι εχθροί του*, p. 93: "at the same time only one in 12 British citizens, had the right to vote while, in France, of the 32 million residents, only 170.000 citizens voted in elections during the Orleanist period [...] Universal suffrage – of the male population, of course – in France was established permanently after the founding of the third Republic in 1875, in Belgium in 1893, in Norway in 1898, in Austria in 1907, in Sweden in 1909, in Italy in 1912 and in Great Britain, the cradle of parliamentarianism, only after the First World War".
22 See also article 94: "[the House] shall amend and annul laws other than constitutional ones".

18 Ideals of freedom in the Greek Revolution and the political discourse of modernity[*]

Konstantinos A. Papageorgiou

Freedom for a nation: Two projects in one?

Over the past two centuries, generations of younger Greeks may have legitimately paused and pondered over the meaning of the first line of Rhigas's Thourios, "Better to live free even if only for one hour than to remain forty years a slave in prison".[1] It is, of course, a battle cry, a protreptic paean, one should not take it literally. Still, we may wonder about the importance of the idea of freedom, the point of sacrificing one's life for it and future generations, and most of all about the enormous responsibility in violently subverting a political status quo for the purpose of establishing a new regime. It is not only about finding out what freedom means and if it is worth the trouble and the sacrifice. It is certainly not a question of individual rationality. A quest for legitimacy of an uprising in the name of freedom raises a question of *responsibility* towards oneself, but also towards other humans and compatriots, ultimately towards the entire world. Of course, these questions could not be raised from the outset, at least not in this form. Yet, they did linger, sometimes more prominently, sometimes in disguise. Before and during the Greek Revolution many great and sophisticated people – as well as simple and less educated ones – expressed their feelings, articulated their thoughts, and attempted to offer reasons of a justifying and protreptic nature. This was not an easy undertaking. The social and political views of people making their living from agriculture (and secondarily commerce), who were particularly conservative and found solace and identity in the Orthodox religion could only with great difficult converse with Enlightenment ideals.[2]

There are many interesting questions to ask here concerning the justificatory potential and the need to explain and convince the necessity of reverting to arms. Although the Greek Revolution is typically associated with the revolutionary spirit of the times, the connection is usually established in a merely explanatory framework. The Greek Revolution was, of course, in a sense, inspired by the great American[3] and French exemplars but how and in what way? We seldom discuss the events in the context of political legitimacy and the ideals of the political and philosophical discourse of modernity.[4]

246   *Konstantinos Papageorgiou*

Thus, in the following I will try to establish this "etiology" in the form of invoking "Freedom" by some of the eminent thinkers of the period – some more and some less philosophical – and place it within a larger context of modern political theorizing.

The Greek struggle for independence holds a prominent place in the imagination of the modern Greeks as a struggle of heroic, "bigger than life", personalities against Ottoman despotism and oppression. Like all similar struggles, the Greek Revolution of 1821 claimed a good and justified cause, to achieve *first and foremost* social and political freedom for a particular group of people. A *second*, parallel project, inextricably connected with the quest for freedom, aimed at resuscitating[5] a nation, an ancient culture, and a people. The idea was to liberate the "descendants" of ancient people and reclaim their rights to the lands of their ancestors. This was essentially a romantic project supported by great poets and thinkers, but it also became an invaluable political instrument in attracting European and American attention to the Greek cause. It ultimately played an important role in forging modern Greek identity. As we will see, major writers and texts usually contain a reference to the ancestors as if the importance of what they have to say has to measure up with their achievements.[6]

This is not a suitable occasion to examine the internal coherence of the romantic aspects of the national project. More relevant for our purposes here is to question the extent to which the hyphenation of the two parallel projects, *the freedom idea* and *the national rebirth idea*, despite its effectiveness on a practical-political level took a toll on the normative level.[7] As the nation (rather than the people and its liberties) became the founding agent of the new political entity, it acquired a practically and politically more effective standing but, normatively and institutionally speaking, it stood on weak ground. Of course, this was nothing unusual in the historical context, but the "supervenience" of romantic nationalism over legitimate political claims nevertheless had some serious side effects.

Firstly, the question of legitimacy was not cast as a question to be answered primarily by fundamental normative-political ideas and principles connected to the two great Revolutions. It was rather roughly molded as an "informal" discourse seeking legitimacy for the cause by invoking history and culture. It was this very idea that seemed in romantic and nationalist eyes to provide *the justifying rationale* as an ideal aspiring to the rediscovery and reemergence of a people and civilization of excellence. The ancient nation and bearer of a great culture *deserved* to reclaim its rightful place among the older and more modern nations and was thus justified to seek self-determination and independence. National liberation was backward-looking and premised on some notion of historical entitlement.[8] Secondly, the idea of the rights of a nation based on historical entitlement, even if loosely established, provided a special kind of legitimacy – analogous *cum grano salis* to the "divine right of kings" – and, thus, eclipsed serious reflection on the underlying political values, in particular the importance of

Ideals of freedom in the Greek Revolution 247

freedom, equality, democracy, rights, rule of law principles, and their institutional underpinning in a new constitution.[9]

What (and how) could justify the cause

What kind of freedom did the Greeks (and those endorsing the "Greek cause") aspire to? What gave them the right to take to arms and revolt against Ottoman rule (or unrule) and seek self-determination and independence? Can we talk of motivating ideals of freedom capable to set the soul of the fighters ablaze but also adequate to justify the struggle in the eye of third parties and neutral observers? The idea of resuscitating an ancient nation is nearly as coherent as wanting to bring back to life a great personality from the past or have a mythic hero, such as Achilles, reborn. It would have been more plausible to either phrase the claim in a less ambitious notion of nationhood, as a claim put forward by a contemporaneous people with a non-idealized actual cultural identity, or revert directly to the idea of a people with an agenda of freedom.[10] In that case what would be the most convincing course to take in order to justify the revolution and the quest for national independence?

A point to start with would concern the legitimacy of an absolutist state like the Ottoman Empire and its imperial authority over ethnic and religious groups living under its rule. Another point would concern the circumstances that called for revolt, for countering arbitrary power as illegitimate and for claiming self-determination and independent statehood. These points that can be dealt here only very cursorily involve not only establishing a right to autonomy but also making the case for independent statehood. A war of independence would ultimately be justified, only if it succeeded to create a legitimate political order. Political scholars and activists writing immediately before and during the Greek Revolution in fact developed their ideals of freedom in harmony with the larger justicatory framework of modernity and reverted to the national rebirth idea mainly for rhetorical purposes and reasons of expediency. Despite appearances the pursuit of deeper normative sense of political legitimacy was present and played an important role at all fronts, including the coming to life of three impressive constitutional texts during the Revolution (1822, 1823, 1827).

A quest for freedom: The contractual and the Republican model

Let us begin by taking as a point of departure two paradigmatic theories that were introduced by modern political thought in the 17th and 18th centuries, the social contract and the republican theory. Their aim was to work out terms of legitimacy and normative limits to state power and, therefore, strongly qualify and constrain a claim to an alleged absolute and God-given power by monarchs and princes. We turn our attention to the social contract theory first. For simplicity, I will abstract from the many

248 *Konstantinos Papageorgiou*

important differences and variations among the protagonists concerning the contracting parties, the terms and content of the contract, etc. There are clearly different viewpoints involved in the construction of social contract theories with nearly infinite variations and not all contractarians are liberal thinkers. However, there is one idea shared by nearly all, namely, that everybody recognized as a party to the agreement should have a say, or somehow "consent" or at least be counted and "represented" in the decision-making procedure.[11] Whatever might be taken as the focus of the contractual agreement, be it security, freedom, happiness, rights, or property, these are goods that need to be guaranteed vis-à-vis everybody. Contract theory has, therefore, a kind of *bound, controlled individualism* inscribed in its program from the very beginning and has been since its inception a theory meant not merely to justify *status quo* but mainly to challenge *de facto* absolutist power; this holds *cum grano salis* even for a more absolutist version like the one constructed by Thomas Hobbes. John Locke, on the other hand, and, in a different and more tragic sense, the republican Algernon Sidney literally risked their heads by challenging power (as did Rousseau in his own way).[12]

An alternative theoretical and political tradition that could also serve as a justifying framework goes back to the writings (and practices) of classical and modern republicanism.[13] In fact, republicanism seems to be at least in some respects superior to social contract theory. As Quentin Skinner convincingly demonstrated, the republican understanding of freedom steers clear of the Scylla of extreme individualism and the Charybdis of a view that conceives freedom as inextricably connected to a substantial human purpose. The apparent antithesis in the conceptualization of liberty between so-called negative and so-called "positive" freedom feeds on this polarity.[14] On the contrary, for republican thought, individuals can only be free as active agents in the public sphere not because there is *per se* a substantial value to be fulfilled in this activity, dictated by some natural feature in humans, but because it is the only way for them to be free from domination by powerful others, including princes. Individuals can never be free simply as individuals without actively engaging and safeguarding the freedom of their Republic. This is a lesson from the experience of the Roman Republic as it was handed down to us from Machiavelli to Milton and Montesquieu.

Let us now return to our main topic and examine which of the two models could be more convincing as normative support for a national uprising like the Greek Revolution. Could we not say that the Christian Orthodox people and other ethnic and religious groups in the Ottoman Empire were in a quasi *state of nature* situation which strongly favoured opting for a common political life under law and freedom? Awkward as it may sound, the Ottoman rule – of which Greeks and others were subjects – did not obviously represent their point of view, did not acknowledge their rights and liberties, did not protect their life, freedom, and property, or, to formulate it in a more Rousseauan manner, it did not manifest the "general will" of free

Ideals of freedom in the Greek Revolution 249

and equal citizens. Yet, in another sense we can plausibly assume that Ottoman rule was after all a kind of *rule*,[15] the millet system was a workable model of peaceful coexistence among religious groups, and some particularly talented, among them many Christians, had the opportunity to climb up the ladder of the Ottoman military and administration. A despotic multiethnic and multicultural Empire, even if oppressive, was not exactly a state of nature but rather an absolutist state. As a temporary conclusion, we can say that some social contract theories but not necessarily all (i.e. those with absolutist leanings like the Hobbesian one) would offer legitimacy to an ethnic and religious uprising against the Ottoman State.

As already mentioned, there are many ways the Greek cause could be accounted for in terms of the political philosophy of modernity. However, there is an important aspect that often escapes our attention. If we say that in this struggle for independence the most central quest was about claiming liberties and rights vis-à-vis a central (but also locally present) imperial power which was deeply unjust and oppressive, then the fact that it was Orthodox Greeks revolting against the Ottoman Turks would appear to be a detail of minor significance. The Greek Revolution could then be seen as closer and more congenial to the great model of the American revolution. The Americans rose against the King neither because they considered themselves culturally or religiously different from the English (certainly not at that time) nor because they cherished a glorious past but rather because they did not anymore feel it right to be considered and treated as subjects of a ruler they did not in any sense control. They did not want to pay taxes imposed by a parliament, or a power for that matter, that did not represent them.

On the other hand, there is a parallel issue of justification, one we are equally prone to underestimate, not completely unrelated to the first one but certainly not identical. The Greeks and later other ethnic groups sought autonomy and self-determination, sovereignty, and independence not only as an expression of their determination to have their rights and liberties acknowledged and respected by a central government. They struggled for self-determination and independence because they wanted to challenge the imperial rule over *their* lands and lives and create their own domain of sovereignty which they hoped would guarantee a more legitimate and successful form of common life and a more free, happy, and fulfilling life for themselves as individuals. The Greeks wanted – not only as individuals but also as a *people* – to establish their *right* to determine themselves and exclusively enjoy *their* rights over *their* lands. They wanted to be masters over their lives. Here is the crux; this claim to sovereignty and independence is a claim of a different normative order because, in a sense, it presupposes *non-reformability*. Children may claim their rights against neglecting or oppressive parents, but changing parents altogether is a different and far more demanding project. Oppression may therefore trigger and explain revolt and the ensuing quest for independence but it does not *per se* justify it.

250 *Konstantinos Papageorgiou*

Otherwise, aiming at a reform of the Ottoman state would suffice (assuming, of course, the capacity for a people to enact reforms over the very authorities that "oppress" them). The Greeks, however, would never have regarded themselves merely as a political group seeking to reform the Empire from within and aiming at its modernization, which does not mean that there were not Orthodox Christians who took a different attitude towards the Empire.[16] This is exactly the point where the republican tradition promises to be superior to the contractual. To articulate it as succinctly as possible: the revolutionary cause and the Greek ideal of freedom had a better claim to legitimacy not simply as a liberal "Rights and Liberties Revolution" (a necessary but not sufficient component), but as a claim of a set of individuals, ultimately a people, in urgent need of public space, resources and institutions in which they could defend and enjoy their Freedom and be masters over their own life. The myth of national reemergence, helpful as it may have been for the politics of the time, had no normative resources and political clout for developing the institutions of the new nation-state.[17] In the remaining, we will try to trace arguments and ideas supportive of such ideals in the writings of eminent figures from the revolutionary period. For this purpose, I would like to highlight some examples from important texts written before or during the Revolution by figures as interesting and disparate as Rhigas Velestinlis, Adamantios Korais, and the anonymous author of *Elliniki Nomarchia*.[18]

A message in the bottle: Rhigas

Even if all these writers are writing in the philosophical climate of the Enlightenment and the political context of the American and the French Revolution, they differ substantially in style, in method, and in political aspirations. However, it will not come as a surprise to discover that their common quest to animate but also offer substantial arguments for the Greek cause is ultimately rooted, directly or indirectly, in the political discourse of modernity. Their commitment to Enlightenment values is manifest also in the fact that the way they invoke the "national rebirth" idea is more politically and rhetorically patriotic than essentially nationalist. It is, after all, not their responsibility that posterity focused more on the "national rebirth" idea rather than on the freedom idea and proved less inspired by the project of creating sovereignty for free people eager to live under the law.

The two projects run parallel to each other in the works of Rhigas. In his adaptation of the work *The Voyage of Young Anacharsis* by Abbé Barthélemy, Rhigas laments the present state of ancient Pherrai. Rhigas's own town of origin is described as a place of sighs where "the frequent, unjust taxation of the Christians ... would have led to the desolation of the town if it was not for its natural graces that made the inhabitants stay and put up with their ordeals so as to be buried where their ancestors lie."[19] One cannot fail to see that the context transforms the text's classicism into a

Ideals of freedom in the Greek Revolution 251

message of liberation. Nevertheless, the urging for liberation and recon-
stitution is founded upon the awareness that the country is currently a sad
relic of what it had once been. In a sense, *Young Anacharsis* could be taken
as a quasi-patriotic call of a classicist who aspires to some kind of return to a
Golden Age but in the actual context, it becomes more than a classicist's
dream. Rhigas simultaneously endorses the national rebirth idea, even if it is
mainly for educative purposes, and this also comes up in his more visual
choices, for example, in the Hercules etching illustrating his Chart of Greece
(Χάρτα της Ελλάδος) and the Head of Alexander etching by Franz Müller
which he personally published.[20] In both cases, the visual vocabulary and
ornamentation is indebted to Greek history and mythology.

On the other hand, Rhigas' thought and political practice are deeply
embedded in Enlightenment principles and ideas, the republicanism of
Montesquieu and Rousseau, and the ideals of the French Revolution are his
models. His "Rights of Man" and his "Constitution" are nearly faithful
adaptations from the respective Declaration and Jacobin Constitution of
1793, of *Year One* of the French Revolution. Rhigas's texts and ideas are not
triggered by a romantic bias for something ideal lying in the remote past. He
reflects on the present and the future and envisages a polity founded on
freedom, equality, and fraternity among citizens and ethnic groups. The
common fate of all the people living under the travails of Ottoman despotism and imperial disintegration is inspirational for him in the sense that
by focusing on the main target which is the overturning of despotic rule he
also detects an interesting potential.

The people inhabiting vast areas of the Empire, like continental Greece, the
Balkans, Asia Minor, and the Archipelago, and sharing a common cause
against tyranny also share a common basis for creating one unique polity. He
sees no difference between "Christians and Turks" and is keen to address and
integrate all groups, be it Greeks, Turks, Jews, Armenians, Vlachs, Albanians,
or Slavs. Rhigas may have underestimated the negative burden of nationalism, religious fanaticism, and ethnic bias, he may have been overoptimistic
in his overall assessment of human nature, but he also made an important
discovery. To be sure, he did not think in terms of a federation, he believed in
a unique sovereignty of one and undivided people consisting of free and equal
citizens, but he also propounded an idea of *equality* (and fraternity) among
ethnic and religious groups, which is far ahead of its time. In that respect,
Rhigas exemplified a far-sightedness that is exemplary. His effort to align with
"neighbouring" peoples exposed to similar conditions of tyrannical oppression may also have been strategic – actually, he failed in this – but most of all,
it was *normative* in the sense that he realized the necessity to explain and
justify the reasons for the revolution and the necessity of a new sovereign
polity first and foremost *vis-à-vis* those most *affected* by it and those most
interested in it. In his fair and inclusive vision, there was room for *all*.[21]

It is uncertain what would have become of his vision; had he had the
chance to live longer and see to its realization. There are reasons to be

252 *Konstantinos Papageorgiou*

skeptical. It was an uncertain, unstable vision, to say the least, but not only because a democratic political culture was practically non-existent, nor because his assessment of humanity as it can be when free from control and oppression was over-optimistic. His view of society was also relatively simplistic, if not naïve. Of course, Rhigas wrote with the experience of tyranny coming from above, not below. He had no idea of the dangers of a "tyranny of the majority" (De Tocqueville) but also of the divisiveness of particular, "sinister interests" (Bentham). Although active in commerce he was lacking a deeper grasp of the complexity of the social world and an awareness of the importance of political and social institutions designed to protect liberty, but also harness private ambition. Rhigas relied too much on removing the obstacles to the formation of a genuine "general will" and expected a natural fraternity and equality to do the rest. To a certain extent, his radical egalitarianism gravitated towards anarchy. He despised social discrimination with good reason, but he also misinterpreted the meaning of hierarchy in cooperative structures or underestimated the importance of trust and responsibility in economic transactions. This may have been enough for a purely agrarian society, but certainly not enough for a commercially oriented society. He relied on the idea of rights and popular control of the executive but he did not seem to be aware of the practical complexities of this mission, including the question of the effectiveness of state functions. Even if the liberated peoples of Southeastern Europe had the best of intentions, it was unclear how they could live together under these circumstances other than through coming under the guidance of a strong, charismatic personality that would rather authoritatively construct than genuinely express the general will of the sovereign, the people. This, however, would have meant a return to some kind of despotism. Bentham, who also seriously cared about social unrest and political transformations in Greece and other parts of the world, would have certainly frowned upon Rhigas's dreams.

A message in the bottle: Korais

Contrary to Rhigas, Adamantios Korais, the great polymath, doctor of medicine, and classical scholar (who descended from the island of Chios, was born in Smyrna and lived in Paris), had no admiration whatsoever for the Byzantines and their successors, "Christian Turks". What he shared with Rhigas was the deep commitment to classical letters and ideas as a trove of a unique moral and political civilization that had developed in the past in this part of the world and which, under favourable conditions, could once again become the solid foundation of the modern descendants of the ancients. Conversely, Rhigas's attitude was less scholarly and more driven by the symbolism of the contrast with the ancient world rather than from the content itself.

Korais's plan was ambitious, maybe not too realistic, but certainly not internally incoherent. His ideal of freedom was a *perfectionist* one and the

Ideals of freedom in the Greek Revolution 253

project of liberating the Greek people from oppression was conceptually connected not only with a thoroughly political but also with a moral reform. In fact, the whole point of fighting tyranny was based on the promise of human development and moral progress. It would make little sense to take up the fight and spill Greek blood only to substitute a tyrannical and corrupt regime for another, equally tyrannical and corrupt. In a certain sense, Korais' approach to the legitimacy question was on the face of it not at all nationalist. He did not claim that a certain people were entitled to freedom and self-determination because of their identity, religion, language, history, and culture.[22]

Korais's point of departure was an interpretation of despotism that was not only political but also moral. For him, despotism's disvalue did not lie merely in the suppression of freedom, or in the unwarranted control of human thought, expression, and action, or in establishing a regime of fear. Korais also entertained a very Greek idea, an interpretation of despotism that one could trace back to Xenophon, Thucydides, and Aristotle, namely that despotic regimes are not only oppressive but also *morally* corrupting, utterly barbaric. Seen from this perspective, the Greek struggle against the Ottoman Empire was justified because it aspired to a polis capable of promoting human excellence. This is the reason why education of the citizens of the future state was a *sine qua non* prerequisite and the reason why he wholeheartedly devoted himself to this task. Of course, this may sound not only perfectionist but also potentially illiberal. Still, Korais adapted Aristotle as an early Millian or a Humboldtian[23] rather than as a communitarian. It was more about setting the terms for individual flourishing and happiness in society rather than subjecting individuals to a higher societal end.

Korais's long-neglected *Notes on the Provisional Constitution of Greece*,[24] unfortunately published too late, actually on the eve of World War II, is a masterpiece of political and constitutional thought. The great Parisian polymath from Chios is clearly indebted to the social contract tradition but closer to a Lockean or Kantian than a Rousseauan reading. Unfortunately, it is impossible to do justice to the richness and profundity of his comments. Some of them, sometimes associated with protestant creeds, are clearly against the grain in the East. His comments against the reference to the Orthodox Church as established religion and in favour of a more radical separation of church and state are to the point, but must have troubled many at the time – perhaps even now. Korais does not mince his words calling the "established church clause" an utter absurdity that has no place where freedom of conscience reigns supreme.[25]

His views on citizenship are also of great interest and patently ahead of his time. He criticizes § β′ of the Constitution, according to which, Greeks can only be individuals who are indigenous and Christians. Korais suggests that as a rule everybody born in Greece should be considered Greek, regardless of religion. Korais's perceptive but also pragmatically balanced views,

254 *Konstantinos Papageorgiou*

developed with moral empathy and sharp judgment, are close in spirit to the careful thoughts Bentham expressed in his own commentary on the same text.[26] Some of Korais' most interesting comments on the constitution fall along the following lines. It would not only be unfair but it would also be utterly inexpedient to exclude or to ban Jews or Muslims since, as he notes, they have suffered all sorts of injustices in the past, and marginalizing them would only turn them inimical towards the new polity of which they found themselves to be part. A special law should impose some barriers in their access to offices, but time and positive experience would eventually allow them to be lifted. After all, nobody would avoid boarding a ship whose captain was an experienced Muslim or Jew, when the alternative would be a boat with an incompetent Christian at the rudder. Otherwise, access to offices is open to all citizens according to their merit and talents. Meritocracy is important and those who want to serve from a higher office need to be specially qualified and excel in moral and intellectual virtues. Korais's approach is in all matters generously inclusive but also wisely republican. For instance, immigrants who have lived three to five years in the land should be cautiously naturalized under the proviso that they give away their previous citizenship. As Korais remarks, "we should be cosmopolitans but not polypolitans; the love for one's country is indivisible"![27]

As we mentioned earlier, Korais's comments on § ζ´ are directly indebted to the social contract tradition, evidently closer to Locke and Kant than Hobbes. Personal security, personal freedom, and property are under the protection of the law, since these three rights provide the main reason why men decided to abandon the "wild state of nature" in order to enter political society. Otherwise, in the state of nature, the rights would be in constant flux ("το δίκαιον εσαλεύετο κατά πάσαν ώραν"). As nothing could be properly considered one's own, it would appear pointless to cultivate and render a property useable. Particularly interesting is the connection to just war. Korais also considers the protection of personal security, freedom, and property as the *only* legitimate foundation to wage a just war. Individuals who cherish their personal freedom and property are willing and justified to fight in order to protect their rights but on the other hand, they would never endanger these values and goods to fight wars for other reasons. Korais comes close to the Kantian intuition that democracy and commerce are basically pacific institutions. These notes on just war are not incidental and somehow they also serve to justify the war of independence under the proviso that democracy and rule of law would finally be accomplished.

Korais' *Notes* include many insightful and sharp observations and they all form part of a consistent whole, a constitutional philosophy for a liberal and humane republic. Some of these insights could be taken as *en passant* observations, but they are not. They are connected to a consistent vision about the right foundations of a polity aspiring to a free and meaningful life under the law. For example, when he writes about fair burden-sharing in taxation, he goes to great lengths to explain how important it is for the state to make its purposes understood by its citizens. Taxes are necessary to protect citizen's rights and the state should be accountable for its expenses. Naming, as well, matters a great deal. Taxes should better be called εισφοραί (contributions) rather than εισπράξεις (collection) as a token of their democratic, non-authoritarian character. In a memorable formulation reminiscent of the triptych of the French Revolution he writes, "Political society is a society of siblings. Everything should be done and everything should be named in the mildest possible tone".[28] This harmonizes with what he says when he discusses freedom of religion; "The deeper purpose of a political society is to eradicate all causes that make people hate each other".[29]

A message in the bottle: *Hellenic Nomarchy*

The third, and perhaps most fascinating, text to be considered is *Hellenic Nomarchy or A Discourse on Freedom,* published in 1806 by an "Anonymous Hellene" and arguably also the most misunderstood one.[30] It is neither a political nor philosophical treatise nor a pamphlet, but rather a hybrid of different literary genres aspiring to be a manifesto. It is as if the author has written it in different psychological states and tried to do many things simultaneously: exhaust his topic from all theoretical angles, explore fundamental ideals and values, add enthusiastic comments and deep insights next to passionate invectives, while occasionally changing from the objectified third-person perspective through a second person plural to an engaged and emotional "We". Although the text seems to be continuously shifting in mood and focus one feels that the Anonymous Hellene has basically one purpose in mind, one that incidentally unfolds as a double mission. The author's intention is to answer a question we asked at the outset, including why aging as a slave in prison makes no sense, why living as a free person even for one hour instead makes far more sense, and, concurrently, to convince its Greek readership that dying for freedom is worth the sacrifice.

Hellenic Nomarchy, consequently, operates on two levels, an intellectual and an emotional one. The first draws on the history of political ideas up to the French Revolution and the second on poetry, philosophy, and history from Homer to Thucydides. As in the case of Rhigas and Korais, the anonymous author of *Hellenic Nomarchy* returns to the past only for the purpose of bringing back to surface inspiring stories, symbols, heroes, and, most of all, attitudes. It is done with an edifying intent, to inspire its readership and render it aware of its duties. He has no intention to use the past, remote or more recent, in order to establish a pedigree that could justify the revolutionary cause. This is the reason that the most substantial parts of the book are dedicated to the meaning of Freedom. The *Hellenic Nomarchy* is therefore also called, Discourse on Freedom, because its point is none other than to articulate and explain the importance of the

256   *Konstantinos Papageorgiou*

fundamental principle that can justify recourse to violence and war: "War is just when it is motived by the need to safeguard mastery over one's own life and freedom".[31]

The Anonymous Hellene starts with a rather straightforward reference to an early Rousseauan idea. Man was happy as long as he could rely on his own powers and live naturally, but from the moment he called on others for aid, he brought disaster upon himself, "the end of natural system and the beginning of the wretched theatre of the human condition". This was a point of no return that man was forced either to accept injustice breeding anarchy and ultimately tyranny, or opt for a form of government that could guarantee security and happiness. Anarchy is a kind of state of nature and its opposite in none other than *nomarchy*, a regime that curbs "natural liberty" and the reign of the imposition of anybody's unruly and indiscriminate will. However, nomarchy is also the opposite of tyranny, the regime where people regard obedience to their master's will as freedom. In nomarchy, on the contrary, freedom is shared by everybody, because freedom is dedicated to the laws that everybody has decided; by obeying these laws one obeys one's own will and is therefore free. Nomarchy is literally the rule of the law and therefore the rule of freedom.[32]

This Rousseauan connection of law and freedom claims its origins not in Social Contract Theory but in the republican or neo-Roman tradition, most likely mediated by Italian 18th-century thinkers working in the context of a Machiavellian understanding of political virtue.[33] Nomarchy, the rule of the law, is not merely a framework to promote human liberty conceived as non-intervention in one's private will, one does not strive to establish a nomarchical regime in order to guarantee one's private interest. In many different ways, the anonymous writer of this text makes it clear that the uprising against tyranny or anarchy (one can safely assume that both vices were typically present in the Ottoman Empire of that period and thus relevant for the Greek cause) was triggered by a deeper understanding of individual freedom. This was part of a political project aspiring to educate demoralized and enslaved people to learn to conceive of themselves as one body. The following impressive characterization of the nature of the slave lies at the core of the entire argument about freedom in nomarchy.

According to Anonymous Hellene slaves are people who die without knowing why. Not only are they condemned to suffer rough treatment, disrespect, and neglect, but they grow old without being able to say if and why they lived. They are not masters of themselves and they have no country of their own, nor honor.[34] Tyranny and slavery are two sides of the same coin, deeply human and socially corrupt. Men living in this state are prone to lose reason and be guided only by indiscriminate, absurd fear.[35] The result is that a slavish soul will never be in harmony with itself, it will always undermine and disintegrate its actual will (if it has one) and perennially strive to appear pleasing to the mind of the tyrant. The slavish

Ideals of freedom in the Greek Revolution 257

soul, a subject under a tyrant's will, will never dare to counter "No, I am not afraid, since my master is the law!"[36] Only in nomarchy, can different ideas and objectives be harmonized by the mere fact that everyone concurs in the importance of the rule of law. This is why everyone who acknowledges the importance of a nomarchical government is also prone and ready to defend it when in danger. Only free people, not slaves can share one common purpose, to defend the foundation upon which everybody's happiness rests.[37] Nomarchical institutions, bonds of deep social friendship, and virtuous mores are necessary to safeguard the regime of freedom. This is why it is far more difficult for a polity to recover that has suffered disintegration from within, rather than a polity conquered by a foreign power. In the former case, the moral resources for resilience and recovery are lacking, not so in the latter.[38]

The "meaning" of the message

If the texts and figures we have highlighted as the main bearers of ideals of freedom in revolutionary Greece were also carriers of a certain "message" to posterity, what could this "message" actually be? Their ideas and intentions were often selectively received, distorted, and – as in the case of Korais – occasionally suppressed. For instance, a lot of ink has been spilled concerning the sharp critique the anonymous author of the Hellenic Nomarchy addresses to the Greek "elites" of the prerevolutionary era, especially the Church, the higher clergy, those holding high positions in the Ottoman administration, and the local potentates. This has obscured the deeper meaning of the text which with hindsight and in the context of the past centuries of political theorizing and discourse seems more robust and thoughtful than initially assumed. These works were not, not preponderantly at least, a paean to a nationalist conception of freedom. Their ideal of freedom was rather inspired and aligned with the rich traditions of political discourse of modernity, the great texts, the figures, the events. Rhigas, Korais, and Anonymous ultimately point the way to a more subtle understanding of the Ideal of Freedom as a justifying principle of the rise of Greeks against the Ottomans. For them, the Greek revolution was not to be seen simply as a liberal uprising merely to promote individual rights and interests, nor as a national revolt triggered by past entitlements. No such simplistic wholesale view was offered. It was rather the attempt to create the real public space and the normative, institutional, and moral resources for a group of individuals to live as free people in their own right. For the project to succeed, not only did they have to fight valiantly and withstand suppression courageously, they also had to negotiate among themselves and *vis-à-vis* others the terms of their future freedom. This last bit was clearly conceived to be in a firm dialogue with the political discourse of modernity, but it was at the same time overlooked or neglected for the sake of other, perhaps more pressing, needs.

258 *Konstantinos Papageorgiou*

Notes

* I am indebted to Paschalis Kitromilides for generously sharing his knowledge during many inspiring discussions. His erudition as well as his more targeted suggestions were invaluable in helping me improve some points in this paper. I also wish to thank Philippos Papageorgiou for his thoughtful comments.

1 Similar applies to the opening verses of Solomos's Hymn to Freedom.

2 Korais's aim in establishing a Greek Library (Ελληνική Βιβλιοθήκη) was to cultivate and instill in the Greek people values that would gradually win them to national independence and enlightenment ideas. The attitudes, practices, and doctrines of faith of the indigenous people were not necessarily conducive to building a modern state inspired by freedom, equality, and fraternity.

3 For a concise account of the relevance of the American Revolution and its main personalities to events in Greece and in particular to the great "enlightener" Adamantios Korais cf. Jonathan Israel, *The Expanding Blaze, How the American Revolution Ignited the World, 1775–1848* (Princeton and Oxford, 2017), 501–511. On the impact of the Declaration of Independence see David Armitage, *The Declaration of Independence, A Global History* (Cambridge, MA and London, 2007), 108.

4 We should conceive the discourse of modernity in a much broader way than the "Enlightenment discourse" placing its beginning as early as the sixteenth century. In my view, the most paradigmatic field of expression of modern political thought is the engaged intellectual achievement of scholastic philosophers, lawyers, and theologians (notably Francisco de Vitoria) raising normative barriers to the ruthless exploitation and destruction of indigenous peoples in the New World.

5 Many authors before, during and after the Revolution invoke the notion of a national "Renaissance" (αναγέννησις). So Georgios N. Filaretos who introduces the first edition (1933) of Adamantios Korais's *Notes on the Provisional Constitution of Greece*, speaks of Rhigas and Korais, as "two angels sent from Heaven to imbue the life of national renaissance to the dying body of Hellas". See Adamantios Korais, *Σημειώσεις εις το Προσωρινόν Πολίτευμα της Ελλάδος* [Notes on the Provisional Constitution of Greece], introduced and ed. Paschalis M. Kitromilides (Athens: Hellenic Parliament Foundation, 2018), 70–71.

6 Cf. Paschalis M. Kitromilides, "From Republican Patriotism to National Sentiment, A reading of *Hellenic Nomarchy*", *European Journal of Political Theory* 5 (2006): 50–60.

7 There is also a question addressed to historians. Can we say that this strategy of hyphenating the two projects had an impact on the overall legitimacy of the struggle?

8 We need to distinguish between this romantic claim based on the objective goodness of a "civilization of excellence" providing a ground for the future and the more "mundane" version of a cultural nationalism which understands itself as founded on a collective right to cultural self-determination. For the latter see Yael Tamir, *Liberal Nationalism* (Princeton, 1993), especially pp. 57–77. The question to be asked is why the "romantic" claim to national life did not take the form of a right to cultural self-determination. I suspect the answer lies in the uncertain grounding of such a claim. The connection to a civilization of excellence was more imagined than real and lacking demonstrability the second-best option was to invoke the ideal proleptically as an agent of cultural and political transformation.

9 It is not by accident that romantic philhellenes like Byron saw themselves trapped in dilemmas with no apparent solution. Byron pleaded - poetically, financially, and politically - for the rebirth of an ideal Hellas, admired the grace and courage of honest warriors, like the Souliotes (e.g. Markos Botsaris) whom he considered

the closest possible to ancient Greek heroes. On the other hand, he was also aware of the danger in the lurking confrontation between on the one hand-seasoned but self-centered fighters (e.g. Kolokotronis) and equally shrewd and self-serving but culturally and intellectually far more differentiated politicians (e.g. Mavrokordatos) on the other. The drama between high-minded idealization and brutal reality is the stuff great art is made of but inadequate as the normative and institutional foundation of a political nation. For interesting insights concerning this drama cf. the impressive account by Roderick Beaton, *Byron at War, Romantic Rebellion, Greek Revolution* (Cambridge, 2013). In this vein, it would be hardly exaggerated to say that modern Greek identity was also steeped in an attitude of historical rather than political legitimacy and the cry for freedom—beautifully expressed by poets such as Solomos and Kalvos on the one hand, Shelley and Byron on the other—leaned towards poetic imagery heavily indebted to a past culture rather than political metaphors pertaining to the life of a people of the present. Thence some misunderstandings on the part of the visionaries of the freedom of the Greeks.

10 For an exemplary analysis of the claims of peoples from a domestic and a global point of view cf. Philip Pettit, *Just Freedom, A Moral Compass for a Complex World* (New York and London, 2014), 109–187. See also Philip Pettit, *On the People's Terms, A Republican Theory and Model of Democracy* (Cambridge, 2004), 130–186.

11 This is a feature we also encounter in Utilitarianism. In assessing collective utility everybody should count as equal.

12 Another rich tradition is the Republican one. We will have more to say towards the end of the paper in relation to one of the most interesting prerevolutionary Greek texts.

13 For a historical introduction and a systematic reconstruction see Philip Pettit, *On the People's Terms: A Republican Theory and Model of Democracy* (Cambridge, 2004), 1–74.

14 Cf. Quentin Skinner, "The republican ideal of political liberty", in *Machiavelli and Republicanism*, eds Gisela Bock, Quentin Skinner, and Maurizio Viroli (Cambridge, 1990), 293–309.

15 On the early stage of Ottoman state formation cf. Cemal Kafadar, *Between Two Worlds, The Construction of the Ottoman State* (Berkeley, Los Angeles, and London, 1995).

16 If this is accurate the focus of attention shifts from the deficit in legitimacy on the side of the rulers to the need for legitimacy on the side of the insurgents who aimed at establishing not just another kind of more legitimate rule but new sovereignty. In the first case, it is those who rule who hold the burden of proof towards their subjects that their power is legitimate and their acts justified and, of course, their claims can be rightfully countered, their acts protested and their authority challenged. In the latter case, however, it is those who want to subvert the rule that was tested and found lacking that have to present an adequate reason for their insurgency and in particular in their claim to self-determination. Furthermore, if in the first case legitimacy is basically a question that remains to be answered between rulers and ruled, in the second the question concerns a wider set of peoples – not just those participating in the established scheme of power. To be sure, in our globalized but inchoately cosmopolitan world deficits of legitimacy concern us all and we care for citizens who strive for political reform in their countries. (In the 1840s Parisian workers adopted the clothing habits of Greek political refugees as a token of solidarity to their cause. See Richard Sennett, the Stranger). But a national revolution and ultimate secession have a qualitative difference, their change is deep, there is much at stake and the

260 *Konstantinos Papageorgiou*

need for justification has a wider scope compared to the challenge of legitimacy that established power is usually confronted with. In fact, the very shift from the need for internal legitimacy vis-à-vis citizens to the need for external legitimacy among peoples also expresses a deeper shift in the understanding of sovereignty and manifests the limits of the justificatory potential of an established structure of power.

17 See Maurizio Viroli, *For Love of Country, An Essay on Patriotism and Nationalism* (Oxford, 1995). On the never-ending debate among Greek historians on the peculiarities of the nationalist project see Konstantinos Papageorgiou, "Nation, Value & History. Normative notes on Greek ethnogenesis" (Unpublished manuscript, Princeton, 2005).

18 These authors have acquired an exemplary position as engaged theorists in the war of Greek independence. They are certainly not unique cases, many other important texts were written either before or during the revolutionary years, including the comments provided from very different angles by personalities abroad such as Byron and Bentham. Cf. the important book by Frederick Rosen, *Bentham, Byron and Greece, Consitutionalism, Nationalism and Early Liberal Political Thought* (Oxford, 1992). On Bentham's interest in political developments in Greece see Konstantinos Papageorgiou and Filimon Peonidis, "Introduction", in *Jeremy Bentham and the Greek Revolution* [Ο Ιερεμίας Μπένθαμ και η Ελληνική Επανάσταση] (Athens, 2005) and Konstantinos Papageorgiou, "Jeremy Bentham and the Greek Revolution: A Philosopher as Political Advisor", *British-Greek Relations. Aspects of Their Recent History* (Athens, 2005), 165–179.

19 *Anacharsis*, 133 (quoted by P. Kitromilides, *Ρήγας Βελεστινλής. Θεωρία και Πράξη* [Rhigas Velestinlis. Theory and Practice] (Athens, 1998), 44).

20 Cf. P. M. Kitromilides, *Enlightenment and Revolution, The Making of Modern Greece* (Cambridge, MA and London, 2013), 212.

21 See further Paschalis M. Kitromilides, "An Enlightenment Perspective on Balkan Cultural Pluralism. The Republican Vision of Rhigas Velestinlis", *History of Political Thought* XXIV (2003): 465–479.

22 See further Paschalis M. Kitromilides, "Adamantios Korais and the Dilemmas of Liberal Nationalism", in *Adamantios Korais and the European Enlightenment*, ed. P. M. Kitromilides (Oxford, 2010), 213–223. http://hdl.handle.net/10442/8673

23 On Mill's indebtedness to Humboldt cf. Konstantinos A. Papageorgiou, "Sicherheit und Autonomie, Zur Strafrechtsphilosophie Wilhelm von Humboldts und John Stuart Mills", *Archiv für Rechts-und Sozialphilosophie*, 76, no. 3 (1990): 324–247.

24 Adamantios Korais, *Σημειώσεις*. See above endnote 5 of this chapter.

25 It is thus not a question of tolerance not to be coerced in one's own "judgements, beliefs, views, and ways of thinking"; tolerance is a virtue of those who show lenience towards evildoers but "religious tolerance among free and equal citizens is both as a word and as a deed a monstrosity", Korais, *Σημειώσεις*, 86.

26 See Papageorgiou and Peonidis, "Introduction", in *Ιερεμίας Μπένθαμ και η Ελληνική Επανάσταση*; and Papageorgiou, "Bentham and the Greek Revolution", 165–179.

27 Korais, *Σημειώσεις*, 106.

28 Ibid., 112

29 Ibid., 89.

30 Cf. Paschalis M. Kitromilides, "From Republican Patriotism to National Sentiment", with many important suggestions concerning the origin of its ideas in the writings of Italian 18th century republicans.

Ideals of freedom in the Greek Revolution 261

31 Anonymous Hellene, *Ελληνική Νομαρχία ήτοι λόγος περί ελευθερίας* [Hellenic Nomarchy, or A Discourse on Freedom] (Athens, 1980), 30.
32 Ibid., 17.
33 P. M. Kitromilides, "From Republican Patriotism to National Sentiment, A Reading of *Hellenic Nomarchy*", 55–57.
34 *Νομαρχία*, 54.
35 Ibid., 55.
36 Ibid., 53.
37 Ibid., 60.
38 Ibid., 76–77.

Index

Abulafia, David 136
Adamopoulos, Aggelis 161
Adelman, Jeremy 25
Adjara 144
Adorno, Theodor 46
Adrianople, Treaty of (1829) 152
Adriatic 154, 164
Aegean, Aegean islands 2, 89, 163, 166, 178, 203–7, 209–13
Aeschylus 228
Aetoliko 204
Africa 8, 14, 20, 40, 60, 84, 218
Ahmed Bey, Khimshiashvili (Hamşizade) 144
Ahıska (Akhaltsikhe) 144
Aigina 204, 206
Ainos 204
Albania 112, 117, 127–28, 130, 141–43, 145–47, 149, 162, 164, 221, 229
Aleppo 142, 145
Alexander I, tsar 36, 55, 82, 85, 126, 129, 131–32, 135, 152
Alexander the Great 129, 251
Alexandria 3, 82, 181, 205–6, 218
Algeria 59–60, 86, 92, 206
Ali Pasha Tepedelenli, Ioannina 36, 144–46, 160, 163, 165
Aliprantis, Christos 11
Alivizatos, Nikos 244
Álvarez, José María 47–48
America 6–8, 19, 21–22, 25–28, 32–35, 37, 39, 45–47, 67, 69, 89, 109, 191, 193–94, 199, 225, 239, 245–46, 249–50; see also United States of America
Anatolia 142–43, 147; see also Asia Minor
Ancona 59–60, 68, 164
Andros 204

Androutsos, Georgios 210
Anscombe, F. 201
Antisthenis 1
Apennines 61
Apostolis, Nikolas 210
Arabia 142, 144
Aragon 49
Archipelago 129, 133, 203, 251; see also Aegean, Aegean islands
Argalasti 144
Argos 182
Argosaronic gulf 193
Argyrokastro see Gjirokastër
Aristophanes 228
Aristotle 3, 253
Armenia 127
Armitage, David 8, 33
Arta 164
Asia 2, 8, 14, 20, 141, 229
Asia Minor 1–2, 76, 154, 162, 192, 204, 229, 251; see also Anatolia
Astrakhan 127
Astros, constitution of (1823) 235, 237–38, 241–43
Athens 71, 95, 97, 99, 101–2, 129–30, 135, 181–82, 219, 224, 228
Austen, Jane 71
Austria 10, 19–20, 22–4, 27, 29, 32, 40, 43, 53–59, 62, 82, 84, 86–88, 97, 101, 103–4, 115–16, 118, 127–28, 140, 152–54, 159, 163, 173, 184, 192, 198, 205–7, 209, 218, 222–23, 225–26, 229, 244; see also Habsburg Empire
Avignon 22
Avlonas see Vlorë
Azov Sea 127
Aztec empire 38

Index   263

Babanzade Abdurrahman Pasha 144
Baghdad 142
Balkans 5, 12, 35–36, 40, 43, 57, 84, 90,
   101, 126, 128, 132, 153–54, 160–65,
   184, 191–94, 200–1, 251
Balsamo, Giorgio 218–19
Banat 155
Barbary coast 203, 207
Barcelona 86
Bárcena, Manuel de la 50
Barère, Bertrand 217
Barthélemy, Abbé Jean-Jacques 250
Basdekis, Tanaş/Thanasis 144
Bass, Gary J. 56
Batavian Republic 23–24, 217
Bavaria 40, 99, 101–2, 117, 221–27
Bayly, Christopher 20, 34, 67
Bazili, Konstantin 130
Bazili, Mikhail 130
Bedouin tribe 145
Behram Pasha 145
Beirut 130
Belgium 19–23, 27, 29–32, 61, 96,
   100–101, 244
Belgrade 30, 144, 151, 154–55, 159, 192
Bell, David 8, 10, 13, 20
Benakis, Panagiotis 161
Bentham, Jeremy 71, 87, 252, 254, 260
Berat 146
Berlin 97, 103, 107
Berlin, Treaty of (1833) 58
Berlioz, Héctor 75
Bern 23, 68
Bessarabia 3, 127
Bew, John 56
Bey, Süleyman 143
Billinger, Robert D. 54
Black Sea 3, 36, 125, 134, 139, 144, 193,
   203, 209
Blanco-White, José María 50
Blaquiere, Edward 71, 77, 87–89
Bonaparte see Bonaparte, Joseph;
   Bonaparte, Louis; Napoleon Bonaparte
Bonaparte, Joseph 86
Bonaparte, Louis 31
Bosnia 142, 229
Botsaris, Markos 258
Boutmy, Émile 33
Bowen, George Ferguson 137
Bowring, John 71, 87
Bozikis, Simos 211
Brâncoveanu, Constantin 154
Brazil 84, 87–88

Brigido, Pompeo de 159
Brinton, Crane 12
Brissot, Jacques Pierre 30
Britain 8, 11, 19, 21, 26–28, 30, 32,
   35–36, 38–40, 49, 51, 53, 56, 58–60, 67,
   70–71, 73, 76, 83, 86–92, 100, 103, 127,
   132, 134, 151–53, 162, 180, 191, 203–4,
   207–10, 218–19, 225, 229, 240, 244;
   see also England
Brussels 25
Bucharest 11, 126, 133, 152, 154
Bucharest, Treaty of (1812) 140,
   142, 151
Bucovina 155
Budapest 164; see also Pest
Bulgaria 126, 132, 134, 229
Buonarotti, Filippo 24
Burke, Edmund 45–46, 91
Bushati Mustafa Pasha 146
Butler, Marilyn 91
Byron, Lord 38, 69, 71, 74–76, 78, 83,
   88, 90–91, 131, 236, 258–60

Cabbarzade dynasty 143
Cádiz 96
Cádiz constitution 25–26, 28, 49, 82, 85–87
Cairo 3
Calabria 88
Campo Formio, Treaty of 23, 159
Canary Islands 47
Candia 228; see also Herakleion
   Canning, Sir Stratford 134
Capodistrias, Ioannis 27, 30n21, 39, 56,
   101–2, 126–27, 129–32, 135, 179, 194,
   208–9, 239–40
Caribbean 8, 20, 32, 35, 39
Carlile, Richard 71
Carlsbad 82
Caroline, queen of Great Britain 91
Carrascosa, Michele 88
Caspian Sea 3
Cassero 221
Castile 46, 49
Catalonia 87
Catania 109
Catherine II, empress of Russia 125,
   127–29, 134, 161–63
Caucasus 139, 142, 144
Cavo d'Oro 205
Ceauşescu, Nicolae 173
Central Greece (Rumeli) 151, 161,
   163–64, 166, 175, 182, 193, 195–96,
   199, 204, 235, 251

264 *Index*

Cephalonia 23, 161, 206
Ceracchi, Giuseppe 24
Cerigo *see* Kythira
Ceulleneer, Charles de 25
Cevdet, Ahmed Pasha 142
Championnet, Jean-Étienne 24
Channel (English) 162
Charles III, king of Spain 46
Charles IV, king of Spain 49
Charles of Bourbon, king of Naples 216, 226
Charles X, king of France 29, 60
Chateaubriand, François-René de 72–3, 77, 82
Chesme, naval battle of 111, 128, 162, 204
Chetta, Nicolò 117
Chile 50–1
Chimara 164, 171
China 34
Chios 55, 130, 183, 206, 252–53
Church, Sir Richard 69
Çıldır (Ardahan) 144
Clare, John 71
Clark, Chris 11
Clavière, Etienne 30
Cloots, Anacharsis 38
Cochrane, Thomas 73, 212
Codrington, Edward 208
Colburn, Henry 70–1
Colin, Alexandre 76
Colletta, Pietro 88
Constantas, Gregorios 46
Constantine Pavlovich, Grand Duke of Russia 129
Constantinople 1–2, 54, 76, 111, 125–26, 129–35, 143, 153–54, 163–64, 195, 197, 199, 206, 216–20, 229
Copenhagen 60
Corfu 2, 23, 126–27, 129, 133, 137, 216, 218
Corinth 164; Bay of 204; Isthmus of 89
Corsica 19–20, 22, 25, 32
Crete 2, 118, 161, 204–6, 208
Crimea 36, 127, 129
Crispi, Giuseppe 117
Croce, Benedetto 119
Cuba 47
Cunningham, Allan 76
Cyclades 193
Cyprus 2, 144, 219
Czartoryski, Adam 130

D'Alembert, Jean-Baptiste le Rond 161
Damascus 3

Danube 2, 131, 142, 155, 163
Danubian principalities 2, 32, 82, 130, 133, 152–55; *see also* Moldavia; Romania; Wallachia
Daskalogiannis, Ioannis 161
Davis, John 11
Davydov, Vasilii 131
De Condorcet, Nicolas 21
De Francesco, Antonino 110
De Hauranne, Duvergier 58
De Galvez, José 46
De Lamartine, Alphonse 74
De Rigny, Henri 178
Delacroix, Eugène 38, 76
Demosthenes 228
Denmark 32, 229
Dervenakia 195
Descartes, René 133
Di Carlo, Eugenio 113
Diaz, Delphine 95
Diderot, Denis 161
Dimitropoulos, Dimitris 211
Dixon, Simon 11
Diyarbekir 145
Djordjević, Dimitrije 151, 193–94
Dniester 163
Dou, Ramón Lázaro 47
Dufour du Pradt, Dominique 10, 51, 72, 77
Dumas, Alexandre 74
Dumouriez, Charles François 22, 30
Düsseldorf 107

Efendi, Halet 141, 145
Efthymiou, Maria 12
Egaña, Juan 50
Egypt 3, 24, 36, 40, 69, 76, 144, 147, 206, 219, 229
Eichtal, François d' 98
Elbasan 146
England 6, 19, 24, 26–9, 31, 45, 49, 59, 69, 71, 73, 75–6, 89–90, 96, 160, 166, 207, 217–22, 225, 228, 249; *see also* Britain
Epictetus 1
Epidaurus 77, 176, 236; constitution of (1822) 87, 166, 175, 178, 235–38, 241–43
Epirus 55, 160–61, 163–64, 166, 198
Ermolov, A.P. 131
Erskine, Thomas, Lord 76
España, José Maria 37
Euboia 206
Euripides 228

Index 265

Fabvier, Charles 25, 69
Falzone, Gaetano 113
Fauriel, Claude 76
Ferdinand I, king of Naples 82, 112, 222
Ferdinand VII, king of Spain 27, 39–40, 49–51, 82
Ferrand, Humbert 75
Fertile Crescent 3
Filaretos, Georgios N 258
Finland 59
Firmin-Didot, Ambroise 76–7
Fischer-Galati, Stephen 151, 193–94
Fiume 164
Florence 61, 109
Foscolo, Ugo 91
Foucault, Michel 184
France 6–8, 10, 13, 19–40, 44–5, 47, 49, 53, 56–61, 67, 69, 72–7, 80, 82–3, 85–92, 96–7, 100–1, 103, 109, 112, 114, 130, 140, 151–52, 159–61, 163–66, 168, 174, 176, 178–80, 183, 191, 194, 199, 203, 207–8, 210, 217–18, 220–23, 225–26, 228–29, 236, 244–45, 250–51, 255
Frangos, George 165
Franklin, Simon 125
Frederic the Great, king of Prussia 19
Funes, Gregorio 49

Galani, Katerina 12
Galaxidi 204
Galdi, Matteo 217
Gallina, Vincenzo 236
García de Paso, Ignácio 95
Garibaldi 97, 118
Gegëria (land of the Gegs) 146, 149
Geneva 19–20, 22–4, 30, 32, 127
Genoa 23–4, 209
Gentile, Giovanni 113
George I, king of Greece 102
Georgia 144
Germany 22–3, 27–9, 32, 37, 40, 53, 67–8, 82–3, 97–9, 163, 166, 196, 217
Gerontas, naval battle of 205
Giarrizzo, Giuseppe 109
Gibraltar 162
Gjirokastër (Argyrokastro) 146
Godebout, Louis 208
Godechot, Jacques 7, 9
Golescu, Dinicu 154
Golitsyn, A.N. 130, 132
Gramvousa 208
Graziani, Raffaele 218

Grigorakis, Tzanetbey 164
Grigorios V, patriarch of Constantinople 55, 130
Gual, Manuel 37
Guatemala 47
Guizot, François 72

Habsburg Empire 2, 67, 97, 153, 160, 163–64; *see also* Austria
Haiti 7–8, 32, 34, 36, 39
Harlaftis, Gelina 12
Harpe, Frederic César de la 23
Hastings, Frank Abney, admiral 212
Helvétius, Claude Adrien 220
Heppner, Harald 12
Herakleion 208; *see also* Candia
Heydenreuter, Reinhard 56
Hobbes, Thomas 248–49, 254
Hobhouse, John Cam 69
Hobsbawm, Eric 8–9, 20, 208
Hoche, General Louis Lazare 24
Hoidas, Dimitrios 181
Holy Places 134
Holy Roman Empire 19
Homer 255
Horkheimer, Max 46
Hugo, Victor 74
Hungary 19, 27–8, 32, 127, 154–55, 164, 192
Hydra 175, 178, 195–98, 203–7, 210, 215, 227

Iberian Peninsula 47, 87, 91; *see also* Portugal; Spain
Ignace, Anne-Claire 95
Ilıcak, Sükrü 11
Inca empire 38
Indies 45
Ioannina 36, 146, 160–61, 163, 165
Ionian islands 2, 23–4, 27, 36, 39, 86, 91–2, 118, 129–30, 134, 137, 153, 159–60, 163–66, 203–5, 207, 209, 212–13, 219, 235
Iran 145, 147
Ireland 19, 24, 32, 59
Iron Gates, Danube 155
Isabella, Maurizio 84
Israel, Jonathan 5, 8, 34
Istanbul *see* Constantinople
Italy 1, 3, 11, 19–20, 23–5, 27–9, 32, 38–41, 46, 53–4, 56, 58–62, 69, 74, 82–8, 90–2, 97, 109–18, 120, 128, 159,

266   Index

161–64, 175, 192, 209, 216–18, 220, 223, 228–29, 236, 244, 256
İzmit (Nicomedia) 144

Jassy 126, 152
Jeffrey, Francis 91
Jelavich, Barbara 192
Jelavich, Charles 192
Jellinek, Georg 33
Jerusalem 3
Joseph II, emperor of Austria 19, 129, 163–64, 171
Joubert, Barthélemy Catherine 24
Jourdan, Annie 10, 199

Kalamata 161
Kalvos, Andreas 259
Kant, Immanuel 253–54
Karadjordje, Djordje Petrovich 36, 154, 191, 194, 199
Karahisar 144
Karakatsouli, Anna 10
Karaosmanzade dynasty 143
Karaosmanzade, Hacı Ömer Agha 143
Karatzas, Constantinos 197
Kardhiq (Gardiki) 146
Kasos 204–6
Kastellorizo 204, 206
Kastoria 126
Katartzis, Dimitrios 3–6
Katsiardi-Hering, Olga 12
Katsonis, Lampros 163
Keats, John 71
Kedourie, Elie 8–9
Kenanoğlu, Ahmed 144
Kiev 126
Kishinev 131
Kitromilides, Paschalis 43, 128
Koca Yusuf Pasha, grand vezir 148
Kodricas, Panayotis 77
Kokkinis, Ioannis 179
Kolettis, Ioannis 98
Kolokotronis, Theodoros 195, 239, 259
Kolonitskii, Boris 34
Komárom 164
Konstantin Nikolaevich, Grand Duke 134
Korais, Adamantios 1, 5–7, 9, 76, 154, 165, 250, 252–55, 257–58
Koron 164
Kosovo 153
Koumoundourakis, Thodorakis 145
Koumoundourakis clan 145

Koundouriotis family 211
Koundouriotis, Lazaros 215
Kraehe, Enno 54
Kranidi 195, 204
Küçük Kaynarca, Treaty of 127, 139, 162
Kurdistan 142, 144–45
Kydonies (Ayvalık)76 204–5
Kythira 2, 23

Lachevardière, Alexandre 73
Lang, Michael 20
Larisa 143
Latin America 8, 25, 43, 73
Laybach, Congress of (1821) 82
Laz region (Asia Minor) 144
Lazkiye (Latakia, Syria) 144
Lee, Richard 48
Leibniz, Gottfried Wilhelm 133
Leipzig 79
Lemaire, Pierre-Auguste 77
Lemnos 206
Leopold, king of Belgium 29
Lepanto, naval battle of 111
Leroux, Pierre 73
Lesvos 206
Libohovë 146
Libohovo see Libohovë
Liège 32
Lisbon 88, 90
Liverpool, Robert Banks Jenkinson, Lord 76
Livorno 3, 111, 161, 164, 209
Locke, John 1, 133, 248, 253–54
Lombardy 23
London 25, 30, 38, 56, 70–2, 75, 83, 87–8, 90–1, 100, 103, 127, 131, 222; Protocol of (1830) 152; Treaty of (1827) 208, 219
Louis XVI, king of France 21
Louverture, Toussaint 36
Loverdos, Agapios 162
Lucca 24
Ludolf, Guglielmo 217
Ludwig I, king of Bavaria 222, 224
Lütfullah Pasha 144

Macedonia 2, 164, 227–29
Machiavelli, Niccolò 248, 256
Madrid 35, 45, 88, 90, 98
Magna Graecia 216, 220
Mahmud II, Ottoman sultan 55–9, 141–42, 145
Maison, Nicolas Joseph, general 80

Makrinitsa 144
Malta 86, 92, 129, 209, 214
Mandalà, Cristina 113
Mandrillon, merchant 21
Mani 145–46, 164, 208–9
Mansolas, Alexandros 101
Maraşlı, Ali Pasha 144
Marina, Francisco Xavier Martínez 50
Mariupol 127
Markides-Poulios brothers 159
Maroutsis, Panos 161
Marseilles 68, 83, 88, 103, 209, 214, 220
Martischang, François-Xavier 95
Martuscelli, Domenico 219–20
Martuscelli, Rocco 219–28
Marx, Karl 33–4
Massachusetts 32
Masson de Morviliers, Nicolas 46
Mavrokordatos, Alexandros 75, 197, 259
Mavromichalis, Constantinos 208–9
Mavromichalis, Elias 208
Mavromichalis, Georgios 209
Mavromichalis, Ioannis 208
Mavromichalis, Petros 145, 208
Mazzini, Giuseppe 28, 83–4, 116
Mediterranean 2, 19–20, 36, 39, 44, 55, 59, 83, 86–7, 90–2, 98, 109–10, 126, 128, 130, 135–36, 152, 162–63, 165, 193–94, 203, 207–9, 216–18, 221
Mehmet Ali, pasha of Egypt 181
Mehmet pasha of Shkodra 160
Meola, Gian Vincenzo 217
Messina 116
Messolonghi 69, 75–6, 204–7
Mexico 25, 50–1
Miaoulis, Andreas 210
Michael the Brave 153
Middle East 36, 130
Milan 119, 217
Mill, John Stuart 253, 260
Milton, John 248
Mina, Francisco, general 25
Miranda, Francisco 38
Modena 58
Modon 164
Moisiodax, Iosipos 2–4, 6, 37
Moldavia 126–27, 130–31, 133–34, 139, 152–53, 155, 229; *see also* Danubian principalities
Moldowallachia 142, 152; *see also* Danubian principalities
Molos, V. 162
Montenegro 161

Montesquieu 44–5, 248, 251
Moore, Barrington, Jr. 33
Moore, Thomas 69
Morea *see* Peloponnese Morelli, Domenico 228–29
Moscow 126
Motzenigos, Demetrios 161
Mount Athos 125, 133–34, 138
Moustoxydis, Andreas 166
Müller, Franz 251
Müller Jürgensen, Claus 95
Munich 226
Muoni, Guido 116
Murat, Joachim 86, 88
Murav'ev, A.N. 133–34, 138
Murray, John 69, 71, 76, 78
Mütevellioğlu, Mahmud 144
Mykonos 129, 204

Nadar, Felix 81
Nafplio 177–78, 182–83, 205, 209, 214, 219, 221, 223–24
Naples 20, 23–6, 60, 75, 82–90, 111–16, 132, 161, 216–23, 227–29
Napoleon Bonaparte 7, 23–5, 28–9, 31–2, 37, 39, 45, 48–9, 51, 82, 85–6, 91, 130, 152, 159, 164–65, 220
Napoleon III, emperor of France 28, 97
Navarino, naval battle of 40, 55, 60, 68, 111, 182, 212, 219, 229
Navarre 49
Naxos 178
Near East 54, 59, 61, 191
Necker, Jacques 21
Negris, Theodoros 175, 197
Nelson, Horatio 90
Nenadović, Aleksa 154
Nesselrode, Karl 126, 132
Netherlands 20–3, 30–2
Nevsky, Alexander 129
New York 212, 221
Nezhin 125–27
Nice 22
Nicholas I 55, 59, 127, 132, 135
Nikolaev 127
North America 20, 34–5, 48, 89
Northern Europe 216–17
Norway 244
Nottinghamshire 69
Nusayri tribes 144

Obolensky, Dimitri 125
Obradović, Dositej 154

268 *Index*

Obrenović, Miloš 151, 191, 194, 199
Ochs, Peter 23
Odessa 125, 127, 130, 155, 165, 209
Ohrid 146
Oitylo 208
Orlov, A.G. 128
Orlov brothers 111, 153, 161
Osman Efendi 144
Othon, king of Greece 29, 40, 101–2,
 117, 132, 221, 225–26, 240
Otto, prince of Bavaria *see* Othon, king
 of Greece

Paine, Thomas 37–8
Palatino 159
Palatinos, Georgios 163
Palatinos, Ioannis 161
Palermo 112–13, 115–16
Palestine 76
Palmer, R. R. 7–9, 33
Panckoucke, Charles-Joseph 46
Panin, N.I. 129
Papagergiou, Konstantinos 13
Papal States 23, 58, 60, 223
Papazolis, Georgios 161
Paraskevas, Anastasios 163–64
Paris 9, 22, 25, 28, 30, 37, 56, 72, 74–7,
 83, 95, 97–8, 100–1, 103, 131, 164, 173,
 252–53, 259
Parma 58, 221
Parry, William 77
Pasha, Alemdar Mustafa 142
Pasha, Derviş Mehmed 145
Pasha, Hacı Ali 144
Pasha, Hurşid Ahmed 145–46
Pasha, İbrahim 69, 177–79, 182
Patmos 204
Patras 102, 206, 227
Paul, tsar of Russia 129
Pavlovitch, S 194
Pazvandoğlu, Osman 140, 160
Pecchio, Giuseppe 71, 87–9
Peloponnese 55, 68–9, 75, 77, 80, 82, 89,
 111, 128, 130–31, 146, 159–62, 164–66,
 177–78, 182, 192, 195–96, 198–99,
 204–6, 209, 219, 224–25, 235
Pepe, Guglielmo 86, 88–92
Peqin 146
Peru 36, 48
Pest 160; *see also* Budapest Peta
battle of 69
Philadelphia 221
Philippidis, Daniel 46

Philippines 47
Pichat, Michel 74
Piedmont 20, 23–6, 58–9, 62, 82–5, 87,
 89, 97, 115
Piraeus 225
Pisa 75
Pittoni, Pier Antonio 159
Plato 228
Platon (Levshin), metropolitan of
 Moscow 127
Poland 19–20, 27–8, 32, 59, 61, 83, 128
Polasky, Janet 34
Poltava 127
Polychroniadis, Constantinos 76
Pontus 2
Poros 204
Portillo Valdés, José Maria 10
Portugal 20, 25–7, 32, 37–9, 45, 51, 61,
 69, 82–92
Potemkin, G.A., Prince 127, 134
Pouqueville, F.C.H.L 76
Prussia 19, 29, 32, 40, 57–8, 99,
 103–4, 229
Pruth river 130, 163
Psara 203–7, 210
Psaro, Grigorios (Anton
 Konstantinovich) 129
Puerto Rico 47
Pushkin, Alexander 11, 131
Putin, Vladimir 125
Pyrenees 43

Rao, Anna Maria 11
Rapisardi, Mario 109–10, 119
Ravenna 236
Raybaud, Maxime 77
Reinerman, Alan J. 54
Rhigas Velestinlis 4–7, 30, 37, 154, 159,
 164, 194, 235, 245, 250–52, 255, 257–58
Rhineland 19, 22–4
Rhodes 206
Rhodophoinikis, C. 197
Richelieu, Armand Jean du Plessis,
 cardinal 72
Ridgway, James 71
Rieti 88
Rio de la Plata 49
Rio y Coronel, Marcos Manuel 51
Rittweger, François 25
Robertson, William 45–6
Rodogno, Davide 56
Romania 12, 28, 133, 142, 150–55;
 see also Danubian principalities

Romanian principalities *see* Danubian principalities
Rome 23–4
Rosanvallon, Pierre 26
Roscio, Juan Germán 50
Rosini, bishop of Pozzuoli 220
Ross, Anna 96
Ross, Ludwig 101
Rossini, Gioachino 75
Roumeli *see* Central Greece
Rousseau, Jean-Jacques 248, 251, 253, 256
Rumelia (Turkey in Europe) 127, 135, 143, 146–47, 162, 229
Russia 3, 11, 20, 24, 29, 34, 36, 39–40, 53, 55–60, 67, 82, 84, 90, 96–7, 111, 125–36, 139–40, 143–44, 147, 151–52, 154, 159–64, 191–92, 194, 197, 199, 207, 209, 217, 221, 225, 228–29
Ryleev, Kondratii 131

Sachtouris, Georgios 206
St Petersburg 56, 85, 126, 131; Protocol of (1826) 64, 132
Saint-Domingue 32, 39
Salzmann, Ariel 142
Samos 175, 193, 204–5
Samothrace 206
Şanizade 142
Santangelo, Giorgio 113
Santarosa, Santorre 82, 118
Santorini 204, 206
Sardinia 23, 208
Savoy 22
Saxony 71
Scalora, Francesco 11
Scheffer, Ary 76
Schroeder, Paul 84
Schulz, Matthias 56
Schulz, Oliver 56
Scott, James 98
Scott, John 71
Scott, Sir Walter 71, 88
Šedivý, Miroslav 10
Seirinidou, Vaso 12
Selim III, Ottoman sultan 36, 184
Selim Sabit Pasha 144
Serbia 12, 36, 40, 132, 134, 142, 144, 150–53, 165, 191–94, 196–99, 201, 229
Sérurier, Jean-Mathieu-Philibert 24
Seville 82, 84
Şeyhzadeoğlu, İbrahim 145
Seyyid Ali Pasha 145
Sgricci, Tommaso 74–5

Shelley, Percy Bysshe 38, 71, 75, 259
Shirinskii-Shikhmatov, S.A 133
Shkodra 146, 160
Shkumbin river 149
Sicily 12, 23, 82–4, 86–7, 90, 96, 109, 112–18, 121
Sidney, Algernon 248
Sidon 144
Siemann, Wolfram 54
Sieyès, Emmanuel 37
Sivas 144
Skinner, Quentin 248
Skocpol, Theda 33
Skopelos 204, 206
Slaviansk 127
Smolenitz 164
Smyrna 165, 178, 216, 218, 252
Solomos, Dionysios 77, 166, 258–59
Sophocles 228
Sotiris, Loudovikos 161
Souda 205
South America 20, 26, 31, 34, 36–7, 84–5, 88
Southeastern Europe 1–2, 7, 10–2, 36, 38, 159–60, 163, 165, 168, 191, 252
Southern Europe 7, 11, 82–92
Southey, Robert 91
Soutsos, Michail 141
Spain 10, 20, 25–9, 32, 34–40, 43–51, 53, 59, 61, 69, 72, 82–92, 95, 98, 110, 218, 226–27
Sparta 3
Spetses 198, 203–4, 206–7, 210
Spiliotakis, Spyridon 99–101, 106
Spini, Giorgio 85
Spiridov, G.A., admiral 128–29, 133
Sporades 204, 208
Stamatis, Constantinos 164
Statella, Antonio 221
Stefanopoli, Dimo 164
Stefanopoli, Niclolò 164
Sterea Ellas *see* Central Greece
Ştirbei, Barbu 154
Stourdza, Alexandre 126, 131–32
Stroganov, G.A., count 130–31
Stuttgart 68
Sugar, Peter 196–97
Süleyman Pasha 144
Sweden 127, 221, 229, 244
Switzerland 19–20, 23–4, 27, 68, 83
Syria 76
Syros 178, 206, 214
Szécheny, Isztvan, count 127

270 *Index*

Taganrog 127, 209
Taglioni, Ferdinando 223
Ternoire, Silvia 220
Thebes 164
Theotokis, Nikiphoros 127
Thermopylae 89
Thessaloniki 164, 216, 218
Thessaly 103, 108, 161, 163–64, 228–29
Thrace 204
Thucydides 228, 253, 255
Tinos 204, 214
Tirana 146
Tocqueville, Alexis de 252
Tombazis, Yakoumakis 210
Tositsa house 181
Toskëria (land of the Tosks) 146
Tournachon, Victor 77, 81
Trabzon (Trebizond) 145
Transylvania 152–55
Trieste 3, 55, 68, 111, 130, 155, 159, 161, 164, 208–9
Trikeri 204
Tripoli *see* Tripolitsa Tripolitsa 55, 69, 178–79
Troezen, constitution of (1827) 27, 31, 235–36, 238–41, 243
Troppau, Congress of (1820) 82
Troppau, Protocol of (1820) 58
Tunisia 206
Túpac Amaru 36
Turcoman tribe 145
Turin 86, 96
Tuscany 23, 161
Tuzcuoğlu, Hopa 144
Tuzcuoğlu Memiş Agha 144
Tuzcuoğlu, Rize 144
Two Sicilies, Kingdom of 12, 39, 58–60, 112, 216, 218–23, 226–29
Tzschirner, Heinrich Gottlieb 71

Ukraine 125, 130
United Colonies 48; *see also* United States of America
United States of America 6, 14–5, 20–1, 30–1, 33–4, 36, 46–7, 55–6, 67, 89, 203, 228, 236, 258

Valais, Switzerland 23
Valaoritis, Aristotelis 118
Van, lake 145

Vatican 109
Vattel, Emmerich de 48
Venezuela 37–8, 47, 50
Venice 2–3, 23, 56, 111, 128, 159–61, 164, 216
Venturi, Franco 32
Versailles 32, 45
Vidin 140, 160
Vienna 57, 86, 97, 103, 155, 159–60, 163–64, 221, 228
Vienna, Congress of 13, 39, 53–4, 57–61, 84, 112, 132, 143, 165–66, 191
Virginia 48
Vitoria, Francisco de 258
Vlachopoulos, Spyros 13
Vladimirescu, Tudor 151, 154
Vlorë (Avlonas) 146
Volos 144
Voltaire, François Marie Arouet 128, 162
Von Humboldt, Alexander 253, 260
Von Metternich, Klemens 1, 10, 13, 26, 53–60, 62, 82, 84–5, 131–32
Vorontsov, S.R., count 127
Vostizza 214
Voulgaris, Evgenios 37, 127–28, 133, 162
Vyzantios, Scarlatos 97

Wahhabis 144
Wallachia 126, 131, 133, 142, 152–55, 229; *see also* Danubian principalities
Washington, D.C. 221
Weyland, Kurt 95
Whittaker, George B. 71
Wilberforce, William 91
William I, king of the Netherlands 31
Wolff, Christian 133
Wordsworth, William 71

Xenophon 228, 253

Yemen 142
Ypsilantis, Alexandros 55, 126, 130–31, 151, 154, 197
Ypsilantis, Dimitrios 197

Zagori, Epirus 198
Zallony, Marc-Philippe 141, 148
Zante 23, 161, 165–66
Zorin, Andrei 129

Printed in the United States
by Baker & Taylor Publisher Services